TRANSCULTURAL PSYCHIATRY

Transcultural Psychiatry

Edited by JOHN L. COX

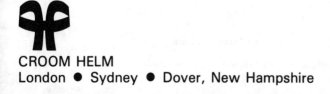

CROOM HELM
London • Sydney • Dover, New Hampshire

© 1986 John L. Cox
Croom Helm Ltd, Provident House, Burrell Row,
Beckenham, Kent BR3 1AT
Croom Helm Australia Pty Ltd, Suite 4, 6th Floor,
64–76 Kippax Street, Surry Hills, NSW 2010 Australia

British Library Cataloguing in Publication Data

Transcultural Psychiatry.
   1. Psychiatry, Transcultural
   I. Cox, John L.
   362.2   RC455.4.E8
   ISBN 0-7099-3428-9

Croom Helm, 51 Washington Street, Dover,
New Hampshire 03820, USA

Library of Congress Cataloging in Publication Data

Transcultural psychiatry.

   Bibliography: p.
   Includes index.
   1. Psychiatry, transcultural.   I. Cox, John L.
(John Lee) (DNLM: 1. Cross-cultural comparison.
2. Mental disorders. 3. Psychiatry. WM 100 T7724)
RC455.4.E8T695   1986   616.89   86-8888
ISBN 0-7099-3428-9

Filmset by Mayhew Typesetting, Bristol, England

Printed and bound in Great Britain by
Biddles Ltd, Guildford and King's Lynn

CONTENTS

List of Contributors
Acknowledgements

1. Introduction   *John L. Cox*   1

2. The Historical Development of Transcultural
    Psychiatry   *H.B.M. Murphy*   7

3. The Epidemiology of Mental Illness across
    Cultures   *Julian Leff*   23

4. Russian Dolls and Chinese Boxes: An
    Anthropological Approach to the Implicit Models of
    Comparative Psychiatry   *Roland Littlewood*   37

5. Migration and Mental Illness   *Philip H. Rack*   59

6. Overseas Students and Expatriates: Sojourners or
    Settlers?   *John L. Cox*   76

7. Psychiatric Services for Ethnic Minority
    Groups   *John Bavington and Abdul Majid*   87

8. Depression in Ethnic Minorities   *Suman Fernando*   107

9. Racism, Prejudice and Mental Illness
    Aggrey W. Burke   139

10. Ideology and Politics in Transcultural
    Psychiatry   *S.P. Sashidharan*   158

11. The Mental Health Impact of British Cultural
    Traditions   *H.B.M. Murphy*   179

12. Transcultural Social Work   *John Triseliotis*   196

13. Culture and Psychiatric Nursing: Implications for
    Training   *Bryn D. Davis*   218

14. Family Therapy Across Cultures   *Annie Lau*   234

Contents

15. The 'Culture-bound Syndromes' of the Dominant Culture: Culture, Psychopathology and Biomedicine *Roland Littlewood and Maurice Lipsedge* 253

16. Chinese Psychiatry: Development and Characteristics *Wen-Shing Tseng* 274

17. Indian and Western Psychiatry: A Comparison *A. Venkoba Rao* 291

18. African and Western Psychiatry: A Comparison *T. Asuni* 306

Index 322

CONTRIBUTORS

Professor T. Asuni MA MD DPM FRCPsych FMCPsych,
Professor and Head of Psychiatry Department,
College of Medicine,
University of Lagos,
Lagos,
Nigeria

formerly Director, United Nations Social Defence Research
Institute, Rome, Italy

Dr John Bavington MB BS DRCOG MRCPsych DPM,
Consultant Psychiatrist,
Lynfield Mount Hospital,
Heights Lane,
Bradford,
West Yorkshire BD9 6DP
UK

Dr Aggrey W. Burke BSc(Hons) MB ChB MRCPsych,
Senior Lecturer and Honorary Consultant Psychiatrist,
St. George's Hospital Medical School,
Department of Psychiatry,
Jenner Wing,
Cranmer Terrace,
Tooting,
London SW17 0RE,
UK

Professor John L. Cox MA DM MRCPsych DPM FRCP(Ed.),
Department of Postgraduate Medicine,
University of Keele,
Keele,
Staffordshire ST5 5BG,
UK

formerly Senior Lecturer, Department of Psychiatry, University of
Edinburgh, UK

Contributors

Dr Bryn D. Davis BSc PhD SRN RMN RNT,
Principal Lecturer,
Department of Community Studies,
Brighton Polytechnic,
Falmer,
Brighton BN1 9PH,
UK

Dr Suman Fernando MA MB BCh MD (Camb.) MRCPsych,
Consultant Psychiatrist,
Chase Farm Hospital,
The Ridgeway,
Enfield,
Middlesex EN2 8JL,
UK

Dr Annie Yin-Har Lau MD DipPsych(OH) FRCP(C) (Canada),
Consultant Psychiatrist,
Redbridge Child Guidance Clinic and King George Hospital,
Ilford IG1 2PL,
UK

Dr Julian Leff BSc MD FRCPsych MRCP,
Assistant Director,
MRC Social Psychiatry Unit,
Outstation: Friern Hospital,
Friern Barnet Road,
London N11 3BP,
UK

Dr Maurice Lipsedge M Phil FRCP FRCPsych,
Consultant Psychiatrist,
Guy's Hospital,
London SE1 9RT,
UK

Dr Roland Littlewood BSc MB BS Dip. Soc. Anthrop. MRCPsych,
Senior Lecturer in Psychiatry,
University of Birmingham,
All Saints Hospital,
Lodge Road,
Birmingham B18 5SD,
UK

Dr Abdul Majid MB BS DPM MRCPsych,
Consultant Psychiatrist,
St. Luke's Hospital,
Middlesborough,
Cleveland TS4 3AF,
UK

Professor H.B.M. Murphy MD PhD,
Emeritus Professor,
Department of Psychiatry,
McGill University,
Montreal,
Canada H4H 1R3

Dr Philip H. Rack MA MB BChir FRCPsych DPM,
Consultant Psychiatrist,
Transcultural Psychiatry Unit,
Lynfield Mount Hospital,
Heights Lane,
Bradford BD9 6DP,
UK

Professor A. Venkoba Rao MD PhD DSc DPM FRCPsych,
Project Officer-in-charge,
Advanced Centre for Research on 'Health and Behaviour',
Indian Council of Medical Research,
Institute of Psychiatry,
Madurai Medical College and Government Rajaji Hospital,
Madurai 625020,
India

Contributors

Dr S.P. Sashidharan MB BS MPhil MRCPsych,
Research Psychiatrist,
MRC Unit for Epidemiological Studies in Psychiatry,
University Department of Psychiatry,
Royal Edinburgh Hospital,
Morningside Park,
Edinburgh EH10 5HF,
UK

Dr John Triseliotis DipSociol, Cert Mental Health, PhD,
Director of Social Work Education,
University of Edinburgh,
Edinburgh EH8 9LL,
UK

Professor Wen-Shing Tseng, MD
Department of Psychiatry,
University of Hawaii School of Medicine,
1356 Lusitana Street,
Honolulu,
Hawaii 96813,
USA

ACKNOWLEDGEMENTS

As my interest in transcultural psychiatry first began during my earlier clinical and academic work at the London Hospital and in Uganda, and was maintained more recently in Edinburgh, I am particularly glad to acknowledge the encouragement and advice that was given to me by Sir Desmond Pond, Professor Allen German, Dr John Orley, Dr Morris Carstairs and Professor H.J. Walton.

It was however, the spark that was ignited at meetings of the Edinburgh, and of the UK, Transcultural Psychiatry Society which provided the energy and motivation to bring together the chapters that comprise this book. The founders of these pioneer organisations therefore have succeeded in one respect at least, and that was to establish a forum where issues in transcultural psychiatry could be discussed and where its inherent tensions could be experienced. I am therefore grateful to the contributors for collaborating so constructively with me.

My sincere thanks also to my secretary, Mrs Marjory Dodd; without her unflagging interest and readiness to carry out considerable correspondence and revision of drafts, the book might not have been completed, or even initiated. I am especially grateful also to my wife, Karin, for her encouragement, and for her helpful comments on my own chapters.

John L. Cox

1 INTRODUCTION

John L. Cox

This book is mainly concerned with those aspects of transcultural psychiatry that have become increasingly important for the optimum development of psychiatric services at the present time. It is not, however, a 'do-it-yourself' primer, and the reader who expects to find a detailed account of the behaviours and beliefs of minority ethnic groups, or who wants specific advice about the development of a less culture-bound psychiatric service, will be disappointed. Indeed, several contributors have emphasised why some aspects of transcultural psychiatry are 'no go' areas not only for research workers but for clinicians as well, especially if such personnel belong to the majority white community.

Since the international conference on transcultural psychiatry held in Bradford ten years ago, there has been much turbulent thinking, not only as to how transcultual psychiatry can 'begin at home', but also about its social and political aspects. Indeed, it has been a chastening experience for many professional health workers to be reminded that for some commentators the subject of transcultural psychiatry may itself be regarded as a further expression of institutional racism.

Several contributors to this book have pointed out that this issue remains of such paramount importance that until the full extent of racism is recognised and remedial action is undertaken by health-service professionals, then other non-racial aspects of transcultural psychiatry must have a lower priority.

Nevertheless it is of interest that one of the first major studies of the relationship of migration to mental illness was not directly linked to British colonial history but was an investigation of Norwegian immigrants to America at the end of the last century. These classic studies by Ødegaard (1932) were important not only because they initiated academic debate about this subject, but also because they showed how Scandinavian migrants, of similar ethnicity to the host society, also experienced difficulties of adjustment in the new country not always so different from those faced by the black community in Britain at the present time.

The range of feeling experienced by these Scandinavian immigrants and the development of paranoid attitudes was lucidly described:

Everywhere you are surrounded by people with strange and unfamiliar ways and customs and you can hardly understand anything of what they say, at any rate when they talk to each other. They do not seem to be as friendly and helpful as the people at home and many of them do their best to profit by your lack of experience. Even if you have not had any disagreeable experience yourself, your imagination is stirred by all the stories you have heard about how crooked and dangerous they may be. You notice that your own appearance, clothing and language points you out to everybody as a greenhorn, and a 'big Swede' at that, and you are frequently met by a mixture of mirth and contempt. You have no friends, no one to associate with and no money for expensive entertainments — frequently you live under the strain of imminent unemployment. You are forced to live among the least attractive types of Americans, because it is cheap in those sections, and this frequently means a considerable lowering of your previous standard of life. There are hundreds of similar things which tend to make you suspicious and bewildered, anxious and lonely. Sexual adjustment also is more difficult than at home, becuase of the lack of social connections, and owing to financial difficulties, and the scarcity of women in the immigrant population.

The constellation of the clinical experience of contributors to this book and their different ethnic and national groupings will, it is hoped, provide the reader with a contemporary critique of transcultural psychiatry, and will also be a useful reminder of the cultural relativity of taken-for-granted social norms, as well as identifying more universal components of social relationships.

Transcultural psychiatry in the last decade has therefore come a long way from Wittkower and Rin's (1965) 'playing safe' definition. This confined the subject to a research perspective only, in which the vista of the scientific observer was extended beyond the scope of one cultural unit on to another. Transcultural psychiatry is now inescapably embedded in ordinary clinical practice. Thus, at the centre of psychiatric practice is the definition of a delusion as a false belief firmly held against all evidence to the contrary, and also *out of keeping with the patient's social and cultural background*. The practitioner therefore has the inevitable task of deciding whether or not an individual patient has such false beliefs (i.e. is deluded), and to make this crucial decision he or she must understand the patient's values, family structure, and religious beliefs, as well as become familiar with the local 'popular' explanations for illness and other misfortunes.

As discussed by several contributors, the main impetus behind this renewed interest in transcultural psychiatry in Britain at the present time has been the immigration of Afro-Caribbeans and Asians over the past 30 years. Because many such migrants have a different ethnic origin, language, dress and family structure from those of the majority community, the provision of adequate medical services for these minorities has caused difficulty for Eurocentric physicians who speak only one language and are not adequately trained for this new clinical situation. However, to relinquish an interest in the provision of these medical services, and to believe that an understanding of the use of interpreters, food prohibitions, naming systems and different explanatory models of illness is less important than an understanding of the pervasive influence of racism may possibly increase yet further the health-service deprivation experienced by some minorities.

Health workers and administrators of various ethnic origins are indeed increasingly asking for information about the characteristics of minority groups as they impinge on the provision of health care. The responsibility for filling in this large educational vacuum is generally and appropriately acknowledged, provided it is realised that such education, if given as facts without attempting to understand the systems of cultural meaning, can be extremely limited or even discriminatory (see Ballard, 1983).

It is therefore fortunate that several books on transcultural psychiatry are now available, for example Leff (1981), Littlewood and Lipsedge (1982), Murphy (1982) and Rack (1982), and also an excellent multi-author book, edited by Edwards *et al*, (1983), which shows how an understanding of drug addiction can only be fully grasped if the sociocultural matrix of the societies is understood. In North America, Kleinman, who is both psychiatrist and anthropologist, has provided most scholarly insights into the relevance of transcultural psychiatry for the delivery of health care in the United States, and particularly for general hospital psychiatrists (Kleinman, 1980). Another useful American book, which largely draws its inspiration from an understanding of minority groups, is by Tseng and McDermott (1981), and a multi-author book edited by Gaw (1982) describes cultural aspects of mental health care in minority groups but also has useful chapters on the implications of these concerns for the training of doctors. An earlier review article by Cox (1977) also emphasised the relevance of transcultural psychiatry to education of overseas psychiatrists in Britain, and included a discussion of methodological research problems. Favazza and Oman (1978) provide an overview of cultural psychiatry, a topic they regard as an essential integrative component of 'scientific psychiatry'.

In addition the contribution of medical anthropologists to medical education by increasing the sensitivity of health professionals to these topics is well described by Helman (1984) in his book, *Culture, Health and Illness*.

This substantial increase in academic literature has helped to facilitate the introduction of courses on transcultural medicine in undergraduate medical teaching, and within the field of postgraduate education transcultural psychiatry is now recognised as important for the training of psychiatrists. Ten years ago this topic was generally regarded not only as exotic, but also as largely irrelevant for postgraduate study.

Kleinman (1978) has strongly recommended that a general hospital doctor would also benefit from a knowledge of transcultural psychiatry when trying to understand 'majority patients', and recommends, for example, that the physician should ask patients *why* they think they have become ill and what other healers have been consulted because of their problems. He or she should also learn to elicit the patient's explanatory model, which can then be contrasted with the medical explanation offered by doctors. It is then suggested that if the discrepancies between these explanations are examined, a fuller understanding of the patient's problems will be obtained and compliance with treatment is more likely to be optimal.

Medical anthropologists have in this way stimulated doctors to recognise the relevance of this sociocultural approach to understanding physical illness and have pointed out what is unusual about those aspects of medical care that are usually taken entirely for granted: why, for example, certain 'sacred cows', such as psychotherapy, or the routine prescription of iron tablets during pregnancy, are regarded by some as particularly sacrosanct even when their efficacy cannot be scientifically proven. They have also described how a culturally sanctioned behaviour such as a medical consultation has an efficacy quite independent of the biomedical 'disease', or the particular psychodynamic theory used by the healer. Helman (1984) has put forward an interesting perspective on these issues and regards the general practitioner as a 'culture broker' who mediates between the patient's folk explanations for minor ailments (such as germs, viruses and head colds) and the hospital consultant who practises technological biomedical science. Okley (1982) has provided a fascinating insight into gypsies' attitudes to health care by describing their refusal to refer a relative with a major paranoid psychosis to a suspect Gorgio hospital. She also observed that childbirth was regarded as polluting, which, paradoxically, led to a greater use of obstetric services than might otherwise have occured.

Transcultural psychiatry has therefore become a rather large 'umbrella' subject that includes many diverse topics and may even emphasise contradictory clinical approaches. However, the extent to which it is taken seriously by health professionals will depend very largely on their own ability to examine the cultural relativity of aspects of health-service provision and medical diagnostic practice which previously were taken entirely for granted, and so were accepted as having a universal validity.

It will also be apparent that the understanding of psychiatric disorder from a transcultural perspective can proceed no further than the extent to which the individual medical practitioner can accept the cultural relativity of long-held, cherished notions about the causes of mental illness, its classification, and its taken-for-granted treatment strategies. Transcultural psychiatry does indeed 'begin at home' and it is therefore appropriate that the present concern with the way in which racial prejudice adversely affects mental health is prominently emphasised throughout this book.

References

Ballard, R. (1983) 'The Significance of Culture', in A.G. Sims and W. Batty (eds.), *Lecture Notes on Behavioural Sciences for Medical Students,* Blackwell Scientific Publications, Oxford

Cox, J.L. (1977) 'Aspects of Transcultural Psychiatry', *British Journal of Psychiatry, 130,* 211–21

Edwards, G., Arif, A. and Jaffe, J. (eds) (1983) *Drug Use and Misuse,* Croom Helm, London

Favazza, A.R. and Oman, M. (1978) 'Overview: Foundations of Cultural Psychiatry', *American Journal of Psychiatry, 135,* 293–303

Gaw, A. (ed.) (1982) *Cross-cultural Psychiatry,* Wright P.S.G., Littleton, Mass. and Bristol

Helman, C. (1984) *Culture, Health and Illness,* Wright P.S.G., Littleton, Mass. and Bristol

Kleinman, A. (1978) 'Clinical Relevance of Anthropological and Cross-Cultural Research: Comments and Strategies', *American Journal of Psychiatry, 135,* 427

Kleinman, A. (1980) *Patients and Healers in the Context of Culture,* University of California Press, Berkeley

Leff, J. (1981) *Psychiatry around the Globe — Transcultural View,* Marcel Dekker, New York

Littlewood, R. and Lipsedge, M. (1982) *Aliens and Alienists, Ethnic Minorities and Psychiatrists,* Penguin Books, London

Murphy, H.B.M. (1982) *Comparative Psychiatry: the International and Intercultural Distribution of Mental Illness,* Springer, Berlin, Heidelberg and New York

Ødergaard, O. (1932) 'Emigration and Insanity', *Acta Psychiatrica et Neurologica Scandinavica,* Suppl. 4

Okley, J.M. (1982) *The Traveller-Gypsies,* Cambridge University Press, Cambridge

Rack, P. (1982) *Race, Culture and Mental Disorders,* Tavistock Publications, London

Tseng, W.S. and McDermott, J.F. (1981) *Culture, Mind and Therapy,* Brunner/Mazel, New York

Wittkower, E.D. and Rin, H. (1965) 'Transcultural Psychiatry', *Archives of General Psychiatry*, *13*, 387–94

2 THE HISTORICAL DEVELOPMENT OF TRANSCULTURAL PSYCHIATRY

H.B.M. Murphy

The Early Signs

Although the early Greek and Arabic physicians make occasional reference to forms of mental disturbance occurring especially in particular peoples, and although Rhazes condemns the ascetic tradition as being unhealthy, the earliest text I have encountered that makes serious reference to a link between culture and mental health is that by the great Arab social historian, Ibn Khaldun, in the fourteenth century. Very conscious of the phychosocial changes that occurred in warrior tribes when they moved from a nomadic, mutually supportive existence to the towns, he describes a growing prevalence of jealousy, distrust, self-indulgence and fear of others. This was in part a rational reaction to the changes in social structure and the failure of the old tribal system to adapt, but at different points in his long, three-volume treatise (Ibn Khaldun, 1967–68) he indicates fairly clearly that he views some of these reactions as irrational (paranoid or phobic) and as contributing to the downfall not only of individual leaders but of whole dynasties. For Ibn Khaldun, a townsman himself, the urbanisation of Arabic peoples in the Middle Ages was pathogenic by reason of culture change, and later histories and travellers' descriptions give support to that conclusion.

Roughly fifty years after Ibn Khaldun's commentary comes the first reliable description of a culture-bound syndrome that I have been able to discover, again in an Islamic society but this time by a European. The Venetian traveller Nicolo Conti visited Java in the 1430s, and brought back from there a description of *amok* which corresponds relatively closely to nineteenth- and twentieth- century descriptions of the same condition (Yule and Burnell, 1886). As I have discussed elsewhere (Murphy, 1972), it is probable that this behaviour pattern was at that time not irrational; but it was an individual act, thus contrasting with that of the berserker who acted wildly only in battle, and in the following century the description of another traveller, Duarte Barbosa (1921), makes it clear that it was linked to cultural beliefs.

The European Awakening

That these first pointers to our field should have come from travellers
and a social historian rather than from medical men is not surprising.
From the Middle Ages through the Renaissance and on till the Counter-
Reformation, most mental disorder apart from simple idiocy was
attributed either to supernatural spirits or to a reverse of fortune. For
this reason an excess of any type of mental disorder in a given population was usually attributed to an attack by evil spirits (as at Salem) or
to mass despair as after the sacking of a town. Even the dancing manias
and other hysterical epidemics confined to a particular religious movement, therefore, were not attributed to the cultural setting. By the sixteenth and seventeenth centuries, however, scientific enquiry into the
causes of associations between phenomena was advancing rapidly, and
one then finds writers hypothesising not that mental illness might be due
to culture, but that cultural change might be due to mental illness! Several
authors at that time were attempting to explain the 'enthusiasms' of certain Puritan sects (including the 'quaking' which was to give one of these
its popular name) as the effect of melancholic 'vapours' of organic origin
(Sena, 1973). Since Elizabethan times, however, physicians and travellers
had also been vaguely aware that melancholia appeared to be commoner
in England than elsewhere (see the collection of texts from that period
by Hunter and MacAlpine, 1963), and in 1733 an Edinburgh-trained
physician brought the matter out into the open with a book entitled *The
English Malady* (Cheyne, 1733). This pointed clearly to the English
middle class as being exceptionally neurotic and thus opened the door
to the idea that such neuroticism might be linked to English customs and
traditions, even though the author himself offers no such definite
explanation for the association.

Once that door was opened, theories were not long in developing.
This was the time when serious writers like Montesquieu were questioning not merely their own governments but their own national customs,
and when the image of the 'noble savage' (to be enshrined by J.J.
Rousseau) was becoming popular. The possibility that English society
might be neurotic because it was 'decadent' (in a moral rather than in
a racial sense) was thus an idea that appealed to the North American
revolutionaries, and before long their leading physician, Benjamin Rush,
was claiming (probably on the basis of clinical observation) that participation in the Revolution was curing women of hysteria whereas the
traditional life under the British monarchy was generating mental disorder
(Rush, 1794).

Nineteenth-Century Trends

Rush's observations, as distinct from his rhetoric, related more to the effect of participation in a mass movement (on the revolutionary side) and a threat to an existing way of life (on the loyalist one) than to culture *per se*; but they did reinforce the idea that mental disorder might be associated with sociocultural complexity, and mental health with simplicity. By the 1820s it was possible for the author of an official report on mental disorder and mental hospitals in Britain to link his findings to the alleged fact that 'not one of our African travellers remarks their having seen a single madman' (Halliday, 1828), and for the rest of the century one finds British psychiatry repeatedly coming back to the idea that a simple (usually rural) lifestyle is a mentally healthy one.

This nineteenth-century British theory held 'civilisation' rather than any particular cultural tradition to be the pathogenic agent, and the solid evidence of rising suicide rates in country after country as their standard of living improved (Murphy, 1982, Chapter 7) seemed to confirm that. However, two other lines of psychiatric enquiry during that century pointed less to civilisation than to particular ethnic backgrounds. At the empirical level, international visits by asylum administrators brought the more alert of them to realise that a presenting syndrome which carried a poor prognosis in one society might not carry the same prognosis in another, and a favoured treatment in the one might be likely to fail in another (Morel, 1845). At the theoretical level, concerns began to be felt regarding racial genetics. It may be of some slight consolation to African or Asian readers who have encountered pejorative references to their own racial backgrounds in the psychiatric literature from the twentieth century to learn that in the 1900s similarly patronising remarks were being made about European peoples. In the USA, the excess of immigrants entering the mental hospitals led many authorities to refer to the 'poor stock' from which the newer waves of immigrants were coming, sometimes recognising the effect of adverse selection but sometimes blaming race. In Europe, the development of the science of genetics of animals and plants led to a theory of 'decadence' being applied to human societies in which there had been either insufficient admixture of gene stocks or an introduction of new and unhealthy strains. At its mildest this theory, when linked to the fact that Janet and Charcot were turning up many cases of hysteria of a type little known elsewhere, led to the opinion that 'among the French . . . there are just more hereditarily tainted individuals than among the German races' (Enke, 1900); at its worst, it led to the ideas of Gobineau regarding Nordic superiority, Latin degeneracy, and the danger of a Jewish or Negro 'taint'.

The Early Twentieth Century

That such racial theories did not get a stronger grip on European psychiatry and that the door remained open to the possibility of other ethnic factors was due to Emil Kraepelin, with his insistence on careful observation and comparison. Not only did he call for systematic comparisons between the mental disorder patterns of different European peoples (a call which has still not been adequately responded to) but he also visited mental hospitals in Singapore and Java to learn for himself how far the syndromes he had differentiated in Europe were common or uncommon there (Kraepelin, 1904). He has been reproached for not having taken a firm stand against the racial theories of some of his contemporaries, but to have done so would have been quite against his own scientific principles since it would have taken much more evidence than was then available to disprove (as distinct from disapprove of) such theories. Moreover, at the very time he was writing, the main targets of European racist theory, the Jews, were beginning to report research into the medical and psychiatric peculiarities of their own people, research which could be interpreted genetically (Fishberg, 1901).

Yet, although Kraepelin's prestige was high, and although he personally would probably have seen very little difficulty in making cross-cultural comparisons within European peoples, the idea of relating European cultural traditions to the type or the amount of mental illness they harboured was not at all attractive to his followers when the cultures were their own. (It was only in the mid-1970s that I was able to persuade colleagues there to write up such a comparison; see Parin and Parin-Matthey, 1978). Soon after Kraepelin wrote, ethnic comparisons became possible with regard to North American immigrant patients, and — as Pilcz (1919/1920) was later to show — the multi-ethnic character of the Austro-Hungarian army offered still better opportunities. But Europe's psychiatrists preferred to follow Freud when he turned his back on the question of cultural differences among his international clientele and chose, in *Totem and Taboo* (1918) to write about hypothetical connections within a culture of which he had no personal knowledge and which anthropologists found extremely difficult to interpret, the Australian Aboriginal one. *Totem and Taboo* is a brilliant theoretical exercise offering a model of approach which many anthropologists have found

inspiring, however much they doubt the validity of his specific interpretations and the second- or third-hand information on which he based
these. However, it unfortunately gave priority to armchair theorising
over the careful and thorough case studies on which his earlier work
was based, and in its original subtitle, 'Uber einige Uebereinstimmungen
in Seelenleben der Wilden und der Neurotiker' (dropped from later editions), it implied a pathological basis to the thinking of primitive peoples
and thus reinforced colonial prejudices.

Thanks in part to Freud's opting for this armchair approach, but probably more to a reluctance to undertake research that would involve them
in the racial controversy, very few psychiatrists in the 1920s and 1930s
undertook direct observations on possible links between culture and either
psychopathology or its treatment. Psychoanalysts were happy to write
papers on various myths and legends, but when the distinguished anthropologist Bronislaw Malinowski came forward with field observations that
invited a rethinking of the Oedipus Complex theory, they neither welcomed these additional data nor encouraged other anthropologists to collect more. Instead, they rejected Malinowski's observations on the
grounds that since they did not fit their theory, they could not be true
(Parsons, 1964). The one location in which, at that time, there was a
real attempt to relate culture to mental health through direct observation
was the Dutch East Indies. However, much of what was written then
on the subject by Van Loon and his colleagues was published in a local
medical journal which the rest of the world never saw, or in texts on
tropical medicine which psychiatrists did not feel concerned them, and
therefore it had very little impact. Gesa Roheim, describing himself as
'the only anthropologist who accepted psychoanalysis without any reservations' (Roheim, 1947, p. 13) did undertake frequent fieldwork with
a psychoanalytic inspiration, but his anxiety to have all his observations
conform to Freudian theory dominated his activities and a rereading of
his reports today is disheartening, so superficial does much of the
fieldwork seem. (In the above-cited text, he labels (p. 16) as 'absurd'
Malinowski's idea that one might be able to *test* Freudian theory by means
of field observations, particularly when one has not had a personal
psychoanalysis.) In advance of their time were symptom-checklist surveys
in Peking, Wulf Sachs' (1937) *Black Hamlet*, and the early work of
Haiti's first psychiatrist (and later Foreign Minister) Louis Mars; but
there was no common audience for them to address.

With the Second World War, the same trends continued, but there
were more persons involved and they therefore began to recognise a
common interest. Particularly in the British and US armed forces,

psychiatrists found themselves faced with the psychiatric care of whole regiments from ethnic backgrounds other than their own, and sometimes with the time to ask themselves why the presenting syndromes seemed to cluster by ethnic group. One thus got, for instance, the excellent comparison of different East Indian subgroups by Williams (1950), and American reports on Puerto Rican and Negro units. At the same time, but quite independently and in relative isolation from each other, individual anthropologists, of whom Georges Devereux was the most active but not the best known, became more confident about opening their mouths on psychiatric matters, and also more skilled at assessing what types and amounts of information were needed to meet medical criteria. (Medical writers were, and still are, much more ignorant about meeting anthropological criteria.)

With the end of the war, the desirability of comparing mental-health needs and problems in different societies led J.R. Rees, who had been head of psychiatric services for the British Army, to found the World Federation for Mental Health and to encourage researchers (including the present writer) to carry out comparative studies. The massive population movements of this time, including repatriation of prisoners and resettlement of refugees, added to the stimulus and opportunity. However, what soon became apparent was that the recent processes (imprisonment, political persecution, search for a new life) which had produced these movements were of more apparent significance than cultural background, so that the cultural aspects got overshadowed by the migrational ones. As a result, individual workers in our field remained about as isolated as before, although they were more numerous.

Since 1950

That situation changed relatively rapidly after 1955, with several groups showing initiative at about the same time. In 1955, the World Federation for Mental Health decided to sponsor an international conference on student mental health in which the question of cultural influences was fully recognised (Funkenstein, 1959). In 1956 the departments of psychiatry and anthropology at McGill University, Montreal, launched a newsletter *Transcultural Research in Mental Health Problems*. In 1957 the American Anthropological Association, on the urging of Marvin Opler, organised a well-planned conference session at its annual meeting (Opler, 1959); and in the same year the Second World Congress of Psychiatry, in Zurich, organised an international round-table discussion of the subject under the chairmanship of the International Association's president, Ewan Cameron. In March 1958 the World Health Organisation accepted an invitation to join the WFMH (and other bodies) in organising a meeting regarding mental health in Africa south of the Sahara at which not just conventional hospital and clinical services were discussed, but also the value of traditional healers. Suddenly, a potential link between cultural background and mental health was receiving some official recognition, and along with that the term 'transcultural psychiatry' for the whole field.

The choice of the term 'transcultural' caused some debate, since 'cultural', 'ethno-cultural', 'cross-cultural' and 'comparative' could also have been used, each carrying a somewhat different connotation. The 'trans' part of the term even caused some unease, since it appeared to imply that the field would be concerned only with features that transcended cultural boundaries, not those that remained within them; but on the other hand it could be taken as implying intercultural comparison, and that was definitely the intention of some of us. Regarding those for whom the field would mainly cater, there were three main targets, namely those who found the influence of culture on mental health an interesting subject for study, those who found mainline psychiatric teaching unsuited to practice in societies with cultures very different from those in which that teaching had developed, and those who sought to add an international dimension to the concerns of social psychiatry. In the McGill group, after I joined it in 1959, it was decided to attempt to bring together, somewhat incongrously, the first and second of these; and when I later became the chairman of the newly formed Transcultural Section of the World Psychiatric Association, the same double target was somewhat dogmatically chosen, which made difficulties for us in the short run. It was obviously appropriate for us, as far as possible, to think internationally rather than locally, and the WPA was an obvious parent body. But most of the WPA's Sections had committees dominated by persons from two or three contiguous countries, making meetings between them relatively easy. The Transcultural Section, because it felt a special duty towards societies with cultures very different from those in which conventional psychiatric teaching had developed, rejected that form and insisted on its committee being drawn equally from different regions of the world, with no concentration of committee members from any one. This quixotic decision meant that the committee virtually never met, or at least could never muster a quorum, even on the occasion of WPA Congresses! However, it is a policy that has probably paid off in the longer run, since the field and its WPA Section became the natural forum for expressing the doubts that non-Western professionals felt regarding the applicability of Western psychiatric teachings to their home societies, while at the same time moderating these doubts with soundly comparative and ethnographic research.

To finish with the 1950s, reference needs to be made to events that appeared very promising at the time, but which circumstances prevented from developing in the way one might have hoped. The first of these was the establishment in 1957 of the Groupo Latino-Americano de Estudios Transculturales, linking psychiatrists in Cuba, Haiti, Mexico and Peru with the intention of carrying out comparative studies. Political and economic forces unfortunately, interfered with that effort, although one of the initial members, Dr J.A. Bustamante, was able after years of difficulty to return to transcultural studies and by the 1980s had made Cuba, despite its small size, one of the Latin American countries in which the most interesting sociocultural research is going on. The second factor was the promise of related work from psychologists at the National Institute for Personnel Research in Johannesburg, South Africa. The Institute was undertaking considerable research into the psychology of the Bantu peoples, research of high quality which, with a slight change of direction, could have been of substantial value in our field; but unfortunately the change in direction did not take place and political factors again influenced the type of work which the Institute subsequently performed. Thirdly, two important classics for our field were published at this time, but neither started any trend even though the approaches they employed were fine models. These were the Hutterites study by Eaton and Weil (1955) and *The Twice-born* by Morris Carstairs (1957). Carstairs was pulled away from his Indian fieldwork to a distinguished British career as professor and vice-chancellor; the other two returned to their earlier career and found other interests.

In the 1960s, the difficulty of organising meetings in our field was only one of the problems to be faced. The McGill newsletter, now called the *Transcultural Psychiatric Research Review*, let workers know what was going on in the field and reminded them that they were not alone; but the number of persons devoting much time to the field was still very small. Both government medical agencies and private foundations supporting medical research expected that research to take place within their own countries, and in so far as international money was available for such work in poorer nations, it was expected to be devoted to the more obvious medical needs of improving nutrition, controlling endemic infections, and restricting population growth. The few of us who did attempt to do cross-cultural psychiatric studies thus had great difficulty in finding funds for these, and often had to subsidise the work from our own pockets. (Some readers may feel that the situation is still unchanged today.) Thus, John Cawte had to organise his important team fieldwork with Australian Aborigines (Cawte, 1972) to coincide with his team's vacations, since it was not specially funded or recognised as official; and the Swiss team of Parin, Morgenthaler and Parin-Matthey (1963) paid for their highly original fieldwork in Africa from their own private psychoanalytic practices. Another problem was that even when local meetings seemed possible, there was disagreement as to whether it was acceptable to organise these for such workers as could pay their own way to them, or whether it was obligatory for the organisers to raise money to cover the travel of colleagues from poorer countries; and one of the regional meetings which the WPA Section attempted to arrange fell through because of this disagreement on ethics. (A different method of bringing an international group together so as to benefit workers in the Third World was to combine it with a vacation tour in some developing world area for richer professionals from the Developed World; but the quality of participation by the latter has proved so uncertain that it is not an approach that many workers in transcultural psychiatry favour.)

With the emphasis on exploring the psychiatric needs of societies with cultures very different from those in which psychiatry developed, and with the further desire to help adapt psychiatric teaching to the needs of these societies, it was natural that transcultural psychiatry came to be recognised as concerned mainly with the Developing World. However, as a matter of principle, some of us at that time felt that the influence of local culture on mental health was likely to be just as important, although perhaps more disguised, within our more advanced societies, and that this should receive its share of attention. At the 1957 meeting of the American Anthropological Association, Marvin Opler (1959) had presented a seminal paper on the difference between Italian-American and Irish-American schizophrenics which led to a number of similar small studies, principally by his own students; and Victor Sanua (1963) extended this approach to include the white Protestant majority, pointing out that some of the results from studies into parental behaviour and schizophrenia might be better explained by differences in the ethnic backgrounds of contrasting samples than by the complex theories which the authors were proposing. But these researchers were non-medical, and I do not think that there was a single psychiatrist at that time who took up their observations and attempted to incorporate them into mainstream teaching.

In the 1960s, the main contributions to transcultural psychiatry were, in my opinion, the following:

(1) The training centre in Dakar, Senegal, led by Henri Collomb and having as its voice that most admirable journal, *Psychopathologie Africaine*. The centre attempted to combine the very different viewpoints of psychoanalysis, colonial medical administration, and anthropology, while teaching routine psychiatric care of the African patient. The journal, with French governmental (CRNS) sponsorship, was able to publish long articles with both clinical and anthropological emphases, and the cross-fertilisation among disciplines there was very rich. Among other publications to which the centre gave rise was *Oedipe Africain* (Ortigues and Ortigues, 1966).

(2) The series of conferences and conference volumes organised by the anthropologist William Lebra at the University of Hawaii in conjunction with the East-West Center, entitled *Mental Health Research in Asia and the Pacific*. In association with these conferences were a number of fellowships for experienced researchers to analyse or write up their work, some of which was also published through the same channels (e.g. that of John Cawte cited earlier). The conference participants and Center fellows came from a wide region, and the quality of presentation obtained was high.

(3) The series of studies of Japanese normal and abnormal psychology organised around the two American researchers, William Caudill and George De Vos. The first focused on child-rearing practices (with careful comparison with American middle-class ones), but covered also clinical syndromes and hospital customs (Schooler, 1974); the second focused on deviancy, achievement motivation and suicide (De Vos, 1973). Initially their approaches were very North American, requiring their Japanese colleagues to adapt to Western concepts, but as their work progressed they learnt increasingly to adopt a more Japanese viewpoint assisted by various Japanese scholars' own efforts — particularly those of Takeo Doi (1973) and Bin Kimura (1971) — to interpret their own culture to the West. Several key papers by Caudill and De Vos were published in the volumes edited by Lebra.

(4) The exceptional efforts of a small number of relatively isolated individuals who broke new ground but for one reason or another were usually not able to carry the same work on into the 1970s. These individuals included:

(a) Thomas Adeoye Lambo who started the Aro village experiment with traditional healers in Nigeria but was pulled away to become the Assistant Director-General of the World Health Organisation;

(b) Margaret Field, who after an anthropological training and extensive fieldwork in Ghana in the 1930s became so fascinated by the mentally disordered persons she was encountering that she returned to Britain for a medical and psychiatric training in order to effect what has become a classic in our field, the study of healing shrines and their patients, entitled *Search for Security* (Field, 1960);

(c) Anne Parsons, daugher of the famous sociologist Talcott Parsons, who undertook highly original studies first of Boston Italian patients and then of Neopolitan ones, but who then died prematurely at the age of 33 (Parsons, 1969).

On the other hand a certain number of false starts occured during that decade. Both at the University of New South Wales and jointly between McGill University and the University of Vermont, training programmes in transcultural psychiatry were formally established but failed to find sufficient financial backing and therefore had only small numbers of trainees in subsequent years. In research, an impressively large-scale mental health survey, contrasting Iban, Malays and Chinese, had its data collection and initial data analysis completed but then ran out of steam, and for the most part has not seen publication.

The 1970s opened impressively for us with the publication of Henri Ellenberger's (1970) massive and important text, *The Discovery of the Unconscious,* and it closed with a flurry of activity in almost all expected directions, but with the development of somewhat divergent trends in different parts of the world.

One of these trends, most obvious in Europe, was a shift from theory towards action, but also a blurring of what the term 'transcultural' was intended to mean. Immigrant minorities, who had been relatively ignored since the 1940s, sprung into prominence again in the 1970s, with transcultural psychiatry now being called upon to help in their care. They consisted in Britain of members of the 'coloured' Commonwealth, in continental Europe of *Gastarbeiters,* and in North America (later) of Vietnamese and other political refugees. The answer which our field provided to that call was a weak one, in part because of our small numbers and in part because of a reluctance to appear to be criticising any people's cultural tradition. Our small numbers meant that whereas answers should have been coming separately as regards each major culture participating in the migrations, they tended to focus on the shared characteristics of migrational stress and social disadvantage rather than on the different value systems and child-rearing practices. This was very obvious at two conferences that took place in 1976, the first in Kiel and the second in Bradford, both of which had the word 'transcultural' in their titles but neither of which had many papers addressing specifically cultural factors. The major problem that became evident at these meetings was that the only mental health practitioners who had a real knowledge of the special mental health problems in particular immigrant cultures were members of these cultures themselves, and both their training and inclination led them to glide over questions of cultural values lest they appeared to be doubting sacred tenets. Only when the culture was a distant one and the writer an outsider, as in Joseph Westermeyer's papers on Indo-Chinese refugees, did one get a true differentiation of cultural and migrational strains. Anthropologists have criticised this trend as not really dealing with culture, but it did offer a chance to apply our knowledge; and before they complain about practitioners from immigrant cultures failing to confront their own backgrounds, they should be more active at examining the values that they themselves grew up with (as Ellenberger did, historically) and push further with the anthropology of complex societies.

The opposing trend also sought to be of practical value in mental health, but in a very different fashion, arguing that the concepts of mental health and mental disorder are culturally based and that both concepts and therapies must stem from the local culture if they are to be effective. This school thus called for the fuller use or at least fuller study of traditional nosologies and healing systems, and challenged the application of Western-based nosologies to other peoples. The best-known exponent of this position was Arthur Kleinman, through his journal *Culture, Medicine and Psychiatry,* and his prize-winning book (1980), but the argument came from the developing world as well as the developed one, as illustrated by Sow's book *Psychiatrie Dynamique Africaine* (1977). Objections to this viewpoint came from hospital psychiatrists who argued that traditional healers succeeded only with the lesser disorders and dumped the major ones on the foreign-trained professionals; but (as I argued at a meeting in Brazil) that case can only be accepted after a systematic comparative evaluation using mutually agreed criteria.

Between these divergent wings, the mainstream of transcultural psychiatry forged ahead, both in recruits and in ideas. The early 1970s saw useful attempts at synthesis in books by Pfeiffer (1971) and Yap (1974) as well as the launching of the journals *Ethos* and *Journal of Cross-cultural Psychology.* The middle years saw the establishment of transcultural psychiatry societies in Britain, the United States, France, Italy and Cuba, and by the end of the decade we had *Culture, Medicine and Psychiatry, Ethnopsychiatrica, Medical Anthropology, the Journal of Psychological Anthropology, Journal of Operational Psychiatry* and *Curare,,* all in principle or in practice catering for our field. (Not all of these societies and journals survived the stringencies of the early 1980s.) At the 1977 congress of the World Psychiatric Association, the Transcultural Section's administrative meeting (which at previous Congresses could scarcely muster a quorum) was almost crowded out, and by this time many other international and national congresses were routinely featuring 'transcultural' symposia in their programmes. Regarding papers, the numbers grew so great that publication of a hard-cover annotated bibliography with over 3600 items became possible (Favazza and Oman, 1977), and the *Transcultural Psychiatric Research Review,* which previously had attempted to abstract every paper of importance in the field, had to abandon that policy and instead commence invited 'overviews' in which the literature on particular sections of the field would be systematically summarised.

From all these publications and studies it is difficult to judge which will prove to have been significant for our field in the future, but I will mention two, one mainly anthropological and the other psychiatric. The first is the international survey of trance and possession states, under the direction of Erika Bourguignon (1973). It is notable for casting light on a hotly debated subject, namely the degree to which such states should be considered pathological, and also because it was probably the first large-scale anthropological study financed over many years by a medical agency, the NIMH. The second was the reporting of the follow-up results from the massive 'International Pilot Study of Schizophrenia' (WHO, 1979, and earlier). In the presentation of these results, as in the planning of the project, cultural variables were almost wholly ignored, but the fact that patients in developing countries showed significantly better outcomes than those in more developed ones changed that. Mainstream psychiatry had been able to ignore earlier evidence of a cultural influence on schizophrenia (e.g. Murphy and Raman, 1973), but it was not able to disregard the WHO findings, and therefore cultural factors began to receive considerably more attention within WHO and elsewhere.

Conclusions

The foregoing history tells us something about our field. First, we see that it has quite deep roots, and ones that extend beyond medicine, but on the other hand these roots are theoretical rather than applied. Secondly, we see that it remained a very restricted field until the mid-1970s, when its expansion threatened a potential split between an 'etic' (comparative and universalist) and an 'emic' (culture-specific) wing. This potential split can be attributed in part to the sudden and rapid expansion of medical anthropology as a separate discipline, but it can also be attributed to a conflict between a preoccupation with what one anthropologist has called, in a letter which evoked many responses, 'exotica' (Estroff, 1978) and the demands of clinical practice. At time of writing the two wings are coming together again, thanks to the growing number of developing-country psychiatrists who seek a representation of their own societies' problems in international teaching, but more is likely to be needed to make our field coherent. Each of the wings just referred to can be interpreted as a way of avoiding a shared problem, that of facing up to the effects that cultural traditions may be having on the disorders and therapies not just of small, distant, cultural groups, but of the world's major cultures. Ellenberger (1970) demonstrated such effects historically, but Estroff's letter insisted that we need to be examining the contemporary process.

References

Barbosa, D. (1921) *The Book of Duarte Barbosa* (Transl. M.L. Dames), Vol. 2, pp. 177–8, Hakluyt Society, London

Bourguignon, E. (ed.) (1973) *Religion, Altered States of Consciousness and Social Change*, Ohio State Univ Press, Columbus

Carstairs, G.M. (1957) *The Twice-born: a Study of a Community of High-caste Hindus*, Hogarth Press, London

Cawte, J.E. (1972) *Cruel, Poor and Brutal Nations*, University of Hawaii Press, Honolulu

Cheyne, G. (1733) *The English Malady: or a Treatise of Nervous Diseases of all Kinds*, Strahan, London

De Vos, G.A. (1973), *Socialization for Achievement: Essays on the Cultural Psychology of the Japanese*, University of Calif. Press, Berkeley

Doi, T. (1973), *The Anatomy of Dependence* (Transl. J. Bester), Kodansha, Tokyo

Eaton, J.W. and Weil, R.J. (1955) *Culture and Mental Disorders*, Free Press, Glencoe, Illinois

Ellenberger, H. (1970) *The Discovery of the Unconscious*, Basic Books, New York

Enke, P. (1900) 'Casuistische Beiträge zur männlichen Hysterie', thesis, Jena University (cited by Decker, H.S. (1977), *Freud in Germany*, International Universities Press, New York

Estroff, S. (1978) 'The Anthropology-Psychiatry Fantasy; Can we Make it a Reality? *Transcultural Psychiatry Research Review 15*, 209–13

Favazza, A.R. and Oman, M. (1977) *Anthropological and Cross-Cultural Themes in Mental Health: an Annotated Bibliography, 1925–1974*, University of Missouri Press, Columbia

Field, M.J. (1960) *Search for Security: an Ethno-Psychiatric Study of Rural Ghana*, Faber, London

Fishberg, M. (1901) 'Comparative pathology of the Jews', *New York Medical Journal*, 538–43, 576–81

Freud, S. (1918) 'Totem und Tabu: über einige, Ubereinstimmungen im Seelenleben der Wilden und der Neurotiker', *Imago, 1*, 17, 213, 301, etc.

Funkenstein, D.H. (ed.) (1959) *The Student and Mental Health, an International View*, WFMH, Cambridge, Mass.

Halliday, A. (1828) *A General View of the Present State of Lunatics and Lunatic Asylums in Britain and Ireland, and some other Kingdoms*, Underwood, London

Hunter, R. and MacAlpine, I. (1963) *Three Hundred Years of Psychiatry*, Oxford University Press, London

Ibn Khaldun (1967–68), *Discours sur l'Histoire Universelle;* 3 vols (transl. V. Monteil), Sinbad Press, Paris

Kimura, B. (1971) Struktur des Selbstbewusstseins beim Japaner im Spiegel der sogenannten 'Anthropophobien' (extended English abstract), *Transcultural Psychiatry Research Review, 8,* 129

Kleinman, A. (1980) *Patients and Healers in the Context of Culture*, University of California Press, Berkeley

Kraepelin, E. (1904) 'Vergleichende Psychiatrie', *Zentrablatt für die gesamte Neurologie und Psychiatrie, 15,* 433–7

Morel, B-A. (1845) 'Pathologie mentale en Belgique, en Hollande, et en Allemagne', *Annales Medico-Psychologiques, 6,* 196–222 and 350–8

Murphy, H.B.M. (1972) 'History and the Evolution of Syndromes: the Striking Case of *Latah* and *Amok*' in M. Hammer, K. Salzinger and S. Sutton (eds), *Psychopathology*, 33–55, Wiley, New York

Murphy, H.B.M. (1982) *Comparative Psychiatry: the International and Intercultural Distribution of Mental Illness*, Springer, Berlin

Murphy, H.B.M. and Raman, A.C. (1973) 'The Chronicity of Schizophrenia in Indigenous Tropical Peoples', *British Journal of Psychiatry, 118,* 489–97

Opler, M.K. (1959) (ed.) *Culture and Mental Health*, Macmillan, New York

Ortigues, M.C. and Ortigues, E. (1966) *Oedipe Africain*, Plon, Paris

Parin, P. and Parin-Matthey, G. (1978), 'The Swiss and South-German Middle-class; an Ethno-psychoanalytic Study', *Journal of Psychological Anthropology 1,* 101–19

Parin, P., Morgenthaler, F. and Parin-Matthey, G. (1963), *Die Weissen denken zuviel*, Atlantis, Zurich

Parsons, A. (1964) 'Is the Oedipus Complex Universal? The Jones-Malinowski Debate Revisited', *Psychoanalytic Study of Society, 3,* 278–28

Parsons, A. (1969) *Belief, Magic and Anomie: Essays in Psychosocial Anthropology*, Free Press, New York

Pfeiffer, W.M. (1971) *Transkulturelle Psychiatrie, Ergebnisse und Probleme*, Geo. Thieme, Stuttgart

Pilcz, A. (1919/20) 'Beitrag zur vergleichenden Rassenpsychiatrie', *Psychiatrisch-neurologische Wochenschrift, 23/24,* 157–62, 179–82

Roheim, G. (1947) 'Introduction: Psychoanalysis and Anthropology', *Psychoanalysis and the Social Sciences*, Vol. 1, International University Press, New York

Rush, B. (1794) *Medical Inquiries and Observations*, p. 24, Dobson, Philadelphia (cited by G. Rosen) (1968) *Madness in Society*, (Harper & Row, New York)

Sachs, W. (1937) *Black Hamlet: the Mind of an African Negro Revealed by Psychoanalysis*, Geoffry Bles, London

Sanua, V.D. (1963) 'The Socio-cultural Aspects of Schizophrenia; Comparison of Protestant and Jewish Schizophrenics', *International Journal of Social Psychiatry, 9,* 27

Schooler, C. (1974) 'William Caudill's Contributions to Japanese Cultural Psychology and Psychiatry; a Memorial', *Transcultural Psychiatry Research Review, 11,* 149

Sena, J.F. (1973) 'Melancholic Madness and the Puritans, *Harvard Theological Review, 66,* 293

Sow, I. (1977) *Psychiatrie Dynamique Africaine*, Payot, Paris

Williams, A.H. (1950) 'A Psychiatric Study of Indian Soldiers on the Arakan', *British Journal of Medical Psychology, 23,* 130–81

World Health Organisation (1979) *Schizophrenia: an International Follow-up Study*, Wiley, New York

Yap, P.M. (1974) *Comparative Psychiatry, a Theoretical Framework*, University of Toronto Press, Toronto

Yule, H. and Burnell, A.C. (1886) *Hobson-Jobson; Being a Glossary of Anglo-Indian Colloquial Words and Phrases* . . . John Murray, London

3 THE EPIDEMIOLOGY OF MENTAL ILLNESS ACROSS CULTURES

Julian Leff

The Contribution of Epidemiology to Psychiatry

Epidemiology is the study of the distribution of disorders in defined populations. The populations studied are commonly defined in terms of age, sex or geographical location, but any measurable characteristic could be used. The advantage of relating disorders to a defined population is that it avoids the biases introduced by the selection of patients for treatment at the various levels of a medical system. For example, Carothers' (1951) statement, distilled from his clinical experience, that depression was rare in Africans was partly influenced by the fact that where psychiatric facilities are scarce they cater almost exclusively for patients with the severest psychiatric disorders. A statement of that kind can only have validity if it is made on the basis of a population survey. Comparisons of the frequency of conditions across cultures can be very misleading if the samples are not based on defined populations.

An illustration of this point is provided by the International Pilot Study of Schizophrenia (IPSS) (WHO, 1979). This was a study of schizophrenia in nine different countries. The pilot nature of this enterprise was stressed in the title, as it was not designed as population-based research but was intended to lay the basis for later epidemiological studies. Consecutive admissions to each centre's psychiatric facility were screened to determine whether they met the inclusion criteria for psychosis, and were then assessed with the Present State Examination (PSE) (Wing *et al.*, 1974). The psychiatrists in each centre made their own clinical diagnoses, and when the distribution of these was compared it was found that there was a striking variation in the proportion of manic patients in the various samples. This ranged from 16 per cent in Aarhus, Denmark, to 5 per cent in London. It was considered worth while mounting an epidemiological study based on case registers to investigate this interesting finding. A case register is one of the most useful epidemiological tools, although it is relatively expensive to set up and maintain. It consists of a list of patients from a defined catchment area, who utilise the medical services for that area. It is continuously updated as new individuals make contact

23

with the various facilities. Patients who cease contact are retained on the register, so that it grows progressively larger and needs a computer to handle the data.

Case registers already existed in two of the IPSS centres, Aarhus, Denmark, and Camberwell, London. An epidemiological study of the first contact rate for mania was therefore initiated in these two centres (Leff *et al.*, 1976). Using diagnoses made by the research psychiatrists, the annual first-admission rate for mania was found to be identical in the two centres, 2.6 per 100 000 population. This result indicates that the difference in proportions of manic patients found in the Aarhus and London groups of the IPSS was an artefact attributable to differences in referral and admission practices.

Incidence and Prevalence

In order to appreciate the potential contribution of epidemiology to psychiatry it is necessary to distinguish between the terms 'incidence' and 'prevalence'. 'Incidence' refers to the rate of appearance of new cases of a particular condition, and is usually measured over the period of a year. Variations in incidence across populations can provide clues to aetiology. Thus the finding that the incidence of schizophrenia was much higher in population A than in population B would lead to a search for differences between the two populations that might explain this, and hence could result in the identification of aetiological factors. Since the aetiology of most psychiatric conditions remains obscure, the theoretical and practical importance of a marked difference in incidence is clear.

Prevalence rates include both first-onset cases and also any subsequent episodes of illness, as well as individuals who remain persistently ill for long periods of time. Prevalence can be related to a particular instant in time (point prevalence), to a specified interval of time (e.g. one-year prevalence) or even to the whole life span of individuals (lifetime prevalence). Prevalence rates inform us about the factors that influence the course of illness, and are important both theoretically and in practical management. Both incidence and prevalence rates represent essential information for the planning of services, with which we will not be concerned in this chapter.

Standardisation of Clinical Assessment

Of course, before being able to calculate incidence or prevalence rates, one has to be able to define what one is counting. This is by no means a simple matter. To take schizophrenia as an example, it appeared from hospital statistics that the admission rate for this condition in the United States was about twice that in England. However, when the PSE was used to assess symptoms and a project team made a standardised diagnosis on both sides of the Atlantic, this difference disappeared. This finding, which emerged from the US/UK project (Cooper *et al.*, 1972), indicated that the term 'schizophrenia' was being used in a very different way by American and British psychiatrists. A parallel study, the IPSS, confirmed this result, and also showed that psychiatrists in Moscow operated an idiosyncratic diagnostic system that incorporated a very broad concept of schizophrenia. However, psychiatrists in seven of the nine centres participating in the IPSS, including cities as diverse as Ibadan in Nigeria, Agra in India, and Cali in Columbia, were in substantial agreement as to the diagnosis of schizophrenia. This reassuring result showed that the situation was not as chaotic as suggested by the US/UK project. However, it underlined the necessity for the employment of standardised clinical assessment and diagnostic techniques in cross-cultural epidemiological studies. As a result the PSE and the Catego program linked to it have become an integral part of the WHO research in psychiatric epidemiology.

Ethnocentric Bias

Although the development of standardised clinical tools marks a major advance in this field, it carries with it an inherent problem. The instruments in general use, like the PSE, have all been developed in Western countries on the basis of experience with Western psychiatric patients. As a consequence they do not include symptoms that are peculiar to non-Western patients. Thus when Leighton *et al.* (1963) mounted their pioneering psychiatric survey of the Yoruba people of Nigeria, they used the Cornell Medical Index which had been developed for a similar study in north east America. They found that they had to supplement the instrument with additional questions tailored to Yoruba complaints, such as: 'Do you ever have creeping feelings in the skin?', and 'Are you troubled by having a feeling of expanded head and goose flesh?' This way of adapting questions developed in the West for local use also has its limitations. In developing countries, the psychiatric services have been closely modelled on Western facilities and deal with only a small fraction of the psychiatrically ill. There is good evidence that people with conditions conforming to folk categories of mental disturbance are taken by preference to the traditional healer and may never be seen by professionals working in the psychiatric facilities. Hence the Western concepts of psychiatric illness, which are incorporated in the internationally accepted instruments, may never be challenged by the indigenous sufferers who do not conform to them.

There is a way of avoiding this ethnocentric bias, namely to develop psychiatric interviews in non-Western countries based on the complaints of people attending traditional healers and taking account of folk categories of illness. Attempts to adopt this approach have been made by Carstairs and Kapur (1976), who constructed the Indian Psychiatric Interview Schedule in Kannada, a South Indian language, and Verma and Wig (1976), who produced the (PGI) Health Questionnaire in Hindi. However, neither group has really started at grass-roots level, in the way that Beiser and his colleagues (1972) have done. They worked with the Serer people of Senegal and built up a native lexicon of disease terms and determined the patterns of behaviour to which they referred. They identified seven categories of disorder, which were classified by the Serer as 'illnesses of the spirit'. They then interviewed a sample of 50 people who were considered to be suffering from an illness of the spirit. Two interviews were conducted, one with a Western psychiatric questionnaire and the other with an unstructured clinical interview administered by psychiatrists who were working in Senegal. By this means it was possible to compare indigenous categories of disturbance with Western psychiatric concepts. From this comparison it emerged that one of the Serer categories, *Pobouh Lang,* or earth eating, had no Western equivalent.

Locally recognised psychiatric conditions in the Third World which have no equivalent in Western countries are of great interest to the epidemiologist for obvious reasons. The issues surrounding these are dealt with in detail in Chapter 15, and will not be discussed further here.

Case-finding Procedures for Schizophrenia

As we have seen, the use of the PSE in conjunction with the Catego diagnostic program defines a group of patients which most psychiatrists round the world would classify as suffering from schizophrenia. This lays a firm basis for epidemiological studies of the incidence and prevalence of this condition, but there are further obstacles to overcome, in particular the collection of a population-based sample. The problems are of a different dimension in a non-Western compared with a Western country. In the latter, psychiatric facilities are well developed and there is usually no hindrance to referral of a psychotic patient to a psychiatrist for diagnosis and treatment. It is probable that a small proportion of patients with a first onset of schizophrenia receive treatment from their general practitioners without referral to a specialist. However, the vast majority of such patients are seen at a psychiatric facility as either in-patients or out-patients. Hence a reasonably accurate estimate of the annual incidence of schizophrenia can be obtained from hospital statistics in a Western country. The use of case registers, as described above, ensures that the figures obtained are based on a defined population, and has the additional advantage that they employ strategies to detect patients from the catchment area who are seen at hospitals unrelated to it. Thus the most accurate estimates of the incidence of schizophrenia in the West are derived from case registers. The available figures come from Western Europe and vary relatively little in the range of ten to fifteen new cases of schizophrenia per year for a population of 100 000.

Case registers are usually set up at a late phase in the development of a psychiatric service, when most areas in a country are well endowed with psychiatric facilities. A different approach is required in a developing country with sparse facilities. To appreciate the scope of the problem it is necessary to consider the variety of actions that may be taken in such a country when an individual develops a schizophrenic illness. If the sufferer behaves in a violent or destructive manner, the first professional contacted may well be a policeman. Where there are no psychiatric facilities nearby, such patients are often housed in prison. Should the disturbance prove to be transient, a patient of this kind may not come to the notice of the psychiatric services at all. Sufferers who present less of a problem with aggression are likely to be taken in the first instance to a traditional healer. Healers in Africa and India are known to use Rauwolfia, which is a potent antipsychotic agent. Harding's (1973) survey of traditional healers in Ibarapa, Nigeria, showed that a significant number of psychotic patients are treated by them and live with the healers for weeks if not months. It is probable that many schizophrenic patients treated in this way recover and return to their families without ever seeing a Western-style practitioner. Others fail to respond to the healer's regime and, when the family's financial support ceases, are turned loose to wander in the bush or else to join the ranks of vagrant psychotics who congregate in the cities (Asuni, 1971). Some patients with an insidious onset of schizophrenia may not even be taken to a traditional healer, but might live out their lives disabled but sheltered by their family.

Studies of Incidence

A consideration of these possible outcomes of a first episode of schizophrenia makes it clear that schizophrenic patients referred to a psychiatric facility in the Third World are a highly selected group and constitute only a small proportion of the total number of cases that need to be included in an incidence figure. As a bare minimum, an incidence survey in a developing country needs to cover prisons, traditional healers and known vagrants, in addition to the psychiatric facilities. The inclusion of a population survey to identify patients living with family members who have never been seen by professionals raises the effort and resources needed to an impractical level. Following the completion of the IPSS, the WHO Mental Health Division initiated case-finding procedures in a selection of ten centres in developing and developed countries, which were designed to yield reasonably comprehensive incidence rates for defined catchment areas. Case-finding networks were established in each centre which encompassed a wide range of potential contact agencies, including modern psychiatric practitioners and medical facilities, and traditional and religious treatment agencies, as well as social services and the prison service. The findings of this important and ambitious study have not yet been published, but preliminary results show a threefold variation in incidence rates across the centres if a broad definition of schizophrenia is employed. With a narrow definition based on the presence of Schneider's first-rank symptoms, the variation in rates is reduced, with a range between seven and fourteen new cases per year per 100 000 population between the ages of 15 and 54. Even the use of the narrow definition of schizophrenia generates enough variation in incidence rates to stimulate the formulation and testing of hypotheses about the aetiology of schizophrenia, which is a desirable outcome of any epidemiological study.

Studies of Prevalence

Having examined the obstacles in the way of studying the incidence of schizophrenia across cultures, we can turn to the work on prevalence. The same issues concerning definition of the illness are raised by prevalence as by incidence studies, but the technical problems affecting case finding are less formidable. The population survey is the principal epidemiological tool required, although it needs to be supplemented by studies of vagrants and surveys of patients residing with traditional healers in developing countries. The main problem is a practical one of sampling a large enough population to be reasonably confident of the prevalence rate obtained. On account of the relative rarity of schizophrenia in the general population, surveys on a heroic scale are required; for example, Dube (1970) screened over 29 000 people living around Agra, and Lin (1953) interviewed almost 20 000 Taiwanese. It is necessary in calculating the rate to use another epidemiological technique, age stratification. Since schizophrenia, like most other major psychiatric conditions, is extremely rare below the age of 15, its incidence and prevalence will be greatly affected by the age structure of the population under study. If related to the size of the whole population, schizophrenia will inevitably appear to be less frequent in a developing country, where half the people are aged under 15, than in a developed country, where the proportion is less than one-third. To make such comparisons valid, it is necessary to express the rates in relation to the proportion at risk for the condition, namely those over 15 years of age. It may also be advisable to establish an upper limit, partly to avoid confusion with psychoses due to organic change in the brain consequent on age, and partly to adjust for the greater longevity in Western countries.

Prevalence of Neurosis

Leff (1981) reviewed the population surveys that have been conducted in developing countries and found that the age-adjusted prevalence rate for schizophrenia varied within fairly narrow limits between 3.3 and 8.0 per 1000 population over the age of 15. The figure of 8.0 was an outlier from a study by Elnagar *et al.*, (1971) and the next highest prevalence rate was 5.6 (Wijesinghe *et al.*, 1978). A dramatic contrast with this narrow range is provided by the prevalence rates for neurosis derived from *the same set of studies*. The lowest rate recorded was 0.8 per 1000 for Taiwan aborigines (Rin and Lin, 1962) and the highest was 67.0 per 1000 for Bengalese (Nandi *et al.*, 1975). This is almost a hundred-fold difference but even so does not represent the upper limit. More recent studies using standardised clinical assessments have yielded much higher prevalence rates for neurosis: 287 per 1000 for women in Buenos Aires (Tarnopolsky *et al.*, 1977) and 269 per 1000 for Ugandan village women (Orley and Wing, 1979). Thus the highest rate recorded is 350 times the lowest. Common sense tells us that this result cannot be taken at its face value, and indeed there are a number of factors responsible for this other than a true difference in prevalence. These will now be explored.

Problems Affecting the Detection of Neurosis

Intensity of Screening

The first factor is the method of screening the population being surveyed. The most economical method of conducting a survey is to use key informants to identify likely cases. Village chiefs, policemen and schoolteachers have been used for this purpose. The usefulness of this strategy depends on developing a good liaison with the informants, and on the degree to which psychiatric conditions are stigmatised and hence kept hidden by sufferers and their relatives. It is likely that most people suffering from psychotic conditions will be known to key informants. However, neurotic conditions will frequently be overlooked. The problem has been studied by Hagnell (1966), who personally interviewed over 3000 inhabitants of Lundby in southern Sweden. In addition to the interviews, Hagnell used three key informants who had lived in the area for at least 25 years and who had actively participated in both official and private events. In some cases their information was extremely accurate when checked with the personal interviews, whereas in others they were completely unaware of psychiatric disturbance in the recent past. For example, in one case a depressive illness five years earlier lasting six months was not mentioned by the key informant.

This kind of discrepancy undermines confidence in the use of key informants to provide information about neuroses. The most expensive alternative is for a psychiatrist to interview each respondent personally, as Hagnell did. However, his survey took well over two years to complete and its type is out of the question in a developing country. A compromise is possible in the form of a two-stage procedure. The first stage is the use of a screening interview to detect 'cases', which can be administered by lay interviewers after a relatively short period of training. Psychiatrists then interview all 'cases', but have to check on the sensitivity of the screening procedure by also seeing a random selection of 'non-cases', say one in ten. This technique was used by Wijesinghe *et al.* (1978) in Sri Lanka. The screening interview consisted of a general health enquiry followed by psychiatric items, and was administered by social workers to 7643 people in a semi-urban area. Criteria for caseness were established, and any subject satisfying them was referred for a full psychiatric examination. This yielded a six-month prevalence rate of 25 per 1000 for neuroses. A random sample of subjects not identified by the screening procedure as 'cases' was also interviewed by the psychiatrists. A substantial proportion of these were found to be suffering from an active neurotic condition. When the prevalence rate was amended to take account of the missed cases, it more than doubled to about 60 per 1000. This indicates that the screening procedure had a low sensitivity to neurosis. It is advisable to check this aspect of screening in pilot studies, and amend the instrument accordingly if indicated, as has been done with the General Health Questionnaire (Goldberg, 1972).

Determination of Caseness

The second factor concerns another technical issue, the method of determining the level of symptoms which would justify an individual being labelled a case. This is a complex problem which raises important theoretical issues (Wing *et al.*, 1981). The simplest approach is to score a series of symptoms on rating scales, to add up the total score on the list of symptoms, and to establish a cut-off point, above which the subject qualifies as a case. Since the aim is to identify subjects in the general population who are as ill as those attending for psychiatric treatment, the cut-off point is adjusted so that virtually all the clients of an outpatient clinic would qualify as cases. This is the approach embodied in the General Health Questionnaire. However, the simple summation of scores ignores the fact that in clinical practice certain symptoms are given more weight than others. Thus a small degree of depression is generally viewed as seriously as a lot of worrying or muscular tension. These variations in the clinical significance ascribed to symptoms have been conceptualised in the form of a hierarchy (Foulds and Bedford, 1975) and are incorporated in an Index of Definition (ID) constructed by Wing *et al.* (1978). The ID contains rules, incorporated in a computer program, that can be applied to PSE data. A subject is allocated by the program to one of eight levels of confidence that the symptoms present indicate a diagnosis of a functional psychosis or neurosis. Levels one to four are non-cases, level five is at the threshold for caseness, and levels six to eight are increasingly more definite. The advantage of the cut-off point for a total score and of the ID system is that they are completely standardised and do not involve any subjective judgements.

A different approach, which does not eliminate clinical judgement, was used in the survey of the Yoruba by Leighton and his colleagues (1963). They compiled a series of narrative descriptions of subjects, some of whom were clear-cut cases, some borderline and some non-cases. They then had to classify each subject interviewed in the survey by comparing him with the illustrative narratives. This technique has the disadvantage of being difficult to replicate, but has been developed further by Brown (1981) and Finlay-Jones (1981). Brown's team used the PSE in population surveys to assess psychiatric symptoms. At weekly rating meetings the interviewer described the type, intensity, and duration of the symptoms of a particular subject to a team of experienced raters. The raters then compared them with narrative descriptions of various types of case and classified the subject by consensus agreement after considerable discusssion. It was possible for the team to achieve acceptable reliability, but a doubt hangs over the communication of their technique to other fresh teams since the criteria for classification are not entirely explicit. Despite the element of subjectivity involved in Brown's approach, when his team's method of assigning caseness was compared with Wing's PSE-ID-Catego system, the prevalence rates of neurosis showed considerable similarity. In view of the ease with which computer classification can be applied, it is likely to displace the kind of consensus ratings employed by Brown, even though they appear to approximate more closely to clinical practice.

The Language of Emotion

The final factor to be considered that may affect the ascertainment of the prevalence of neurosis in developing countries is language. We have already discussed ways in which schedules developed in the West may be biased against the detection of indigenous varieties of psychiatric disturbance. A further loss of sensitivity may occur when a schedule is translated from a Western to a non-Western language. This is exemplified by the process of translation of the PSE from English into the seven other languages represented by the centres in the IPSS. Difficulties were encountered when translating various neurotic symptoms into Yoruba and Chinese. In particular the words 'depression' and 'anxiety' seemed to have no direct equivalents in Yoruba. In the original translation they were represented by phrases, which were later back-translated as 'the heart is weak' and 'the heart is not at rest'. The problem with Chinese was that only a single word could be found to stand for 'anxiety', 'tension' and 'worrying', these symptoms being clearly differentiated in the original English version of the PSE. Similar gaps in the vocabulary of emotion are found in a number of African languages. Cheetham and Cheetham (1976) reported that depression is a word unknown to the Xhosa people of South Africa, and Gillis *et al.* (1982) encountered similar problems in translating the PSE into Xhosa as had bedevilled the Yoruba translation. Orley (unpublished manuscript) also had difficulty in finding specific words for anxiety and depression when translating the PSE into Luganda.

This phenomenon is by no means confined to African languages.

Manson and Shore (1985) constructed an American Indian Depression Schedule in the Hopi language and found that there was no word or phrase equivalent to the term 'depression'. Ekman *et al.* (1969) studied the recognition of emotional expressions by the South Fore people of New Guinea. They concluded that it was doubtful whether the meaning of a particular emotional concept was adequately conveyed by translating a single English word into a single South Fore word. Marsella (1979), in reviewing cross-cultural studies of depression, noted that work on indigenous categories of mental disorder in Malaysia, Borneo, Africa and among American Indians revealed that there were no concepts that represented depression as a disease, a symptom or a syndrome.

Leff (1981) has incorporated this evidence into a theory concerning the development of the language of emotional expression. The kernel of the theory is that over time there has been a shift in focus from the bodily expression of distress to its communication through language, with a consequent progressive differentiation of the vocabulary of emotion. This historical process has occurred unevenly, so that in many cultures today emotional distress is still communicated through a rich variety of somatic symptoms. One of the pieces of evidence cited by Leff to substantiate this theory is the disappearance of conversion hysteria in the West whereas it persists as a common form of neurosis in the Third World.

There are two interesting cross-cultural studies of the frequency of hysteria in soldiers during the Second World War. Abse (1950) studied psychiatric admissions to the Indian Military Hospital in Delhi during the year 1944 and found the proportion of hysteria to be 57 per cent whereas that of anxiety states was 12 per cent. Comparable figures from a British military hospital showed reversal of these proportions, with 24 per cent suffering from hysteria and 50 per cent from anxiety states. A very similar picture was presented by Williams (1950), who was a psychiatrist appointed to a mixed Indian and British division fighting in Burma. Although soliders from both cultures faced the same high degree of stress, the pattern of neurotic symptoms in each was quite different. Over 50 per cent of the British referrals presented with an anxiety state and only 7 per cent with hysteria, whereas the proportions among Indian patients were 10 per cent with anxiety states and 32 per cent with hysteria. Hysteria remains a common form of presentation at psychiatric facilities throughout the Third World, constituting around 20 per cent of all neurotic patients. In the West, however, hysteria has become a rarity.

Conversion hysteria is a specific form of bodily expression of emotional distress. The psychological origin of the symptoms is usually relatively easy to determine. However, the cultural factors that influence the geographical distribution of hysteria also operate on a host of somatic complaints which are only distinguished with difficulty from the symptoms of organic diseases. Indeed clients with this mode of presentation of distress are seen in large numbers in general medical facilities in the Third World (Harding *et al.*, 1980). We have already encountered one example of the effect this has on epidemiological research, namely the need that Leighton *et al.* (1963) found to supplement their American survey instrument with somatic symptoms for use with the Yoruba. However, the addition of suitable questions about somatic complaints does not contribute towards differentiating emotional distress presented in this form from organic disease. This issue is crucial for the determination of the prevalence of neurosis in developing countries, yet is beyond the resources of most population surveys. The fact that malnutrition and parasitic diseases are endemic causes of physical symptoms in many Third World countries means that a psychiatric survey needs the back-up facility of a pathology laboratory to differentiate between psychological and physical illnesses. Very few population surveys in developing countries have had this available, and in its absence psychiatric conditions presenting with bodily complaints are unlikely to be identified. Hence prevalence rates for neurosis that have been established by population surveys in the Third World are likely to be underestimates.

A Role for Culture

To sum up, we have considered three sources of variability in the detection of neurotic conditions in population surveys: the degree of intensity of the screening procedure, the arbitrary nature of judgements concerning caseness, and the somatic presentation of emotional distress. These undoubtedly account for much of the diversity of prevalence rates of neurosis that have been ascertained. However, we need to ask whether there is a cultural variation distinct from that attributable to these technical issues. We can begin to answer this question by referring to the study of Orley and Wing (1979), comparing prevalence rates for neurosis in two Ugandan villages and a suburb of London. This study represents a technical innovation in that the same standardised interview technique, the PSE, was used in both surveys, and also the same standardised method of determining caseness, the ID-Catego computerised system. The PSE does not attempt to detect neurosis presenting somatically, so that Orley's Ugandan survey almost certainly underestimated prevalence. Nevertheless, the rate of neurosis at ID level five or above was 269 per

1000 for women aged 18 to 65. The comparable rate for London women derived from the survey by Wing *et al.* (1978) was 106 per 1000. We cannot invoke any of the technical problems discussed above to explain the fact that the Ugandan prevalence rate was two-and-a-half times the London rate, so this finding should stimulate a search for cultural factors.

The work presented in this chapter shows that it is essential to get the basic epidemiological techniques right before we can invoke cultural factors to explain differences in incidence and prevalence. Technical advances in this field have now reached the point where we can proceed to test theories about the influence of culture on the aetiology and course of psychiatric disorders.

References

Abse, D.W. (1950) *The Diagnosis of Hysteria*, John Wright, Bristol

Asuni, T. (1971) 'Vagrant Psychotics in Abeokuta', *Journal of the National Medical Association (New York)*, *63*, 173–80

Beiser, M., Ravel, J.L., Collomb, H. and Englehoff, C. (1972) 'Assessing Psychiatric Disorder among the Serer of Senegal', *Journal of Nervous and Mental Disease*, *154*, 141–51

Brown, G.W. (1981) 'Aetiological Studies and the Definition of a Case', in J.K. Wing, P. Bebbington and L.N. Robbins, (eds), *What is a Case?*, pp. 62–9, Grant McIntyre, London

Carothers, J.C. (1951) 'Frontal Lobe Function and the African', *Journal of Mental Science*, *97*, 12–48

Carstairs, G.M. and Kapur, R.L. (1976) *The Great Universe of Kota*, Hogarth Press, London

Cheetham, W.S. and Cheetham, R.J. (1976), 'Concepts of Mental Illness amongst the Xhosa People in South Africa', *Australia and New Zealand Journal of Psychiatry*, *10*, 39–45

Cooper, J.E., Kendell, R.E., Gurland, B.J., Sharpe, L., Copeland, J.R.M. and Simon, R. (1972) *Psychiatric Diagnosis in New York and London*, Maudsley Monograph No.20, Oxford University Press, London

Dube, K.C. (1970) 'A Study of Prevalence and Biosocial Variables in Mental Illness in a Rural and an Urban Community in Uttar Pradesh, India, *Acta Psychiatrica Scandinavica*, *46*, 327–59

Ekman, P., Sorenson, E.R. and Friesen, W.V. (1969) 'Pancultural Elements in Facial Displays of Emotion', *Science 164*, 86–8

Elnagar, M.N., Maitra, P. and Rao, M.N. (1971) 'Mental Health in an Indian Rural Community', *British Journal of Psychiatry*, *118*, 499–503

Finlay-Jones, R. (1981) 'The Diagnosis of a Case by a Global Rating Method', in J.K. Wing, P. Bebbington and L.N. Robins, (eds), *What is a Case?* pp. 70–5, Grant McIntyre, London

Foulds, G.A. and Bedford, A. (1975) 'Hierarchy of Classes of Personal Illness', *Psychological Medicine*, *5*, 181–92

Gillis, L.S., Elk, R., Ben-Arie, O. and Teggin, A. (1982) 'The Present State Examination: Experiences with Xhosa-speaking Psychiatric Patients', *British Journal of Psychiatry*, *141*, 143–7

Goldberg, D.P. (1972) *The Detection of Psychiatric Illness by Questionnaire*, Oxford University Press, London

Hagnell, O. (1966) *A Prospective Study of the Incidence of Mental Disorder*, Norstedts, Stockholm

Harding, T. (1973) 'Psychosis in a Rural West African Community', *Social Psychiatry, 8*, 198–203

Harding, T.W., De Arango, M.V., Baltazar, J., Climent, C.E., Ibrahim, H.H.A., Ladrido-Ignacio, L., Srinavasa Murthy, R. and Wig, N.N. (1980) 'Mental Disorders in Primary Health Care: a Study of their Frequency and Diagnosis in Four Developing Countries', *Psychological Medicine, 10*, 231–41

Leighton, A.H., Lambo, T.A., Hughes, C.C., Leighton, D.C., Murphy, J.M. and Macklin, D.B. (1963), *Psychiatric Disorder among the Yoruba*, Cornell University Press, New York

Leff, J. (1981) *Psychiatry around the Globe*, Dekker, New York

Leff, J.P., Fischer, M. and Bertelson, A. (1976) 'A Cross-national Epidemiological Study of Mania', *British Journal of Psychiatry, 129*, 428–37

Lin, T. (1953) 'A Study of the Incidence of Mental Disorder in Chinese and Other Cultures', *Psychiatry, 16*, 313–36

Manson, S.M. and Shore, J.H. (1985) 'The Depressive Experience in a Northwest Plateau American Indian Community: Indigenous Models of Explanation and Psychiatric Diagnosis', In R. Morris and E. Foulkes (eds), *The Diagnostic Endeavour: Anthropological Applications to the Psychiatric Interview*, Reidel, Amsterdam

Marsella, A.J. (1979) 'Depressive Experience and Disorder across Cultures', in H. Triandis and J. Draguns (eds), *Handbook of Crosscultural Psychology*, Vol. 5, Allyn and Bacon, Boston

Nandi, D.N., Ajmany, S., Ganguli, H., Bannerjee, G., Boral, G.C., Ghosh, A. and Sarkar, S. (1975) 'Psychiatric Disorders in a Rural Community in West Bengal — an Epidemiological Study', *Indian Journal of Psychiatry, 17*, 87–99

Orley, J. and Wing, J.K. (1979) 'Psychiatric Disorders in Two African Villages', *Archives of General Psychiatry, 36*, 513–20

Rin, H. and Lin, T. (1962) 'Mental Illness among Formosan Aborigines as Compared with the Chinese in Taiwan', *Journal of Mental Science, 108*, 134–46

Tarnopolsky, A., Caetano, R., Levav, I., Del Olmo, G., Campillo, C. and Pinheiro, H. (1977) 'Prelevance of Psychiatric Morbidity in an Industrial Suburb of Buenos Aires', *Social Psychiatry, 12*, 75–88

Verma, S.K. and Wig, N.N. (1976) 'PGI Health Questionnaire N-2: Construction and Initial Try Outs', *Indian Journal of Clinical Psychology, 3*, 135–42

Wijesinghe, C.P., Dissanayake, S.A.W. and Dassanayake, P.V.I.N. (1978) 'Survey of Psychiatric Morbidity in a Semi-urban Population in Sri Lanka', *Acta Psychiatrica Scandinavica, 58*, 413–41

Williams, A.H., (1950) 'A Psychiatric Study of Indian Soldiers in The Arakan', *British Journal of Medical Psychology, 23*, 130–81

Wing, J.K., Cooper, J.E. and Sartorius, N. (1974) *Measurement and Classification of Psychiatric Symptoms*, Cambridge University Press, London

Wing, J.K. Mann, S.A., Leff, J.P. and Nixon, J.M. (1978), 'The Concept of a Case in Psychiatric Population Surveys', *Psychological Medicine, 8*, 203–17

Wing, J.K., Bebbington, P. and Robins, L.N. (1981) 'Theory-testing in Psychiatric Epidemiology', in J.K. Wing, P. Bebbington, and L.N. Robins (eds), *What is a Case?*, pp. 1–8, Grant McIntyre, London

World Health Organisation (1979) *Schizophrenia. An International Follow-up Study*, Wiley, New York

4 RUSSIAN DOLLS AND CHINESE BOXES: AN ANTHROPOLOGICAL APPROACH TO THE IMPLICIT MODELS OF COMPARATIVE PSYCHIATRY†

Roland Littlewood

Any problem in psychopathology becomes a problem of symbol functioning, a matter of seeking to understand and interpret eccentric symbol performance.

Harry Stack Sullivan

Social Anthropology and British Psychiatry

Many British psychiatrists, notably Aubrey Lewis (1958) and Morris Carstairs, have looked to anthropology to clarify the relationship between psychopathology and culture. Though there were close historical links between the two disciplines earlier this century, particularly in the work of C.G. Seligman and W.H.R. Rivers, less than five contemporary British psychiatrists have taken an anthropological training; the teaching of the social sciences to medical students and trainee psychiatrists remains the preserve of sociologists. By contrast, many American universities, notably Harvard and Hawaii, not only have joint appointments in psychiatry and social anthropology, but also offer postgraduate training courses for future research workers. Arthur Kleinman, Professor of Psychiatry at Harvard, has suggested (1980) that the co-operation of anthropology and psychiatry is essential to achieve the 'full potentialities of a culturally appropriate, human, integrated practice of clinical care'. A number of medical journals edited in North America (*Culture, Medicine and Psychiatry; Transcultural Psychiatric Research Review; Journal of Operational Psychiatry; Social Science and Medicine; Medical Anthropology*) have a particular interest in social anthropology. By contrast the last specific mention of the psychiatric relevance of anthropology in a British journal was that by Loudon in 1972.

†This chapter is an expanded version of the paper 'Social Anthropology in Relation to Psychiatry', *British Journal of Psychiatry, 146* (1985), pp. 552–4.

The syllabus for the examination for Membership of the Royal College of Psychiatrists in Britain includes social anthropology, but no essay question has ever been set in this area, and the guidelines of the Association of University Teachers of Psychiatry (AUTP) restrict themselves to a single sentence: 'Knowledge of social anthropology need not be extensive but should include an understanding of cultural differenees in family and social roles, particularly as they apply to ethnic minorities in this country; and the range of human development as it is shown by its variations in different societies' (AUTP, 1982). Teaching of social anthropology to psychiatrists in Britain is minimal, and I should imagine I am unusual in giving eight lectures to the Guy's Hospital MRC Psych course.

The AUTP guidelines emphasise not the theoretical approach of social anthropology, but empirical information about particular communities, especially their forms of socialisation. In this chapter I am taking as self-evident the idea that psychopathology of all types can only be manifest in a cultural field, often in relation to certain core social values, and that in psychiatric practice some knowledge of 'local' social structure, values, behaviour, and conceptualisation of distress and mental illness is essential (*British Medical Journal,* 1981). Instead of answering questions of the 'Is this a delusion?' type (perhaps the most common request by colleagues to the ethnographically inclined clinician (Littlewood, 1980; Gaines, 1982), I wish to look at the implicit model of comparative psychiatry, the Russian Dolls of my title, through a mildly anthropological lens.

The Imperial Legacy

The mention of ethnic minorities by the AUTP is characteristic. Most of the chapters in this volume are concerned with minorities, and the British Transcultural Psychiatry Society has devoted its exclusive attention to them. In Britain 'transcultural psychiatry' is now synonymous with 'the psychiatry of ethnic minorities'. Patient and therapist may belong to different subcultures, e.g. a minority and a majority culture. (The programmatic value-free study of the relationship between psychopathology and culture now prefers the designation of *cross-cultural psychiatry, comparative psychiatry* or, simply, *cultural psychiatry.*) Although the consequent revival of psychiatric interest in social anthropology is welcome, it is unfortunate that it is largely attributable to anxieties on our part at working with minorities whose patterns of mental illness are erroneously perceived as more 'cultural' than our textbook paradigms (Littlewood and Lipsedge, 1982). The theoretical models of transcultural psychiatry have yet to be applied with any seriousness to Western societies (see Chapter 15); as Hahn (1983) puts it, culture-bound syndromes 'are what other people have, not us'.

The origins of transcultural psychiatry lie in the European colonial empires, particularly in Africa and the Pacific, and in the Indian Reservations of North America. Psychiatrists working in these areas would occasionally leave their hospitals for brief forays into the local community, where traditional patterns of ritual and belief were seized upon and labelled as 'culture-bound syndromes' (Littlewood and Lipsedge, 1985). As German (1972) has observed, transcultural psychiatry 'was based on work carried out by a host of short-term visitors (producing) a wealth of data about some strange ritual of an obscure tribe, analysed with style and erudition, but without comment on general trends particularly as they relate to the more mundane aspects of clinical psychiatry'. Transcultural psychiatry has been bedevilled by this pursuit of exotic syndromes, relegating them quite understandably to 'the twilight zone of psychiatric phenomena' (Hughes, 1985), marginal both to the corpus of general psychiatric theory and to the practice of psychiatry in the developing world. Emphasis on the exotic precluded the serious situating of comparative psychiatry in its social context (Kleinman, 1977) and directed attention from more immediate problems, besides providing yet another justification of the strangeness or inferiority of non-Europeans.

The idea that non-Europeans were 'in a lower state of intellectual development' (Kraepelin, 1904) produced novel mental states: 'hyperidic states', 'catastrophic reactions', 'malignant anxiety', 'simple responses', and 'primitive reactions' (Kiev, 1972). Manschreck and Petri (1978) describe the approach as a 'preoccupation with cultureness, superficial assessment of cultural variables [and] remoteness from anthropological studies of normative behaviour in the same settings'. Littlewood and Lipsedge (1982) suggest that the pathologisation of indigenous cultures played a significant role in the legitimation of colonial endeavours. Religion was equated with obsessional neurosis and witchcraft with paranoia (Lewis, I.M. 1977). A particular claim that has continued to trouble anthropologists was the idea that the inspirational healer or *shaman* was invariably mentally ill (Littlewood and Lipsedge, 1985).

The study of 'culture-bound syndromes' has frequently been merely the hearsay repetition of previous descriptions, usually in their most bizarre form, distorting the significance and context of the phenomena

(Neutra *et al.*, 1977); in the case of *susto* and the 'possession states', observed behaviour was confused with local exegesis (Littlewood and Lipsedge, 1985). It now seems that *windigo* (a reaction supposedly found among North American Indians and Inuit in which an individual became possessed by a cannibalistic vampire) is merely the solidification of psychiatric folklore, a 'near mythical syndrome' (Neutra *et al.*, 1977) with perhaps three actual instances and a state which has never been observed by Westerners. Similar doubt has been cast on 'voodoo death' (the splendidly named *thanatomania*) (Mauss, 1950; Lewis, S.A., 1977).

That such 'reactions' merely demonstrate professional helplessness in the face of patterns for which we lack intellectual tools is well exemplified by the recent descriptions in Britain of 'the Begum syndrome' (Galbraith, 1980), and (incredibly) 'New Cross Psychosis'. Exotic (and unintelligible) syndromes are delineated and then pushed into the margins; interpretations of their mechanism or meaning are couched in the form of 'suggestion' or 'culture' *tout court*. Transcultural psychiatry in Britain has been regarded with suspicion by anthropologists precisely because of its unstated ethnocentric assumptions and its lack of methodological rigour (Lewis, I.M., 1977). Ioan Lewis, Professor of Social Anthropology at the London School of Economics and an anthropologist who is sympathetic to psychiatry, notes that a dialogue 'between those who study the culturally standardised symbolism of societies and those who study the idiosyncratic personal symbolism of individuals seems obvious', but regretfully adds 'the rather limited fruits which [transcultural psychiatry] has so far produced merely provided for British social anthropologists additional confirmation of the undesirability of all liaisons of this sort' (Lewis, I.M., 1977).

The Social Anthropological Approach

What then of social anthropology? Since it separated itself from physical anthropology (the study of human biological variation) last century and left the latter to engage at that time in racist justifications for European supremacy along the lines of cranial capacity and the like (e.g. Baker, 1974), it too has been principally concerned with the study of the societies colonised by Europeans. Although there remains a continuing emphasis on small-scale, bounded and homogeneous communities, contemporary anthropologists have turned also to look at European and urban societies and particular environments within them; indeed perhaps the most influential work emanating from the social sciences for the practice of psychiatry has been the book *Asylums*, by the anthropologist Goffman (1968), a participant-observation study of the life of a traditional mental hospital. Recent studies have looked at housing estates (Owens, 1981), domestic violence (Martin, 1978; Dobash and Dobash, 1980) and women's refuges (Pahl, 1984).

Anthropology is less differentiated from other social sciences by subject matter than by its theoretical approach and method of participant observation; conducting 'fieldwork', the ethnographer lives in a community for a year or more, speaking the local language and, in varying degrees, becoming an active member of that society. Fieldwork provides as much of a rite of passage to the anthropologist's professional future and status as does a personal psychoanalysis for the aspiring analyst. Often exhilarating, it provides

> a salutary if sometimes demoralising experience of discovering how inadequate initial explanatory hypotheses can be . . . Quite apart from the aspect of personal ordeal and discovery, fieldwork involves testing the edge of theoretical concepts against the bone and gristle of ideas and everyday existence of ordinary people living in another cultural world from one's own. (Loudon, 1972)

Social anthropologists were historically distinctive in their insistence that cultural differences could not be predicated upon racial differences. Whereas early theorists like Tylor and Frazer could still assume an evolution of culture, the notion of a 'primitive mentality' was later discarded, particularly since Evans-Pritchard's demonstration (1937) that witchcraft was not so much a set of mistaken beliefs as an empirical and adaptive mode of social organisation. Anthropology proposes that societies differ not by psychological *processes* but by *vehicles* of thought: conceptual structures and classifications of space and time, the sexes and the natural world, which are coded in symbols, particularly language, and which 'lie outside the boundaries of the individual as such, in that inter-subjective world of common understandings into which all human individuals are born, in which they pursue their separate careers, and which they leave persisting behind them after they die' (Geertz, 1966).

While looking at the whole society, anthropologists may concentrate on specific cultural complexes, each of which may articulate a whole set of questions, including individual personality, marital relations and kin ties, the conceptualisation of the world, the distribution of labour and economic resources, medical nosologies and healing practices. Such specific analytical complexes may themselves be derived from local kinship systems, from concepts of gender or caste, or from traditional anthropological tools: reciprocity or such binary distinctions as nature/culture. Themes of this type are manifest in symbols which are seen to refer simultaneously to multiple levels of local reality and are often represented in key rituals.

Rather than relying on statistical samples of discrete units of the social universe separated out from the rest (as does sociology), anthropology endeavours to look at the total culture. It thus assumes that mental illness is not only a function of such objective indices as social class or the availability of services, but also of the considerably less tangible idea of the unique experience of being a member of a particular society: a society with its own characteristic web of economic constraints, social relations and beliefs (Littlewood, 1980).

Thus, a psychiatric approach which is based on anthropology will be meaning-centred. Such an *ethnopsychiatry* starts from the concepts of normality and abnormality held by a particular community (Kleinman, 1977). It is concerned with the relationship between public and private symbolism and how the individual makes sense of his or her personal situation given the intellectual tools available (Littlewood, 1984a). It attempts to explain how these tools, whether they are systems of magic or medicine, religion or psychology, reflect the physical environment of the community and its political organisation.

Ethnopsychiatry offers an alternative to traditional social psychiatry by regarding psychopathology not as a particular individual's state of mind at a given time or as nature thinly disguised, but as a cultural datum with complex linguistic, political and historical determinants. It approaches the mind through the examination of shared cultural categories of thought and action rather than through the statistical study of individuals. It is non-psychological in that the symbols which bind a society together and which articulate both private and public concerns are regarded not as the products of individual experience and motivation, however generalised, but primarily as the ordering of social reality (see Chapter 15).

Such an approach is rather different from the usual model of comparative psychiatry in which the individual represents a basic psychological or physiological core, surrounded by a series of envelopes, awaiting unpacking by a cultural psychiatrist. Although usually unstated, the epistemological underpinnings of the model are sketched out by Yap (1974). Instead it offers an approach in which human identity, behaviour and thought can only occur within an available social context and world view. As the psychologist Rom Harré has recently suggested (Harré,

1983), it implies that much of the endeavour of academic psychology and psychiatry is the reification and amplification of what is basically European folk psychology.

Schools of Social Anthropology

Anthropological schools differ as to what they regard as the major determining aspects of a culture. Various starting points — the history and diffusion of technology, patterns of morbidity or environmental constraints, organisation of labour, relations with other societies, social regulation, cognitive patterns, psychological needs — have all been regarded as primary; workers in identical societies have placed greater emphasis on different features depending on their own theoretical approach. Different anthropological approaches may thus be compared to Chinese boxes: entry to and exit from the models depend upon how the data are handled.

The 'classical' period of *functionalism* between the 1920s and 1950s conceived of societies as closed homeostatic systems in which beliefs and institutions served to organise and preserve a community in accordance with individual needs (Malinowski, 1922). In tribal societies such values are articulated primarily in terms of complex systems of kinship whose study accounts for much of the mystification of anthropology for the outsider. A lucid introduction to kinship is provided by Fox (1967), and the classic papers in Radcliffe-Brown and Forde (1976) illustrate a major kinship debate of the period, between those who emphasise the indigenous notion of *descent* and those who favour *alliance.*

By contrast, *structuralism,* associated especially with the French ethnographer Lévi-Strauss (1963), assumes, like George Kelly, that man is primarily motivated by a need to make sense of his situation. It postulates systems of cognitive universals, particularly binary symbolism (systems of dual classification), which may be represented in symbols of the natural world such as the sexes, the morphology of the human body or physiological states (Douglas, 1973a; Needham, 1973).

The opposing perspective of *cultural materialism* places greater determining power on the environment: thus Rappaport (1968) demonstrates that, in New Guinea, patterns of ritual warfare are closely tied to the maximum capacity for domestic livestock. *Marxist anthropology* (Godelier, 1973) also emphasises ecological and technological constraints and offers explanations for two questions which are problematic for the functionalist or structuralist: the presence of divergent interests inside bounded societies and the mechanism of cultural change. Another currently influential 'conflict theory' is that of *women's anthropology* (Ardener, 1975), which attempts to show how dominant symbolism and ideology in any society reflect men's interests and experiences, and how women always have to use the dominant conceptual system to attain a personal perspective; this offers us a fruitful model for the examination of individual experience including psychopathology (Littlewood, 1980).

Although many of the founders of social anthropology, such as Rivers, Seligman and McDougall, were psychiatrists or psychologists, the discipline has prospered as it discarded explanations based on individual psychology. Because of the influence of Durkheim and Mauss (1903), British anthropology is closer to French anthropology than to the more psychological American discipline, a rather different situation from that found in psychiatry. Durkheim believed that the symbols by which we organise our experience are themselves direct reflections of the social order. Thus the organisation of the universe reflects the organisation of the community. Douglas (1973a) shows how the boundaries of the body physical parallel those of the body politic, and suggests that dissociative states ('psychological loosening') are more prominent in egalitarian and individualistic societies ('social loosening'). She points out (Douglas, 1970) that notions of purity are not inaccurate cognitive stabs at empirical reality but part of a comprehensive system of social classification. A collection of papers edited by her (Douglas, 1973b) emphasises how, in a variety of situations, individual experience is only possible through collective notions of time, space, identity and causality. Durkheim's attempt to avoid psychological explanations of social phenomena tended to 'squeeze out' psychology as the middle term between sociology and physiology (e.g. Mauss, 1950); whether he was successful is debateable and all anthropologists contain implicit and unstated psychological assumptions, often of a rather naive type (Lewis, I.M., 1977; Jahoda, 1982).

American anthropology, however, has been strongly influenced by psychoanalysis, particularly in the *culture and personality* school which offered a notion of culture as primarily a reflection of the socialisation of the young child. It is books by workers in this school (Kluckholm, Lifton, Mead, Erikson, Benedict, Kardiner) which are particularly likely to be read by psychiatrists. The starting point of the culture and personality approach was Freud's 'Totem and Taboo' (1913) and, although his conjectural psychohistory of man's origins was discarded, the psychoanalytic equation of archaic and tribal man, child and neurotic was continued in normative and evaluative comments on American society (e.g. Mead, 1949). Benedict (1935) suggests that patterns of what is regarded as psychopathology in Western societies (and thus by psychoanalysis) may be the chosen cultural norm in others.

Through the work of Bateson (1972) and others, culture and personality theorists developed an interest in psychopathology, notably in the now discarded notion of the 'double-bind' theory of schizophrenia. Although considerably less influential than previously, they have reintroduced the individual into studies of collective beliefs and behaviour. European social anthropology has tended to neglect questions of individual personality and the differences between individuals in a given society, and to regard the particular person as a passive carrier of *collective representations* shared by all members. For the psychoanalytically inclined anthropologist, the solution was the reverse: collective notions were the sum of a series of individual experiences. By contrast, the French psychoanalyst Devereux (1978) suggests that psychological and sociological explanations of any symbol or behaviour are both equally valid and equally necessary. Turner (1967) relates private to public meaning by suggesting that any symbol can be regarded as having two 'poles': one articulates the shared cognitive requirements of the social order whereas the other is shaped by, and gains its power through, its relationship to personal affective experience.

Medical Anthropology

The newer American school of Medical Anthropology has followed the Europeans in emphasising indigenous conceptualisations of healing and disease as logical systems in their own right, an approach sometimes known as ethnoscience. It employs the useful distinction between 'illness' (the indigenous experience and conceptualisation) and 'disease' (the theoretical systematisation of illness, as in Western scientific biomedicine). Contemporary American anthropologists interested in medicine are now looking at the cultural underpinning of genetic disease, population dynamics, nutrition and fertility, healing practices, medical ethics, health-care organisation and patient choice among health-care alternatives in pluralistic societies (Chrisman and Maretzki, 1982). The most influential medical anthropologist is probably Arthur Kleinman who provides (1980) a wealth of comparative data and a theoretical schema for studying those medical interactions in which patient and professional employ different explanatory models of disease (Kleinman, 1982). Kleinman (1977) has been critical of much comparative psychiatry, particularly of the notion of the 'somatisation' of distress in reactions regarded as 'really psychological', and also of comparative studies like the International Pilot Study of Schizophrenia for their attempt to contrast psychopathology across cultures by focusing on patterns which are themselves taken as culture-free. He emphasises that 'the new cross-cultural psychiatry' must start from local conceptualisations of sickness before attempting generalised comparisons.

Western biomedicine (and thus psychiatry) makes certain assumptions: that it represents an external reality of actually existing disease entities; that a disease can be defined as a deviation from normal, standardised, biological functioning, and that it has a specific pathogenesis and pathology; that the taxonomy of diseases can be applied universally; and that biomedical knowledge, because of its scientific foundations, is 'neutral', both in its theory and in its application (Lock, 1984). Much of current work in medical anthropology is concerned with questioning these assumptions and demonstrating the social bases of biomedical theory. Estroff (1982) offers a sensitive approach to the lifestyles and values of chronic psychiatric patients, and Rhodes (1984) discusses the metaphors used by psychiatrist and patient when negotiating the dosages of psychotropic drugs.

The papers in Marsella and White (1982) provide an overview of current developments in 'the new cross-cultural psychiatry', particularly the study of indigenous medical classifications. Descriptions of such medical systems with a particular emphasis on how they are organised are found in Crapanzano (1973), Fabrega and Silver (1973), Lewis (1975) and Janzen (1978). As lay medical theories do not necessarily employ our own distinction between psychiatric disorders and other medical conditions, such medical classifications offer much of interest to the psychiatrist, particularly in their detailed descriptions of how distress is experienced, recognised and treated within the constraints of a particular world view. Gaines (1982) notes that the clinical encounter between doctor and patient is socially constructed: 'meanings are brought to it, and exchanged by actors through the employment, patterned and idiosyncratic, of various symbolic forms'. Critics of a pure ethnoscience approach point out that local classifications cannot be considered in isolation from their political and cultural context (Good, 1977). Quite complex societies may offer considerable scope for individual perspectives in the absence of a developed psychological theory (Heelas and Lock, 1981), suggesting that the primacy of psychological explanations in the West may be secondary to other social determinants (Harré, 1983). By contrast, traditional transcultural psychiatry dismisses our lay theories as irrelevant (Yap, 1974, p. 73).

That clinical reality is socially constructed does not imply 'sociological reductionism' or the impossibility of comparison (cf. Yap, 1974). Indeed medical anthropology offers psychiatry a fresh approach to the question of biological universals and one which does not assume the biologically reductionist core/envelope distinction. Thus the Melanesian reaction *kuru* is perhaps of greater interest since the demonstration of its association with a slow virus (Lindenbaum, 1979). The suggestion in the *Journal of Nervous and Mental Disease* that *latah* was a modification of the universal startle reflex (Simons, 1980) precipitated a series of papers and comments on the role of biological universals in the culture-bound syndromes (summarised in Littlewood and Lipsedge, 1985). Physiological abnormalities in certain instances of a culture-bound reaction do not preclude the possibility that the majority of cases are 'modelled' on an organic minority, or alternatively that social meanings are imposed on a single 'organic' type or series of types to produce a unitary syndrome. The presence of invariate biological changes in any particular reaction, as in *kuru*, is likely to remove it from the domain of transcultural psychiatry, but not from that of medical anthropology. Littlewood (1984b) has reconsidered the old 'culture and personality' suggestion that psychopathology may have an active social role.

Culture-bound Psychopathology

Although anthropologists are not, of course, independent of implicit folk models or political assumptions, this discipline, unlike psychiatry or psychology, does contain within itself the tools for a self-reflexive examination of them (Littlewood, 1983b). An anthropological approach to psychiatric phenomena allows for the conceptualisation of the psychiatrist and his or her values by the patient (Littlewood, 1980, 1983a). Conversely, transcultural psychiatry often perceives a reflexive and socially rooted approach as 'negative . . . a sort of conspiracy theory' or as sociological reductionism (Littlewood, 1983b). Much of its literature tells us more about the historical relationship between Europeans and non-Europeans than about the relationship of psychopathology to culture. I shall turn to look at this question in relation to the notion of 'culture-bound' psychopathology.

Since the beginning of this century, psychiatrists have tended to distinguish between the essential *pathogenic* determinants of a mental disorder, necessary and sufficient to cause it, and those *pathoplastic* factors which are associated with individual variation. This distinction was loosely tied to the classic nineteenth-century German distinction between form and content. (Yap (1974) traces the origin of this distinction to Indo-European subject/predicate grammar, whereas Lewontin *et al.* (1984) more plausibly suggest that it is associated with Descartes and the bourgeois revolutions, with their tendency to analyse wholes in terms of the underlying properties of their parts.) Thus pathoplastic factors gave 'content, colouring and contour to individual illnesses whose basic form and character have already been biologically established' (Birnbaum, 1923).

This model was most applicable to those psychoses that had demonstrable biological origins: the hallucinations of alcoholic delirium (form) could be coded in the particular concepts of a culture (content), and the confabulations of the damaged brain in the immediate preoccupations of the individual (Weinstein, 1962). The possibility of a distinction between form and content was more problematic in the absence of clear organic pathology where the pathogenic/pathoplastic distinction was employed in symptomatology alone (e.g. Yap, 1974). Pathogenicity became associated with those symptoms which *characterised* a particular reaction: for Bleuler (1911) such characteristic symptoms were primary, directly related to the underlying biological cause.

In his statement of the aims of comparative psychiatry, Kraepelin (1904) suggested that it was the *universal* symptoms that were pathogenic, though 'reliable comparison is of course only possible if we are able to draw clear distinctions between identifiable illnesses'. This proved difficult, given the worldwide variety of symptoms and the desire to fit them into a restricted number of universal categories. The 'culture-bound syndromes' described as specific to particular communities were taken as variants of the classic disorders described in Europe. Mental illness in Java, said Kraepelin, showed 'broadly the same clinical picture as we see in our country . . . The overall similarity far outweighed the deviant features.' He then proceeded to equate *amok* with both epilepsy and catatonia.

What were the 'deviant features', and what was being compared with what? If one looked, for instance, at delusions of persecution by neighbours, the delusion was form and the 'neighbours' content but 'persecution' was variously one or the other. Textbooks of comparative psychiatry suggested that local reactions were 'not new diagnostic entities: they are in fact similar to those already known in the West' (Kiev, 1972), although windigo was variously described as depression, schizophrenia, hysteria and anxiety (Yap, 1951; Parker, 1960; Kiev,

1972; Leff, 1981). Culture bound syndromes were thus regarded on phenomenological grounds not as 'real' existing entities but as local and erroneous conceptualisations which shaped certain universal reactions, although the psychiatric observers might disagree as to which reactions. Carr (1978) notes that researchers focused on the overt symptomatology and ignored the social setting, 'supposedly the defining criterion in the culture-bound syndromes'. Like Kleinman (1977), Manschrek and Petri (1978) suggest the quest for fitting syndromes into universal categories is pointless: 'such research is self-fulfilling in its aim to determine universal features of behaviour in cross-cultural settings because these features constitute its only object'.

Culture itself was not then regarded as primary: it acted as a sort of confusing soup which passively filled in the biological matrix. 'Symptoms may be masked or distorted by psychological states or cultural values, but it is assumed that underneath this "noise" is a specific disease with its own distinguishing and differentiating features' (Mishler, 1981). This (i) denial of the cultural rooting of psychopathology, together with (ii) the equation of characteristic and pathogenic symptoms, and (iii) the assumption that symptoms observed in European patients were more clearly pathogenic and culture free, led to the widely held belief that depression did not occur in non-Europeans (Littlewood and Lipsedge, 1982). If European psychiatrists were at times puzzled about the cultural incrustations they saw adhering to the familiar 'real' illness, at other times they were struck by the 'barrenness of the clinical picture . . . In more primitive culture schizophrenia is "a poor imitation of European forms"' (Yap, 1951). Greater familiarity with psychopathology outside European societies has, however, suggested that Western depressive symptoms may be only a culture-specific variant of universal patterns, salient because chosen for remark by local culture (Waxler, 1977; Littlewood, 1985). Fabrega (1982) has suggested that the same may be true of schizophrenia.

Whether a particular reaction is described as a 'ritual' or a 'syndrome' often seems to depend upon which type of Western professional first described it. Many of the phenomena described by cultural psychiatrists as pathological have been studied by anthropologists as social institutions, as meaningful and functional as systems of kinship or political organisation (e.g. Kenny, 1981). Culture-bound syndromes are representations in the individual of symbolic themes concerning social relations and which occur in certain personal and historical situations. They articulate both personal predicament and public concerns usually relations between age groups or the sexes (Newman, 1964; Lewis, 1966) 'by mystical pressure upon their superiors in circumstances of deprivation and frustration when few other sanctions are available to them' (Lewis, 1966). An anthropological approach offers both a functionalist explanation of how a pattern of this type serves as a sub-system of the wider social whole and of how the individual uses latent social mechanisms to adjust his or her situation, but it also suggests a meaning of the pattern for both individual and community (see Chapter 15).

Changing Patterns of Psychopathology

The form/content model has difficulty not only in comparing reactions across cultures, but also in dealing with changing patterns of psychopathology in a single society. Whereas it offers a heuristic explanation of the changing psychopathology of schizophrenia (form remains constant but content reflects changing social preoccupations — Klaf and Hamilton, 1961), it is less applicable to considering the disappearance of such reactions as conversion hysteria or the development of new ones — agoraphobia, Briquet's syndrome, anorexia nervosa, exhibitionism, self-poisoning or, perhaps, the chronic pain syndromes. It seems difficult to understand their appearance, function and meaning without taking into account the whole social context, including the relationship between doctor and patient, and between lay and professional notions of sickness. This has been done with a certain degree of success in the case of conversion hysteria (Ellenberger, 1970).

Interest has recently been expressed in the social origins of the 'classic' culture-bound syndromes. Murphy (1973) suggests that *latah* may have originated as a mimicry by local men of the unintelligible demands of European colonialists. Similarly, *piblokto* (arctic hysteria), when first described by Peary among Smith Sound Inuit, was apparently limited to dogs; Peary's presence precipitated an epidemic among humans since when it has remained endemic (Neutra *et al.*, 1977). From the Eskimo perspective on power relations it appears that human : dog :: European : Eskimo. Murphy (1973) points out that until the eighteenth century the *amok* was a hero: the reaction was an acceptable response to an unacceptable insult or injury. European colonialism devalued this institution, and what had been a conscious, although risky, social act became increasingly pathological: 'the heroic legend remained and offered a model frequently acted upon' (Murphy, 1973). Cultures are likely to provide latent patterns of this type, which can be used 'inappropriately' by abnormal individuals (Littlewood, 1983a). Thus, with time, culture-bound syndromes and other patterns become increasingly 'abnormal' in their own social terms; though the 'signs of election' to the status of *shaman* may historically include incipient mental illness (among other signs), the occupant of the shamanic role appears to be more likely to be disturbed than formerly (Murphy, 1964). In Western Europe, *tarrantism* and *fascination* (evil eye) become first pathology and then folkloric curiosities.

To assume that patterns change is not to assume an 'evolution' but to recognise that, as social institutions, the cultural complexes we term syndromes are each appropriate to, and articulate, a particular model of social and political organisation. It is perhaps not surprising that 'culture-bound' syndromes are found in women in male-orientated societies, and in communities faced with European domination. Both are 'culturally excluded' groups, prevented from participating in the dominant culture through which everyday individual identity is attained. Thus, perforce, they have resorted to 'mystical sanctions' outside everyday jural relationships and power (Chapter 15).

Although we know that psychopathology may alter with time, it is often difficult to observe the individual steps of the mutation given the slow adaptation of culture compared with an individual clinical history. Migration and rapid culture change are frequently regarded simply as the cause of psychopathology (Chapter 5) rather than as useful examples of concomitant variation. The temporary evacuation of the islanders of Tristan da Cunha to Britain in the face of a volcanic eruption suggested that it was the same islanders who had 'hysterical' Tristan symptoms who later developed British 'psychosomatic' complaints (Rawnsley and Loudon, 1964). *Latah* has been noted among Europeans resident in Malay communities, whereas by contrast premigration culture-bound psychopathology among Oriental Jews in Israel has been described as occurring more than fifteen years after migration in adolescence. Although one must allow for the effects of forced migration, racism, acculturation and the persistence of premigration subcultures in the new society, there appear to be three questions of interest (Littlewood and Lipsedge, 1985):

(1) At what age is the original pattern 'laid down'?
(2) How does it change phenomenologically and functionally?
(3) Why does it change?

A follow-up study of a group of West Indians who had migrated to Britain and who were diagnosed as having an acute psychotic reaction (*bouffée délirante*) suggested that, with repeated hospitalisations, the symptoms increasingly resembled classical depression (Littlewood and Lipsedge, 1985). A similar pattern has been found among French-speaking African patients in France (Leroy *et al.*, 1982). Another example is a Bengali patient of mine in whose female line there was a tradition of spirit-mediumship. Soon after her marriage her husband left her to come to Britain. While living in difficult relations with his family in Bangladesh, she became possessed; her social status was thus enhanced and she later joined her husband in East London. Their precarious economic situation was threatened after some years by obligations incurred by his younger brother's marriage in Bangladesh and she developed dissociative 'hysterical' symptoms. Diagnosed as ill by their *imam* she entered hospital and in the course of family therapy her symptoms subsequently became more 'depressive'. A further domestic crisis was signalled by her telephoning and threatening to take an overdose of drugs.

It would of course be erroneous to suggest that either of these reactions were 'really depressive' or 'depressive equivalents'. However, it is not unreasonable to examine the relationship between them and 'classical' (Western) patterns of depression: whereas the latter is characterised solely on phenomenological grounds, the social context of parasuicide offers close parallels with non-European culture-bound reactions (Chapter 15). 'Depression' itself is culture-bound to the context of a pervasive biomedical ethos (Murphy, 1978) and its associated psychological notions of self-hood (Marsella and White, 1982); in these examples it is difficult to distinguish the relative influences of the hospitalisation or family therapy themselves from the pervasive 'psychologising' norms of the majority culture.

Bouffées délirantes seem to have a certain relationship to the normative states of dissociation in Afro-American possession trance; in the French-speaking Caribbean (where they are most common) they are associated with a similar local exegesis in terms of possession. Given the occurrence of these 'ritual' possession states in non-ritualised situations (induction of anaesthesia, car accidents — Métraux, 1959; Philippe and Romain, 1979), it is arguable that *bouffées délirantes* are a further deritualistiaon of trance possession in increasingly informal circumstances but serving similar functions of self-expression, social mobilisation and status adjustment in a crisis. Alternatively the two may have existed together, sharing many common features and distinguished principally by the extent of ritual context. Philippe and Romain (1979) suggest a similar relation between Haitian ritual possession and *indisposition*, a local syndrome of vertigo and other somatic complaints. Caribbean culture is not of course 'indigenous', and the original existence of a possession/*bouffée délirante* complex is likely to be closely tied to black/white relations in the period of slavery, colonialism and after: the phenomenology and meaning of Haitian possession states incorporate 'a conception of history' (Larose, 1977). So far from our traditional culture-bound syndromes existing as observations by one conceptual system (biomedicine) of another social institution, they may exist specifically as intermediate points of an historical change, midway between socially rewarded behaviours and socially devalued patterns of depression which accompany industrialisation and its associated medical-isation (Littlewood and Lipsedge, 1985). To compare reactions in this way, we have to take into account not only phenomenology, but social and historical context and local exegesis.

To suggest an association between states recognised as pathological by psychiatry and normative social patterns is not to pathologise the latter. Quite the reverse. It is to suggest that many of the patterns we regard as pathological are only so by their development in relation to a domi-nant biomedicine. It is not to explain away cultural institutions by regard-ing them as pathological in origin, but to resituate much of such pathology in social terms. Rather than the 'pathologisation of culture', we have, if I may be forgiven an inelegant expression, the 'enculturation of pathology'.

Reading about Social Anthropology for Psychiatrists

Anthropological papers of psychiatric interest are to be found in Klein-man's journal *Culture, Medicine and Psychiatry,* in *Social Science and Medicine,* and in the *Medical Anthropology Newsletter.* The *Transcultural Psychiatric Research Review* from McGill University provides summaries of papers published elsewhere, together with review articles. Anthro-pological monographs are comparatively jargon-free and easily access-ible to the psychiatrist, but a useful short textbook is that by Lewis (1976), who, like Turner (1967), is particularly sympathetic to a rapprochement with psychiatry. In his introduction to *Symbols and Sentiments* (Lewis, I.M., 1977), he outlines the 'phobic reaction of British anthropology towards psychoanalysis and psychology'. Jahoda (1982) has discussed anthropology from the psychologist's perspective; Landy (1977) and Kiev (1964) offer selections of key papers in psychiatric anthropology suitable for teaching, and Helman (1984) reviews the field of medical anthro-pology with an emphasis on Britain. Kleinman (1980) and Marsella and

White (1982) offer theoretical schemata for psychiatric anthropology, and the papers in Chrisman and Maretzki (1982) describe the immediate practical relevance of anthropology for clinical practice. The definitive textbook of cultural psychiatry is that by Murphy (1982), which is refreshing for the cultural relativity with which he discusses psychopathology in the West. For teaching psychiatric trainees, discussion of previously circulated papers is more appropriate than formal lectures, and the best single paper is perhaps Victor Turner's 'An Ndembu Doctor in Practice' (Turner, 1964). In what follows I have marked with an asterisk fifteen books and papers which together provide an overview. Paperback editions have been selected where available. The headings below are arbitrary, and thus there is much on kinship and social organisation in Evans-Pritchard's *The Nuer* (1940) which I have placed under 'Religion, Cosmology and Symbolism'.

Classic Functionalist Descriptions. Firth, 1936; Malinowski, 1922; see also in Lewis, 1976 (*).

Kinship and Social Organisation. Fox, 1967; Radcliffe-Brown and Forde, 1976.

Religion, Cosmology and Symbolism. Douglas, 1970, 1973a, 1973b (*); Durkheim and Evans-Pritchard, 1937 (*), 1940; Mauss, 1950; Geertz, 1966 (*); Lewis, 1966 (*), 1976; Lévi-Strauss, 1963; Lienhardt, 1961; Needham, 1973; Rappaport, 1968; Turner, 1967 (*).

'Critical Anthropology'. Ardener, 1975 (*); Godelier, 1973.

The Relation between Anthropology and Psychology. Bateson, 1972; Benedict, 1935 (*); Devereux, 1978; Heelas and Lock, 1981; Jahoda, 1982 (*), Kiev, 1964 (*); Lewis, I.M., 1977; Littlewood, 1980 (*), 1984a, 1984b; Loudon, 1972; Mauss, 1950; Mead, 1949; Simons, 1980.

Medical Anthropology and 'the New Cross-cultural Psychiatry'. Chrisman and Maretzki, 1982; Crapanzano, 1973 (*); Estroff, 1982; Fabrega, 1982; Fabrega and Silver, 1973; Gaines, 1982; Good, 1977; Helman, 1984; Hughes, 1985; Janzen, 1978; Kleinman, 1977, 1980 (*), 1982; Landy, 1977 (*); Lewis, 1975; Lindenbaum, 1979; Littlewood, 1985; Lock, 1984; Marsella and White, 1982 (*); Mishler, 1981; Neutra *et al.*, 1977; Philippe and Romain, 1979; Rhodes, 1984.

References

Ardener, E. (1975) 'Belief and the Problem of Women', in S. Ardener (ed.), *Perceiving Women*, Dent, London

Association of University Teachers of Psychiatry (1982) 'Sciences Basic to Psychiatry: AUTP Guidelines', *Bulletin of the Royal College of Psychiatrists.*, 6, 54

Baker, J.R. (1974) *Race*, Oxford University Press, Oxford

Bateson, G. (1972) *Steps to an Ecology of Mind*, Chandler, New York

Benedict, R. (1935) *Patterns of Culture*, Routledge & Kegan Paul, London

Birnbaum, K. (1923) 'Der Aufbau der Psychose', Translated as 'The Making of a Psychosis', in S.R. Hirsch and M. Shepherd (eds) *Themes and Variations in European Psychiatry*, 1974, Wright, Bristol

Bleuler, E. (1911) *Dementia Praecox*, International Universities Press, New York

British Medical Journal (1981) (Editorial) 'More Anthropology and Less Sleep for Medical Students', *British Medical Journal*, 281, 1662

Carr, J.E. (1978) 'Ethno-behaviourism and the Culture-bound Syndromes: the Case of Amok', *Culture, Medicine and Psychiatry*, 2, 269

Chrisman, N.J. and Maretzki, T.W. (eds) (1982) *Clinically Applied Anthropology: Anthropologists in Health Science Settings*, Reidel, Dordrecht

Crapanzano, V. (1973) *The Hamadsha: a Study in Moroccan Ethnopsychiatry*, University of California Press, Berkeley

Devereux, G. (1978) *Ethnopsychoanalysis*, University of California Press, Berkeley

Dobash, R.E. and Dobash, R. (1980), *Violence against Wives*, Open Books, London

Douglas, M. (1970) *Purity and Danger: an Analysis of Concepts of Pollution and Taboo*, Penguin, Harmondsworth

Douglas, M. (1973a) *Natural Symbols: Explorations in Cosmology*, Penguin, Harmondsworth

Douglas, M. (ed.) (1973b) *Rules and Meanings: the Anthropology of Everyday Knowledge*, Penguin, Harmondsworth

Durkheim, E. and Mauss, M. (1903) *Primitive Classification*, Routledge and Kegan Paul, London

Ellenberger, H.F. (1970) *The Discovery of the Unconscious*, Allen Lane, London

Estroff, S.E. (1982) 'Long-term Psychiatric Clients in an American Community', In: N.J. Chrisman and T.W. Maretzki (eds), *Clinically Applied Anthropology: Anthropologists in Health Science Settings*, Reidel, Dordrecht

Evans-Pritchard, E.E. (1937) *Witchcraft, Oracles and Magic among the Azande*, Oxford University Press, Oxford

Evans-Pritchard, E.E. (1940) *The Nuer*, Oxford University Press, Oxford

Fabrega, H. (1982) 'Culture and Psychiatric Illness', in A.J. Marsella and G. White (eds), *Cultural Conceptions of Mental Health and Therapy*, Reidel, Dordrecht

Fabrega, H. and Silver, D.B. (1973) *Illness and Shamanistic Curing in Zinacantan*, Stanford University Press, Stanford

Firth, R. (1936) *We the Tikopia* (1957) Beacon, New York

Fox, R. (1967) *Kinship and Marriage*, Penguin, Harmondsworth

Freud, S. (1913) 'Totem and Taboo' (1960), Routledge and Kegan Paul, London

Gaines, A. (1982) 'Knowledge and Practice: Anthropological Ideas and Psychiatric Practice', in N.J. Chrisman and T.W. Maretzki (eds), *Clinically Applied Anthropology: Anthropologists in Health Science Settings*, Reidel, Dordrecht

Galbraith, J. (1980) Begin the Begun, *World Medicine*, 14 June, 77

Geertz, C. (1966) 'Religion as a Cultural System', in M. Banton, *Anthropological Approaches to Religion*, Tavistock, London

German, A. (1972) 'Aspects of Clinical Psychiatry in Sub-Saharan Africa', *British Journal of Psychiatry*, 121, 461

Godelier, M. (1973) *Perspectives in Marxist Anthropology*, Cambridge University Press, Cambridge

Goffman, E. (1968) *Asylums*, Penguin, Harmondsworth

Good, B.J. (1977) 'The Heart of What's the Matter: The Semantics of Illness in Iran', *Culture, Medicine and Psychiatry, 1*, 25

Hahn, R.A. (1983) 'Culture-bound Syndromes Unbound', International Congress of Anthropology and Ethnology, Vancouver

Harré, R. (1983) *Personal Being: a Theory of Individual Psychology*, Blackwell, Oxford

Heelas, P. and Lock, A. (ed.) (1981) *Indigenous Psychologies: the Anthropology of the Self*, Academic Press, London

Helman, C. (1984) *Culture, Health and Illness*, Wright, Bristol

Hughes, C.C. (1985) 'Culture-bound or Construct-bound? The Syndromes and DSM-III' in R.C. Simons and C.C. Hughes (eds), *The Culture-bound Syndromes: Folk Illnesses of Psychiatric and Anthropological Interest*, Reidel, Dordrecht

Jahoda, G. (1982) *Psychology and Anthropology: a Psychological Perspective*, Academic Press, London

Janzen, J.M. (1978) *The Quest for Therapy: Medical Pluralism in Lower Zaire*, University of California Press, Berkeley

Kenny, M.G. (1981) 'Multiple Personality and Spirit Possession', *Psychiatry, 44*, 327

Kiev, A. (ed.) (1964) *Magic, Faith and Healing*, Free Press, New York

Kiev, A. (1972) *Transcultural Psychiatry*, Penguin, Harmondsworth

Klaf, F.S. and Hamilton, J.G. (1961) Schizophrenia — a Hundred Years Ago and Today, *Journal of Mental Science, 107*, 817

Kleinman, A. (1977) 'Depression, Somatization and the "New Cross-cultural Psychiatry" *Social Science and Medicine, 11*, 3–10

Kleinman, A. (1980) *Patients and Healers in the Context of Culture*, University of California Press, Berkeley

Kleinman, A. (1982) 'Clinically Applied Anthropology on a Psychiatric Liasion Service', in N.J. Chrisman and T.W. Maretzki (eds), *Clinically Applied Anthropology: Anthropologists in Health Science Settings*, Reidel, Dordrecht

Kraepelin, E. (1904) 'Vergleichende Psychiatrie' Translated as 'Comparative Psychiatry', in S.R. Hirsch and M. Shepherd (eds) *Themes and Variations in European Psychiatry*, 1974, Wright, Bristol

Landy, D. (ed.) (1977) *Culture, Disease and Healing: Studies in Medical Anthropology*, Macmillan, New York

Larose, S. (1977) 'The Meaning of Africa in Haitian Vodu', in I.M. Lewis (ed.), *Symbols and Sentiments*, Academic Press, London

Leff, J. (1981) *Psychiatry around the Globe: a Transcultural View*, Decker, New York

Leroy, C., Alby, J.M. and Ferreri, M. (1982) 'Dysthymie et Bouffées délirantes chez les Transplantés d'Origine noire', *Psychopathologie Africaine, 18*, 281

Lévi-Strauss, C. (1963) *Structural Anthropology*, Penguin, Harmondsworth

Lewis, A.J. (1958) 'Social Psychiatry', in *Lectures on the Scientific Basis of Medicine*, Vol. VI, Athlone Press, London

Lewis, G. (1975) *Knowledge of Illness in a Sepik Society*, Humanities Press, New York

Lewis, I.M. (1966) Spirit Possession and Deprivation Cults, *Man (N.S), I*, 307–29

Lewis, I.M. (1976) *Social Anthropology in Perspective*, Penguin, Harmondsworth

Lewis, I.M. (ed.) (1977) *Symbols and Sentiments*, 'Introduction', Academic Press, London

Lewis, S.A. (1977) 'Fear of Sorcery and the Problem of Death by Suggestion', in J. Blacking, *The Anthropology of the Body*, Academic Press, London

Lewontin, R.C., Rose, S. and Kamin, L.J. (1984) *Not in our Genes: Biology, Ideology and Human Nature*, Pantheon, New York

Lienhardt, G. (1961) *Divinity and Experience*, Clarendon Press, Oxford

Lindenbaum, S. (1979) *Kuru Sorcery: Disease and Danger in the New Guinea Highlands*, Mayfield, Palo Alto

Littlewood, R. (1980) 'Anthropology and Psychiatry; an Alternative Approach', *British Journal of Medical Psychology, 53,* 213

Littlewood, R. (1983a) 'The Antinomiam Hasid', *British Journal of Medical Psychology, 56,* 67

Littlewood, R. (1983b) 'The Theory and Practice of Puzzlement: a Reply to Murphy', *Transcultural Psychiatry Research Review, 20,* 67

Littlewood, R. (1984a) 'The Individual Articulation of Shared Symbols', *Journal of Operational Psychiatry, 15,* 17

Littlewood, R. (1984b) 'The Imitation of Madness: the Influence of Psychopathology upon Culture', *Social Science and Medicine, 19,* 705

Littlewood, R. (1985) 'An Indigenous Conceptualisation of Reactive Depression in Trinidad', *Psychological Medicine, 15,* 275

Littlewood, R. and Lipsedge, M. (1982) *Alien and Alienists: Ethnic Minorities and Psychiatry,* Penguin, London

Littlewood, R. and Lipsedge, M. (1985) 'Culture-Bound Syndromes', in K. Granville-Grossman (ed.), *Recent Advances in Psychiatry — 5,* Churchill Livingstone, Edinburgh

Lock, M. (1984) 'Licorice in Leviathan: the Medicalisation of Care for the Japanese Elder-ly', *Culture, Medicine and Psychiatry, 8,* 121–39

Loudon, J.B. (1972) 'Social Anthropology and Psychiatry', *Psychological Medicine, 2,* 1

Malinowski, B. (1922) *Argonauts of the Western Pacific,* Routledge & Kegan Paul, London

Manschreck, T.C. and Petri, M. (1978) 'The Atypical Psychoses', *Culture, Medicine and Psychiatry, 2,* 233

Marsella, A.J. and White, G. (1982) *Cultural Conceptions of Mental Health and Therapy,* Reidel, Dordrecht

Martin, J.P. (ed.) (1978) *Violence in the Family,* Wiley, Chichester

Mauss, M. (1950) *Sociologie et Anthropologie,* Presses Universitaires de France, Paris

Mead, M. (1949) *Male and Female,* Penguin, Harmondsworth

Métraux, A. (1959) *Voodoo,* Oxford University Press, Oxford

Mishler, E.G. (1981) *Social Contexts of Health, Illness and Patient Care,* Cambridge University Press, New York

Murphy, H.B.M. (1973) 'History and Evolution of Syndromes: the Striking Case of Latah and Amok', in M. Hammer, *Psychopathology,* Wiley, New York

Murphy, H.B.M. (1978) 'The Advent of Guilt Feelings as a Common Depressive Symptom', *Psychiatry, 41,* 229

Murphy, H.B.M. (1982) *Comparative Psychiatry,* Springer, Berlin

Murphy, J. (1964) 'Psychotherapeutic Aspects of Shamanism on St. Lawrence Island', in A. Kiev (ed.), *Magic, Faith and Healing,* Free Press, New York

Needham, R. (ed.) (1973) *Right and Left: Essays in Dual Symbolic Classification,* Chicago University Press, Chicago

Neutra, R., Levy, J.E. and Parker, D. (1977) 'Cultural Expectations versus Reality in Navajo Seizure Patterns and Sick Roles', *Culture Medicine and Psychiatry, 1,* 255

Newman, P.L. (1964) ' "Wild Man" Behaviour in a New Guinea Highlands Community', *American Anthropologist, 66,* 1

Owens, P. (1981) 'Family, Kinship and Welfare', PhD thesis, Cambridge University

Pahl, J. (1984) *Private Violence and Public Policy,* Routledge & Kegan Paul, London

Parker, S. (1960) 'The Windigo Psychosis', *American Anthropologist, 62,* 602

Philippe, J.L. and Romain, J.B. (1979) 'Indisposition in Haiti', *Social Science and Medicine, 13,* 129

Radcliffe-Brown, A.R. and Forde, D. (eds) (1976) *African Systems of Kinship and Marriage,* Oxford University Press, Oxford

Rappaport, R.A. (1968) *Pigs for the Ancestors: Ritual in the Ecology of a New Guinea People,* Yale University Press, New Haven

Rawnsley, K. and Loudon, J.B. (1964) 'Epidemiology of Mental Disorder in a Closed Community', *British Journal of Psychiatry, 110,* 830

Rhodes, L.A. (1984) ' "This Will Clear Your Mind": the Use of Metaphors for Medication in Psychiatric Settings', *Culture, Medicine and Psychiatry, 8*, 49–70

Simons, R.C. (1980) 'The Resolution of the Latah Paradox', *Journal of Nervous and Mental Diseases, 168*, 195

Turner, V.W. (1964) 'An Ndembu Doctor in Practice', in A. Kiev (ed.), *Magic, Faith and Healing*, Free Press, New York

Turner, V.W. (1967) *The Forest of Symbols*. Cornell University Press, Ithaca

Waxler, N.E. (1977) 'Is Mental Illness Cured in Traditional Societies? A Theoretical Analysis', *Culture, Medicine and Psychiatry, 1*, 233

Weinstein, E. (1962) *Cultural Aspects of Delusion*, Free Press, New York

Yap, P.M. (1951) 'Mental Diseases Peculiar to Certain Cultures', *Journal of Mental Science, 97*, 313–27

Yap, P.M. (1974) *Comparative Psychiatry: a Theoretical Framework*, University of Toronto Press, Toronto

5 MIGRATION AND MENTAL ILLNESS

Philip H. Rack

Migration means leaving home and setting up a new home in a different place: the term usually indicates *either* a considerable geographical distance between the two places (e.g. between countries) *or* some important differences between them (e.g. rural to urban), and commonly both. Migration may be permanent, cyclic or temporary; if temporary, the duration amounts to something more than a visit. It is not a new phenomenon but its scale has increased dramatically in the twentieth century, and there can be few communities in the world which are not affected by it in some way.

Migration has been studied by historians, geographers, sociologists and many others. (See, for example, Jackson, 1969; McNeill and Adams, 1978.) It is an appropriate subject for behavioural and social scientists for several reasons, not least because it raises important questions about adaptability. It is no small matter to pull up one's roots, abandon familiar places and people, and transplant to a new environment. The migrant's *adaptive capacity* is tested; and severely tested if the two environments are very different. The differences may include climate, language, environmental hazards and diet: these are obvious (though in practice they are often underestimated). Others are much more subtle: they include the cultural and political attitudes of the new society, and the social role changes demanded of the newcomer. Very large differences in social mores may have the effect of challenging the migrant's habitual behaviour patterns, beliefs, and value systems, and even of threatening his or her sense of personal identity. Stonequist (1937) described the 'marginal man', stranded between two cultures, unable to identify fully with either — a position inherently stressful. Park (1928) commented on the 'sense of moral dichotomy and conflict [which] is probably characteristic of every immigrant during the period of transition when old habits are being discarded and new ones are not yet formed. It is inevitably a period of inner turmoil'.

At the present time, with technological and social change in almost every part of the world occurring at an unparalleled rate, even the person who never leaves his or her birthplace experiences great changes and has to make great adaptations. In a sense, we are all 'marginal'

59

nowadays. We all experience the 'inner turmoil' of that condition. Our individual futures, perhaps the future of the species, depend as never before on adaptation, and psychological adaptation pre-eminently. This is arguably the most important subject for scientific consideration at this time. Migration provides a case study.

The clinician has more pragmatic reasons for paying attention to this subject. Because of international migration, many communities — especially in industrial centres — have become multiracial and multicultural. The health worker in such communities is likely to encounter patients or clients from backgrounds with which he or she is unfamiliar (Rack, 1982a). It is this cultural mixing, and the need to understand differences, which have provoked the recent upsurge of interest in transcultural psychiatry in Britain. Previously, 'transcultural' referred to the strange maladies of peculiar people in remote places, the so-called 'culture-bound' syndromes of koro, amok, susto, and so on. For practical purposes this 'exotic psychiatry' can now be relegated to a footnote; transcultural psychiatry has more immediate applications in the clinics of Bradford, Birmingham or Brixton. Migration affects not only the recipients but also the givers of health care. There are issues about the position of overseas doctors and nurses in the British Health Service which have not received the attention they deserve.

Systematic research on migration and mental health began in America in the nineteenth century. As early as 1850 there was a paper with the blunt title, 'On Insane Foreigners' (Ranney, 1850) which, with other reports, claimed that immigrants were disproportionately represented in American asylums. The original statistics were misleading because age/sex standardisation was omitted, but even when this was corrected (Pollock, 1913) an apparent excess remained. Two explanations were offered, and debated as if they were mutually exclusive:

(a) *the stress-of-migration hypothesis:* high breakdown rates are caused by the psychological trauma, isolation, oppression and other vicissitudes experienced in migration and settlement;
(b) *the self-selection hypothesis:* migrant groups include a disproportionate number of people predisposed to mental instability.

(We can perhaps detect here the beginnings of a polarisation which still persists, between those who are inclined to blame the host society for making life difficult for immigrants, and those who are predisposed to regard the immigrants themselves as incompetent and responsible for their own misfortunes.)

Ødegaard was one of the first to use methodical epidemiological techniques. He surveyed Norwegian immigrants in America and compared them not only with native-born Americans but also with Norwegians who remained at home and migrants who returned home (Ødegaard, 1932, 1945; Astrup and Ødegaard, 1960). The findings confirmed a high rate of breakdown among transatlantic migrants. Ødegaard favoured the self-selection explanation: he suggested that migration was attractive to people with weak social relationships, who were poorly integrated in their original societies, and he believed that such people were particularly liable to develop schizophrenia. Later studies included data on internal migration within Norway, and here the findings were more complex. Migrants into Oslo from other parts of Norway had higher breakdown rates than the Oslo-born but this was the exception: elsewhere in the country internal migrants had lower breakdown rates than those who stayed in the same place.

That was one of the first recorded examples of migrants having *low* rates. Others followed, notably including studies by Murphy in Canada, Singapore and Israel. Migration is *not* always associated with higher breakdown rates. This observation alters the nature of the question:

> Instead of asking *why* migrants have higher rates of mental disorder than non-migrants, we started asking *under what conditions* do migrants have higher rates, and this swung the focus of our attention away from migration as such towards the conditions that attend it, a switch that brought new hopes since although we could hardly expect to stop migration we could now think of changing some of the attendant conditions. (Murphy, 1977)

Murphy suggested that the selection process and the adjustment processes would each vary according to attitudes and expectations in both sending and receiving countries. He stressed the differences in rural-to-urban/urban-to-urban migration, solitary/group migration, and forced/voluntary migration, as well as the more obvious variables of geographical distance and cultural change. Murphy has also drawn attention to the importance of obtaining baseline data in the country of origin. He notes that the prevalence of schizophrenia in the general population appears to be high in (for example) Croatia and Ireland. If a high incidence is found in emigrants from those countries, it might simply reflect that difference, and be nothing to do with the migration process.

The dangers of generalisation are further illustrated by the careful research of Krupinski and his colleagues in Australia, who have shown that for one group of European migrants in that country the breakdown rates are high, and for another group they are also high, but for quite different reasons and with different clinical consequences (Krupinski *et al.*, 1973).

In Britain, several small studies carried out in the 1960s seemed to show a high incidence of breakdown among Asian and Afro-Caribbean immigrants, but most of these reports suffered from small sample size and insufficient attention to age/sex standardisation. More recently we have the results of one national survey (Cochrane, 1977) and three regional surveys (Hitch, 1975; Carpenter and Brockington, 1980; Dean *et al.*, 1981). They are all based on hospital admissions data and their reliability depends on, among other things, the correct recording of birthplace in hospital records, which cannot always be assumed. The findings of these four studies are summarised in Table 5.1. They are contradictory: Asian-born subjects had higher admission rates than the indigenous population in some places but lower in others, and there was considerable variation among the Caribbean-born. Cochrane showed that in England and Wales the immigrants with the highest breakdown rates were those from Ireland and Scotland (Cochrane, 1977). There is also evidence that those who came to Britain from Eastern Europe immediately after the war are a particularly vulnerable group (Hitch, 1975; Hitch and Rack, 1980). (More detailed and comprehensive reviews of research in this area are to be found in Sanua, 1969; Murphy, 1973, 1977; Lipsedge and Littlewood, 1979; Eitinger and Schwarz, 1981; and Rack, 1982a, 1982b).

It becomes apparent that the relationship between migration and mental illness is not simple. We should not be tempted to choose between the stress-of-migration and the self-selection hypotheses, since, in any given individual or group, both these factors — and others — may apply. If we are to get any further with the subject, we must stop asking oversimplified questions and using overinclusive generalisations and ill-defined categories. It might be useful to start by considering the category 'mental illness' and the category 'migration'. Some thoughts on these two subjects form the remainder of this chapter.

What constitutes mental disorder? Or, rather, what determines its apparent incidence? Hospital admission rates provide only a very crude measure of morbidity in any given population. A person comes into contact with psychiatrists because it is believed that (a) he or she needs help, and (b) the kind of help required is that which a psychiatrist can provide: the decision is made by (i) the person concerned, or (ii) a third

Table 5.1: Hospital Admissions Data, Summary

Country of birth	England and Wales 1971 (Cochrane, 1977) All admissions		Bradford 1968–70 (Hitch, 1975)		Manchester 1973–75 (Carpenter and Brockington, 1980) First admissions only		South-East England 1976 (Dean et al., 1981)	
	Male	Female	Male	Female	Male	Female	Male	Female
Britain (base rate)	100	100	100	100	100	100	100	100
West Indies	103	113	72[a]	22[a]	156[d]	185[d]*	136*	156*
Africa							121[b]	129[b]
India	85	79	88	59[a]	236[c]*	325[c]*	149*	123*
Pakistan	68	68	134	191*			59*	55

Notes

There are substantial differences in the rates quoted by different authors for the British-born patients in their series. Presumably these reflect differences in the organisation and utilisation of psychiatric services in different areas. Therefore to obtain rough comparability the rates for each immigrant group have been converted to a percentage of the rates given for British-born patients in the same sample.

* indicates statistically significant difference from British-born rate ($p < 0.01$) calculated by the authors in each case.

a Hitch comments that the numbers in these categories were too small for any important conclusions to be drawn.

b includes ethnic Africans and ethnic Indians (refugees from Kenya and Uganda).

c all Asians amalgamated, including Bangladeshis.

d includes 'negroes from sub-Saharan Africa' (13 per cent of sample).

Source: Rack (1982b)

party (family, friends, neighbours, police, magistrates, etc.). The decision is influenced by the availability and acceptability of psychiatrists and of alternatives. For example, in a particular refugee resettlement programme the workers have ready access to psychiatric advice and use it frequently; whereas in another programme (possibly dealing with an identical population) there are no such channels of referral, but an efficient non-medical system of counselling and casework. The statistics will show high psychiatric morbidity in the first case and low in the second. Acceptability also varies: in the 1970s Britain received a number of refugees from both Chile and Argentina. Resettlement workers found that their Argentinian clients were often quite happy with the suggestion of referral to a psychiatrist, since experience in their own country led them to believe that psychiatrists were helpful people. Many Chileans, on the other hand, had a very negative image of psychiatry and were alarmed when referral was suggested. The stigma attached to 'madness' is a major obstacle to psychiatric referral among many groups (e.g. many Asians in Britain).

Unhappiness and anxiety are common experiences and most such feelings are coped with by the individual with or without group support. Who decides which cases require extra help, and, once that is agreed, who decides to call in a psychiatrist, rather than a priest, guru, village elder, pir or hakim? Are these alternatives available in the particular migrant group? There are differences and even contradictions between cultures in deciding whether a particular item of behaviour is socially acceptable or not: in some Muslim societies a young man who has the temerity to disagree violently with his father and reject his authority is acting so far outside cultural norms that his family may suppose him to be mad and place him under psychiatric care. Among Vietnamese refugees in Britain, many have become so depressed that they have spoken openly of suicide: but their friends did not see this as an indication for psychiatric referral.

When the question of mental illness is raised not by the patient or his friends, but by social workers, doctors, police or magistrates, other factors operate, particularly when these agents do not know the patient personally and are unfamiliar with his or her cultural norms. We have described these 'diagnostic pitfalls' in detail elsewhere (Rack, 1982b). Unusual behaviour can be attributed to mental illness when it is in fact an expression of justified distress or anger. There is also the question of racist harassment which may be overt or subtle. Amrit Wilson, when describing the kinds of harassment to which black people in Britain are exposed, states: 'This kind of stress, caused strictly by the state, was never mentioned by the doctors we spoke to, instead they redefine it as "neurosis", an individual problem . . .' (Wilson, 1981). There is growing evidence, some of which is discussed elsewhere in this book, that members of ethnic minorities, when they come into contact with psychiatric services, do not always receive equal treatment.

Taking all these factors into account, it is probably fair to say that the artefacts and irrelevant variables which determine whether a member of an immigrant group is referred to mental health services (and therefore swells the statistics of psychiatric morbidity) are so great that conclusions drawn from such statistics are of little value.

A different approach is to carry out sample surveys in the 'normal' (i.e. non-referred) population using standardised questionnaires or interview techniques. This was attempted by Cochrane and his colleagues in Birmingham. They used the Langner 22-item questionnaire on population samples of English, Indian and Pakistani origin, and it is very interesting to note that, with this technique, the Indian and Pakistani samples revealed *less* emotional or mental disorder than the English-born (Cochrane, 1977; Cochrane and Stopes-Roe, 1977, 1981). Such research is enormously difficult and the picture it produces is incomplete, but when combined with accurate descriptive accounts it tells us more about that group than measuring psychiatric referral rates, and should have higher research priority.

The other term that requires clarification is 'migrant'. There are important differences between different groups of migrants. It is tempting to make comparisons between (for example) the Indians and the Chinese in Britain, or compare findings in Canada, Australia, Germany or Israel — but these are likely to be misleading if the factors involved in the migrations are not differentiated. Since Ravenstein formulated his 'Laws of Migration' a century ago (Ravenstein, 1889), sociologists have put forward theories, models and schemata to classify migration patterns. Many of them are developed around the positive and negative influences which operate at the places of origin and destination (so-called 'pull-factors' and 'push-factors'). Lee (1965) takes this further. He states that migrants are seldom typical of the population from which they come. Some are above-average in initiative, enterprise and foresight. He refers to this as positive selection, and we can conveniently name them the 'high aspirers'. Others are the unsuccessful, unsettled or deprived, which Lee describes as negative selection and we may call 'low achievers'. Lee suggests that the high aspirers are influenced mainly by pull factors, whereas low achievers are mainly affected by push factors. He goes on to postulate that the greater the obstacles which have to be overcome in the migration, the more the high aspirer/pull factor group will predominate, and vice versa.

We could try this model out on two extreme examples. The first is a Chinese entrepreneur from Hong Kong coming to Britain. He was not obliged to leave home (push factors are not strong) but he perceived advantages in Britain (pull factors). The obstacles were considerable (distance, finance, language). We may therefore expect him to be in the high aspirer category. By contrast an Irishman who came to Britain because he could not obtain work at home (push factor) had few obstacles to overcome, and may belong in the low achiever group. Neither migrant is typical of his compatriots in the place of origin, but their atypicality is quite different in the two cases. It is tempting to link this with the observation (Cochrane, 1977) that the Irish in England have a very high rate of mental illness whereas the Chinese seem to have one of the lowest: but the temptation must be resisted because, although a classification system that takes acccount of motivation is an advance on those that do not, Lee's model is still only three-dimensional, and there are many other dimensions to be considered.

An alternative, which has been proposed by the present author (Rack, 1982b, 1983) and may be worth developing further, is based on a set of stereotypes: the *Gastarbeiter,* exile, and settler.

The *Gastarbeiter* is a migrant worker. The German word is preferred here because of its international acceptance and because in Britain the term 'migrant worker' implies a particular legal status. The stereotypical *Gastarbeiter* is a young man from a rural area who migrates to an industrial city in his own country or abroad in search of work. Initially he leaves his family behind, and his original aim is to stay in the new environment for as long as it takes to amass sufficient wealth to return home and re-establish himself securely. His long-term aim is to improve his economic and social position back home, and to this end he is prepared to work long hours and live economically. As much as possible of his earnings is sent home as remittances for the support of his family and to be banked against his return. He has no intention of remaining permanently abroad so he is not highly motivated to learn about the new culture or any more of the language than necessary. He probably lives in lodgings with compatriots, and is prepared to do whatever work he can get. His emotional roots remain in his country of origin and he lives on news from home.

Gastarbeiter migration is a result of industrialisation. The movement is from rural to urban, and the pull of the city is greatest for people in economically undeveloped rural areas. Historical examples of

Figure 5.1: The Centripetal Flow of *Gastarbeiter* Migration in Europe 1950–70

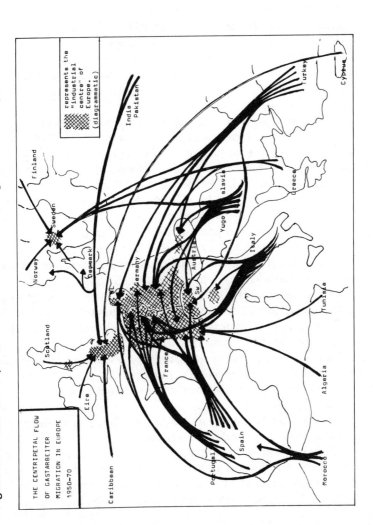

Gastarbeiter migration include the Irish labour force which in succcessive centuries constructed the British canal, railway and motorway systems. Similar situations exist throughout the world wherever industrialisation creates a need for unskilled labour and there is a rural hinterland from which it can be obtained. In Europe during the post-war economic boom, industrial centres of central Europe attracted workers from the rural periphery and Turkey, amounting to about 15 million by 1976; in Switzerland they were 25 per cent of the total labour force (see Figure 5.1). A graphic and beautifully illustrated description of this migration is the work of Berger and Mohr (1975). Other examples of *Gastarbeiter* migration are the Mexican workers in southern USA, Koreans in Japan, and the rural-to-urban movement within and between countries in South America. For the receiving country, *Gastarbeiters* are convenient as they provide a short-term or seasonal labour force which is disposable: when no longer required, the immigrants are expelled (Power and Hardman, 1976).

In Britain, when labour was required in the boom years of 1950–70, *Gastarbeiters* were recruited from the traditional source (Ireland) and to some extent from the rural areas of Europe: but also from parts of the former British Empire, notably the Caribbean islands, Pakistan, North India and Bangladesh. Unlike the Turks and Yugoslavs in Germany or Switzerland, the Asians and Afro-Caribbeans in Britain were not on short-term work permits: as Commonwealth citizens they had (up to 1963) the right to come and stay permanently if they wished. This is an important difference which will be discussed later; the point to consider at present is that, at the outset, most of them had the motivation and intentions of *Gastarbeiters* as described above.

Our second category is the settler. As typical examples, let us imagine a young married couple: they have adventurous ideas and are aiming to find a better life for themselves and their children in a land of greater opportunity. Possibly they feel thwarted and cramped at home, and disillusioned in a society which they find restrictive or in some other way unsatisfactory. They intend to put down new roots. The aim is not to return home wealthy (like the *Gastarbeiter*) but to make a new home permanently and become successful in the new environment. They are predisposed to take a positive view of the differences they encounter, abandon old customs and learn new ones.

This kind of migration is not rural-to-urban, but from 'old country' to 'new country'. Most of the movement from Europe to North America, Canada, Australia and New Zealand in the last hundred years has been of 'settler' type, and perhaps the post-war immigration to Israel may be so described though it had, of course, an additional ideological motivation.

Once established in the new country, the settler can afford to remember his roots. His children and grandchildren may even view the old country with nostalgic affection and take pride in their Scots, or Greek, or Italian ancestry: but at the time of migrating the settler is more or less repudiating his roots and aiming for assimilation into a new culture.

Our third major category is exiles. These are people whose migration was involuntary, who had to leave their homelands because of military or political upheaval, or famine or other disaster. At the time of departure they may have been refugees, but that term becomes inappropiate after a time. We cannot construct a stereotype of the refugee, as there are tremendous differences between groups. Sometimes a whole population is uprooted (as in the case of the Asians expelled from Uganda by Amin); in other circumstances there may be a highly selected group of political activists or persons considered undesirable by the regime (as was the case with the Chileans, Czechs and Hungarians). Occasionally people who have gone abroad for other reasons become refugees *sur place* because of a political change during their absence (there are Iranian and African students in Britain who are in that position). The change of cultures may be enormous and shocking (as with the Vietnamese in Britain) or minimal (as with the Afghans in Pakistan).

There is however, one generalisation which we can make about this group, and it is to do with grief. With the possible exception of some refugees *sur place*, they have all experienced extreme trauma. There is the trauma of enforced uprooting, the misery of permanent separation from loved people and places, which has been well described as a bereavement. On top of that there may well have been the horror of a concentration camp, torture by secret police, hunger, danger, violent death witnessed and feared, and feelings of despair, guilt and remorse to complicate the mourning process and obstruct rehabilitation. Depression, paranoia and other psychotic or neurotic symptoms are common among refugees after they reach safety, and this is not surprising: there is growing recogntition recently of long-term sequelae extending into old age (Baker, 1983).

The three categories are shown in Figure 5.2. They are not comprehensive. They do not include the overseas student (discussed more fully in Chapter 6), who has something in common with the *Gastarbeiter* in that he or she is transient, staying abroad temporarily in order to improve prospects at home later, but differs in coming (probably) from an urban and sophisticated background; nor the international diplomat

Figure 5.2: Three Categories of Migrant (for explanation see text)

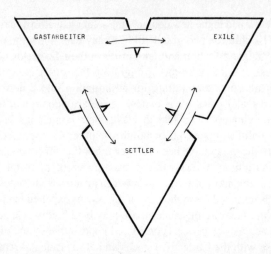

or businessman with a series of postings; nor the different kind of *Gastarbeiter* migration exemplified by the British engineer on a contract in, say, Saudi Arabia; to include every aspect of migration we should also mention the conqueror, and his successor the colonial administrator or 'white settler'. Perhaps Figure 5.2 could be extended to accomodate these and others. The purpose of the triangle is to suggest that, although a particular migrant may not conform exactly to any of the three stereotypes, it is usually possible to place him somewhere within the triangle, in the general direction of one or other of the apices. So placed, he will have things in common with other people placed at the same location. Our first hypothesis is that what they have in common will include psychological and emotional variables including the incidence and types of mental illness. This may not be true but it is testable.

The arrows within the triangle are intended to indicate the possibility of movement from one category to another over time. Some groups of political refugees see themselves as temporary exiles and spend their time planning for the day when they will return and reclaim power: they have (at that stage) no interest in integration. There are some exiles who retain their national identities with fierce determination, remaining (for example) Ukrainian or Estonian after 40 years in Britain. Others, however, move towards the position of settler. The Asians who came to Britain as refugees from Uganda had received a brutal lesson in the consequences of separatism, and many of them were determined to adopt British ways as quickly as possible. Not infrequently an exile who has moved into the settler group (in self-image), moves some way back again in old age. Similarly with *Gastarbeiters*. We have already noted that those who came to Britain from commonwealth countries usually saw the move as temporary. Many of them still subscribe to what has been called 'the myth of return' (Anwar, 1979). Muslims in particular view much of British culture with great misgiving, and are determined to retain their own traditions — even though these may have altered considerably in the home country while they have been away. But they were granted the legal status of settlers, which meant that they could bring wives and children to Britain if they wished; and they cannot prevent their children being exposed to British influences. The children become settlers, but the parents have not yet decided.

The bridges in Figure 5.2 symbolise the fact that this transition from one self-image to another may not be an easy process. It involves a series of adjustments and compromises, which are seldom made by clear thinking and rational decisions but are usually only part-recognised and part-resolved. Clinical experience suggests that many of the conflicts (internal and interpersonal) that afflict Asian patients in Britain at the present time are connected with this self-image adjustment problem. The bridges represent problem areas for them. Perhaps this is true generally: that is our second hypothesis, which is also testable.

No diagram can encompass all the complexities of the subject. If these conceptual models do nothing else, they should at least indicate the absurdity of writing about 'migrants' and making epidemiological comparisons of them, as if they formed a unitary and homogeneous group. We require a multiaxial classification system, and it does not exist. Most research reports that compare (for example) the hospital admission rates of a particular 'ethnic minority' with those of the 'indigenous population' take note of age, sex, marital status, and not much else. What else do we need to know? Here are some suggestions:

(1) At the time of referral or data collection, how long ago did the subject migrate (assuming the study is about migrants and does not include their children and grandchildren born in the new country, which confuses the issue further)?
(2) At what age did the subject migrate? (Although this may be calculated from the first question, it is an important question in itself, particularly for people who migrated during childhood and have attended school in the new country: how many years of school?)
(3) Motives for migration (using a classification system such as push/pull; high aspirer/low achiever; or gastarbeiter/settler/exile; distinction should

Figure 5.3: Questions Addressed to Immigrants

Is the new culture valued,
and to be adopted?

	YES	NO
YES	INTEGRATION	SEPARATISM
NO	ASSIMILATION	MARGINALITY

Is the old culture valued, and to be retained?

Figure 5.4: Questions Adressed to the Host Community

Are newcomers helped
and encouraged to adopt
the host culture and
rewarded for doing so?

	YES	NO
YES	INTEGRATION	SEPARATION
NO	ASSIMILATION	REJECTION

Are racial differences and alternative lifestyles respected?

also be made between *pioneers* and *followers,* the latter including spouses and other dependants of the pioneers).

(4) The difficulty of migration, and its perceived reversibility. (Number and frequency of return visits, if any, may be relevant to this.)

(5) Preparedness (knowledge of language beforehand, expectations, understanding of new environment).

(6) How great was the difference? (Climatic, dietary, religious, etc., and specifically including whether the previous environment was urban (educated, sophisticated, cosmopolitan?) or rural (traditional, restricted, uneducated?.) A cultural-distance scale is needed.

(7) Experience immediately before and during the journey. (This applies particularly to refugees.)

(8) Whether migrated alone or in a group, and whether a compatriot group or ethnic enclave was available to join on arrival.

(9) Intentions at the beginning about duration of stay, and any changes of mind or ambivalence since.

(10) Attitude to the culture of the new country, and to previous culture. A useful model which has been developed by Canadian workers is reproduced as Figure 5.3. We might predict that mental distress would be greatest for those in the 'marginality' category, least for those in the 'integration' category, and intermediate in the other two: this could be tested.

(11) How distinctive was the migrant on arrival and since (dress, complexion, customs, etc.)?

(12) Social, economic and political climate in the new country (including tolerance, racial prejudice and discrimination, employment opportunities, etc.). A model similar to that mentioned above (10) may be useful, and a version is illustrated as Figure 5.4. Comparison of the two sets of answers, in a given case, could be a way of spotlighting some problems.

(13) Previous life experiences. (There is some evidence that the problems of migrating adults are intensified if they have experienced a previous migration in childhood.)

(14) What are the base-rates for mental illness in the country of origin?

These questions are not all equally applicable to every group, and some specific additions and amplifications may be needed; but in time such a list might form the basis of a multiaxial model for research purposes. Clinical data fitted into such a model would be meaningful and instructive, which is not really the case at present.

In summary, the intention of this chapter is to show that if the enquiry is represented by an equation:

Relationship

Mental disorder ◄——————————————————

—————————————————————► Migration

we are unlikely to make progress on the nature of the relationship if we persist in treating mental disorder and migration as simple unitary concepts. The complex and protean nature of 'mental disorder' is generally acknowledged, and the present discussion is not exhaustive but focuses on a few variables which are frequently overlooked or underestimated. 'Migration' is also multi-faceted, and its complexities have not been thoroughly explored in the psychiatric literature. Unless this is done, there is no point in continuing to amass epidemiological research data about the relationship. Some possible lines of approach are suggested.

References

Anwar, M. (1979) *The Myth of Return*, Heinemann, London

Astrup, C. and Ødegaard, O. (1960) 'Internal Migration and Mental Disease in Norway', *Psychiatric Quarterly*, Suppl. 34, 116

Baker, R. (1983) (ed.) *The Psychosocial Problems of Refugees* The British Refugee Council, London

Berger, J. and Mohr, J. (1967) *Seventh Man*, Penguin, Harmondsworth

Carpenter, L. and Brockington, I.F. (1980) 'A Study of Mental Illness in Asians, West Indians and Africans Living in Manchester, *British Journal of Psychiatry, 137*, 201

Cochrane, R. (1977) 'Mental Illness in Immigrants to England and Wales: an Analysis of Mental Hospital Admissions 1971', *Social Psychiatry, 12*, 25

Cochrane, R. and Stopes-Roe, M. (1977) 'Psychological and Social Adjustment of Asian Immigrants to Britain: a Community Survey', *Social Psychology, 12*, 195

Cochrane, R. and Stopes-Roe, M. (1981) 'Psychological Symptom Levels in Indian Immigrants to Britain: a Comparison with Native English', *Psychological Medicine, 11*, 319

Dean, G., Walsh, D., Downing, H., and Shelley, E. (1981) 'First Admissions of Native Born and Immigrants to Psychiatric Hospitals in South-East England 1976', *British Journal of Psychiatry, 139*, 506

Eitinger, L. and Schwartz, D. (eds) (1981) *Stangers in the World*, Hans Huber, Berne

Hitch, P.J. (1975) 'Migration and Mental Illness in a Northern City', Unpublished PhD Thesis, Bradford University

Hitch, P.J. and Rack, P.H. (1980) 'Mental Illness among Polish and Russian Refugees in Bradford', *British Journal of Psychiatry, 137*, 206

Jackson, J.A. (ed.) (1969) *Migration: Sociological Studies*, Cambridge University Press, Cambridge

Krupinski, J., Stoller, A. and Wallace, L. (1973) 'Psychiatric Disorders in Eastern European Refugees now in Australia', *Social Science and Medicine, 7*, 31

Lee, E. (1965) *A Theory of Migration* reprinted in J.A. Jackson (ed.) (1969) *Migration: Sociological Studies*, Cambridge University Press, Cambridge

Lipsedge, M. and Littlewood, R. (1979) 'Recent Advances in Transcultural Psychiatry', in K. Granville-Grossman (ed.) *Recent Advances in Clinical Psychiatry III*, Churchill-Livingstone, London

McNeil, W.H. and Adams, R.S. (1978) *Human Migration: Patterns and Policies*, University Press, Bloomington

Murphy, H.B.M. (1973) 'Migration and the Major Mental Disorders: a Reappraisal', in C.A. Zwingmann, and M. Pfister-Ammende (eds), *Uprooting and After*, Springer, New York

Murphy, H.B.M. (1977) 'Migration, Culture, and Mental Health', *Psychological Medicine*, 7, 677

Ødegaard, O. (1932) 'Emigration and Insanity', *Acta Psychiatrica Scandinavica* Copenhagen Supplement No 4.

Ødegaard, O. (1945) 'Distribution of Mental Diseases in Norway', *Acta Psychiatrica Neurologica*, 20, 247

Park, R. (1928) 'Human Migration and the Marginal Man', *Amer. J. Sociol.*, XXXIII (6), 881. Reprinted in J. Stone (ed.) (1977) *Race, Ethnicity and Social Change*, Mass: Duxbury Press, North Scituate

Pollock, H.M. (1913) 'A Statistical Study of the Foreign-born Insane in New York State Hospitals', *State Hospitals Bulletin*, 5, 10–27 (Special Number)

Power, J. and Hardman, A. (1976) *Western Europe's Migrant Workers* (revised 1978), Minority Rights Group, London

Rack, P.H. (1982a) 'Migration and Mental Illness: a Review of Recent Research in Britain', *Transcultural Psychiatry Research Review*, xix (3) 151 McGill University, Montreal

Rack, P.H. (1982b) *Race, Culture and Mental Disorder*, Tavistock, London

Rack, P.H. (1983) 'Migration and Mental Health: a Matrix of Variables', paper presented at Transcultural Psychiatry Symposium, World Congress of Psychiatry, Vienna 1983, to be published in *Psychiatry: the State of the Art*, Vol. 8, Plenum, New York

Ranney, M.H. (1850) 'On Insane Foreigners', *American Journal of Insanity*, 7, 53

Ravenstein, E.G. (1889) 'The Laws of Migration', *Journal of the Royal Statistical Society'*, 52, 288

Sanua, V.D. (1969) *'Immigration, Migration and Mental Illness: A Review of the Literature with Special Emphasis on Schizophrenia'*, in E.B. Brady, *Behaviour in New Environments*, Sage, Beverley Hills

Stonequist, E.V. (1937) *The Marginal Man* (reissued 1961) Russell & Russell, New York

Wilson, A. (1981) *Black People and the Health Service*, Brent Community Health Council, London

6 OVERSEAS STUDENTS AND EXPATRIATES: SOJOURNERS OR SETTLERS?

John L. Cox

Introduction

Overseas students and expatriates have in common their experience as 'sojourners' living temporarily in a strange land and their need to meet specific work objectives within a limited period of time. They are therefore different from migrant 'settlers', who intend to remain in the new country and may not therefore expect to return 'home'. Such settlers may change their nationality or their cultural allegiance.

Teachers and university administrators have become more aware in the last decade of the work difficulties experienced by student sojourners, and of their contribution to university communities. The effect of the increased tuition fees has been to reduce substantially the number of foreign students in Britain, and indirectly threaten the survival of some academic departments. Furthermore the economic, political and ethical aspects of international education have become important for governments as well as for international organisations; a recent World Health Organization publication, for example, entitled *Uprooting and Health: Psychosocial Problems of Students from Abroad* (Zwingmann and Gunn, 1983) has helped to initiate discussion about the welfare of students who choose to study overseas. The increase in the number of overseas students in Britain from oil-producing countries, and the reduction from New Commonwealth countries, have underlined how political and economic factors may determine not only the number of such students but also their country of origin.

The British expatriate, however, unlike the overseas student, does not usually pay fees to an educational institution but is nevertheless similarly affected by political and economic considerations. Furthermore the expatriate is in a paid post and usually employed by a multinational business, academic institution, national government or, less commonly, by a missionary or philanthropic society. Although an expatriate does not go overseas to obtain a specific educational qualification, other stringent work objectives may have to be met, and the expatriate must ensure that the type of work undertaken does not preclude eventual return to the home country. The expatriate also needs to understand the culture

76

of the host society to achieve these work objectives, but to avoid becoming excessively identified with the foreign culture, which would make re-adjustment to the home society more difficult.

Although expatriates and overseas students are therefore somewhat different in their age range, motivation to travel and work objectives, both groups are nevertheless sojourners in an alien land and may therefore suddenly be sent home because of work failure, loss of economic support or because of political unrest. The precarious adjustment of many student sojourners is illustrated by the plight of students exiled from Chile and from certain Middle Eastern countries. Such students may have had to leave their country suddenly, and so experience profound grief because of this abrupt uprooting (see Munoz, 1980).

Another difficulty may occur if the sojourner fails to achieve the academic tasks set by government, multinational business or educational authority, and so is afraid of 'losing face' or of having severe financial penalties imposed. The longer this unhappy sojourner remains overseas because of such difficulties, the more likely he is to experience problems when returning home, and reverse culture shock can be more difficult to overcome (see Gullahorn and Gullahorn, 1963).

Overseas Students

The number of students undertaking their higher education overseas in 1975 is shown in Table 6.1. The largest number (a quarter of a million) were from Asia and study in North America, Europe or the USSR; the number of North American students in Europe, or of Europeans who travel to America, is much smaller. In Britain the number of overseas students doubled from 55 087 in 1961 to 114 064 in 1975, an increase that resulted from the planned expansion of tertiary education at that time. Similarly Torrey *et al.* (1970) found a 10-fold increase in the number of overseas students in the United States since 1948; and in the academic year 1968–1969 10 per cent of the entire student population were from overseas.

However, according to the recent statistics on the number of overseas students in the United Kingdom between 1979–1980 and 1983–84 published by the British Council (1985), there has been a 37 per cent slump in the number of overseas students in Britain (from 88 037 students in 1979–80 to 55 608 in 1983–84). This decrease is largely because of the British government's controversial decision to charge a full 'economic' fee, although other explanations may include overseas

Table 6.1: Flow of Student Population 1975

1. From Asia	to North America	111 206
	to Europe and USSR	86 000
2. From Africa	to Europe and USSR	61 315
3. From North America	to Europe and USSR	26 648
4. From South America	to North America	17 141
	to Europe and USSR	14 822
5. From Arab States	to Europe and USSR	47 413
	to Asia	20 517
6. From Europe	to North America	29 634
	to other European states and USSR	104 853

countries having become more self-sufficient, a lack of motivation of British universities to enrol overseas students, and also awareness that racial discrimination is increasingly found in British universities.

Push-Pull Factors

A closer understanding of the motivation to study overseas can be gained by determining the influence of 'push' and 'pull' factors. Those factors which *push* a student to travel overseas include:

(a) the home govenment's need for administrative professional personnel, which in turn determines the availability of scholarships to study overseas.

(b) the attitudes of the student's family to a European education, which may be regarded as particularly desirable and prestigious.

(c) the wish to explore a new country and to take independent travel initiatives and so to achieve greater personal autonomy.

(d) political oppression, i.e. students who are political refugees and were forced to leave their home university, for example students from Uganda who had to contend with an increasingly hostile environment that devalued academic success.

(e) the inability of the home university to offer a complete degree course, e.g. Lesothan law students needing to study in Edinburgh; many such students were unhappy about this arrangement and were not reconciled to this 'forced' migration.

The *pull* factors include:

(a) the financial benefit to the host country of receiving educational fees.

(b)   the work contribution that a foreign student can make, e.g. postgraduate doctors in Britain who may occupy a third of training posts in some medical specialities.

(c)   the need to remain friendly with oil-producing countries and to fulfil obligations to Commonwealth countries.

(d)   an obligation to provide university courses not available in the home country, such as courses in engineering, agriculture or medicine.

(e)   the advantage to the university of having an 'international reputation', which will increase its influence overseas.

It is clear that these social, psychological and political 'push-pull factors' are complex and interlock to a considerable extent. The students themselves, however, are not usually aware that their decision to study overseas is so complex; only when political problems occur or economic difficulties are encountered do they realise their particular vulnerability.

Another way of conceptualising the difficulties of overseas students is discussed by Reed *et al.* (1978) who consider their problems of adjusting to three different social roles: that of a 'student' who conforms to the demands of an academic institution, i.e. who studies on a prescribed course and takes examinations; a 'client' who pays for an education and expects good value for money; and a 'visitor' who is subject to immigration laws that could shorten the stay in the foreign country or restrict the entry of dependents.

Bearing these factors in mind, it is not surprising that the adjustment of overseas students to the foreign country is not always straightforward and that many students are afraid of being pushed out by examination failure or by an arbitrary decision of sponsors. Some may even wish to return home prematurely because of excessive nostalgia or as a result of experiencing racial discrimination.

The difficulties that African students may experience are shown in Table 6.2. Anumonye (1967) has usefully classified their problems into those that were inevitable, such as the British weather, and those that could be avoided, such as loneliness or ethnocentricity.

Zwingmann and Pfister-Ammende (1973) have conceptualised many of these difficulties by referring to them as 'uprooting problems', a term that appropriately emphasises how self-esteem is maintained by cognitive, social and affective roots which interact with the primary milieu, so that an uprooting disorder results when these roots are severed. The experience of being severely uprooted may then lead to the development of a depressive illness or anxiety neurosis, which may require psychiatric treatment. However, the relationship of uprooting difficulties to

Table 6.2: Common Causes of Psychological Stress for African Students in Britain

Inevitable problems	Avoidable problems
British peculiarities	Financial stress
Racial discrimination	Misunderstanding and mistrust
Accommodation difficulties	Teacher-student difficulties
Separation reactions	Vocational guidance problems
Age-determined problems	Loneliness in Britain
Language and adjustment	Married student's problems
Sexual problems	Over-identification
Career-choice restrictions	Academic inadequacy
Study-method discrepancies	Ethnocentricism
Dietary difficulties	General disillusionment
Personality problems	Employment difficulties
British climate	Poor embassy support

examination performance is not clear; anxiety, for example, can be a spur to academic achievement but if it becomes excessive it may prevent studying, by impairing concentration. The relationship between anxiety and studying ability is complicated further if there are language difficulties, or if there are teaching-method discrepancies between the home and the overseas country.

In our study of 121 overseas students at Edinburgh University, their academic progress and psychological problems were determined during the first year, and final degree results were also obtained. The sample was, however, somewhat heterogeneous and included students from North America, British nationals living overseas, as well as students from other West European countries; the proportion of students from Africa and Asia was surprisingly small (22 per cent).

One purpose of this study was to determine if there was any relationship between academic performance and cultural distance between the home culture and that found in Edinburgh. We therefore attempted to measure this distance, and developed a 'cultural distance scale'. This scale consisted of ten items, which included language, clothes, food preferences, religious belief and courtship behaviour; each item was rated on a three point scale according to the extent to which the student's home subculture was similar to, or different from, that found in Edinburgh (Babiker *et al.*, 1980). This scale, though having face validity, could not, however, measure more subtle cultural variables, such as the authority relationships within the family, the sex-role differences or the types of family ritual.

Students were interviewed shortly after matriculation and more extensively during the following February or March. At this second interview details of the life events experienced since the student was accepted by the university were obtained, and we also recorded if the student had been depressed or anxious (see Miller *et al.*, 1981, for details of method).

We found that overseas students *were* less likely than home students to pass their first-year examinations and so gain entry to the second year: 31 per cent of overseas students 'failed' compared with 21 per cent of home students. However, the relationship between this examination failure and psychiatric disturbance or adjustment problems was not clear. Only psychiatric symptoms in the Easter term were associated with examination failure, and only eight students had a definite psychiatric disorder: four were depressed, two had anxiety neuroses, one an eating disorder, and one further student had psychiatric symptoms associated with migraine (Cox *et al.*, 1981).

The prevalence of psychiatric morbidity in these first-year overseas students was therefore no greater than that found in all students at Belfast, Kampala and Edinburgh (see German and Arya, 1969). Furthermore, those students who failed their first-year examinations were not necessarily those most likely to have experienced adverse racial prejudice. Thus three of the four students from The Netherlands, for example, failed, but they were unlikely to have experienced racial discrimination.

Our results showed that it was difficulties experienced *after* arriving in Britain, such as language and study-method problems, that were closely related to academic difficulties, and that cultural distance had no relationship to academic success. This finding was similar to that of Furnham and Trezise (1983). Furthermore, we found no relationship between success in obtaining a degree and nationality or ethnicity.

Health-service Considerations

The vulnerability of students to political unrest was apparent from clinical work at Makerere University, during the oppressive regime of Idi Amin. At this time the number of new referrals almost doubled between 1972 and 1973, and there was also a 50 per cent increase in the number of students who attended the mental health clinic (Cox and Muhangi, 1975). There were four student suicides at that time, compared with only one in the previous years. This excessively high suicide rate in a university of only 3 500 students was partly related to the *anomie* that affected the students and teachers, which was a result of the demoralisation caused by a military government. Academic achievement was an undesired goal: an attitude that impaired the motivation of students to study and of teachers to teach.

Reed *et al.* (1978) have suggested that universities should designate a special tutor to assist overseas students, and should also provide an adequate counselling service. To be effective this tutor/counsellor needs to be familiar with the educational demands of the institution, as well as with the specific stresses of the sojourner such as homesickness, political problems, language difficulties and racial prejudice. A full understanding of the stages of bereavement and culture shock is helpful when assisting overseas students who are recently uprooted from their own country.

Another task of this tutor is to ensure that other welfare personnel are familiar with these distinctive problems, and also to maintain close liaison with teachers and with university administrators. A psychiatrist may have an important role in facilitating this communication between welfare agencies, as well as in treating the more seriously disturbed student. The psychiatrist may have to alert academic colleagues to the multifarious ways in which psychiatric disorder can be recognised (such as by a complaint of a headache or by unexpected exam failure) and may have to point out that a rushed decision to repatriate a student is rarely wise (Cox, 1983).

Foreign Medical Graduates: Student and Expatriate

The foreign medical graduate, whether in Britain or the USA (Garetz and Garetz, 1973; Davidson, 1982), is a particularly vulnerable migrant. A postgraduate doctor not only is a student who wants to obtain a professional qualification but also is an expatriate who needs paid employment and is competing with the UK doctors. Most such overseas doctors are therefore in a 'double-bind' situation; on the one hand they know the National Health Service could not continue without their employment (Smith, 1980), but on the other hand they are aware that competition with local graduates is increasing and that recent immigration laws may pre-empt their stay in Britain for longer than four years.

A career survey of members of the Royal College of Psychiatrists showed that overseas psychiatrists were increasingly being squeezed out from the more popular senior registrar and consultant posts and that many were uncertain about their future plans. Only rarely did Asian doctors intend to return to their native country, however, and most were more likely to seek work in the Middle East or in North America (Bhate *et al.*, 1986).

This increased competition with UK graduates for posts in the National Health Service has already resulted in fewer overseas doctors obtaining such training posts. This situation is regarded by some as being appropriate nationalism (looking after your own students) but by others as a further example of racial discrimination.

Expatriate Stress

It is a strange irony that although the problems of overseas students in the UK are now more widely recognised by administrators, teachers and university welfare services, the problems of British personnel who work overseas are more rarely appreciated. It is only recently that a conference was organised by Maurice Lipsedge on this topic, although in 1900 the distinctive problems experienced by an expatriate doctor living on the remote island of St. Helena were familiar to colonial administrators such as G. Martinu (personal communication from Professor McRae):

> The environment of the island of St. Helena is such as to have a dramatic effect on the personalities of the expatriates. Isolation in time and distance from the outside world, very limited social and virtually no recreational facilities must, and from observation do, have a pronounced effect on those thrown together in such surroundings. It is probable that the effect on the majority is merely to exaggerate any personality defect to a degree in which it becomes a burden on other members of the community. Hence, friendships tend to be short-lived and animosities prolonged and fierce. Recurrent fits of depression and neurotic illnesses of one sort or another are all too common in such circumstances. For most, if not all, the periodic loss of perspective inevitable in such a circumscribed life must be endured and overcome without the assistance of the many diversions taken so much for granted in a larger community.

Somewhat similar difficulties were observed by Culpin (1935) and were included in his description of 'tropical neurasthenia'. Culpin, however, believed that the popular physical explanations for this condition, such as overindulgence in games, bridge and dinner parties or the brightness of the sun's rays, excess alcohol and comparative air stagnation, were unlikely to be correct, and that psychological factors were more important. Thus treatment of tropical neurasthenia, Culpin thought, was best commenced by asking the expatriate 'What is worrying you?', rather than by giving advice to take a long leave or to have teeth attended to.

Forsyth (1933) recognised the relationship of expatriate difficulties to personality factors and observed that individuals with 'neurotic or temperamental infirmity' were predisposed to 'tropical neurasthenia'. Climate and conditions of service could only 'pull the trigger', and could not load the gun.

More recent reports about the psychological problems experienced by expatriates employed by multinational companies indicate that 'tropical neurasthenia' is not only of historical interest, but is also of much contemporary importance. Caplan (1983), for example, found that up to 30 per cent of expatriates returned home prematurely because of family worries, alcoholism or psychiatric disorder. He found that many multinational companies were aware of this very high 'failure rate', and even budgeted extra monies when planning their overseas developments.

The reasons why an expatriate works overseas may therefore need to be considered, and would include the lack of suitable employment, inadequate salary and poor working conditions in the home society, as well as family problems and a curiosity about other people's lifestyle. The wish to assist with the education and health-service provision of another country is also a common motivation, and some expatriates are mainly motivated by religious or philanthropic ideals. Preoccupation with half-forgotten colonial myths, images of tropical relaxation, the lure of increased salaries, as well as the prospect of being a big fish in a small pond, are further factors to consider.

The manpower priorities of the overseas country and its willingness to attract business enterprise by financial incentives will also influence the number of expatriates recruited. A British doctor, for example, is more likely to work in a country where the salary is supplemented by the Ministry of Overseas Development, and yet the level of such supplementation is a political decision. Some East African countries no longer receive such overseas aid, so British doctors and other professional workers are therefore less likely to work in these countries.

When considering the specific difficulties that an expatriate may experience, the problems for the family should also be recognised. Thus the wives' migration may be likened to that of a forced exile, so that the stability of the marriage as well as the wife's personality may determine whether or not the overseas placement is satisfactory. Some expatriates return home prematurely because of unexpected marital problems. In a prospective study of expatriate couples, Caplan is presently investigating the extent to which the coping ability of an expatriate prior to the migration predicts subsequent breakdown and the extent to which such factors as meeting the employees at the airport, giving practical help to settle in and providing sporting facilities will ameliorate stress. There is, however, a need for more prospective studies with different groups of expatriates. These would contribute substantially to the migration literature as well as assist in the development of better welfare services.

It is possible, for example, that a more detailed screening of expatriates, possibly excluding those with major marital problems, a history of major psychiatric disorder or those severely depressed, would reduce the 'drop-out' rate, and be an advantage to the business company or missionary society. However, the finding of King (1975), in a survey of 130 professional US personnel working overseas, that depression was common and generally had a good prognosis is a reminder that an affective illness should not necessarily preclude recruitment or indicate the need for the expatriate to return home. Welfare personnel need to be familiar with the psychological aspects of uprooting, and to have a detailed knowledge of the psychology of separation, as well as of the common psychiatric disorders.

Expatriates who have spent an extended period of time overseas, or who have identified closely with the host society, will benefit from being informed about the stages of reverse culture shock on return home. Reorientation courses and opportunities for appropriate nostalgia are also helpful for such returned migrants.

Expatriates' children may become distressed by being uprooted from friends or school and so require support and practical assistance with their adjustment to the new 'home' environment. Some will have been born overseas, and so for them the return home is then more similar to the experience of the expatriate moving to an alien land.

Although the difficulties for overseas students and expatriates have been described in this chapter, for many such sojourners the migration has not only been a personally enriching experience but also enabled new work tasks to be undertaken. There is however, a pressing need for more studies of the psychological adjustments of such migrants, and of the extent to which the migration experience initiates, or protects against, psychiatric disorder.

References

Anumonye, A. (1967) 'Psychological Stresses among African Students in Britain', *Scottish Medical Journal, 12,* 314

Babiker, I.E., Cox, J.L. and Miller, P. McC. (1980) 'The Measurement of Cultural Distance and its Relationship to Medical Consultations, Symptomatology and Examination Performance of Overseas Students at Edinburgh University', *Social Psychiatry, 15,* 109–16

Bhate, S., Sagovsky, R. and Cox, J.L. (1986) 'Career Survey of Successful Candidates in Membership of Royal College of Psychiatrists Examination', *Bulletin of the Royal College of Psychiatrists, 10*, April

British Council (1985) *Statistics of Overseas Students in the United Kingdom 1983–84*, British Council, London

Caplan, R. (1983) 'Developing a Psychological Screening Procedure for the Selection of Expatriates', Paper presented at Conference on Expatriate Stress, London

Cox, J.L. (1983) 'Role of the Psychiatrist in the Treatment of Mental Illness in Students from Abroad', in C.A.A. Zwingmann and A.D.G. Gunn (eds), *Uprooting and Health: Psychosocial Problems of Students from Abroad*, pp. 59–61, World Health Organisation, Geneva

Cox, J.L. and Muhangi, J. (1975) 'Problems of Mental Illness among Makerere University Students with Special Reference to the Period 1970–1973', *East African Medical Journal, 52*, 615–18

Cox, J.L., Babiker, I.E. and Miller, P.McC. (1981) 'Psychiatric Problems and First-year Examinations in Overseas Students at Edinburgh University', *Journal of Adolescence, 4*, 261–70

Culpin, M. (1935) 'Neurasthenia in the Tropics', *The Practitioner, 85*, 146–54

Davidson, L. (1982) 'Foreign Medical Graduates: Transcultural Psychiatric Perspectives', *Journal of the American Academy of Psychoanalysis, 10*, 211–24

Forsyth, D. (1933) 'Comment in Discussion on "An Examination of Tropical Neurasthenia"', *Proceedings of the Royal Society of Medicine, xxvi*, 921

Furnham, A. and Trezise, L. (1983) 'The Mental Health of Foreign Students', *Social Science and Medicine, 17*, 365–70

Garetz, F.K. and Garetz, D. (1973) 'Alternative Models of Training Foreign Physicians in Psychiatry', *Psychiatric Quarterly, 47*, 132–8

German, G.A. and Arya, O.P. (1969) 'Psychiatric Morbidity amongst a Ugandan Student Population', *British Journal of Psychiatry, 115*, 1323–9

Gullahorn, J.T. and Gullahorn, J.F. (1963) 'An Extension of the U Curve Hypothesis', *Journal of Social Issues, 19*, 33–47

King, L.J. (1975) 'The Depressive Syndrome: a Follow-up Study of 130 Professionals Working Overseas', *American Journal of Psychiatry, 132*, 636–40

Miller, P.McC., Babiker, I.E. and Cox, J.L. (1981) 'Background, Life Circumstances, Symptoms and Academic Performance in Overseas Students', *African Journal of Psychiatry, 8*, 1–11

Munoz, L. (1980) 'Exile as Bereavement: Socio-psychological Manifestation of Chilean Exiles in Great Britain', *British Journal of Medical Psychology, 53*, 227–32

Reed, B., Hutton, J. and Bazalgett, J. (1978) *Freedom to Study. Requirements of Overseas Students in the U.K.*, Overseas Students Trust, London

Smith, D.J. (1980) *Overseas Doctors in the National Health Service*, Policy Studies Institute, London

Torrey, E.F., Van Rheenan, F.J. and Katchadourian, H.A. (1970) 'Problems of Foreign Students: An Overview', *Journal of the American College Health Association, 19*, 83–6

Zwingmann, C.A.A. and Gunn, A.D.G. (eds) (1983) *Uprooting and Health: Psychosocial Problems of Students from Abroad*, World Health Organization, Geneva

Zwingmann, C.A.A. and Pfister-Ammende, M. (1973) *Uprooting and After*, Springer, New York

7 PSYCHIATRIC SERVICES FOR ETHNIC MINORITY GROUPS

John Bavington and Abdul Majid

Introduction: Psychosocial Problems of Migrants in Britain

In this chapter, we wish to consider some aspects of provision of psychiatric services for minority ethnic groups in cities where there are large ethnic minorities, e.g. Hispanics in New York, Afghans in Islamabad or Pakistanis in Bradford, or many races in the Arabian Gulf states. The best approach for psychiatric services will depend on various factors to do with the local situation. The present chapter concentrates on the situation in Britain and draws mainly on experiences with Asian groups.

According to 1981 figures mentioned by Brown (1983), the total number of the coloured population from the New Commonwealth and from Pakistan is just over 2.2 million, which constitutes 4.1% of the total population of the United Kingdom. About 40% of this population was born in Britain; a further 1.4 per cent came from Ireland, and many such Irish immigrants retain their roots within their home country. East Europeans (Polish, Ukranian, Baltic, Yugoslavian, Hungarian, Czechoslovakian, etc.) form other substantial ethnic minorities, and there are smaller populations from Cyprus, Italy, other European countries, Chile, Argentina, Vietnam, China and East or West Africa. Any of these may present particular needs for the National Health Service. In some large cities, such as London, Birmingham, Leicester, Wolverhampton or Bradford, such ethnic minorities may represent 20 per cent or more of the total population. Britain is therefore indeed a multi-racial, multi-cultural and multi-coloured society.

It is well known that many such immigrants and refugees experience distinctive social and environmental stresses. First, there are problems of dislocation, culture shock and the subsequent need to adjust to the new situation. This process of acculturation to the new society can be distressing and may involve a fundamental change in the whole orientation of the individual; he may have to relinquish his traditional cultural and religious beliefs and learn the meaning of new symbols and also readjust his social behaviour. This readjustment can be painful and is associated with the fear of losing personal identity. Such cultural adaptation to an unfamiliar environment takes time; living on the fringes of two cultures can be a cause of constant frustration and of intense personal insecurity. Such acculturation can be associated with severe anxiety or depression and may induce a psychosomatic illness.

Secondly, these difficulties of adaptation are exacerbated by the social situation in which many immigrants live. Thus many are forced to live in deprived areas of large industrial cities that have been described as 'pathological zones'. In such zones there is a high rate of unemployment, crime, infant mortality and malnutrition. Although at first most of these migrants were able to earn well and so fulfill to some extent their initial hope of financial improvement for themselves and their family at home, downward social mobility was often the price to be paid for the economic improvement. Thus many professionals, including doctors, found that their aspirations for work in Britain were unrealistic, and many skilled persons were reduced to working as unskilled labourers. The poor current economic situation has hit minority ethnic groups particularly severely, so that after many years of unpleasant work there is an ageing population of immigrants for whom 'the bubble has burst', which has resulted in a loss of social role and purpose, especially for men.

Thirdly, there is the ever-present and pervasive attitude of racial superiority, so powerfully present in British society. Lord David Pitt pointed out that such racial prejudice and discrimination were undoubtedly the most urgent and serious problems facing the minority ethnic groups, and their effects on mental health cannot be ignored. The host society is often openly hostile and prejudiced against minority ethnic groups who consequently feel most insecure and threatened. Their customs, habits and attitudes are not only questioned by the majority but are also ridiculed, which can undermine the individual's own sense of identity and self-esteem. Such racial discrimination has been aggravated by the present poor economic climate in the UK, and minority groups, especially those distinguished by their skin colour, are then used as scapegoats for economic ills and so become the victims of increased racial discrimination.

However, although these stresses are experienced by the majority of such ethnic minorities in the United Kingdom, they are not necessarily the main causes of mental disorder. What additional factors are likely, therefore, to precipitate mental illnesses? Every society may have its own specific stresses which could lead to such a breakdown (Bavington, 1982). Furthermore, societies will have their own ways of dealing with and alleviating the impact of such stress factors. In the immigrant situation, however, these cultural resources and supports are weakened or even absent, and certain aspects of the structure of that society are therefore perceived of as being vulnerable.

In our experience, loneliness and a feeling of isolation were particularly common among minorities. A quarter of depressed Asian women, for example, had none of their immediate family in Britain and were therefore deprived of important social supports and comfort. Sometimes married Asian women are intensely unhappy because they are unable to adapt to new ways of life in Britain compared to the rural village life from which they may have come. They find the cold climate frightening and rarely go beyond the corner shop because of culture-bound social restrictions; a few may be particularly lonely while their husbands are at work and while their children are at school if they do not have the opportunity to enjoy other women's company which at home would have been more available, providing emotional support and allowing feelings to be more directly expressed. Some Asian husbands cannot recognise this aspect of their wives' emotional needs. Such wives therefore can become severely depressed and often complain of physical symptoms (Majid, 1981).

Conflicts within the family are a common cause of stress which could be related to mental illness in Asian culture. They include the tension between a young wife and her mother-in-law, marital unhappiness, and also more complex family troubles perhaps triggered by disputes over marriage arrangements or the financial obligations within an extended family. Such problems are well recognised and there are established procedures to resolve them. Where these difficulties arise in Asians living in the United Kingdom, however, it may be impossible to use these procedures because of the distance from home as well as the fragmentation of the community network. Thus a young wife who has recently arrived in the UK experiences unhappiness living with her husband's family. She will find difficulty obtaining assistance from her father, uncle or brothers, relatives who would normally have been available to help her at home.

One other common cause of stress relating to acculturation is the difference in outlook between the first-generation immigrant and the second generation who have been born in Britain or were living there since childhood. This problem mostly affects teenage girls and relates to such issues as personal autonomy, choice of boyfriend and, for some ethnic minorities, the conflict between arranged and Western marriages. Many parents find it difficult to accept that their daughters may wish to choose whom they go out with or even to decide for themselves to marry a British boy. This problem may increase in the future, and results not uncommonly in increases of stress which take the form of taking overdoses or other behavioural problems. In addition, anxiety and depression can also be provoked among the parents of such children.

Presentation of Mental Illness

Any consideration of what would constitute appropriate psychiatric services for minority groups must also take into account the frequency and presentation of mental illness among immigrants. Rack (1982) and Littlewood and Lipsedge (1982) are in agreement that the pattern and frequency of illness in migrants vary greatly depending on their reason for migration, their country of origin and the social situation in the host country of the immigrant.

In the United Kingdom earlier studies (Hashmi, 1968; Pinto, 1970; Carpenter and Brockington, 1980; Dean *et al.*, 1981; Hitch, 1981) suggested higher rates of mental illness than for native British among the New Commonwealth community, but more recent work indicates lower rates for Asian groups, whether measured by hospital admission rate or in community surveys (Cochrane, 1979).

Higher incidences of schizophrenia were found by Hashmi (1968), Pinto (1970), Cochrane (1977), especially in Pakistanis in the United Kingdom, and some relate this to the social, financial and political difficulties encountered by this group. The higher incidence of schizophrenia might also be explained by the fact that some psychiatrists may tend to overdiagnose this illness, especially in its paranoid form; and overlook the fact that these paranoid symptoms might be a justifiable reaction to hostility from the host community.

We have much clinical evidence that depressed Asian patients commonly present with somatic symptoms. Usually they complain of vague pains in the abdomen or 'all over' the body, have difficulty in breathing, and experience headache and also peculiar sensations of hot and cold which often start off in the legs and spread to the abdomen, chest and head (Majid, 1981). Often they deny having a depressed mood, although closer scrutiny will reveal that they have been tearful, and had insomnia, lack of appetite and loss of weight. Most are reluctant to admit to having difficulties in adjusting to the new society or in having any problems in their own personal or marital life. Such depressed patients are often nor readily identified by doctors and many are referred to other physicians where they undergo unnecessary and often costly further medical investigations.

Psychiatric Service Provision

A mental health service that is appropriate to the needs of a particular ethnic minority community or to situations of ethnic diversity can best be developed if attention is given to the basic general principles of good medical practice. It has often been said, for example, that transcultural psychiatry is nothing more than 'good psychiatry'. Thus a good psychiatric service will depend on knowledge of the characteristics of the population it seeks to serve obtained as a result of close contact and links with the community. A criticism of much provision of services in the United Kingdom at the present time is that it often suffers from an 'ivory tower complex', being too distant geographically and emotionally and so more limited and rigid in its interpretation of and response to psychiatric problems. If the delivery of psychiatric services is indeed of this type, then it is most likely that the ethnic minorities will be particularly adversely affected by its inadequacies.

There is considerable evidence that minorities in Britain underutilise the benefits of the National Health Service for a number of reasons. One such reason concerns the attitude and feelings of the minority community towards the concept of mental illness, and their interpretation of emotional disturbance or abnormal behaviour. Thus they may believe that a mental illness is caused by supernatural power, and so cannot appreciate the role of the doctor in its cure. Moreover, in the extended family, personal worries and financial disputes that affect individuals are regarded as a problem for the whole family to solve, so that disclosure of this information to outsiders is regarded as shameful and would cause disgrace to the family. Many social and voluntary agencies are regarded with fear and suspicion, so contact is avoided unless it is absolutely necessary. This heavy reliance on the intra-familial resources is to some extent brought about by the social isolation of the minorities themselves, which may reinforce the prejudiced, racist outlook that locates the problem within the ethnic minority. In this way the majority community avoids having to examine the weaknesses and deficiencies in the delivery of health services. Roger Ballard, an anthropologist with particular experience of illness behaviour in minority ethnic groups, has observed that there is a strong tendency for the host community to regard minority cultural practices, at least those that impinge on professional work, as being essentially pathological. He gives examples such as purdah, cousin marriages, vegetarian diet, and the use of traditional medicines and cosmetics (Ballard, 1983a).

Good medical practice clearly implies an openness of approach to the minority community which will lead to a greater awareness of their needs as they are perceived by the community and so allow more flexibility and modification of existing patterns of service. Furthermore, such Health Service provision would also indicate the strengths and resources of the local community to assist with medical problems.

An important aspect of this style of clinical practice is the method of communication which in many instances requires the overcoming of language differences as a priority.

However, professional health workers closely involved with the provision of services for ethnic minorities need not just language competence but also what Ballard has called 'cultural competence', i.e. the ability to understand and work with a patient from a different culture in his or her own terms. This must be regarded as equally important as adequate language if good communication is to be achieved, since culture itself is 'a vehicle for communication'.

To achieve this cultural sensitivity, health professionals need to become more aware of their own culture and how this may influence their attitude towards patients as well as their clinical judgement. What might be involved in such a shift of perspective? Clearly the creation of a specialist team would provide a high level of cultural and linguistic resources to assist more especially minority group members. However, this is not often possible, nor in certain specific instances is it necessarily desirable. Our clinical experience has shown that it is not necessary to acquire vast detailed knowledge about unfamiliar customs and practices, and such knowledge may further increase the attitude that the lifestyles of minority groups are misguided, unnatural or even backward. Ballard (1983b) has said that it is not just the information that is obtained that is important, but also how such information is used. Some information about minority ethnic groups is of course valuable, but of more importance is the perception of what the issues are and also a commitment to start from the patient's own perception of the world and responding to his or her own cultural categories rather than imposing one's own. Doctors, Roger Ballard says, do not require a stereotype rule of thumb, such as 'this is how minority group X behave'.

There is also an inherent danger in supplying cultural information if this is divorced from the more demanding and challenging tasks of 'changing deeply entrenched and taken for granted social conventions' (Ballard, 1983b). A basic amount of knowledge may be fairly easily acquired given an attitude of openness and an ability to listen and learn from others. There is no shortage of suitable material describing social customs of ethnic minorities (see Henley, 1979), but such literature should be used as a supplement to the more dynamic learning that takes place when there is a better communication between patient and health professionals, which is here being advocated.

This principle of approach to clinical problems is fundamental to the provision of appropriate psychiatric services to all populations and is relevant when considering the effect of other differences such as those relating to class, gender or religion.

Language and Interpreters

In psychiatry, communication with the patient by use of language is particularly important for successful clinical practice. At present in many such clinical situations, a translator or interpreter is used, such as a son or daughter, or, more rarely, a professional, paid interpreter. Indeed in British hospitals it is often the practice to use a junior doctor from the same country to interpret. None of these practices, however, is satisfactory, and indeed there are many instances when gross inadequacies in communication have resulted in inappropriate management.

In Bradford it has been possible to create a clinical team which is multidisciplinary and also multilingual. In this instance the interpreter speaks on behalf of the team, which is not the same as interpreting for the team. The critical difference (as Rack, 1982, has pointed out) is that the person asking the questions understands their significance and the importance of the answers, and so participates in the diagnostic decision-making. In our opinion the best solution is to recruit suitable bilingual professionals, and this should certainly prove possible in cities with large ethnic minorities. It is our contention that such a policy will eventually minimise the need for interpreters. If this principle were applied to all categories of staff, including receptionists, clerks, canteen servers, porters, cleaners, etc., the beneficial effects would be felt generally over the whole service. However, this policy has only rarely been attempted and it is likely that the less satisfactory method of using an interpreter service will be continued. What might an ideal interpreter provide? A good interpreter should have an adequate command of both languages, and be familiar with the psychiatric and sociological terms and cultural background of the patients. He should have a pleasant and sociable personality and be capable of making linguistic and cultural interpretation.

No doubt there are individual examples of such a person, but they are rare in the National Health Service. Any improvement in the quality and quantity of interpreters will need to tackle these issues.

Bradford College has pioneered a course to prepare and equip multi-lingual personnel to function effectively in such situations, and individuals who have had this training can provide a better standard of interpreting services. However, to attract such specialist staff it is necessary to improve their status and to remunerate them as independent professionals. Rack (1982) has summarised the training content that such interpreters should receive:

> They must be fluently bilingual to start with but this is not a sufficient criterion any more than an ability to read English is an adequate qualification for a secretary. They should have the sort of educational background and personal characteristics that we would expect in any other important Health Service employee. Like Medical Secretaries, they should be given background knowledge of the meaning of medical terms and the convention and ethics of medical situations, a need to understand how patients feel and have a working knowledge of the organisation of that part of the service in which they are employed, so that they can answer patients' questions and reassure them. Their training must give them sufficient confidence to speak up boldly when they perceive that the two sides are misunderstanding each other. It is not always easy to tell a Consultant that he is on the wrong track altogether because he has failed to see the significance of some point of cultural difference; nor is it easy for the Consultant to accept such correction until he has learned to regard the interpreter as a professional colleague whose competence and acumen may be trusted.

Such a person would be most effective if he or she were to become a regular and long-term member of the clinical team, although this would obviously not be possible where the numbers needing the particular language would be small.

Assessment and Diagnosis

Professor Yamamoto (1978) refers to 'cross-cultural mis-diagnosis', and Rack (1982) describes the cultural pitfalls in recognising psychiatric conditions. Clearly psychiatric services for minority groups will need to be aware of the dangers inherent in attempting to evaluate and interpret

symptoms and behaviour presentation across cultural and language differences, which are liable to be accentuated by the unfamiliar background.
One of these dangers is the assumption that familiar Western diagnostic
categories can be used and applied to different ethnic groups. It would
be wiser to remain somewhat unattached to these classifications, and some
recent developments in transcultural psychiatry have advocated a more
phenomenological approach in which indigenous categories are identified
and used as the basis for cross-cultural comparisons (e.g. Kleinman,
1977).

There is still, however, the need to have an appropriate understanding of the phenomena in order to make appropriate responses and avoid
either over-reactions or the failure to recognise treatable conditions.
Assessment of patients from ethnic minority groups needs special attention, and various factors such as unfamiliar presentation, language and
communication barriers, etc. may complicate the diagnosis and management as patients may be misunderstood, misinterpreted and passed from
one discipline of medicine to another, undergoing unnecessary investigations which may have adverse effects on their mental health.

Physicians treating members of ethnic minority groups should make
every effort to have a proper assessment of the case, which includes a
thorough history from the patient and relatives as well as accurate medical
and mental-state examinations. Behaviour needs to be carefully evaluated
by skilled personnel, and because of its diagnostic impoortance the risk
of misinterpretation across social and cultural boundaries must be
recognised. Important questions need to be borne in mind, such as 'Is
it deviant, abnormal and to what degree?' 'Is it considered 'illness' or
viewed rather as badness, awkwardness or laziness?'; 'Is it regarded as
"madness" or as a more understandable and culturally familiar way of
expressing distress;'. Such questions framed in an acceptable manner
can be usefully put to relatives, although the answers to them should
not necessarily be taken completely at their face value. Familiarity with
the language and culture will obviously facilitate better answers, but will
not by any means entirely remove the ambiguities inherent in the concept
of 'mental illness'.

A large element in the skill of working across culture is to be able
to appreciate both our own liability to biases in clinical interpretations,
and also the factors that influence the patients' presentation; symptoms
very rarely appear 'pure' but are the product of various processes and
influences, many of which have to do with culture. What is presented
is influenced by the perception and expectations of the setting, so that
knowledge about how an Asian patient will view the doctor/patient

relationship is important. To complain of emotions may be thought irrelevant but a physical symptom will certainly not be. The threshold for
awareness and differentiation of various emotional states (like guilt or
sadness) may also differ: for example, it seems easier to acknowledge
unhappiness if the reason or cause is an acceptable loss than if it is connected with some painful family conflict. The individual's own interpretation and conception of his illness may determine the choice of the
symptom, as for example the Asian patient's belief that hot gases go
to the brain, or that diet or spiritual influences cause illness. 'Every
culture structures its experience with the available cultural tools and even
the experiences of psychosis can be expressed in terms of religion, family
or social conflict' (Littlewood and Lipsedge, 1982). Part of this includes
ideas of illness behaviour and the culturally influenced use of the sick
role in certain situations. Awareness of these dynamics may be very
valuable in determining the most appropriate response or avoiding inappropriate ones which might prolong the illness state. As Littlewood
and Lipsedge have observed:

> The extent to which a patient sees himself as ill and in need of treat-
> ment varies with his culture. What may be endured in India requires
> therapy in New York. What is insane behaviour in Barbados may not
> be in Jamaica. Acceptance of the role of a mental patient depends
> on our beliefs about the nature of mental illness and whether any
> stigma is associated with it.

Treatment and Management

What ways of, or approaches to, management and treatment are likely
to require modification for a minority group? After all it might be thought
that biological treatments could be given without any such modification
being necessary. It should, however, be remembered that the impact of
any treatment is influenced by the views and beliefs of the patient and
the setting in which the treatment is delivered. Hence it is important to
be aware of the expectations of the patient and family, and of the possibility that they are unfamiliar with the whole concept of "psychological
illness". Ideas about the potential dangers of Western medicine (often
considered by Asians as 'hot' and hence potentially harmful) or the value
of injection, or information on the significance of timing and diet in relation to the taking of drugs are important.

The dosages of drugs may differ between ethnic groups. It has been the general clinical experience of psychiatrists working in Third World countries that a satisfactory therapeutic response can be obtained with lower doses of phenothiazines or anti-depressants than would be used in a Western country. Some studies (cf. Allen *et al.*, 1977; Zeigler and Biggs, 1977; Lewis *et al.*, 1980; Rack, 1980) have shown higher blood levels in black or Asian patients than in white subjects after the same dose of tricyclic antidepressants has been given, so administering the same initial dose for an Asian as for a white patient is more likely to produce side-effects, and hence non-compliance.

Rack (1982) has commented that there is sufficient evidence to suggest that:

(1) when new drugs are introduced, their efficacy and toxicity should be assessed for each separate ethnic or racial group (it is not sufficient to carry out controlled clinical trials in one country and then utilise the drugs worldwide without local confirmatory trials);

(2) the practitioner prescribing for members of other races should be prepared to use low doses and increase gradually if necessary. This recommendation certainly applies to tricyclic anti-depressants in Asian subjects, and it may well apply to other categories of drugs for other groups.

Where admission is required, it is important that the ward staff have some awareness of the possible difficulties related to culture that might be experienced.

The patient who is admitted to a hospital ward in which he is unable to communicate with anyone at all may feel apprehensive and tense. With the best of intentions one can hardly prevent such a patient being alarmed by unfamiliar and incomprehensible routines or bored to distraction by social isolation. In such a situation the strategy most patients usually adopt is to observe what others are doing and to copy them. Clearly, in a psychiatric ward, this can cause additional complications. In innumerable ways such as misunderstandings about eating or toilet habits, religious observances, behaviour towards other patients, lack of common language debars non-English speaking patients from therapeutic activities in a psychiatric ward. They often cannot talk through their problems with staff or with patients in group activities. Occupational therapy is a meaningless concept to most Asians. (Rack, 1982)

An uneducated, rural Asian woman is especially likely to find the situation strange and bewildering, particularly if the ward is mixed and there are no provisions for a separate 'purdah' area. So far there are very few psychiatric nurses with Asian languages.

Another vulnerable patient is the refugee for whom the walls of the institution and the loss of personal freedom evoke traumatic memories. Elderly people who are confused in their own homes usually become even more disorientated in a strange environment and this effect is exacerbated if verbal communication is impossible. (Rack, 1982)

Dietary needs should also be considered. It should be viewed as equally important that the patient receives the food with which he is familiar as it is to ensure the correct diet for, say a diabetic. In either case to provide the wrong diet would be regarded as examples of bad medical practice. A flexible ward policy would at least allow relatives to bring food from home, a potentially important source of comfort in an alien situation.

There are likely to be any number of other possible issues in which existing hospital and clinic facilities and practices may create discomfort, distress and misunderstandings for the ethnic minority patients. Very often the main reason for the unhappiness is the incomprehension, intolerance or insensitivity of the staff concerned, for example: in the matter of using the correct name or form of address; in appreciating the hygiene beliefs and religious practices and the significance of certain personal items, such as *taawiz* (amulet) so often worn by Asians; or how to relate to alternative forms of treatment (e.g. *hakim*) which the patient may wish to use at the same time. Another source of contention for ward staff has been the number of visitors arriving because of the importance given to visiting in many other cultures. In all such matters it is a question of clear and simple good professional practice for those concerned to equip themselves responsibly with the relevant information. Those who do so will be amply rewarded.

Psychotherapy

There has been considerable debate concerning the applicability of psychological methods of treatment across culture. The psychotherapies commonly practised in Britain have their roots in the Western world, and they were devised, developed and formulated on the basis of a Western philosophy of life which in many respects contradicts the traditional beliefs and ideology of those who have come from other parts of the world and have different religious and value systems. Western psychotherapy places an unequivocal emphasis on individualism and self-understanding, and aims towards the greater maturity of the individual. In contrast, in most Third World cultures, the individual identity is seldom recognised and there is less stress on the autonomy of the individual and greater emphasis is given to interdependency.

One reaction to these differences has been the tendency to jump to the conclusion that 'psychotherapy' is not generally usable for most ethnic minority patients. This feeling, combined with the inadequate provision of staff with appropriate language and cultural knowledge, has resulted in less use of psychotherapy in favour of drug treatments, at least in the United Kingdom.

However, rather than rule out altogether the value of such methods of help, a better approach would be to consider what might be a relevant and acceptable form of psychotherapy. Such an approach would need, for example, to recognise the basic concept of dependence and interdependence and also ideas of illness and expectations of treatment for most Asian patients. It would attempt to provide a culturally consonant therapy approach. In Britain, unfortunately, inclusion of cultural concepts in the therapeutic process has so far received very little interest, which might be due to the fact that Western experts find it very difficult to believe that ideas perceived in the West may not be applicable to people from other parts of the world. Yet Margaret Mead (1948) rightly emphasised that thought originating in the Euro-American culture may not have universal validity. The objective of psychotherapy for Afro-Asians must be based on their sociocultural roots, religious beliefs and concepts of health and life in general. Considerable research and work are needed in this respect, and in Britain there is a unique opportunity to develop such therapeutic methods. Doubt has been similarly cast on the possibility of using group-therapy techniques, but again it seems perfectly possible to apply the general concept of group dynamics with sensitivity to cultural concepts. In Bradford an Urdu/Hindi/Punjabi mixed weekly group for patients has now been running for over a year with growing acceptance and support, so much so that it may shortly have to split into two groups. Therapeutic community methods have also been found to be transportable across cultural frontiers (Currer, 1975; Bavington, 1984). Even mixed groups and community meetings can be used acceptably, and in one unit they came to be called 'The Family Meeting'. It was found that the richer concept of the family was a useful way to evoke caring responses in the group. Because of the frequency with which stresses and illness appear to arise from family conflict, and because of the importance of the extended family in the culture of some of the minorities in Britain, it might be thought that some form of family therapy would be particularly suitable in such cases. This may well prove to be so and indeed Ballard has proposed 'a family reconciliation service' aiming to enlist the high premium placed on family unity. Such an approach would certainly be very different from Western types of family therapy, but experience in Bradford has indicated that it is possible to work therapeutically with a family focus (Hitch, 1981).

Physicians treating patients from other cultures must be fully aware of the problems of cross-cultural psychotherapy. Several techniques and approaches have been suggested by experts, mostly from America, which are mainly designed to enable the therapist to be aware of his own as well as the patient's background and value systems, in order to minimise the discrepancy between the patient's expectation and the therapist's practice. It has been suggested that therapists should have formal training in cultural anthropology with a view to understanding cultural factors that influence psychotherapy. The therapist must be fully aware of his own prejudices and has to be flexible and prepared to learn from his patients and to exchange ideas with them. One important aspect of such learning is racism awareness training, such as, for example, the regular staff 'sensitivity group' under the leadership of Dr Aggrey Burke at St. George's Hospital, London.

It should be remembered that, in all psychotherapy, one underlying element is to challenge or question cultural assumptions, and in that sense all psychotherapy is 'counter-culture'. Part of any therapy interaction is the negotiation and dialogue that must proceed between the differing views and expectations of client and therapist.

In most situations of ethnic diversity in the United Kingdom, the structure of the psychiatric services is to provide for the majority and is not adapted to the needs of any minority group, who consequently often derive less benefit and indeed sometimes experience harm as a result of their contact with the health services.

The Transcultural Psychiatry Unit at Lynfield Mount Hospital, Bradford, is one example of an attempt to provide a relevant psychiatric service and has been described by Rack (1982). It incorporates many of the ideas discussed in the previous sections. This unit consists of a multidisciplinary team, most of whom have relevant languages in addition to English and have varied cultural experiences and backgrounds. The majority can give only part of their time to the services of the unit, whose primary aim is to provide suitable psychiatric help to the members of the various ethnic minorities in Bradford. This is mainly achieved through a weekly clinic when most team members are present, and for the few inpatients there is a weekly special review/round on the ward in which most of the Unit's patients stay. It has not been possible, nor it considered desirable, to provide a totally separate ward, and there is flexibility also as to when patients attend the hospital, for example some have expressed preference to attend the same outpatient clinic as the majority white population. Although most of the patients come from the hospital's catchment area, increasingly the advice of the Unit is being sought on behalf of patients who live outside the catchment area or in relation to problems which are not strictly 'psychiatric' and for which hospital referral would be inappropriate. Colleagues seeking advice in such cases are usually invited to join the lunchtime staff meeting. These weekly meetings provide the opportunity for wider discussions and 'constitute an on-going exercise in mutual education from which everyone benefits, the indigenous English members probably most of all' (Rack, 1982).

This meeting has become a forum for raising questions, considering ideas, looking at deficiencies in the services, formulating new initiatives (such as the Urdu group referred to earlier) or considering possible research projects. Quite often, friends in associated professions or neighbouring areas may join the group, perhaps to explore some particular issue or share some relevant interest or concern. Examples include a teacher of deaf Asian children, a lecturer in applied anthropology, an Asian worker making video films in several Asian languages to publicise the local social services, a sociology lecturer, and two workers starting an Asian women's group in Leeds.

In addition, once every month, this meeting is replaced by an open meeting, usually attended by up to 100 people from various local services and agencies. In all these ways, it is hoped that the Unit will continue to develop and improve the range and relevance of the service provided.

Although it is not possible to lay down any universally applicable blueprint, it is suggested that some such model of a special psychiatric clinic should be considered in other areas of the country with a high concentration of ethnic minority people. Such a centre would provide adequate clinical care by staff who are particularly interested, and in possession of expert knowledge and experience. It would especially respond to the most obvious issues of language and the effects of cultural differences on presentation, assessment, diagnosis, treatment and management. It should be used as a centre for research, especially for the development of culturally relevant diagnostic techniques and treatment methods, and for teaching on transcultural psychiatry. Such a centre should physically be located close to the minority community so that a trusting relationship can be established, and so that regular contact with members of the family and the community can be maintained. This process of being accepted and trusted can constitute a major challenge. The family may view the clinic's presence as an intrusion unless it is persuaded of the intrinsic value of the treatment methods proposed. This requires patience, understanding of the community's view on mental illness, and the ability to convince family members of the rationality of intervention methods and the competence of the mental health workers. Psychotherapeutic support for the patients and their families, by helping them gain insight and resolve the conflicts arising out of migration and breakdown of family bonds, is usually of much greater benefit than prescibing drugs. The aim of such therapy is to help the individual overcome the problems of adaptation to the new society by removing the internal conflict about learning new values, and to reward socialisation in either native or ethnic groups which will result in increased security. Such treatment is time-consuming and demands expert knowledge, but is also most rewarding.

Good psychiatry is largely about effective communication across whatever barriers may be present — about being able to listen to and understand what is being expressed in situations of pain and distress, both verbally, non-verbally and through the language of the culture. Poor communication has repeatedly emerged in our experience as the area in which the most glaring and unforgivable failures have occurred, and attention to this need must be considered one of the most basic aspects in any programme of better services for ethnic minorities.

References and Further Reading

Adebimpe, V.R. (1981) 'Overview: White Norms and Psychiatric Diagnosis of Black Patients', *American Journal of Psychiatry, 138*, 279–85

Allen, J.J., Rack, P.H. and Vaddadi, K.S. (1977) 'Differences in the Effects of Clomipramine on English and Asian Volunteers, *Postgraduate Medical Journal, 53*, Suppl. 4, 79

Anon. 1976, 'Multi-cultural Problems', *New Psychiatry*, 8 July

Anon. 1980, 'Paranoia and Immigrants', *British Medical Journal, 281*, 1613–14

Bal, P. (1981) 'Communicating with Non-English Speaking Patients', *British Medical Journal, 283*, 368

Ballard, R. (1983a) 'Racial Inequality, Ethnic Diversity and Social Policy. Applied Anthropology in Urban Britain', Paper presented at the ASA Decennial Conference

Ballard, R. (1983b) 'The Significance of Culture', in *Lecture Notes in Behavioural Sciences for Medical Students*, A.G. Sims and W. Batty (eds), Blackwell Scientific, Oxford

Ballard, R. (1983c) 'Appropriate Style of Service Delivery to Asian Clients The Case for a Family Reconciliation Service' (unpublished)

Ballard, R. (1983d) 'The Implications of Cultural Diversity for Medical Practice. An Anthropological Perspective' (unpublished)

Bavington, J. (1982) 'The Stress which Leads to Distress', Paper read at the 4th Pakistan Psychiatric Society International Conference, Islamabad

Bavington, J. (1984) 'A Frontier Mental Health Venture', Paper presented at 5th International Conference of the Pakistan Psychiatric Society, Peshawar

Beecham, L. (1983) 'Health Problems of Ethnic Minorities', *British Medical Journal, 3286*, 1226–7

Bernard, V.W. (1953) 'Psychoanalysis and Members of Minority Groups', *Journal of the American Psychoanalysts' Association, 1*, 256–67

Bhatti, F.M. (1976) 'Language Difficulties and Social Isolation: the Case of South Asian Women in Britain', *New Community, 115*

Bradshaw, W.H. (1978) 'Training Psychiatrists for Working with Blacks in Basic Residency Programs', *American Journal of Psychiatry, 135*, 1520–4

Brown, C. (1983) 'Ethnic Pluralism in Britain: the Demographic and Legal Background', *Ethnic Pluralism and Public Policy*, N, Glazan and K. Young (eds), Lexington Books, Toronto/Heineman London

Burke, A.W. (1974), 'First Admissions and Planning in Jamaica', *Social Psychiatry, 9*, 39, pp. 9–45

Cameron, J. (1982) 'Study Centre Helps G.P.s to Treat Ethnic Minorities', *Pulse,* January,2

Carpenter, L and Brockington, I.F. (1980) 'A Study of Mental Illness in Asians, West Indians and Africans Living in Manchester, *British Journal of Psychiatry, 137*, 201–5

Carstairs, G.M. (1958) 'Some Problems of Psychiatry in Patients from Alien Cultures', *Lancet,* 1217–20

Carstairs, G.M. and Kapur, R.L. (1976) *The Great Universe of Kota*, Hogarth Press, London

Cochrane, R. (1977) 'Mental Illness in Immigrants to England and Wales: an Analysis of Mental Hospital Admissions in 1971', *Social Psychiatry, 12*, 25–35

Cochrane, R. (1979) 'Psychological and Behavioural Disturbance in West Indians, Indians and Pakistanis in Britain', *British Journal of Psychiatry, 134*, 201–10

Cochrane, R. and Stopes-Roe, M. (1977) 'Psychological and Social Adjustment of Asian Immigrants to Britain', *Social Psychiatry, 12*, 195–206

Collomb, H. (1967) 'Methodological Problems in Cross-cultural Research', *International Journal of Psychiatry, 3*, 17–19

Commission for Racial Equality (1978a) *Five Views of Multi-racial Britain*, CRE, London

Commission for Racial Equality (1978b) *Ethnic Minorities in Britain: Statistical Background*, CRE, London

Community Relations Commission (1976a) 'Between Two Cultures', *Modern Medicine*, October, 45–51

Community Relations Commission (1976b) 'Between Two Cultures: a Study of Relationships between Generations in the Asian Community in Britain', CRC, London

Community Relations Commission (1976c) *Aspects of Mental Health in Multi-cultural Society*, CRC, London

Cox, J.L. (1976) 'Psychiatric Assessment of the Immigrant Patient', *British Journal of Hospital Medicine*, July, 38–40

Cox, J.L. (1982) 'Medical Management, Culture and Mental Illness', *British Journal of Hospital Medicine*, May, 533–8

Currer, C. (1975) 'An Attempt to Apply the Therapeutic Community Approach to Treatment' (unpublished)

Dean, G. Walsh, D., Downing, H. and Shelly, E. (1981) 'First Admission of Native-born and Immigrants to Psychiatric Hospitals in South-East England, 1976', *British Journal of Psychiatry, 139*, 506–12

El-Islam, M.F. and Ahmed, S.A. (1971) 'Traditional Interpretation and Treatment of Mental Illness in an Arab Psychiatric Clinic', *Journal of Cross-cultural Psychology, 2,* 301–7

Finney, J.C. (ed.) (1969) *Culture Change, Mental Health and Poverty,* University of Kentucky Press, Lexington

Forrest, D. and Sims, P. (1982) 'Health Advisory Services and the Immigrant', *Health Trends, 14,* 10–13

Foulks, E.F. (1980) 'The Concept of Culture in Psychiatric Residency Education', *American Journal of Psychiatry, 137,* 811–16

Harding, R.K. and Looney, J.G. (1977) 'Problems of South-east Asian Children in a Refugee Camp', *American Journal of Psychiatry, 134,* 407–11

Hashmi, F. (1968) 'Community Psychiatric Problems among Birmingham Immigrants', *British Journal of Social Psychiatry, 2,* 196–201

Henley, A. (1979) *The Asian Patient in Hospital and at Home,* The Kings Fund, London

Hitch, P. (1981) 'The Policies of Intervention in Asian Families', Paper presented at the TCPS Workshop, Leicester, *1980 Bulletin of Transcultural Psychiatry Society* (UK), March

Jones, I.H. (1972) 'Psychiatric Disorders among Aborigines of the Australian Western Desert', *Social Science and Medicine, 6,* 263–7

Kiev, A. (1972) *Transcultural Psychiatry,* Penguin Books, Harmondsworth

Kinzie, J.D. (1972) 'Cross-cultural Psychotherapy: the Malaysian experience', *American Journal of Psychiatry, 26,* 220–31

Kinzie, T.K.A., Breckenridge, B. and Bloom, R. (1980) 'An Indochinese Refugee Psychiatric Clinic', *American Journal of Psychiatry, 137,* 1429–32

Kleinman, A. (1977) 'Depression, Somatisation and the New Cross-cultural Psychiatry', *Social Science and Medicine, 11,* 3–10

Kline, L.Y. (1969) 'Some Factors in the Psychiatric Treatment of Spanish-Americans', *American Journal of Psychiatry, 125,* 1674–81

Kohler, D. (1974) *Ethnic Minorities in Britain, Statistical Data,* London

Krupinski, J. (1967) 'Sociological Aspects of Mental Ill Health in Migrants', *Social Science and Medicine, 1,* 267–81

Krupinski, J., Stoller, A. and Wallace, L. (1973) 'Psychiatric Disorders in East European Refugees Now in Australia', *Social Science and Medicine, 7,* 31–49

Lancet (1981) 'Notes and News: Ethnic Minorities and the NHS', *Lancet,* 1327

Leighton, A.H. (1965) 'Cultural Change and Psychiatric Disorder', in Reuck and Porter (eds), *Transcultural Psychiatry,* Ciba Foundation Symposium, pp. 217–35, Little, Brown & Co, Boston

Leighton, A.H., Lambo, T.A. and Hughes, C.C. (1963) *Psychiatric Disorder among the Yoruba,* Cornell University Press, New York

Leininger, M. (ed.) (1978) *Transcultural Nursing: Concept, Theory and Practice,* Wiley, New York

Levitt, H.N. (1967) A Report of a Symposium on the Medical and Social Problems of an Immigrant Population in Britain, held at the Royal Society of Physicians, London, 26, May, 1967

Lewis, P., Vaddadi, K.S., Rack, P.H. and Allen, J.J. (1980) 'Ethnic Differences in Drug Response', *Postgraduate Medical Journal, 56,* Suppl. 1, 46–9

Lin Tsung-Yi (1982) 'Discussion: Cultural Aspects of Mental Health Care for Asian Americans' in A. Gaw (ed.), *Cross-cultural Psychiatry,* pp. 69–73, John Wright, Boston

Lin, K.M., and Tazuma, L. and Masuda, M. (1979) 'Adaptational Problems of Vietnamese Refugees', *Archives of General Psychiatry, 36,* 955–61

Littlewood, R. and Lipsedge, M. (1982) *Aliens and Alienists, Ethnic Minorities and Psychiatrists,* Penguin, London

Majid, A. (1981) 'Mental Health of Asian Immigrants in the UK', paper presented at the Regional Meeting of World Psychiatric Associations, New York

Malzberg, B. (1940) *Social and Biological Aspects of Mental Disease*, New York State Hospitals Press, Utica

Malzberg, G. and Lee, E.S. (1956) *Migration and Mental Disease*, Social Science Research Council, New York

Marcos, L.R. (1979) 'Effects of Interpreters on the Evaluation of Psychotherapy in Non-English-speaking Patients', *American Journal of Psychiatry, 136*, 171-4

Mattison, R.A. and Ky, D.D. (1978) 'Vietnamese Refugee Care — Psychiatric Observation', *Minnesota Medicine, 61*, 33-6

Mead, M. (1948) 'Collective Guilt', *Lancet, 2*, pp. 303-4

Morice, R. (1978) 'Psychiatric Diagnosis in a Transcultural Setting', *British Journal of Psychiatry, 132*, 87-95

Murphy, H.B.M., Wittkower, E.D. and Chance, N.W. (1964) 'A Cross-cultural Enquiry into the Symptomatology of Depression', *Transcultural Psychiatry Research Review, 1*, 5-18

Murphy, M. (1973) 'Current Trends in Transcultural Psychiatry', *Proceedings of the Royal Society of Medicine, 66*, 711-16

Murphy, M. and Raman, A.C. (1971) 'The Chronicity of Schizophrenia in Indigenous Tropical Peoples', *British Journal of Psychiatry, 118*, 489-97

Neki, J.S. (1973) 'Psychiatry in South-East Asia', *British Journal of Psychiatry, 123*, 257

Ødegaard, O. (1932) 'Emigration and Insanity', *Acta Psychiatrica et Neurologica*, Suppl. 4

Pardes, H. (1982) 'Foreword', in A. Gaw (ed.), *Cross-cultural Psychiatry*, John Wright, Boston

Pierce, C.M. (1976) 'Teaching Cross-racial Therapy', American Psychiatric Association, The Working Paper of the 1975 Conference on Education of Psychiatrists, pp. 224-7

Pinderhughes, C. (1973) *Racism and Mental Health*, Pittsburgh University Press, Pittsburgh

Pinto, R.T. (1970) 'A Study of Psychiatric Illness in the Cumberland Area', M. Phil. Dissertion, University of London

Prince, R.H. and Wittkower, E.D. (1964) 'The Care of the Mentally Ill in a Changing Culture', *American Journal of Psychiatry, 18*, 644-8 Oct. 1964.

Qureshi, S.M. (1980) 'Health Problems of Asian Immigrants', *Medicos, 2* (5)

Rack, P.H. (1980) 'Ethnic Differences in Depression and its Responses to Treatment', *Journal of Medical Research*, Suppl. 3, 20-3

Rack, P.H. (1982) *Race, Culture and Mental Disorder*, Tavistock, London

Racy, J. (1980) 'Somatization in Saudi Women: a Therapeutic Challenge', *British Journal of Psychiatry, 137*, 212-16

Rahe, R.H., Looney, J.G., Ward, H.W. *et al.* (1978) 'Psychiatric Consultation in a Vietnamese Refugee Camp', *American Journal of Psychiatry, 135*, 185-90

Richardson, E. and Henryk-Gutt, R. (1982) 'Diagnosis of Psychiatric Illness in Immigrant Patients', *British Journal of Clinical and Social Psychiatry, 1*, 78-81

Rose, E.J.B. (1969) *Colour and Citizenship, A Report on British Race Relations*, Oxford University Press, London

Seguin, C.A. (1956) 'Migration and Psychosomatic Disadaptation', *Psychosomatic Medicine, 18*, 404-49

Sifullah Khan, V. (1979) *Minority Families in Britain: Support and Stress*, Macmillan, London

Styles, W. (1977) 'Are we Failing our Immigrant Patients?', *Modern Medicine*, 45-50

Tristram, U. (1981) 'Psychiatric Care Thrives on the Family Approach', *Hospital Doctor*, September, 16

Walton, H. (1962) 'Psychiatric Practice in a Multiracial Society', *Comprehensive Psychiatry, 3*, 255-67

Walton, H.J. (1969) in J.S. Neki (ed.), *Mental Health Services in the Developing World* Commonwealth Foundation, London

Wing, J.K., Cooper, J.E. and Sartorius, N. (1974) *The Measurement and Classification of Psychiatric Symptoms*, Cambridge University Press, Cambridge

Wintrob, R.M. (1976) 'Belief and Behaviour: Cultural Factors in the Recognition and Treatment of Mental Illness', *Current Perspectives in Cultural Psychiatry*, 103–11

Wittkower, E.D. and Rin, H. (1965) 'Transcultural Psychiatry', *Archives of General Psychiatry, 13*, 387–94

World Health Organisation (1976) 'Mental Health Service in Europe', WHO, Geneva

Yamamoto, J. (1978) 'Therapy for Asian Americans', *Journal of the National Medical Association, 70*, 267–70

Yap, P.M. (1951) 'Mental Diseases Peculiar to Certain cultures: a Survey of Comparative Psychiatry', *Journal of Mental Science, 97*, 313–27

Zeigler, V.E. and Biggs, J.T. (1977) 'Tricyclic Plasma Levels. Effects of Age, Race, Sex and Smoking', *Journal of the American Medical Association, 238*, 2167

8 DEPRESSION IN ETHNIC MINORITIES

Suman Fernando

Introduction

Depression has a long history in Western medicine. In early Greek times, the condition was designated as the illness of melancholia described by Hippocrates (Jones, 1823) and Arataeus (Adams, 1856). Descriptions of depression by European writers in the Middle Ages have been recorded by Lewis (1934). The concept of melancholia was widened during the sixteenth and seventeenth centuries to such an extent that 'melancholic' became a popular way of describing people in English literature (Lyons, 1971). As psychiatry developed into a discipline in Western Europe, the concept of melancholia as a part of a manic-depressive illness was established by Kraeplin in 1896 (Defendorf, 1902). The term 'depression' replaced melancholia shortly afterwards at the suggestion of Meyer (1905).

The use of the word 'depression' in contemporary psychiatry is complex. It may denote a mood, a symptom or a syndrome (Mendels, 1970). When used as a diagnosis (rather than a mood or symptom) its meaning is not always clear for the simple reason that it has changed considerably over the last half century; Kraeplin's understanding of depression as a biological change has been influenced by insights from psychoanalytic writing, social studies, behavioural observations and cognitive psychology. Since the publication of 'Mourning and Melancholia' by Freud (1917), psychoanalytic literature has produced a variety of concepts for understanding depression (Mendelson, 1974). Ideas of 'mourning' and 'guilt' as a part of depressive psychopathology have been incorporated into general psychiatric thinking, with guilt being seen as a part of 'aggression' or 'hostility'. However, it is the organic approach to depression that has dominated the British psychiatric scene with its emphasis on a biochemical/biological aetiology of psychiatric illness in general. Nevertheless, views put forward by researchers such as Brown and Harris (1978) are beginning to have some effect on British psychiatry by providing models that can be used to conceptualise ways in which social factors and psychological states interact in giving rise to depression. Other views of depression that are creeping into British psychiatry are those concerned with a learned-helplessness model of depression (Seligman, 1975) and a cognitive theory of depression (Beck, 1967).

Recently, transcultural psychiatrists have commented upon so-called 'cultural pitfalls in the recognition of depression and anxiety' (Rack, 1982), drawing attention to two particular parameters along which culturally determined variations in symptomatology occur — those of 'somatisation' and 'guilt'. The view has grown that some so-called 'exotic syndromes' or 'culture-bound' disorders are extreme variations of depression caused by the pathoplastic effect of culture on a basic disturbance which is cross-culturally valid (Marsella, 1980). However, in noting the variety of ways in which depression is said to be manifested, Marsella (1978) questions the validity of the concept of depression across cultures:

> It may well be the case that depression is a disorder of the Western world and is not universal. Or, perhaps it would be more accurate to say that depression is a disorder associated with cultures that are characterised by particular epistemological orientation. Specifically, cultures which tend to psychologize experience. In these instances, experiential states become labelled and interpreted psychologically and this adds the components of depressed mood, guilt, self depreciation, and suicidal ideation. At this level, the experience of depression assumes meaning which is clearly different to that associated with the early somatic experience of the problem.

Since psychiatry has arisen within a West European cultural framework, its development is strongly influenced by philosophies and fashions prevalent in Western society — although the influences may not be those present in current societies. Thus, psychiatry, as we know it, is geared to a 'world view' (Huffard, 1977) inherent in European culture; in particular such features as the mind/body dichotomy, naturalistic (as opposed to supernaturalistic) explanations for personal phenomena, and a more or less materialistic approach to life. Furthermore, psychiatry developed in Europe at a time when European culture was permeated by the ideology of racism which arose in the context of colonialism and slavery (Davidson, 1984). Depression was seen, until recently, as a malady of mature and sophisticated people and quoted as being uncommon among Africans well into the 1950s (Prince, 1968). The Negro was said to have 'a simple nature which gives little thought to the future' so that 'depression is rarely encountered even under circumstances in which a white person would be overwhelmed by it' (Green,

1914). The black man was said to lack an individual mind — a sense of being a person — sharing some sort of tribal or communal mind where he made little distinction between himself and the outside world (Levy-Bruhl, 1910). Contemporary theory and practice continue to reflect racist ideology. In a recent review of depression, Bebbington (1978) refers to 'primitve' cultures as synonymous with non-Western cultures, and goes on to argue that depression in terms of symptomatology recognised in West Europeans and Americans is the norm 'against which cross-cultural anomalies can be tested'.

A recent review of scientific studies into racial differentiation (Jones, 1981) concludes that the concept of a racial type or race 'is no longer a very useful one in human biology'. But racial differentiation based on obvious physical characteristics such as skin colour is a social reality in Britain (Cashmore and Troyna, 1983) closely affecting the lives of ethnic minorities. Psychiatry is not an exact science and has few if any objective criteria for the recognition of illness categories (Ingleby, 1981). Its diagnostic system has low reliability and limited validity (Kendell, 1975). The usefulness of psychiatry as an institution or profession is questionable (Szasz, 1967; Torrey, 1975). But psychiatry based on a medical model of illness categorisation dominates the mental health services in Britain (Treacher and Baruch, 1981) as a sociopolitical reality. Depressive illness in ethnic minorities will therefore be analysed in a social context. No attempt will be made to describe or discuss clinical practice as such. There will be no direct advice to health workers or potential patients, no guidelines for diagnosis or treatment. The aim of this chapter is to provide an ambience — as it were — within which health workers and others can begin to understand the complex issues involved in using helpfully and realistically the psychiatric concept of depression. In order to do so, we start by taking a sociocultural view of depression. Then we consider what it means to an individual to be depressed. A short discussion on the social psychological position of ethnic minorities in British society is followed by a discussion of some social psychiatric aspects of depression in individuals from black and ethnic minority communities. The views expressed in this chapter are those of the author (unless quoted otherwise), based on his personal experience and critical reading of the relevant literature.

Sociocultural Perspectives in Understanding Depression

Cultural psychiatry is akin to family psychiatry in that it is a way of trying to understand emotional disorder in the context of the non-material aspects of a person's life, his or her values, beliefs, attitudes and habits — but with a wider reference group than family. Sociocultural psychiatry — or cultural psychiatry — is then seen as a perspective or a way of looking at people rather than as a discipline or subdiscipline of psychiatry. However, our primary interest is the individual. This section examines certain sociocultural factors that have been researched in relation to depression in order to see how a sociocultural perspective can illuminate our understanding of the depressed individual. The subject is approached from a clinician's point of view by picking on certain areas which may be useful in practice for the understanding and treatment of depressed people, particularly people from minority ethnic groups in this country. Later there is a brief review of cross-cultural studies into the epidemiology and content of depression, in so far as they throw light on depression in ethnic minorities.

An important question in research is the definition of the term 'culture'. In a broad sense it is applied to all aspects of an individual's environment, but generally refers to its non-material aspects that the person holds in common with other individuals forming a group. For example, it refers to child-rearing habits, family systems, and ethical values or attitudes common to a group. When we speak of culture in the context of research, we generally use such criteria as nationality of origin, religious affiliation, race or even colour to denote membership of what we assume to be cultural groups. But the validity of such criteira is arguable. When a particular group is designated as a cultural group, we assume that the individuals within that group have certain similarities of behaviour, belief and attitudes. If a sense of belonging to a group develops, the group is usually called an 'ethnic' group (Cashmore and Troyna, 1983). However, not all ethnic grops are cultural groups; a sense of belonging to a group may not stem from culture but from some other factor. In a cross-cultural study, the groups chosen for study must be valid in respect of cultural differences. If the boundary is defined by a characteristic such as race (however that is defined) or religion, then the groups so defined should be termed racial groups or religious groups rather than cultural groups. If ethnicity is used, the study is a cross-ethnic study.

Apart from the problem of definition of boundaries, various other methodological difficulties are evident in the field of cross-cultural research. Firstly, there is the problem of defining depression. The UK-US diagnostic study (Cooper *et al.*, 1972) has shown that there are considerable differences in diagnostic criteria and threshold for symptom recognition between two countries which use the same basic language and adhere to a similar broad conceptual framework. The differences become compounded where diagnoses are made across national and linguistic boundaries with errors caused by observer bias, patient compliance and communication problems. An even greater problem is the basic (unanswered) question as to whether depression as defined in modern psychiatry is an universal concept or one that is ethnocentric to West European culture. In a recent review, Fabrega (1974) asks, 'if that which is signified by the term depression is a psychological entity, then why and how are the underlying psychobiological changes of depression transformed into the form we see and recognise in our everyday clinical work?' While conceding that we do not have the answer to this question, Fabrega justifies the study of depresssion cross-culturally using the Western analogue of depression 'as a guide line — or a first approximation, to be refined and modified'. However, the major drawback here is that of 'category fallacy' (Kleinman, 1977) which means the use of illness categories derived in one cultural setting for the understanding of illness patterns in a different culture. One way of avoiding category fallacy is to start off by examining symptom patterns identified by methods indigenous to the culture under study — as in a study in South India (Carstairs and Kapur, 1976) — and then proceeding to delineate syndromes. Here, too, one comes up against the problem of the boundaries of normality and the difficulty in applying such boundaries cross-culturally. For example, psychological states (such as spirit possession) or behaviour patterns (such as alcohol consumption) which are regarded as normal in one culture may be seen as abnormal from a different standpoint. It has been shown in Sri Lanka that a combination of social withdrawal, lack of energy and feeling of sadness (commonly labelled 'depression' in Western societies) receives relatively little attention as an illness (Waxler, 1977) and very little treatment (Wijesinghe *et al.*, 1978).

The practical problems of valid sampling are compounded in cross-cultural studies by differences between groups in help-seeking practices and the availability of services — both of which may be culturally as well as politically determined.

The problems of cross-cultural research into depression may be summarised as follows: variability in criteria for defining the boundaries of a cultural group; dubious diagnostic reliability in the recognition and definition of depression across geographical, linguistic and political boundaries; doubtful universality of the concept of depressive illness; variation in the boundaries of normality across cultures; and sampling errors arising from variations in service provision and help-seeking practices.

It is the opinion of the author that these problems are seldom dealt with adequately in cross-cultural research, and therefore the conclusions of all such studies must be viewed with extreme caution.

Gender and Marriage

Studies in the United Kingdom show that women have a higher rate of depression when compared with men in nearly all age groups, both in hospital practice (e.g. Norris, 1959) and general practice (e.g. Porter, 1970). The usual female/male ratio is about three to one. Cross-cultural studies have shown that female preponderance is limited to certain cultural groups. Kraeplin (1913) thought that the sex ratio was near unity in Brazil. Others have found that men predominate among Maori's of New Zealand (Rawnsley, 1968) but women predominate among Chinese in Hong Kong (Yap, 1965a). In a hierarchical classification of depressive symptoms in an Indian study (Carstairs and Kapur, 1976) 4 per cent of men and 3 per cent of women suffered depressive symptoms in the total sample, but in one group (the Bants) none of the men had depression whereas 9 per cent of the women reported such symptoms. Clearly, the male-female difference is likely to be a sociocultural phenomenon — perhaps related to the status of men and women in the community.

A study of depression in East London (Fernando, 1973) found that unmarried men may be a particularly vulnerable group in the Jewish community of that area, although most community surveys in Britain show a preponderance of depression in married people as opposed to single people (e.g. Porter, 1970). But marital status cannot be looked at in isolation. In a culture where marital discord is a common cause of mental stress, marriage is likely to be associated with emotional breakdown, whereas in a society where most marriages are stable, those who lack its stabilising influence may be over-represented in a group of psychiatric patients. Indeed the crucial matter is perhaps what actually happens within the marriage. Brown and Harris (1978) found that women in Camberwell were protected from depression by having an intimate and close relationship with a husband. In non-Western or even perhaps in non-urban cultures the husband/wife relationship may not be all that crucial. The relationship that is potentially protective (in Brown's terminology) in an arranged marriage where a women goes to live with her in-laws may be that with her mother-in-law rather than her husband. For example, the author treated an Indian patient who appeared to have been protected from depression by the support she received by her close relationship with a brother. She became depressed when her husband was about to join her and set up home, taking her away from her brother. Another example is a Hindu patient of Indian origin who presented with severe depression. Antidepressants had managed to keep her going but repeated relapses contintued to occur until the case was evaluated in a cultural-family perspective. She had what seemed to be an ideal Western-type marriage. She and her husband shared roles. She had a job outside the home and she had a close intimate relationship with her husband. Once they were into marital therapy it became evident that she was very guilty about what she saw as her domination of her husband and an inadequacy of her role in mothering her children. Her feeling of helplessness in this situation was worked through very quickly in a few sessions with therapists who represented the dyadic relationship which so frightened her. The conclusion is that it is not merely a matter of looking at the husband/wife relationship but of considering the roles and relationships within the family in the context of cultural expectations and values, looking for psychopathological entities such as loss of self-esteem and helplessness.

Social Class

The study of social class as an aetiological factor in depressive illness has produced conflicting findings. Studies in London indicate their depression rates are highest among working-class mothers of pre-school children (Richman, 1976). But Brown and Harris (1978) found that the class difference whereby working-class women are particularly prone to depression is explicable in terms of certain risks to a woman with children — the lack of an intimate relationship with her husband, the early loss of a mother and the presence of several children under 14 living at home. Social mobility may be a more productive parameter in this field of research than social class *per se*.

An American study (Hollingshead and Redlich, 1958) showed that psychiatric illness as a whole was related to upward social mobility of class-three patients. The most vulnerable people were those who had moved up the social scale, but still felt dissatisfied with their achievement. A study in East London showed that socioeconomic dissatisfaction is an important concomitant of depression among Jews, but less important among Protestants (Fernando, 1975). Perhaps this particular difference between Jews and Protestants hinges upon aspiration derived from values instilled during childhood and/or based upon those of the peer group. The high level of socioeconomic aspiration characteristic of Jewish immigrants of 70 to 90 years ago (Krausz, 1971) is likely to apply to other ethnic minority groups also. For example, Pirani (1974) found that Asian and West Indian adolescents have 'unrealistically high' aspirations when compared with their native counterparts in Bristol, and Dove (1975) reported similar findings in Tottenham. Psychiatrists sometimes tend to encourage people to face reality with respect to job expectation. In a situation of limited opportunity, facing reality may leave youngsters from some minority groups with a sense of dissatisfaction and therefore a vulnerability to depression later on — possibly through a gradual sapping of self-esteem and a prolonged feeling of hopelessness.

Epidemiology and Content of Depression

Cultural differences in the incidence of depression have been quoted for over 70 years. Manic depressive psychosis was considered to be particularly prevalent among European Jews compared with Christians (e.g. Mayer-Gross *et al.,* 1960). Objective studies in New York (e.g. Malzberg, 1973) confirmed that the Jewish rate for affective illness was higher than that in other American ethnic groups. This is not seen in Israel (Hes, 1960), but Ashkenazi Jews of European origin were found to have higher rates than Sephardic Jews of Oriental and Spanish origin, both in Israel (Hes, 1960; Halevi, 1963) and in Holland (Grewel, 1967). Brown and Harris (1978) found that the prevalence of depression in North Uist is about half that in Camberwell. There are many reports of cross-cultural differences of this type: it is their meaning that is so difficult to evaluate. When manic depression was found to be relatively common among the Hutterites of North America (Eaton and Weil, 1955) and rare among people in North Sweden (Book, 1953), social cohesiveness was postulated as the factor involved. Hutterites live in closely knit hierarchical families with strong kinship ties, whereas Swedes in the North lead relatively isolated lives in loosely structured groups. However, the connection between social cohesiveness and depression is unlikely to be a simple one. And in any case, the concept is too wide to be useful in practice. The study in North Uist seemed to show that the rate of depression among women decreased with their degree of integration with the community whereas the rate of anxiety increased. In an East End study (Fernando, 1975) the three variables that were associated with depression among Jews (namely a weakening of ethnic links, a waning of religious conformity and a history of paternal inadequacy) represented a similar situation to a falling off of integration. The degree of integration with an ethnic group is obviously linked to one's personal ethnic identity. Conflict in identity formation could well result in poor self-esteem — a forerunner of depression.

At this point the limitations of cross-cultural epidemiology should be noted. Although depression has been recognised as an illness in Western medicine since the time of Hippocrates, exactly similar states have not been delineated in other systems of medicine although there are references to similar states in Indian writings (Singh, 1975; Venkoba Rao, 1975). In a review of research into the epidemiology of depression across cultures, Sartorius (1973) claimed that a core illness of depression is universally recognised. The common core identified among depressed patients attending hospitals and clinics in Japan, Iran, Canada and Switzerland (Jablensky *et al.*, 1981) included sadness, anxiety, loss of interest, difficulty in concentration, and feelings of inadequacy and worthlessness. But the type of case identified as depression by most psychiatrists is not limited to this core illness (Kleinman, 1977). Moreover, studies of indigenous categories of mental disorder in Malaysia, Borneo, Africa and North America have revealed no concepts that represented depression as either a symptom or a syndrome (Marsella, 1980). It is the author's view that international cross-cultural studies of the epidemiology of depression are likely to be misleading since they do not deal adequately with the problem of category fallacy noted earlier. The contention by Bebbington (1978), in a review of such studies, that the use of the Present State Examination (PSE) is a way round this problem is mistaken. According to the instructions manual for its use (Wing *et al.*, 1974), the PSE is a method of standardising a clinical interview 'firmly grounded in the practice of the European School of Psychiatry'. Moreover it was originally devised in Britain and is seemingly unaffected in successive editions by cross-cultural observations. A recent attempt by the World Health Organization (Sartorius *et al.*, 1980) to devise a more flexible measure of depression — namely the Standardized Assessment of Depressive Disorders (WHO/SADD) — also fails to meet the problem of category fallacy.

International studies on the content — rather than prevalence — of depression across cultures, while suffering from the drawbacks noted earlier, may serve to widen our understanding of the concept of depression in its applicationn to ethnic minorities, particularly when they differ markedly from the majority community in terms of cultural factors. In the 1960s, researchers in Canada (Murphy *et al.*, 1964) sent questionnaires on clinical findings in depression to psychiatrists in 30 different countries in Africa, Asia, Australia, the Middle East and both American continents. The questionnaire enquired after symptom patterns in depressive illness seen in these countries, defining the illness in terms of four pathognomonic symptoms, namely depression of mood, diurnal mood changes, insomnia with early waking and diminution of interest in the social environment. The analysis of the answers to these questionnaires provides tentative clues to the possible effect that culture and religion may have on symptom patterns among depressives: suicidal ruminations seem to be inversely proportional to the extent to which somatic manifestations appear in the case of North American depressives, but in Latin America these two tendencies are not related; intensity of religious belief and the degree of guilt go together among Christians, but in Muslems guilt is not related to religiousness. A study of depressed patients in East London found that the relationship between religiousness and hostility was different among Jews to that among Roman Catholics, but Protestants were similar to Jews in this respect (Fernando, 1969). Chance (1964) analysed the questionnaires referred to earlier to find that severe feelings of guilt may be more prevalent in highly cohesive societies than in less cohesive ones. This tallies with the high incidence of guilt-ridden depression among Hutterites, who live in closely knit communities (Eaton and Weil, 1955) and the clinical impressions of a psychoanalyst (Fromm-Reichmann, 1949). But studies in Taiwan (Lin, 1953) and Hong Kong (Yap, 1965a) suggest a relative lack of guilt feelings among depressed Japanese and Chinese patients — and Japanese and Chinese cultures are unlikely to lack cohesiveness.

Pfieffer (1970) suggests that ideas of guilt reflect cultural norms and internalisation of external authority — a more fundamental approach to the genesis of guilt than merely relating it to social cohesiveness. Ruth Benedict (1947) and Margaret Mead (1950) classified societies into shame and guilt cultures depending on the type of social control relied upon. Shame cultures were seen as emphasising external agents to arouse objective fear whereas guilt cultures emphasised self-control. However, shame and guilt have been found to coexist in both Samoan and Caucasian cultural groups (Grinder and McMichael, 1963), casting doubt on the usefulness of the shame/guilt classification. Yap (1965a), too, questioned the validity of this classification and postulated that a sense of failure underlies both shame and guilt. He suggested that this failure is related to a feeling of having violated other people's values in the case of shame, and one's own internal values in the case of guilt. Kimura (1965) observed that guilt feelings in Japanese represent a sense of failure of the 'we' relationship, whereas in Germans they represent a sense of failure of duty towards oneself or one's conscience. Murphy (1973) postulates that the expression of guilt is pathoplastically affected by culture to the extent that the culture promotes the ability of the individual within it to differentiate 'self' from 'other'. In a culture where this separation is slight, failure may be expressed as a loss of group membership. If the separation is stronger, failure may be felt as other people being critical or as feelings of shame. When differentiation between self and other is well established, then failure is felt as a deserved punishment for one's sins, little to do with what other people think.

The somatic presentation of depression (as opposed to the predominantly psychological presentation) has been reported in various cultural groups: Chinese (Tseng, 1975; Kleinman, 1977), African (Binitie, 1975), Indian (Teja *et al.*, 1971; Gada, 1982), Afghan (Waziri, 1973), Saudi Arabian (Racy, 1970), and French Canadian (Murphy, 1974). However, these observations must be seen in the context of 'explanatory models' of illness (Kleinman, 1980) within a culture as well as methodological drawbacks of the studies concerned. In a recent review, Kirmayer (1984) states:

> At present there is insufficient data to support the claim that some cultures are more prone to somatisation than others. In particular, it has not been established whether rates of somatic presentation of major depression are any greater in non-Western cultures than among North American patients in primary care. If such a cross-cultural difference is substantiated by further studies, the next step would be to determine whether differences in the frequency of somatisation present when education and availability of psychologically orientated services are controlled.

It has been pointed out that there are advantages in limiting cross-cultural study in such a way as to keep the groups compared within one national, linguistic, political and geographical framework (Carstairs, 1965). A study comparing two groups of British-born people living in East London (Fernando, 1973) shows the advantages of this approach. Some of the findings were summarised as follows (Fernando, 1978):

> First, Jewish and Protestant depressives were similar in many ways including illness rating, the incidence of family history of psychiatric illness, and outcome of illness. Secondly, depression in Jews (but not that in Protestants) was associated with weak fathers in childhood, loosening of ethnic links, and waning of religious conformity. Thirdly, Jewish depressives were different from Protestant depressives on certain aspects of hostility, although normal Jews and normal Protestants did not differ in this way. Fourthly, Jewish depressives showed a different distribution on a subgrouping of depression from that shown by Protestant depressives.

This last finding referred to the observation that, when depression was typed on an endogenous-reactive scale, Jews tended to fall into one or other extreme type whereas Protestants congregated in the middle. Another finding (Fernando, 1973) was that a sense of failure in socioeconomic achievement was associated with depression among Jews but not among Protestants. These findings were interpreted in terms of a relationship between marginality and depression among Jews, repressed anger showing itself as extra-punitive hostility among Jewish depressives, a need for caution in applying a classificatory system cross-culturally, and relatively high aspiration levels among Jews which were culturally determined. However, if the findings are examined in the context of the East End of the 1930s and institutionalised attitudes towards Jewish people, somewhat different conclusions may be drawn. Jews may have achieved as much as others but they had to struggle a great deal to do so, adopting various manoeuvres to bypass discrimination, for example changing names and such like. 'Straight-forward' achievement in open competition was frequently blocked. The consequent sense of failure (as a psychological concomitant) is then understandable as a reflection of anti-semitism. The particular vulnerability to depression of marginal Jews may have reflected their relative lack of protection from blows to self-esteem arising from anti-semitism. The difference in diagnostic subgrouping may reflect the attitudes within an ethnocentric psychiatry towards Jewish individuals and their ways of expressing emotion. The point here is that purely cultural interpretations may miss important issues that determine depression in ethnic minorities. Culture interacts with social pressures in the final analysis of an illness such as depression.

A major subcultural comparative study done outside Britain was on three South Indian rural communities defined on the basis of caste (Carstairs and Kapur, 1976). Since categorisation (with Western nosology) was avoided, depressive disorders as such was not identified. It was observed that somatic symptoms (in the course of emotional disorder) were commoner among literates when compared with illiterates, and such symptoms reflected prevailing cultural beliefs. Marsella *et al.*, (1973) have reported a comparative study of the expressions of depression among three American ethnic groups, using factor analysis of symptom checklists. The Japanese Americans were found to have a strong interpersonal component in the expression of depression; Chinese Americans showed a strong somatic component; and Caucasian Americans manifested 'existential' patterns. The authors attributed their findings to differences in the 'self' structure derived from cultural traditions.

The issue of Black-White differences in the presentation of depression in the United States led to two studies which used sophisticated observational ratings and took some care in controlling for factors such as age and social differences between samples. Tonks *et al.* (1970) found that when the two racial groups were matched on social-class status and severity of illness, only the variable 'helplessness' differentiated the two groups, Blacks scoring lower than Whites. However, the (apparently) greater self-reliance of black depressives may not reflect their true feelings since no allowance was made for the fact that the questionnaires used in the study were administered by white people. A much larger study (Raskin *et al.*, 1975) in which age, social-class distribution and sex were controlled found that black and white depressives did not differ on gross symptom presentation but did so on a number of hostility variables:

> There was a greater tendency towards negativism and the introjection of anger in Blacks than in Whites. In addition, depressed black males indicated that they were more likely than their white counterparts to strike back, either verbally or physically, when they felt their rights were being violated.

The researchers commented on the feelings of helplessness and frustration engendered by these competing drives (in black patients) — a factor that could aggravate depression.

Conclusions

Methodological problems of cross-cultural research have not been overcome sufficiently to negate the doubt expressed by Kessel (1965) about the value of international studies. However, the following points may be noted:

(1) Cross-cultural observation on guilt and somatic symptoms in depression are worth noting with caution. The way hostility is handled may be culturally determined to some extent but feelings of resentment, negativism and aggression must be evaluated in the context of social and political forces in the society as well as cultural influences. It is the author's clinical impression that conceptualising the dynamics of depression in terms of anger and guilt is a useful way of understanding depressed people of all cultures. However, one should modify these concepts to recognise a sense of failure (instead of guilt) and a sense of resentment (in place of anger).

(2) The effect of sexual roles and marriage in promoting depression must be seen in the light of culturally determined values and expectations.

A close relationship with a supportive individual may be an important protective factor for women, but exactly who this should be is likely to be culturally determined. Particular groups such as unmarried Jewish men may be specifically vulnerable to depression, but this may depend on cultural factors such as the status ascribed to marriage in the culture.
(3) Rapid social mobility and/or a feeling of dissatisfaction in the face of high aspiration for socioeconomic achievement may be an important factor in the genesis of depression in some minority ethnic groups.
(4) Integration into the community may protect women from depression in the case of isolated communities, and stress arising from marginality with identity problems may give rise to depression among members of minority ethnic groups.
(5) Cultural interpretations of research findings must be balanced with a consideration of social issues prevalent in the society being studied as well as the culture of psychiatry itself.

The Depressed Individual

Depression is generally defined in terms of a syndrome composed of symptoms presented by a (depressed) individual. Current psychiatry arising within a dualistic philosophy of a mind-body dichotomy divides symptoms into psychological and somatic (physical) symptoms. Cross-cultural studies indicate the fallacy of such a view, but also suggest that some kind of experiential state (called depression in current psychiatric terminology) may be identifiable as an illness. If this state is looked at in a holistic framework of the inner experience of individuals, the artificiality of dividing up feelings arising from the experience on the basis of external criteria and psychiatric philosophy is evident. However, our approach — to be realistic and practical — needs to come to terms with (Western) psychiatry and its methods. The question is how to do so. The approaches of Kleinman (1982) may offer some openings. In a recent paper he examines the relationship between neurasthenia (as diagnosed in China) and depressive disorder (as diagnosed in the USA). Kleinman describes how biology and culture are intertwined in the evolution of illness patterns, identified as one or other condition. He points out that much of our clinical work and research is hampered by an apparent need to take an 'unidimensional view of an innately multidimensional reality'. This is perhaps particularly so in traditional Western scientific thought, but not so in advanced science and eastern mysticism (Capra, 1976).
Depression, then, is not conceptualised primarily as a syndrome

recognised by a list of symptoms, but as a disturbance at a deeper level. It is the name for an experience of a disturbed equilibrium in a human being where the symptoms form the interface between the individual and the outside world. The central 'core' of this disturbance has been described by Aaron Beck (1971). A depressed individual perceives the self as worthless, the outer world meaningless and the future as hopeless. The self, the outer world and the future should not be conceptualised in purely psychological terms since (for instance) the self includes one's bodily sensations as well as feelings. A sense of failure, a sense of being 'cut off' from external and internal reality (Rowe, 1978), a diminution of self-esteem, and possibly a release of hostility, seem to underlie the symptoms expressed in the somatic, cognitive or behavioural manifestations of depression. To these aspects of 'psychopathology' we should add the concept of helplessness delineated by Seligman (1975). The depressed individual must also be sen in a social context. Although the details of their model are likely to vary from society to society, we could for the time being accept the overall scheme put forward by Brown and Harris (1978) for the social origins of depression. A complex interaction between background factors, provoking factors and cognitive sets (of personality) result in responses which may lead to depression. In brief, a person with high vulnerability and low (cognitive) self-esteem in the face of provoking factors (such as blows to self-esteem) feels hopeless. If this is not resolved, depression ensues. A simplified version of this model has been incorporated into a scheme (Figure 8.1) showing the psychopathology of depression and the psychosocial concepts we use during treatment, namely support and coping. The lowering of self-esteem can be a vulnerability factor if it is a blow which precipitates depression; similarly for a sense of loss or failure and helplessness. The demarcation between a provoking factor and vulnerability factor is not strict — really a matter of when the change takes place and how deeply it is internalised. The disturbance or breakdown (with its psychopathology) may lead to depression or be resolved depending on circumstances and inner strength (i.e. support and coping). The depressed individual seen in these terms could be considered as a person. But then what is so special (psychologically) in being a person from an ethnic minority? The next section will attempt to answer this question before considering sociopsychiatric aspects of depression in such an individual.

Ethnic Minorities

In examining the social psychology of minority groups, Tajfel (1982) has described how categories of people designated by the majority as being 'different' gradually accept the difference and/or become aware of being considered different: 'It may be a long time before the outside consensus results in creating clear-cut group boundaries, formal institutionalised rules and the specific features of informal social behaviour', but as this feeling of common membership develops, a recognisable minority group emerges. It should be noted that the term 'minority' does not necessarily apply to numbers but to the social position of the group which is referred to as a minority group. According to Wagley and Harris (1958) five criteria serve to define minorities:

(1) Minorities are subordinate segments of complex state societies;
(2) minorities have special physical or cultural traits which are held in low esteem by the dominant segments of the society;
(3) minorities are self-conscious units bound together by the special traits which their members share and by the special disabilities which these bring;
(4) membership in a minority is transmitted by a rule of descent which is capable of affiliating succeeding generations even in the absence of readily apparent special cultural or physical traits; and
(5) minority peoples, by choice or necessity, tend to marry within a group.

Thus, minorities are 'self-conscious' units of people who have in common certain similarities and social disadvantages. If such a unit is categorised in terms of racial characteristics alone, it is a racial minority; if cultural criteria alone are used, it should be referred to as a cultural minority. The term 'ethnic minority' is used when the members of such a group or category 'feel themselves, or are thought to be, bound together by common ties of race or nationality or culture' (Morris, 1968) and identify themselves with the group. It is a sense of belonging (to the group) among its members that is crucial. The criteria by which such a group is defined may be mainly or even entirely racial — indeed in a racist society this is very likely to be the case. Hicks (1981) has argued that the minority (ethnic) experience in Britain is largely shaped by a 'climate of prejudice and discrimination' created by several factors: ethnocentric attitudes arising from a cultural heritage, the power arrangements within society, and the prejudice among individuals (Simpson and Yinger, 1972). Colonial attitudes in British society with its implied

Figure 8.1: Genesis of Depression: Socio-psychological Aspects

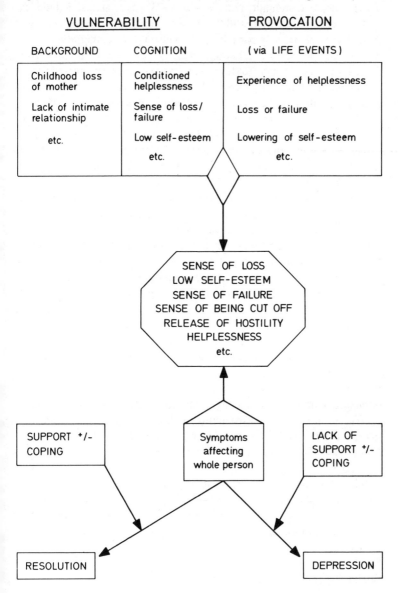

cultural superiority (Rushdie, 1982) and racism in the cultural heritage of the majority community (Katznelson, 1973) have ensured that the 'external consensus' (Tafjel, 1982) defining ethnic minorities is largely to do with racism and only partially to do with culture, immigration, social class or any of the other criteria on which ethnic minorities differ from the majority community. In short, a racist society has pressurised certain people within it to think of themselves as belonging to one or more subgroups, resulting in the emergence of ethnic minorities based on racial definitions. Through this process of 'emergent ethnicity' (Yancey *et al.*, 1976) immigration from Trinidad, Jamaica and other Caribbean Islands has led to a 'West Indian' ethnic group; the descendants of immigrants from the Asian sub-continent have emerged as an 'Asian' ethnic group; similarly, other groups such as Chinese, Irish, Jewish, Romany (Gypsy) and Turkish minorities flourish as more or less separate ethnic minorities in a plural society. However, as racism continues, various ethnic groups are being merged together into a single black ethnic minority. Many Asian, Chinese, Greek, Turkish, and West Indian people are perceived and identify themselves as black British. Meanwhile many 'white' people continue to belong to minority ethnic groups identifying as Jewish, Irish, etc. Although they are subject to variable degreees of discrimination — sometimes firmly institutionalised (e.g. anti semitism and hostility towards Irish and Romany people) — external pressures are not the main reasons for this. Internal needs of individuals to belong to groups, historical allegiance, social behaviour, language, and religion all play some part. Clearly these factors are involved in determining ethnic identity of 'black' people too, but the importance of these cultural factors is insignificant (psychologically at any rate) in contrast to the external pressures. In general, self-definition and the labelling of others always interact in determining the ethnic identity of an individual, but their interaction takes place in the sociopolitical context in which the person lives (Bell, 1975).

The ethnic plurality of British society fashioned by external pressures and the needs and culture of individuals within it is a changing scene. In order to encompass the position, it is proposed to use the phrase 'black and ethnic minorities' to cover all major ethnic minorities.

Social Psychiatry of Depression

Earlier discussions have shown that: (1) depression is an individual experience in a social context, and (2) the social context of a person from a black or ethnic minority is defined by cultural difference, minority status and racism. Hence it is appropriate to consider depression in terms of the effects on the individual of culture, minority status, and racism. It should be stated at the outset that the author views the last of these as the most important of these factors. Therefore, the section on culture and minority status will be fairly brief to lead on to the final section.

Culture

The meaning of depression was discussed earlier. A person who feels a sense of loss, low self-esteem or helplessness would exhibit these feelings in terms of (culturally fashioned) symptoms and behaviour. People from ethnic minority groups in Britain are likely to show many of the symptoms and behaviour shown by patients from the majority ethnic group(s). But in some cases the overall symptom pattern may be at considerable variance with that, although if one investigates the symptoms and behaviour in terms of their meaning to the individual, depressive psychopathology is evident. Difficulties and misconceptions arise because of culture when the therapist or diagnostician does not look very closely into the patient as a person but merely uses a symptom inventory as a basis for diagnosis and treatment. In such an instance, symptoms and behaviour pattern may not add up to give the typical (Western) picture of depression. A misdiagnosis may then result, particularly if the culturally determined mode of illness presentation is perceived as a 'bizarre' state. On the other hand, a failure to recognise depression may result from a rejection of a patient's complaints on the basis that they are 'cultural'. This situation is not usually a cultural problem but rather one of racism. For example, the complaint by a black patient of mental fatigue or bewitchment may be dismissed as 'cultural', thereby avoiding the need to take it seriously.

Just as ethnic minorities in Britain are rarely completely isolated in lifestyle from the majority community, types of illness which are completely different from those within the majority community are unlikely to occur. Therefore 'culture-specific' disorders which are considered by psychiatrists to be 'depressive equivalents' (Marsella, 1980) are unlikely to be seen in Britain. But some elements of such disorders may colour the generalised clinical picture of depression. For example, the author has seen a British Chinese man whose emotional disturbance (though characterised by symptoms such as lack of interest, panic attacks and insomnia) also included a feeling that his penis was shrinking — as in the koro syndrome (Yap, 1965b). Similarly, a patient of Indian origin may present to a doctor with a fear of losing semen, as described among

Indian patients (Carstairs, 1956). However, in all these cases, the underlying psychopathology of depression is discernible. Sometimes the somatic symptoms are easily recognisable as a part of a patient's illness experience determined by the personal, social and cultural reaction to 'disease' (Kleinman, 1980).

Somatic symptoms or hypochondriasis are commonly presented by depressed patients from ethnic minority groups of Asian or African origin. The usual approach is to consider this to be 'somatisation' of emotional distress on the implicit assumption that the 'real' distress is a psychological one. Rack (1982) argues that an alternative explanation is that a somatic complaint is a metaphor or that physical symptoms are the only ones acceptable to the patient. All these views stem from a definition of depression (in both specialist and lay circles) that is ethnocentric to West European culture. The long standing emphasis on a mind-body dichotomy and a more recent preoccupation with the pre-eminence of mental feelings over bodily ones have resulted in a totally 'psychologised' concept of depression. If we decodify this disturbance and accept it as a cross-cultural entity where the total person is affected (as proposed earlier in discussing depressive experience), the problem of diagnosis disappears. In other words, low self-esteem, helplessness, etc. apply to all aspects of a whole person — not just to mind or body.

The recognition of guilt is another so-called problem in dealing with depression among some ethnic minority groups. Guilt, like depression, is an individual experience — and they are both concepts that are culture bound in interpretation. Indeed a superficial evaluation — such as a symptom inventory — may fail to elicit 'guilt' as expected on the basis of current psychiatric practice. However, current practice has failed to take on board insights obtained from transcultural observations (see earlier). The primary disturbance underlying depression is a sense of failure rather than guilt — and failure can be experienced in an individual, family or social context. Again, as in the case of somatic symptoms, the problem of recognising guilt in order to diagnose depression disappears if one goes into some depth in assessing a patient.

Minority Status

Jews have been ethnic minority groups in West European society for hundreds of years. In reviewing the sources of mental stress in American Jews, Rinder (1963) postulated the following liabilities:

(1) minority status in a predominantly Christian society;
(2) high level of aspiration instilled in youth;

(3) high expectancy of parents from children;
(4) need to achieve in order to gain recognition;
(5) ambiguities of identity; and
(6) high rate of social mobility upwards.

All these, except perhaps the last one, may apply to all British ethnic minorities. Research in East London (Fernando, 1973) indicated that depression among Jews may be linked to marginality — a psychological state arising from a dual cultural identification (Ruesch *et al.*, 1948). In some ways, this is the opposite of a psychological state that would arise from a firmly held ethnic identity. The psychological effect that minority experience has on a person's self-worth (and self-image) depends on two factors: first, the views, attitudes, behaviour and social institutions of the dominant majority community; and secondly, the reaction to these by the individual who sees himself/herself as a part of a minority. Hostile views and attitudes, together with institutionalised practices that devalue the minority group concerned, have a negative effect on personal worth. (It should be noted that the term 'minority' is not used in a numerical sense but in the context of power and prestige: belonging to a powerful or highly prestigious group which is numerically small, such as Royalty or a professional group, has a positive effect on self-image.)

The individual who is subject to negative influences on self-esteem may deal with them in various ways. The person may counteract the ill-effects by drawing on positive sources of self-worth within his or her own ethnic groups, often — though not necessarily — developing a strong ethnic identity in the process of doing so. If it is to provide a source of positive self-worth for the individual, the minority ethnic group as a psychosocial entity needs symbols and traditions reflecting its separate identity — in particular an identity that is perceived as valuable by the individuals who form the group. An enhancement of such 'separateness' may be a necessary form of social intervention in dealing with depression. In other words, a sense of belonging to a minority ethnic group and taking pride in its special qualities can have a positive value for individuals living in a society where that same group is negatively rated by the majority community. In such a situation, both marginality as well as cultural identification with the majority community (acculturation) may be risky from the point of view of propensity to depression.

It was seen earlier that the minority experience can affect the self-image of an individual in negative or positive ways depending on the social climate in society as a whole. In Britain today, individuals who are perceived as 'black' or 'ethnic' develop a strong minority ethnic identity to counteract the attacks on their self-esteem in the way described in the next section on racism.

Racism

A general definition of racism based on a description by Ann and Michael Dummett (1982) is that it is about behaviour that arises from a belief (a racist belief) that people can be differentiated from one another mainly or entirely on the basis of their ancestral lineage (referred to as races) often identified by some physical characteristic (e.g. skin colour) but sometimes by a behavioural characteristic (e.g. mannerisms), and that groups of people so categorised are to be treated as different in terms of their rights, capabilities and basic needs, with one or more groups being inferior to others. It should be noted that racism is incorporated into social structures, laws and educational systems. Racism in British and American society is now mainly related to skin colour. The US Commission on Civil Rights defines it as 'any attitude, action or institutionalised structure which subordinates a person or group because of his or her colour' (Shapiro, 1974). Although racial prejudice is an obvious stress to anyone who experiences it, institutionalised racism is much more than just that. Its damage is subtly destructive to the individual. Its role in the aetiology of depression can be examined by considering three aspects of the psychopathology shown in Figure 8.1, namely low self-esteem, sense of loss, and helplessness.

Saifullah Khan (1982) describes how people living in two or more sociocultural systems identify with them to different degrees, while synthesising their identifications in order to make meaning out of their particular circumstances. This synthesis becomes very complicated in a racist society where one culture is held to be dominant over another and real power is held by the dominant group. A consequence of this is shown up in a study by Weinreich (1979) of identity formation in adolescents. His findings are typified in a description of changes in self-evaluation in the case of John, a boy of West-Indian parentage. As John became more positive and his behaviour more controlled, he developed a dislike of his own skin colour and dissociated himself from his own community. But according to Weinrich, cross-ethnic identification leads to 'identity diffusion' (Erickson, 1968) — a sort of confusion of values — rather than self-rejection. Similar findings were reported among Jewish adolescents by Sanua (1959). An increase of inner maladjustment accompanied 'better' social adjustment among successive generations.

Identity (and adjustment within that identity) is closely related to self-concept and self-esteem. A simplified approach is that each person forms an individual identity by internalising 'bits' from people within families, cultural groups and wider society, as well as concepts about experiences, memories and situations. The self-concept or self-image is the combination of these — a person's picture of himself or herself. One's evaluation and feelings about self-image are what is called self-esteem (Coppersmith, 1975). Early research suggested that black children in Britain and the United States had negative evaluations of their self-image (i.e. low self-esteem) and an insecure sense of identity. An understanding of this is that black children had a black cultural identity, but incorporated the negative feelings towards that identity which is prevalent in white society. In other words devaluation of a person's culture is incorporated by the person to give low self-esteem. But it is not culture as some theoretical concept that is devalued in a racist society; it is the person himself or herself who is devalued, including his or her skin colour, mannerisms and way of life. If these sorts of value are incorporated by (for example) a black person, he could be said to 'hate' his black identity and have low self-esteem. Thus commenting on Jewish self-hatred, Sartre (1948) stated that the Jew 'is poisoned by the stereotype that others have of him'. However, it is clear that alternative strategies are possible. People of many minority groups have sufficient sources of self-pride to draw on and do not often introject negative values of the minority culture. Indeed the relevance of the data on self-esteem to present-day British children of black and ethnic minority groups has been seriously challenged by Maureen Stone (1981), who believes that it is not a high or low self-esteem but 'structural forces in society' (i.e. power structure) which largely determine achievement. It would seem, therefore, that if black children have sources of self-pride to draw on in building up self-esteem, they do not introject negative values about themselves that are held by white society. Further, knowledge and awareness should protect one's self-esteem: As Remi Kapo (1981) states: 'The identity of anyone *aware* of being victimized is always clear-cut'. Perhaps this is why Jewish minorities managed to maintain self-esteem through generations of anti-semitism, and why strong ethnic links often arise among minorities in racist societies. If this is true for British minority groups today, blows to self-esteem arising from recent experience (i.e. as a provoking factor) are more important than low self-esteem as a personality attribute (i.e. a vulnerability factor).

Loss is a concept of some value for the understanding of depression. Since we live in a society which promotes the expectation of achievement in terms of merit, if a person expects to get something valuable and then does not do so (be it a job, examination or visa), the result is anger (through frustration) and/or a sense of 'loss'. Clearly, such a loss is more likely in a subtly racist society which does not acknowledge that racism plays a part in the giving of jobs, medical services or ordinary rewards in daily life. In Freud's original thesis, melancholia resembles mourning in that it occurs after the loss of a loved person or the loss of some abstraction (Freud, 1917). In lay terms, a loss of this type is more than a setback or impediment: it is at best a crisis of confidence, at worst a breakdown of personal security. Bibring (1953) postulated that depression is 'the ego's shocking awareness of its helplessness in regard to its aspirations'. Many people from black and ethnic minorities do not recognise the racist source of impediments to their achievement. However, when they do, the feeling of helplessness could be overwhelming. In this sense racism is a provoking factor in causing depression.

The learned helplessness model of depression (Seligman, 1975) is based on animal experiments. When dogs were given repeated and random shocks from which they could not escape because they were yoked in a box, many animals lost their ability to help themselves, i.e. to escape from noxious stimuli even when they could do so. Helpless dogs became submissive, lost weight and appetite, and became sexually deficient. Other experiments showed that deprivation of control over the situation was crucial. Exposure to experiences over which they have no control (and over which they *expect* control) has its analogies in human life experiences. Repeated exposure will result in conditioned helplessness where the sense of helplessness is a personality attribute. Racism is then creating a vulnerability factor — but hopefully one that is reversible.

The discussion so far suggests that racism is not just an added stress to black and ethnic minorities, but a pathogen that generates depression in the individual. Figure 8.2 indicates some ways in which racism affects self-esteem, causes (psychological) losses, and promotes a sense of helplessness. The earlier discussion of the effects of racism within a social model of depression is expanded in Figure 8.3. Clearly these observations have implications for health professinals and the public at large.

In dealing with a depressed person one should try to identify the blows to self-esteem in recent events that arise from racism. An awareness of what happens is important because the patient has to develop strategies to safeguard self-esteem; finding alternative sources of self-pride may mean identifying with (for example) black movements, seeking ethnic therapists, or finding models (to identify with) that do not represent the dominant racial groups. The positive effect of such identification will

Figure 8.2: How Institutional Racism Poisons the Person

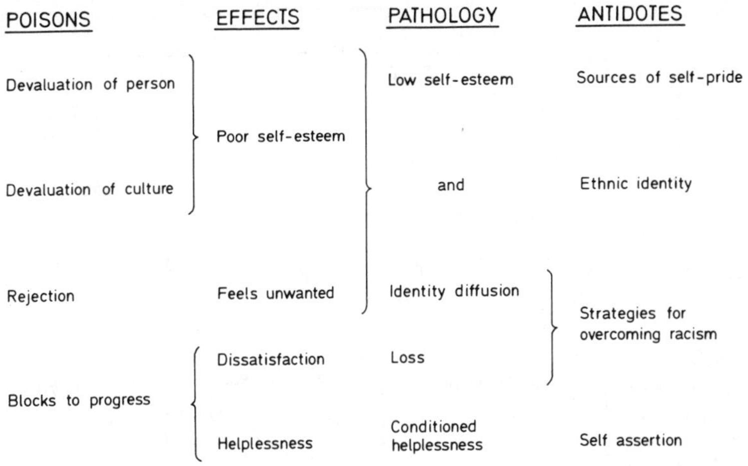

POISONS	EFFECTS	PATHOLOGY	ANTIDOTES
Devaluation of person		Low self-esteem	Sources of self-pride
	Poor self-esteem		
Devaluation of culture		and	Ethnic identity
Rejection	Feels unwanted	Identity diffusion	Strategies for overcoming racism
Blocks to progress	Dissatisfaction	Loss	
	Helplessness	Conditioned helplessness	Self assertion

counteract the negative effect that comes from accepting the ethos of the social system in general. In order to do this a person has to distance himself or herself psychologically from the wider society. The best way of doing this is to recognise and understand the injustices of that society. Hospital wards and hostels often claim to be therapeutic communities. A community that aims to treat depressed black and ethnic minority people who have been exposed to racism must have within it leaders who come from these minorities and are willing to accept their ethnic identity fully. Finally, if the replenishment of self-esteem cannot be sustained through normal channels — and many of these may be blocked — so-called deviant behaviour might have to be accepted as a way of bolstering self-esteem. Violent outbursts and attacks on the system may have to be accepted as inevitable. If a person is perceived as having become depressed by suffering a loss, understanding what has happened must be a prelude to developing ways of compensating for the loss and forming strategies to overcome similar losses. Avoiding the issue by advising patients to 'accept' and lower expectations without understanding the situation is not helpful. Treatment within a model of depression caused by learned helplessness is to encourage strategies for self-assertion and control over events — not a 'coming to terms' or changing cognitive sets. Thus, if this model is used and racism is identified as the restrictive yoke which prevents patients from controlling their environment, the treatment is to encourage ways of resistance and self-assertion.

Figure 8.3: How Institutionalised Racism Causes Depression

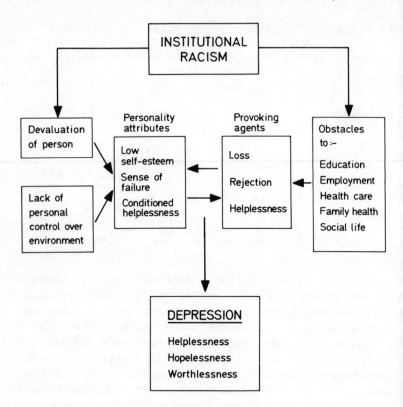

This final section has taken a 'victim' approach to the genesis of depression. However, in depression (as in any psychiatric illness) the individual concerned — the patient — is implicated in the genesis of the condition one way or another. Therefore individual physical and psychological treatment must play a part in management. But the emphasis on social causes and intervention is deliberate and necessary. When we deal with depression among people who are victims of a social condition, be it racism or unemployment, it is all too easy to see the individual as a problem. We then see solutions merely in terms of changing or treating the individual, colluding in or even exacerbating the virulence of the social pathogen concerned. To ignore this and regard depression (or any other psychiatric illness) in British ethnic minorities as no different from an illness that affects the majority community is to do both psychiatry and ethnic minorities a great disservice — at least in the present social climate.

Summary

The current understanding of depression as a psychiatric illness must be seen in the context of the culture of psychiatry itself — in particular its ethnocentricity and racist heritage. The aim of the chapter is to examine depression in a social framework so as to provide an approach which would enable health workers and others to use the concept of depression helpfully in a society with black and ethnic minorities. Although the findings of cross-cultural studies must be viewed with caution, a sociocultural perspective in understanding depression shows the significance of culture in determining symptomatology and the relationship of depression to gender roles, marriage and social mobility.

Depression is an individual experience in a social context. Symptoms are the interface between the individual having the experience and others — both people and society in general. In the case of black and ethnic minorities, the social context is concerned with the criteria that differentiate them from the majority community, namely culture, minority status (in terms of power) and racism. The culture (of an individual) affects the nature of presenting symptoms and the significance of life experience. Marginality may promote vulnerability to depression, and a strong ethnic identity provides protection from blows to self-esteem in a society that devalues the status of minorities. Racism causes depression by promoting blows to self-esteem, inducing experiences of loss, and placing individuals in a position of helplessness. Treatment should encompass these effects by helping people concerned to understand the nature of racism, to assert themselves, and to find ways of building up self-esteem.

References

Adams, F. (1856) (Editor and Translator) *The Extant Works of Aretaeus, the Cappado-cian*, Sydenham Society, London

Bebbington, P.E. (1978) 'The Epidemiology of Depressive Disorder', *Culture, Medicine and Psychiatry, 2*, 297–341

Beck, A.T. (1967) *Depression: Clinical, Experimental and Theoretical Aspects*, Hoeber, New York

Beck, A.T. (1971) 'Cognition, Affect and Psychopathology', *Archives of General Psychiatry, 24*, 495–500

Bell, D. (1975) 'Ethnicity and Social Change', in N. Glazer and D.P. Moynihan (eds), *Ethnicity. Theory and Practice*, pp. 141–74, Harvard University Press, Cambridge, Mass

Benedict, R. (1947) *The Chrysanthemum and the Sword*, Secker and Warburg, London

Bibring, E. (1953) 'The Mechanism of Depression', in P. Greenacre (ed.), *Affective Disorders*, pp. 13–48, International Universities Press, New York

Binitie, R. (1975) 'A Factor-analytical Study of Depression across Cultures (African and European)', *British Journal of Psychiatry, 127*, 559–63

Book, J.A. (1953) 'A Genetic and Neuropsychiatric Investigation of a North-Swedish Population', *Acta Genetica (Basel), 4*, 1–189

Brown, G.W. and Harris, T. (1978) *Social Origins of Depression*, Tavistock, London

Capra, F. (1976) *The Tao of Physics*, Fontana, London

Carstairs, G.M. (1956) 'Hinjra and Jiryan', *British Journal of Medical Psychology, 29*, 128–38.

Carstairs, G.M. (1965) 'Group Discussion', in A.V.S. De Reuck and R. Porter (eds), *Transcultural Psychiatry*, pp. 357–83, Churchill, London

Carstairs, G.M. and Kapur, R.C. (1976) *The Great Universe of Kota: Stress Charge and Mental Disorder in an Indian Village*, Hogarth Press, London

Cashmore, E.E. and Troyna, B. (1983) *Introduction to Race Relations*, Routledge and Kegan Paul, London

Chance, N.A. (1964) 'A Cross-Cultural Study of Social Cohesion and Depression', *Transcultural Psychiatric Research Review, 1*, 19–26

Cooper, J., Kendell, R., Gurland, B., Sharpe, L., Copeland, J. and Simon, R. (1972) *Psychiatric Diagnosis in New York and London: a Comparative Study of Mental Hospital Admissions*, Oxford University Press, London

Coopersmith, S. (1975) 'Self-concept, Race and Education', in G.K. Verma and C. Bagley (eds) *Race and Education across Cultures*, pp. 145–67, Heinmann, London

Davidson, B. (1984) *The Story of Africa*, Mitchell Beazley, London

Defendorf, A. (1902) *Clinical Psychiatry. A Textbook for Students and Physicians*, abstracted and adapted from 6th German edn of Kraepelin's *Lehrbuch der Psychiatrie*, Macmillan, New York

Dove, L. (1975) 'The Hopes of Immigrant School Children', *New Society*, 10 April, 1975, 63–5

Dummett, M. and A. (1982) 'The Role of Government in Britain's Racial Crisis', in C. Husband (ed.), *Race in Britain. Continuity and Change*, pp. 97–127, Hutchinson, London

Eaton, J. and Weil, R. (1955) *Culture and Mental Disorders: A Comparative Study of the Hutterites and Other Populations*, Free Press, Glencoe, Illinois

Erickson, E.H. (1968) *Identity, Youth and Crisis*, Faber and Faber, London

Fabrega, H. (1974) 'Problems Implicit in the Cultural and Social Study of Depression', *Psychomosomatic Medicine*, *36*, 377–98

Fernando, S.J.M. (1969) 'Cultural Differences in the Hostility of Depressed Patients', *British Journal of Medical Psychology*, *42*, 67–74

Fernando, S.J.M. (1973) 'Sociocultural Factors in Depressive Illness: a Comparative Study of Jewish and Non-Jewish Patients in East London', MD thesis, University of Cambridge

Fernando, S.J.M. (1975) 'A Cross-cultural Study of Some Familial and Social Factors in Depressive Illness', *British Journal of Psychiatry*, *127*, 46–53

Fernando, S.J.M. (1978) 'Aspects of Depression in a Jewish Minority Group', *Psychiatria Clinica*, *11*, 23–33

Freud, S. (1917) 'Mourning and Melancholia', in J. Strachey (ed.), *The Standard Edition of the Complete Psychological Works of Sigmund Freud*, Vol. 14, pp. 243–58, Hogarth Press, London

Fromm-Reichmann, F. (1949) 'Intensive Psychotherapy of Manic-depressives. A Preliminary Report', *Confinia Neurologica*, *9*, 158–65

Gada, M.T. (1982) 'A Cross-cultural Study of Symptomatology of Depression — Eastern versus Western Patients', *International Journal of Social Psychiatry*, *28*, 195–202

Green, E.M. (1914) 'Psychoses among Negroes — a Comparative Study', *Journal of Nervous and Mental Diseases*, *41*, 697–708

Grewel, F. (1967) 'Psychiatric Differences in Ashkenazim and Sephardim', *Psychiatria Neurologia Neurochirurgia*, *70*, 339–47

Grinder, R.E. and McMichael, R.E. (1963) 'Cultural Influence on Conscience Development: Resistance to Temptation and Guilt among Samoans and American Caucasians', *Journal of Abnormal and Social Psychology*, *66*, 503–7

Halevi, H.S. (1963) 'Frequency of Mental Illness among Jews in Israel', *International Journal of Social Psychiatry*, *9*, 268–82

Hes, J.P. (1960) 'Manic-depressive Illness in Israel', *American Journal of Psychiatry*, *116*, 1082–6

Hicks, D.W. (1981) *Minorities. A Teachers Resource Book for the Multi-ethnic Curriculum*, Heinemann, London

Hollingshead, A.B. and Redlich, F.C. (1958) *Social Class and Mental Illness. A Community Study*, Wiley, New York

Huffard, D. (1977) 'Christian Religious Healing', *Journal of Operational Psychiatry*, *8* (2), 22–7

Ingleby, D. (1981) 'Understanding Mental Illness', in D. Ingleby (ed.), *Critical Psychiatry. The Politics of Mental Health*, pp. 23–71, Penguin, Harmondsworth

Jablensky, A., Sartorius, N., Gulbinat, W. and Ernberg, G. (1981) 'Characteristics of Depressive Patients Contacting Psychiatric Services in Four Cultures', *Acta Psychiatrica Scandinavica*, *63*, 367–83

Jones, J.S. (1981) 'How Different are Human Races?' *Nature*, *293*, 188–90

Jones, W.H.S. (1823) *Hippocrates with an English Translation*, Heinemann, London

Kapo, R. (1981) *A Savage Culture*, Quartet Books, London

Katznelson, I. (1973) *Black Men, White Cities*, Oxford University Press, London

Kendell, R.E. (1975) *The Role of Diagnosis in Psychiatry*, Blackwell Scientific Publications, Oxford

Kessel, N. (1965) 'Are International Comparisons Timely?', *Millbank Memorial Foundation Quarterly*, *53*, (2), 199–204

Kimura, Van B. (1965) 'Vergleichende Untersuchungen uber depressive Erkrankungen in Japan und in Deutschland', *Fortschritte de Neurologie-Psychiatrie*, *33*, 202–15

Kirmayer, L.J. (1984) 'Culture, Affect and Somatization', *Transcultural Psychiatric Research Review*, *21*, 159–88

Kleinman, A.M. (1977) 'Depression, Somatisation and the "New Cross-cultural Psychiatry"', *Social Science and Medicine*, *11*, 3–10

Kleinman, A. (1980) *Patients and Healers in the Context of Culture*, University of California

Press, Berkeley

Kleinman, A. (1982) 'Neurasthenia and Depression: a Study of Somatization and Culture in China', *Culture Medicine and Psychiatry, 6,* 117–90

Kraepelin, E. (1913) *'Manic Depressive Insanity and Paranoia',* translation of *Lehrbuch der Psychiatrie,* 8th edn, Vols iii and iv, by R.M. Barclay, Livingstone, Edinburgh

Krausz, E. (1971) *Ethnic Minorities in Britain,* MacGibbon and Kee, London

Levy-Bruhl, L. (1910) *Les Fonctions mentales dans les sociétés inférieures,* Alcan, Paris. Quoted by Littlewood and Lipsedge (1982)

Lewis, A.J. (1934) 'Melancholia: A Historical Review', *Journal of Mental Science, 23,* 1–42

Lin, T. (1953) 'A Study of the Incidence of Mental Disorder in Chinese and Other Cultures', *Psychiatry, 16,* 313–36

Littlewood, R. and Lipsedge, M. (1982) *Aliens and Alienists: Ethnic Minorities and Psychiatry,* Penguin, London

Lyons, B.G. (1971) *Voices of Melancholy,* Routledge and Kegan Paul, London

Malzberg, B. (1973) 'Mental Illness among Jews in New York State, 1960–1961. A Study of Ethnic Variation in Incidence', *Acta Psychiatrica Scandinavica, 49,* 479–518

Marsella, A.J. (1978) 'Thoughts on Cross-cultural Studies on the Epidemiology of Depression', *Culture, Medicine and Psychiatry, 2,* 343–57

Marsella, A.J. (1980) 'Depressive Experience and Disorder across Cultures', in H.C. Triandis and J.G. Draguns (eds), *Handbook of Cross-cultural Psychopathology,* Vol. 6, Ch. 6, pp. 237–89, Allyn and Bacon, Boston

Marsella, A.J., Kinzie, D. and Gordon, P. (1973) 'Ethnic Variations in the Expression of Depression', *Journal of Cross-cultural Psychology, 4,* 435–58

Mayer-Gross, W., Slater, E. and Roth, M. (1960) *Clinical Psychiatry,* 2nd edn, Cassell, London

Mead, M. (1950) 'Some Anthropological Considerations Concerning Guilt', in M.L. Reymert, (ed.), *Feelings and Emotions,* pp. 362–73, McGraw-Hill, New York

Mendels, J. (1970) *Concepts of Depression,* Wiley, London

Mendelson, M. (1974) *Psychoanalytic Concepts of Depression,* 2nd edn, Spectrum Publications, New York

Meyer, A. (1905) 'Society Proceedings of New York Neurological Society, November 1904', *Journal of Nervous and Mental Diseases, 32,* 112–20

Morris, H.S. (1968) 'Ethnic Groups', in *International Encyclopedia of the Social Sciences,* Vol. 5, Macmillan Free Press, New York. Quoted by Tajfel (1982)

Murphy, H.B.M. (1973) 'Current Trends in Transcultural Psychiatry', *Proceedings of the Royal Society of Medicine, 66,* 711–16

Murphy, H.B.M. (1974) 'Differences between Mental Disorders of French Canadians and British Canadians', *Canadian Psychiatry Association Journal, 19,* 247–57

Murphy, H.B.M., Wittkower, E.D. and Chance, N.E. (1964) 'A Cross-cultural Enquiry into Symptomatology of Depression', *Transcultural Psychiatric Research Review, 1,* 5–18

Norris, U. (1959) *Mental Illness in London,* Maudsley Monograph No. 6, Institute of Psychiatry, and Chapman Hall, London

Pfeiffer, W.M. (1970) 'Transcultural Psychiatry — Results and Problems', *Transcultural Psychiatric Research Review, 7,* 113–18

Pirani, M. (1974) 'Aspirations and Expectations of English and Immigrant Youth', *New Community, 3,* 73–8

Porter, A.M.W. (1970) 'Depressive Illness in a General Practice. A Demographic Study and a Controlled Trial of Imipramine', *British Medical Journal, 1,* 773–78

Prince, R. (1968) 'The Changing Picture of Depressive Syndromes in Africa', *Canadian Journal of African Studies, 1,* 177–92

Rack, P. (1982) *Race, Culture and Mental Disorder,* Tavistock Publications, London

Racy, J. (1970) 'Psychiatry in the Arab East', *Acta Psychiatrica Scandinavica, Suppl., 211,* 1–171

Raskin, A., Crook, T.H. and Herman, K.D. (1975) 'Psychiatric History and Symptom

Differences in Black and White Depressed In-patients', *Journal of Consulting and Clinical Psychology, 43,* 73–80

Rawnsley, K. (1968) 'Epidemiology of Affective Disorders', in A. Coppen and A. Walk (eds), *Recent Developments in Affective Disorders,* pp. 27–36, Headley, Ashford

Richman, N. (1976) 'Depression in Mothers of Pre-school Children', *Journal of Child Psychology and Psychiatry, 17,* 75–8

Rinder, I.D. (1963) 'Mental Health of Jewish Urbanites. A Review of Literature and Predictions', *International Journal of Social Psychiatry, 9,* 104–9

Rowe, D. (1978) *The Experience of Depression,* Wiley, New York

Ruesch, J., Jacobson, A. and Loeb, M.B. (1948) 'Acculturation and Illness', *Psychology Monographs, 62* (5), 1–40

Rushdie, S. (1982) 'The New Empire within Britain', *New Society,* 9 December, 417–21

Saifullah Khan, V. (1982) 'The Role of the Culture of Dominance in Structuring the Experience of Ethnic Minorities', in C. Husband (ed.), *'Race' in Britain. Continuity and Change,* pp. 197–215, Hutchinson, London

Sanua, V.D. (1959) 'Differences in Personality Adjustment among Different Generations of American Jews and non-Jews', in M.K. Opler (ed.), *Culture and Mental Disorder,* pp. 443–66, Macmillan, New York

Sartorius, N. (1973) 'Culture and the Epidemiology of Depression', *Psychiatrica Neurologia Neurochirurgia, 76,* 479–87

Sartorius, N., Jablensky, A., Gulbinat, W. and Ernberg, G. (1980) 'WHO Collaborative Study: Assessment of Depressive Disorders', *Psychological Medicine, 10,* 743–9

Satre, J.P. (1948) *Antisemite and Jew,* Schoken Books, New York

Seligman, M.E.P. (1975) *Helplessness. On Depression Development and Death,* W.H. Freeman, San Francisco

Shapiro, R.M. (1974) 'Racism and Community Mental Health', Unpublished paper quoted by Wilkeson, 1982.

Simpson, G.E. and Yinger, J.M. (1972) *Racial and Cultural Minorities,* 4th edn, Harper and Row, London

Singh, R. (1975) 'Depression in Ancient Indian Literature', *Indian Journal of Psychiatry, 17,* 148–53

Stone, M. (1981) *The Education of the Black Child in Britain,* Fontana, London

Szasz, T.S. (1967) 'The Myth of Mental Illness', in T.J. Scheff (ed.), *Mental Illness and Social Process,* pp. 242–65, Harper and Row, New York

Tajfel, H. (1982) 'The Social Psychology of Minorities', in C. Husband (ed.), *'Race' in Britain. Continuity and Change,* pp. 216–58, Hutchinson, London

Teja, J.S., Narang, R.L. and Aggarwal, A.K. (1971) 'Depression across Cultures', *British Journal of Psychiatry, 119,* 253–60

Tonks, C.M., Paykel, E.S. and Klerman, G.L. (1970) 'Clinical Depression among Negroes', *American Journal of Psychiatry, 127,* 329–35

Torrey, E. (1975) *The Death of Psychiatry,* Penguin Books, New York

Treacher, A. and Baruch, G. (1981) 'Towards a Critical History of the Psychiatric Profession', in D. Ingleby (ed.), *Critical Psychiatry. The Politics of Mental Health,* pp. 120–49, Penguin Books, Harmondsworth

Tseng, W. (1975) 'The Nature of Somatic Complaints among Psychiatric Patients: the Chinese Case', *Comprehensive Psychiatry, 116,* 237–45

Venkoba Rao, A. (1975) 'India', in J.G. Howells (ed.), *World History of Psychiatry, 26.* pp. 624–49, Balliere Tindall, London

Wagley, C. and Harris, M. (1958) *Minorities in the New World,* Columbia University Press, New York. Quoted by Tajfel (1982)

Waxler, N. (1977) 'Is Mental Illness Cured in Traditional Societies? A Theoretical Analysis', *Culture, Medicine and Psychiatry, 1,* 233–53

Waziri, R. (1973) 'Symptomatology of Depressive Illness in Afghanistan', *American Journal of Psychiatry, 130* (2), 213–17

Weinreich, P. (1979) 'Cross-ethnic Identification and Self Rejection in a Black Adolescent', in G.K. Verma and C. Bagley (eds), *Race, Education and Identity*, pp. 157–75, Macmillan, London

Wijesinghe, C.P., Dassanayake, S.A.W. and Dassanayake, P.V.L.N. (1978) 'Survey of Psychiatric Morbidity in a Semi-urban Population in Sri Lanka', *Acta Psychiatrica Scandinavica, 58*, 413–41

Wilkeson, A.G. (1982) 'A Resident's Perspective', in A. Gaw (ed.), *Cross-cultural Psychiatry*, pp. 285–300, John Wright PSG, Boston

Wing, J.K., Cooper, J.E. and Sartorius, N. (1974) *Measurement and Classification of Psychiatric Symptoms. An Instruction Manual for the P.S.E. and Catego Program*, Cambridge University Press, London

Yancey, W.L., Ericksen, E.P. and Juliani, R.N. (1976) 'Emergent Ethnicity: a Review and Reformulation', *American Sociology Review, 41*, 391–402

Yap, P.M. (1965a) 'Phenomenology of Affective Disorders in Chinese and Other Cultures', in A.V.S. DeRueck and R. Porter (eds), *Transcultural Psychiatry*, pp. 84–108, Churchill, London

Yap, P.M. (1965b) 'Koro — A Culture-bound Depersonalisation Syndrome', *British Journal of Psychiatry, 111*, 43–50

9   RACISM, PREJUDICE AND MENTAL ILLNESS

Aggrey W. Burke

The discipline of transcultural psychiatry covers wide areas of human function in normals (persons and groups), deviants and the ill. The discipline seeks an understanding of the total person and his/her group in relation to others and in the society. The scope of investigation should include those aspects of function (health, adjustment, illness) in this individual and group that arise because of difference from other individuals and groups, and result in fears, antagonisms and negative attitudes among and between such individuals and groups. In this chapter we will consider the role of 'race' in promoting the life-chances of some but also in reducing the likelihood that individuals or whole communities will have an opportunity to maintain mental health or to recover from mental illness or incapacity.

Five aspects of race may be identified. First, prejudice is an individual attitude of derogation. As a result of this attitude there will be the avoidance, discrimination or attack of another individual. Race is but one of many targets for derogatory attitudes; secondly, institutional racism is a theory of racial superiority of Whites as a basis of black (non-white) exploitation; thirdly, individual orientations to this theory of racism are conditioned by emotional factors; fourthly, individual reactions by those affected by racism are 'frustration' reactions. Fifthly, the symbolic quality of black as bad and unwanted and white as better and desirable has significance in personal attractions and relationships. For example, the sheepish 'ugly', 'scared' White is attracted to 'foreign' things and placed in the 'New World' and repulsed by the old order. Not surprisingly relationships may be imbued with such values and this may be true in life or at work. The foregoing would suggest that counsellors and psychotherapists should consider the significance of race-related material in their analysis of human function and behaviour (see Burke, 1984c, d).

In the present chapter it is not our intention to bring about a unified view of individual race-related behaviours, namely attitude (prejudice), orientation to racism, reactions of those affected by racism, and those which instead are group (racism) or relationship related.

Derogatory attitude in an individual may exist in a setting devoid of politically based racism (see Byrne and Wong, 1962) and may have nothing to do with race. However, as an orientation or reaction to racism will be present in those living in racist society, the nature of interactions between groups and individuals will vary according to personal experience (McCord *et al.*, 1960), institutional constraints and attitudes of those in power. There will be difficulty in reaching a conclusion on the relative significance of the individual factor and the institutional one, given the further problem of distinguishing action from reaction. For example, according to Chapman (1967) '. . . many guests — West Indians in particular — arrive in England expecting to encounter colour prejudice and consequently are extremely sensitive and often look for an insult when none is intended. Some children are aggressively defensive and this unfortunate attitude serves to isolate them further'. In this instance the worker identifies a number of demographic variables, as, for example, migrant status, age group and race, as well as social change (rural-urban). It is the author's view that social shift (mobility) interacts in an adverse manner with racial difference in a population that is low status by virtue of immigration. The arrival of the black man in the European or North American country is viewed with apprehension; the welcoming party do not intend an insult but somehow the guest experiences this. The analysis allows us to identify insensitivity of the host along with sensitivity of the guest. Insulting behaviour (real or fantasy) by the host is followed by easily identifiable aggressive reaction by the guest, and prejudice by the host leads to withdrawal by the adult guests.

According to Jaspers (1963), *prejudices* may often lead to the conclusion of what is definitely knowable and what we believe. Jaspers held that, when such prejudices exist, these would have the unconscious effect of weighing on the individual in such a paralysing manner that, in the psychiatric setting (for scientific methods to be followed), it would be necessary to try and free ourselves from these prejudices. Jaspers gives a lucid account of the subject. He notes that prejudices in the area of philosophy touch on moralistic and theological tendencies and therefore involve value judgements. From the point of view of the clinician the issue of empathy is best understood as having two components: first, that which may be learned and is scientific; and secondly, that which is intuitive. Without the latter the scientific method is hampered and cannot be employed. If racism exists and derogatory attitudes are commonly found, the worker may have difficulty in weighing the relative significance of intuitive skill with scientific method. Therefore, it is unlikely that the clinician will attain an adequate level of empathy if he identifies with the institution of racism and is dealing with a 'guest', a person deemed to be low in status and possessing other qualities meriting exploitation for financial gain (Essien-Udom, 1975). In this regard reference should be made to the political variable as described by Fanon (1967), Freire (1968) and Herskovits (1971). Fanon was a psychiatrist in a colonised country in North Africa, Freire was an educator in Latin America, and Herskovits was an anthropologist seeking an understanding of life in a slave population in Haiti in the West Indies. All three bring to light the fact that gross deprivation of a social and psychological kind is a consequence of political domination of so-called subordinate groups by 'exploiters in a superior position'. With the migration of people from colonised areas of black settlement into the midst of the colonisers, the practice of race contact in social and work relations (in earlier times this contact was based on ascribed status positions) is commonplace and based on living and work relationships. Progress has been slow and unfortunately free movement of blacks is not yet possible in any part of the white world. Therefore majority populations in some areas (e.g. South Africa), or majority black populations in parts of others (e.g. the United States of America) are in open revolt, and new black groups in Western Europe are demanding equal opportunities. This would suggest that the joint issues of prejudice and racism should be given careful consideration and subjected to study if psychiatric practice in these advanced countries is to be improved upon.

In his discussion of this issue of prejudice, Jaspers also identifies the use of false analogy. Indeed, as the psyche cannot be observed and therefore can be studied only by metaphor and simile, this will inevitably lead to prejudice. Finally, Jaspers identified prejudice which will interfere with objective collection of data necessary for diagnosis in the field of medicine. Jaspers notes that if, indeed, it is true that prejudice will falsify our view, then those factors that enable and enhance that view (positive falsification) should be distinguished from those that prevent that view (negative falsification). His term for the former was presupposition and he believed that when such presuppositions were wrongly taken as absolutes they would then become prejudices. In Western Europe and the Americas the global practice of racism has resulted in the situation in which false presuppositions on race have been incorporated as truths in everyday life.

In modern usage the term *racism* applies almost entirely to Black/White relations in various parts of the world. This wide and imprecise context serves no useful function if the investigator is interested in identifying psychiatric consequences, or, indeed, personality determinants of the attack (action) and counter-attack (reaction) of dominant and subordinate groups in the dyadic relationship inherent in the black/white organisation. This subject has been fully described by the present author (Burke 1984a, b). The psychiatric consequences of racism cannot be understood without making a full analysis of the mythology, belief system, and specific conditions of the ideology so well described by Essien-Udom (1975). Among specific conditions mentioned by this worker the first is that of physical appearance; the second relates to the belief about the correspondence between the physical, cultural, moral and intellectual differences among the various racial groups; the third, the social actions which are based on those beliefs. The term 'race' is a sociological one which in part has significance because of the ideology. The word 'race' should be distinguished from 'culture' and 'ethnic'. Race as crudely defined is that aspect of appearance (including dress), language or grouping which distinguishes the individual or group. Culture by contrast has to do with learned behaviour and the dynamic change inevitable in new environments or as a result of social change. 'Ethnic' describes those cultural or subcultural groups that can be demarcated by a common tradition or origin.

The growth of racism has taken place over a considerable period. Hart (1980) argues that slavery in the English colonies, being more identified with race in master-servant relations than elsewhere in Latin America or in non-English colonies of the Caribbean, became the ground on which the belief system grew. Those beliefs were to be incorporated in what became part of a pseudo-scientific theory. The Church was to be involved and initially slaves were not admitted to Christianity. Eventually this practice was reversed but seating arrangements maintained the difference necessary to reinforce second-classness in the hostage population. Froude (1888) writes of the despicable attitude of masters, and almost 100 years later Walvin (1973) notes a similar practice in metropolitan areas. Indeed, if, as Froude observed, abolition of slavery had the negative effect of separating the two groups even more than they had been before, it would follow that greater liberation through migration could only further increase the dichotomy.

During this period the practice of reporting information on race, whether in the media, in literature or in history, was subject to bias and distortion. It was the reporting of the behaviour of a lower group by a higher group which held attitudes aimed at maintaining institutional racism. For example, Froude was to write of the lack of morals among the Blacks. He believed that it would be impossible for the Whites to be ruled by this group. He hypothesised that the Blacks would wish revenge as the relationships between the two groups were too embittered for peace to ensue. It could well be that Froude talked for the many and that his sentiments were to lead to restrictive practices concerning migration of the Blacks (hence broken families) and the strengthening of racism in 'host' countries (see Fryer, 1984). When Froude looked at those problems, he preferred to identify the characteristics of the subordinate. This stereotype was one of an inferior race being docile, good tempered, excellent and faithful servants with notions of right and wrong scarcely formed. This stereotype was actively maintained throughout colonisation, and only since Blacks migrated to northern cities in the United States or to 'White' reserves in Europe was there an opportunity to question this stereotype.

The factors that lead to group behaviour in institutional settings have been well studied by Goffman (1971). He described five types of 'institutions' in modern-day society: those for voluntary retreat are distinguished from those with tasks, for example boarding schools, colonial compounds, work camps. Three others are identified for care and protection: firstly, for the care of the indigent; secondly for those presenting with medical and psychological problems that threaten society, for example leprosy, tuberculosis or madness; finally, the third of this group and the fifth in the total sample serves the purpose of containing both individuals and groups which are deemed to be bad (penal) or inferior (subnormal intelligence or subordinate status) and are therefore unwanted and unwelcome in normal society. Although Goffman cites jails, prisoner of war camps and concentration camps in this last group, he makes no mention of the widespread and pervasive practice of racism itself.

Psychological Factors

Elsewhere, the present author has considered those manifestations of racism which may be of importance to transcultural psychiatry. The basic condition of racism is of a sado-masochistic kind and is found in the white population only. Racism among Whites must be distinguished from racism-related disorders in Blacks. The latter result from a basic sense of loss (of face, will and dignity) and the fear of further loss/exclusion by death or other method. The racism-related disorders are grief-like in kind. The experience of institutional racism is low among Whites but high among Blacks. The same is true concerning the experience of individual racism (Burke, 1984b). Recently this subject has not received much attention (see Burke, 1984c, d) but was studied earlier by Mannoni (1964) in Madagascar, and by Fanon (1967) in Algeria. Colonisers and colonised are bonded together in a dyad of oppression. The sub-jugated resist this opression and strive for freedom. In America, McKay (1968) studied the problem in Harlem, New York, and in the Carib-bean, Williams (1973) gives a clear description of the psychological effect of African slavery and Indian indenture on racism lines. More recently, Pillay (1984) and Burke (1985b) describe racism and mental illness in South Africa and Britain, respectively. The simple fact is that no one can come to terms with the horrors of racism resulting in racism-related disorders without grasping the significance of mass extermination or other forms of mortality, as for example, the 50 per cent who died during the slave passage from Africa to the New World (see Williams, 1973). This worker's description of the conditions during that period suggest that life had no value and that the fate meted out to slaves was one of humilia-tion and certain premature death. Extermination is therefore one impor-tant aspect of racism. Related to this is an absence of guilt in the exterminator and the fear of extermination by the subordinated.

When slavery was abolished, handsome compensations were paid to the owners and harsher attitudes led to a retreat by some of the slave population; the practice of whipping into docility continued, a practice which Williams described as 'degrading to the point which sugar cultiva-tion required' (see Williams, 1973, p. 109). The recent experience of Jews in Nazi Germany merits close attention in this context.

The present author has studied psychological aspects of racism and has found the evidence of a number of specific *individual orientations to racism*. This may be identified in group settings which use group analytical methods to explore race (see Burke, 1984c, d). Five individual orientations have been identified:

(1) Over-reaction maintains the superior position because of fear.
(2) Under-reaction stems from sadness and leads to patronage, look-ing after, do-gooding and making of token gestures.
(3) The non-reactor is paralysed by anxiety and is unable to react.
(4) The catastrophic reaction is that of the angry, the aggressive and the irrational, all of whom are prepared to justify their position by aggressive methods.
(5) The stereotyped reaction is that of individuals lacking in individual-ity who prefer to follow the group. The underlying emotion is apathy.

The nature of the therapeutic relationship which should develop and thus may exist between the client or patient from a 'subordinate' group and a worker from the 'superordinate' one has been of greater concern to workers in this area of race-related disorder than the reverse situation of superordinate client and subordinate worker. In the therapy setting there is evidence (Burke, 1985a) that, even with the linking of client and worker by ethnic group, issues of race may be important considerations. However, it is the pairing of therapist and patient by race that exposes worker and client to the ascribed roles of racism, i.e. white worker, black patient, which merits greater attention than that of the reversed situation of black worker, white client. It will be found that workers will identify with one of five orientations to racism, and clients/patients will show counter-reactions appropriate to their own experience and emotion (apathy, anxiety or anger) and to worker orientation. With these diverse patterns of work relationship, the worker in social services (casework or family work), those in probation and those in psychotherapy or psychiatry should be equipped to deal with race-related aspects of transference, counter-transference, resistance and refusal. These issues of race have been studied in North America (see Grier and Cobbs, 1969; Devore and Schlesinger, 1981; Bass *et al.*, 1981). In an earlier period, psychoanalysts studied cultural issues. Thus Horney (1960) discussed the significance of the aggressive tendency in the cultural situation and showed how self-preservation instincts are complemented by aggressive tendencies. The two will develop separately in contrasting groups which are deemed to be cultural by Horney. In the present context, however, note should be made of the fact that both develop in the institution of racism. Herskovits (1969) and Klein (1975) have discussed hatred from the point of view both of its origins and of its consequences. Klein believed that greed, envy and hatred fuelled aggressive tendencies. She also noted that putting in (introjection) and putting out (projection) were the primary factors that contributed to the identifications, resulting in greed, envy and hatred. The analyst is in a position to make a link between the sociopolitical institution and the individual identification with it. None the less, none have sought to make such a link concerning the racism that dehumanised black people in many parts of the world. The consequence of this omission has been that although atrocities have been perpetrated in such populations for a long time, this did not prevent widespread Second World War atrocities in Europe. Subsequent to this there have been racist acts of barbarism in apartheid South Africa and in migrant refugee and 'black' populations elsewhere. The essential feature of such atrocities is, of course, the fact that greed is coupled with repressed hatred, the outcome being victimisation, oppression and all forms of exclusion from society.

An example of *exclusion* is afforded by a study of the psychiatric aspects of repatriation from a migrant society to a formerly colonised one. It is but an extension of the over-representation of such populations in institutional settings including mental hospitals (Cochrane, 1977; Dean *et al.*, 1981) and locked wards in such hospitals (Bolton, 1984). These practices have the inevitable consequence of increasing stigma leading to a worsening of mental condition in hostage populations who eventually lose all sense of motivation and become apathetic. This syndrome of apathy seems characteristic of repatriated patients (Burke, 1973) but may now have become identified as being the result of exclusion of subordinated groups. This is an example of the interaction of institutional racism, the individual orientation of 'host' population members and the reaction of 'hostage' persons. In psychiatry it will be found that mental (social) control is but one aspect of a trio of duties which the professional doctor, nurse, social worker, psychologist, occupational therapist or ancillary worker must fulfil. The professional worker is obliged to deal with mental (social) illness and mental (social) health as the other sides of this triangle, but must at all times exercise powers to protect family, community, society and in effect the individual.

Should it be found that black populations are effectively segregated in education, housing and employment, it may be argued that the subordinate, superordinate racism principle is indeed being followed. The evidence available suggests that health-care systems may be no different in so far as Blacks may be experiencing a lesser form of care than Whites (see Burke, 1984b; Carstairs, 1984; Mercer, 1984, Pillay, 1984). The simple fact is that racism is indeed pervasive and widespread. The South African tragedy as described by Pillay may appear to be more pernicious than Western World racism but the effects may be no different. Indeed, workers must work with patients. A shortfall in service provision may often be due to racism as an institution. However, the worker's or planner's orientation to this institution may dictate certain strategies (e.g. the virtual absence of psychotherapy for Blacks). The insidious undermining of black families, by social deprivation and restrictive migration policies and child-care operations, merits attention. In this instance it will be found that stereotyped views on the black psyche and family contribute to mental illness which, if associated with black counter-reaction by withdrawal or anger, leads to failure in 'treatment' or 'mental control' instead. Essentially such outcome phenomena may be due to individual white orientations (stereotyped or patronising under-reaction), black counter-reactions and subsequent white non-reaction (apathy) or over-reaction (involuntary admission, locked wards, secure hospitals).

Catastrophic reaction may lead to a further shortfall in care, and if evidence detailed by the black media of repatriation, beatings during detention and the far too common tragedy of death in hospital is found to be true, this would suggest that racism generates undue suffering of black folk.

Here in Britain the most significant consequence of social deprivation in Blacks (a direct result of institutional racism) may be the increasing evidence of apathy and the high prevalence of frustration syndromes which will be found in large sections of the black population and also in Whites excluded from adequate living standards. One extreme form of expression of this frustration is the urban riot. This was experienced among similar groups in Asia, Africa, North America and the Caribbean. Workers in Britain have studied the phenomenon with regard to cause (Field and Southgate, 1982) and effects (Bhat *et al.*, 1984a, b). The urban riot is a community phenomenon which seems to result from a feeling of oppression and a reaction to poor social conditions in dilapidated ghetto areas (Moinat *et al.*, 1972). Therefore, this major inevitable consequence of racism is an example of a form of racism-related behaviour.

On other occasions the subordinated group will elect to demonstrate frustration through more readily acceptable modes. Thus, for example, the present author has described an increase in psychosomatic disorders and depression among vulnerable populations exposed to racism (Burke, 1984b). Once again there is evidence of racism as the cause, and it should be evident that the reaction of the group suffering disorder will be to use medical services more frequently than the group not suffering from disorder. A further complication, however, is that a mounting up of cases deemed to be physically or mentally ill results in overcrowding of specific facilities used for the treatment or control of mental illness. This may in part be seen as a justification for acts of therapeutic desperation, as for example the belief that mental patients would be better off in the harsh and deplorable conditions in home environments than in difficult conditions in the Western World where economies are stronger than, and services far superior to, those in previously colonised areas.

A Jamaican Study: Repatriation

In the immediate post-war period, Pfister-Ammende (1955) carried out a unique study on the distribution of psychiatric disorder in more than 7500 refugees and a repatriated group of slightly larger size. On comparing disorder in each of these two groups and the native population of Switzerland, it was found that there was an increase in illness rate in the two former groups. There was an even greater increase of serious depression in refugees as compared with repatriated patients. In the Caribbean, workers have been interested in the phenomena of paranoid reaction (Prange, 1958) and other pathologies in patients who had been repatriated home from England (Burke, 1973; Mahy, 1973). Throughout the Caribbean it became evident that up to one in seven admissions to mental hospitals had returned home from Britain. The health of this group was somewhat worse than that of patients who had not migrated; repatriates were withdrawn and apathetic; locals were not at all like this. This observation countered previous evidence that the repatriation of mental patients was well intentioned and sincere and had a basis in common sense or scientific investigation. Patients who were repatriated from Holland (Tolsma, 1971) France (Frey, 1961) and Britain (Asuni, 1968) to original countries were described as having a good outcome, but unfortunately all of these studies suffered poor methodology and employed loose criteria for adequate follow-up.

When the present author investigated the extent of mental illness (relapse) and premature mortality in a sample of 56 cases repatriated home to Jamaica about 42 months prior to making a follow-up study, the evidence supported the view that the nonsensical practice stemmed from an ideology rooted in racial theory. The population for study was a consecutive series of 66 cases among whom six were not fully traced (though known about) and four were excluded for good reasons. Data on illness in England were used alongside field-survey and hospital data on readmission in Jamaica. Attempts were made to interview patients through relatives, neighbours and hospital personnel involved in their management, and to this end a semi-structured interview form was used which included data on mental, social, psychological and material factors.

The sample was made up of 41 males and 15 females, mean age 24.6 years (SD 8.3 years). At the time of migration to England there were only four older than 35. Within two years of arrival in England one-fifth (10) had been admitted to mental hospital. When application was made for funding for repatriation, each of the 56 cases was under treatment. All had been admitted to mental hospitals and after extensive investigations in the home country it was concluded that repatriation would be beneficial and should take place. When this did in fact take place, the majority (36) had been living in Britain for more than ten years; a quarter had drifted from their families and friends; two-fifths showed features of residential instability; and two-thirds could not keep down a job. More than two-thirds had been admitted to hospital on a compulsory order and in half of them this followed a court procedure. There were seven who had been admitted to a special hospital designated for dangerous mental patients. This association with police contact or with the use of the Mental Health Act or with the criminal courts, locked wards and special hospitals raises issues of fundamental importance to racial analysis, and it is probable that these practices and the interaction between them is of some significance in the apathy syndrome picked up in the home country but often already developing before the final journey home. This issue has been discussed regarding detention (Mercer, 1984) by the police (Humphrey, 1972) and child care (Small, 1984). The simple fact is that the mini-institutions of Goffman are unlikely to have as damaging a role on human function and on human relationship as the macro institution of racism. It is for this reason that the feature of the apathy syndrome is so commonly found in this macro institution. Detailed study of all case notes concerning patients returning home indicated that the initiative for this procedure was that of the authorities. However, as many have passed through a number of services; some had suffered humiliation in court and were sentenced to locked wards; most had experienced the stigma of illness and had a poor prospect for rehabilitation, it is understandable that eventually these patients agreed to being repatriated. Moreover, as more than half had been detained as inpatients for over two years, the situation for them was grim and more similar to imprisonment than to hospitalisation. This reality must be set against the inevitable difficulty in rural environments in the home country.

It was surprising to find that fewer than half the cases deemed to be suffering from serious mental illness on departure had been admitted to hospital for mental illness since return, and almost a quarter had managed to find employment. In fact at the time of the field survey there were only six receiving mental treatment in hospital. None the less it is an alarming fact that nine were living in the bush and seven others were dead (five of these deaths might have been self-inflicted). This unusually high suicide rate of 2 per cent per annum is cause for concern and provides evidence of an undesirable consequence of racism itself. The evidence suggests that in Jamaica practices of suicide and living in the bush are commonly found and are extreme forms of racism-related behaviour. Press reports in Britain and evidence elsewhere (Hendin, 1969) suggest that suicide and retreat by dropping out are frequent occurences. This subject has been fully discussed by others (Black Health Workers, 1983).

Results among 56 repatriated patients in Jamaica indicated that a poor outcome was experienced by three-fifths. Like workers in the United

States of America (see Adebimpe, 1981), we were unable to confirm British evidence of high rates of misdiagnosis in a cohort of patients of similar background (Littlewood and Lipsedge, 1982). Racism frequently results in an orientation of over-reaction and detention. Diagnosis may be a justification for such practices. Our investigation revealed that clinicians and related staff had been concerned about social and psychiatric issues but that this concern was overshadowed by individual attitudes (prejudice) and their own orientation to group ideology (racism). Therefore the procedure of repatriation was unlikely to have been therapeutic as therapy had not been intended in the first place. A creative approach might have been input by skilled workers sharing background factors, who might have been able to pinpoint difficulties in the two environments and provide therapy directed at reducing the effects of such difficulties. It was interesting to find that in support of our contention that individual and group factors contributed to the final decision, there was evidence that a good outcome was associated with low intelligence and not high intelligence, which elsewhere is found to be positively associated with outcome among psychiatric patients. Workers have challenged racial views on intelligence and education, and more recently Stone (1981) has investigated erroneous ideas on self-concept of 'Blacks' in Britain.

Current Practice

In normal practice it is unusual to find evidence of discrimination consequent on prejudice in open every-day therapeutic contact between workers/therapists and patients. None the less there are frequent verbal reports from nurses who have been openly abused or even spat on by patients who believe that black staff should have no contact with them. Language difference is a secondary source of resistance by white patients to black nurses and doctors working in general practices or psychiatric facilities. This 'cloak' of language may serve the purpose of hiding deeply felt prejudicial ideas. Therefore it may be difficult to reach the conclusion that prejudice exists. More commonly, white staff cry out for training on black culture — the hidden agenda being, first, how their own prejudicial position leads to incapacity and sometimes to discriminatory practice; and secondly how much they resist change. Black patients have been slow in reporting dismay simply because of fear of the consequences. None the less, evidence is being systematically reported of unpleasant incidents which seem to be the outcome of individual attitudes (prejudice) or institutional constraints (racism) (see Da Cocodia, 1984).

The evidence on institutional racism has been noted earlier in this paper. Essentially the mental (social) control aspect of psychiatry is far more evident among Blacks than mental illness treatment and mental health promotion aspects, which instead are predominant white concerns. Blacks are selectively shunted to locked wards and facilities. Moreover, despite a less than 5 per cent distribution in the population, Blacks make up half the children in care in many areas, and half the patients in secure psychiatric units in selected psychiatric settings. The extent of the tragedy is best understood by making reference to reports of brutalisation in South African psychiatry (Burke, 1985b). However, from the clinical standpoint, it is recommended that the method of study of the multiple effects of racism and problems arising from this issue should be the case-study method.

Case Examples

At the individual level, 'under-reaction', with its patronising attitude, may lead to the witholding of services. For example, a young woman of 22 years of age who had migrated from Port of Spain, Trinidad and Tobago, to London some seven years earlier became unsettled following childbirth. Her family noted a deterioration in behaviour and social function and became concerned for the well-being of her six-month-old baby. The social services department and general practitioner were informed of their concern. However, little note was taken of this information as behaviour was believed to be cultural and not indicative of social disorganisation. Soon after this the patient destroyed all her furniture and was seen by neighbours to be in a daze and in her own world. Neighbours were alarmed, and with this pressure on social workers, the psychiatrist was called in. Unfortunately, the psychiatrist and his team were not convinced. Once again withdrawn and strange behaviour were believed to be 'cultural'. The situation deteriorated further and eventually the child was taken away under the care of the local authority. It is perhaps of interest that in the particular residential area of this case study the local authority, which knew of the high distribution of black families, did not provide day nurseries or other child-support facilities. They preferred instead to have an energetic child-care fostering/adoption network.

Over-reactions are more commonly found. Bolton (1984) found evidence of speedy removal to locked wards of Blacks deemed uncooperative. Psychiatric reporting for courts or between departments shows an obsession with ideas of Blacks being bad, big Blacks somewhat worse, and big Black males — particularly those who have had any contact with the police — as the most dangerous of all cases. In one particular case a 26-year-old male patient who had spent a three-year period in prison reappeared in a remand facility some 12 months following release on parole and was found to be showing features of excitement. The history revealed evidence of unhappiness in childhood, rejection by his mother, maladjustment in adolescence, and isolation and despair in adulthood. The patient had been recurrently depressed but remained bitter about his past. He had no history of psychiatric illness requiring treatment. On examination the patient was sensitive, suspicious and unsettled. He was desparate and during the previous three-monthh period had turned to God for help. Despite his agreement to take treatment and a rapid repsonse to injection therapy, psychiatric personnel believed that being black and big and with a previous offence he presented a substantial risk to society. Elsewhere it was believed that this patient might have been better treated in the community as a condition of a probation order than by being detained in a prison facility. Control seemed to win the day and in this case it is unfortunate that big and black seemed more important considerations than the treatability of mental disorder. The need to control patients of this kind is justified by using unduly high doses of drugs on some occasions.

The sado-masochistic quality of racism may be studied in all post-colonial societies, from the Far East through Asia and Africa and into the Americas, which have experienced widespread exploitation of black manpower in the interests of white institutions. Thus racism is an integral part of the present civilisation. It may be studied wherever native Blacks have been systematically exterminated (North America, Australia, New Zealand) or demoralised (South Africa), or where migrant Blacks have settled in Europe and the Americas. In the former situation, racism is maintained by brutalisation and by peverse acts of barbarism carried out by psychopathic and normal Whites at all levels of society.

Atrocities will also be widespread in the areas of black settlement. At the individual level, blackness is experienced by all who feel different or are deemed to be different. Clinical material supports the view that an act of abuse, attack, terror or torture, whether emotional, psychological or physical, will have the effect of leading to psychic trauma (which may be long-lasting) (Eaton *et al.*, 1982) and of causing mental illness. *Race* 'attack' is experienced as *rape* of the 'total' person; many become hardened to repeated attack; a minority become vulnerable to any insult; and eventually some succumb. A 22-year-old female patient was referred to the author because of an acute onset of symptoms following physical attack by a white man and the subsequent failure of professionals in her living area to respond to her needs. It was alleged that the patient had been grabbed at the neck and brought to the floor. The background history was of normal adjustment prior to migration and since marriage. She worked as a social worker and related well in all situations. On examination the patient was fearful and agitated. Since the incident she complained of feeling persecuted, of being watched, and of hearing voices telling her bad things; her mood was depressed, appetite and sleep were disturbed; she could not cope with life; had lost interests and concentration; felt worthless and saw no hope in the future; she gave no history of previous psychiatric disturbance and was surprised that she had become frightened and distrustful of and angry with white neighbours, friends and strangers having contact with her. Treatment was aimed at relieving the experience, reducing anxiety and dealing with angry feelings of revenge.

The concept of a multiracial or 'melting-pot' society is one that acknowledges that all people are part of one race of human beings and that no group is superior to any other. This concept should also recognise that geographical, ethnic and cultural factors will shape the development and living syle of diverse communities. This should mean that whenever attempts are made to deny these tenets of multiculturalism, this is done in order to maintain racism. An example is afforded by the misguided one-way practice of transracial fostering and adoption of black children into white families (Small, 1984). This practice may be demoralising to the black community, emotionally damaging to extended families and real parents of the children, and traumatic in a psychic sense to the children being used as pawns of racism. Inevitably there will be a proportion of white parents who will be involved in this transracial process because of symbolic identifications with 'black' (different), despite their manifest prejudicial attitudes and/or their destructive orientations to racism. When cases come to the attention of psychiatry, it may be found that members of the new family have avoided the reality of race.

When a 24-year-old divorcee came to see me, he complained of recent feelings of apathy and despair and of always feeling that he wasn't wanted because of being black. From the age of ten this was associated with bouts of irritability, anger and aggression. He had been adopted into the parental family of his white mother despite their open condemnation of blacks living in Britain. They discouraged contact with black persons and were intolerant of black social and cultural activities. The patient's mother had been brought up in a sibship of four but had never been comfortable in the family setting. She craved the attention of her parents and welcomed their material support. The patient himself longed for contact with his own father and at the first opportunity escaped from his suburban home to seek black companionship and approval. His attendance at the clinic was precipitated when his grandparents moved into an old people's home and his own mother made increasing emotional demands on him. At interview the patient welcomed the opportunity to discuss matters of race with a black therapist. He was a sensitive man who had become depressed and was unable to work in the period of trying to deal with his mother's demands and his own inner-self needs.

Conclusion

In this chapter an attempt has been made to identify specific aspects of human function likely to be affected by racism or prejudice and in some instances resulting in mental illness or a lowering of mental health chances or prevention of a recovery from such impairments. It is unlikely that psychiatry will be able to address itself to the ethical or moral questions that arise in the context of racism if the political issue — the basis of racism — is not recognised and confronted. In dealing with the black person, medical responsibility should not be seen to be a rationale for the continued practice of social control, but clearly sometimes this is indeed the case. For too long psychiatry has chosen to shield itself from criticism on the vexed question of social control of groups unsettled by inequality and reacting to this by apathy (the retreat) or instead by anger and eruption (the riot). The field of racism will make demands on patients and staff alike. Indeed, with any action of one party there will be a matched counter-reaction in the other. Therefore if patient-staff conflict is to reduce, creative matching of like with like by race will have to be entertained alongside strategies aimed at undoing, first, politically motivated but firmly held beliefs on racism, and, secondly, individual prejudice. The evidence points to the conclusion that racism does lead to mental illness; firstly, by fermenting and maintaining social deprivation and so impairing chances of attaining mental health; secondly, by institutional factors which have the effect of witholding care; thirdly, by bully-boy/girl strategies of humiliating Blacks into subordination and inflicting sado-masochistic attacks on them; and finally when this fails by implementing methods of social/medical control. Of interest is the fact that in the modern world our greatest concern is with extreme forms of racism-related behaviours (riot, aggression syndromes, suicide, withdrawal, paranoid reactions) rather than with the moderate but less evident forms (psychosomatic, depression and anxiety) of this condition, or the implied or real acts of abuse, terror and attack which are indices of racism itself. The more widespread issue of prejudice is an individual attitude which may invoke race, but is as likely to be related to some other 'stigma'-generating marker.

References

Adebimpe, V.R. (1981) 'Overview: White Norms and Psychiatric Diagnosis of Black Patients', *American Journal of Psychiatry, 138*, (3), 279–85

Asuni, T. (1968) 'The Review of Nigerian Students Repatriated on Psychiatric Grounds', *West African Medical Journal, 17*, 3–7

Bass, B.A., Wyatt, G.E. and Powell, G.J. (1982) *The Afro-American Family. Assessment, Treatment, and Research Issues*, Grune & Stratton, New York

Bhat, A., Burke, A.W., Falkowski, W., Mason, T., Norton, K., Rao, B., Samanarayake, B. and Sibisi, C. (1984a) 'The Causes of and Solutions for Rioting in Britain in the Summer of 1981', *International Journal of Social Psychiatry, 30* 4–8

Bhat, A., Burke A.W., Falkowski, W., Mason, T. Norton, K., Rao, B., Samanarayake, B. and Sibisi, C. (1984b) 'Psychiatric Workers as Emotional Beings: the Emotional Reactions of Staff Following the Brixton Riots', *International Journal of Social Psychiatry, 30* 9–14

Black Health Workers and Patients Group (1983) 'Psychiatry and the Corporate State', *Race and Class, 25*, 49–64

Bolton, P. (1984) 'Management of Compulsorily Admitted Patients to a High Security Unit', *International Journal of Social Psychiatry, 30* 77–84

Burke, A.W. (1973) 'The Consequences of Unplanned Repatriation', *British Journal of Psychiatry, 23* (572), 109–11

Burke, A.W. (1984a) 'Is Racism a Causatory Factor in Mental Illness? An Introduction', *International Journal of Social Psychiatry, 30* 1–3

Burke, A.W. (1984b) 'Racism and Psychological Disturbance among West Indians in Britain', *International Journal of Social Psychiatry, 30* 50–68

Burke, A.W. (1984c) 'The Multi-racial Small Group on Race: Theoretical Issues and Practical Considerations', *International Journal of Social Psychiatry, 30* (1 & 2), 89–95

Burke, A.W. (1984d) 'The Outcome of the Multi-racial Small Group Experience: Summary Report', *International Journal of Social Psychiatry, 30* 96–101

Burke, A.W. (1985a) 'The Practice of Social Work in Modern Race Society', The Kenneth Brill Lecture at the British Association of Social Workers, Swansea, April 1985

Burke, A.W. (1985b) 'Mental Health and Apartheid. World Psychiatric Association Conference Report', *International Journal of Social Psychiatry, 31* (2), 145–8

Byrne, D. and Wong, T.J. (1962) 'Racial Prejudice, Interpersonal Attraction, and Assumed Dissimilarity of Attitudes', *Journal of Abnormal and Social Psychology, 65*, 246–53

Carstairs, M. (1984) 'Political and Factional Obstacles to Attaining "Health for All by the Year 2000" ', *International Journal of Social Psychiatry, 30* (1 & 2), 143–7

Chapman, R.D. (1967) 'In Two Worlds: Immigrant School Leavers', *Mental Health, 26*, 14–16

Cochrane, R. (1977) 'Mental Illness in Immigrants to England and Wales: an Analysis of Mental Hospital Admissions, 1971', *Social Psychiatry, 12* 25–35

Da-Cocodia, L. (1984) 'The Probable Effects of Racism in Nursing and Related Disciplines', *International Journal of Social Psychiatry, 30* (1 & 2), 17–21

Dean, G., Walsh, D., Downing, H. and Shelly, E. (1981) 'First Admissions of Native-Born and Immigrants to Psychiatric Hospitals in South-East England, 1976', *British Journal of Psychiatry, 139*, 506–12

Devore, W. and Schlesinger, E.G. (1981) *Ethnic-sensitive Social Work Practice*, C.V. Mosby, New York

Essien-Udom, E.U. (1975) 'Tribalism and Racism', in L. Kuper (ed), *Race, Science and Society*, pp. 234–261, Unesco Press/Allen & Unwin, London

Eaton, W.W., Sigal, J.J. and Weinfeld, M. (1982) 'Impairment in Holocaust Survivors after 33 Years: Data from an Unbiased Community Sample', *American Journal of Psychiatry, 139*, 773–7

Fanon, F. (1967) *The Wretched of the Earth*, Penguin Books, London

Field, S. and Southgate, P. (1982) *Public Disorder*, HMSO, London

Freire, P. (1968) *Pedagogy of the Oppressed,* Seabury Press, New York

Frey, F. (1961) 'Evolution, après le retour en Algérie,, des maladies mentales contractées en metropole par les travailleurs Musulmans', *L'Hygiene Mentale, 50*, 244–9

Froude, J.A. (1888) *The English in the West Indies*, Longmans, London

Fryer, P. (1984) *Staying Power. The History of Black People in Britain*, Pluto Press, London

Goffman, E. (1971) *Asylums*, Penguin Books, London

Grier, W.H. and Cobbs, P.M. (1969) *Black Rage*, Johnathan Cape, London

Hart, R. (1980) *Slaves who Abolished Slavery, Vol. 1, Blacks in Bondage*, p. 107, Institute of Social and Economic Research, University of West Indies, Jamaica

Hendin, H. (1969) *Black Suicide*, Allen Lane, London

Herskovits, M.J. (1969) 'Freudian Mechanisms in Primitive Negro Psychology', in S. Herskovits (ed.), *The New World Negro*, pp. 135–44, Minerva Press, New York

Herskovits, M.J. (1971) *Life in a Haitian Valley*, Anchor Books/Doubleday, New York

Horney, K. (1960) '[Culture and Aggression] Einige Gedanken und Bedenken zu Freud'd Todestrieb und Destruktionstrieb', *American Journal of Psychoanalysis, 20*, 130–8

Humphrey, D. (1972) *Police Power and Black People*, Panther, London

Jaspers, K. (1963) *General Psychopathology*, pp. 16–22, Manchester University Press, Manchester

Klein, M. (1975) *Envy and Gratitude*, Hogarth Press, London

Littlewood, R. and Lipsedge, M. (1982) *Aliens and Alienists, Ethnic Minorites and Psychiatry*, Penguin, London

McCord, W., McCord, J. and Howard, A. (1960) 'Early Familial Experiences and Bigotry', *American Sociological Review, 25*, 717–22

McKay, C. (1968) *Harlem: Negro Metropolis*, Harcourt Brace Jovanovich, New York

Mahy, G.E. (1973) 'The Psychotic West Indian Returning from Britain', *West Indian Medical Journal, 22*, 189–90

Mannoni, O. (1964) *Prospero and Caliban. The Psychology of Colonisation*, 18, 142, Praeger, New York

Mercer, K. (1984) 'Black Communities' Experience of Psychiatric Services', *International Journal of Social Psychiatry, 30* (1 & 2), 22–7

Moinat, S.M., Raine, W.J., Burbeck, S.L. and Davison, K.K. (1972) 'Black Ghetto Residents as Rioters', *Journal of Social Issues, 28*, 45–62

Pillay, H.M. (1984) 'The Concepts, "Causation", "Racism" and "Mental Illness" ', *International Journal of Social Psychiatry, 30* (1 & 2), 29–39

Pfister-Ammende, M. (1955) 'The Symptomatology, Treatment and Prognosis in Mentally Ill Refugees and Repatriates in Switzerland', in *Flight and Resettlement*, H.B.M. Murphy (ed.), pp. 147–72, UNESCO, Paris and Geneva

Prange, A.J.Jr (1958) 'An Interpretation of Cultural Isolation and Alien's Paranoid Reaction', *International Journal of Social Psychology, 4*, 254–63

Small, J.W. (1984) 'The Crisis in Adoption', *International Journal of Social Psychiatry,*

30, (1 & 2), 129–34

Stone, M. (1981) *The Education of the Black Child in Britain*, Fontana, London

Tolsma, F.J. (1971) 'Acute Psychosis in Foreign Labourers in the Netherlands', Paper given at Post-graduate Course, June–July, Curaçao

Walvin, J. (1973) *Black and White. The Negro and English Society 1555–1945*, pp. 72 and 202, Allen Lane, London

Williams, E. (1973) *From Columbus to Castro: the History of the Caribbean 1492–1969*, Andre Deutsch, London

10 IDEOLOGY AND POLITICS IN TRANSCULTURAL PSYCHIATRY

S. P. Sashidharan

the triumphant communiqués from the mission are in fact a source
of information concerning the implantation of foreign influences in
the core of the colonized people . . . The Church in the colonies is
the white people's Church, the foreigner's Church. She does not call
the native to God's ways but to the ways of the white man, of the
master, of the oppressor . . . (Fanon, 1961)

This chapter deals with some fundamental issues in transcultural
psychiatry.[1] These are to do with the definition of the subject, its uses
or functions, and its rapid growth as a specialty within psychiatry. In
dealing with these issues, this chapter assumes a critical position in relation to much of what is generally considered to fall within the concerns
of transcultural psychiatry.

Very few people have attempted to define or specify what transcultural
psychiatry is about. Although there is some agreement on what the subject matter of transcultural psychiatry should be, the boundaries that exist,
which demarcate transcultural psychiatry from psychiatry in general, are
often vaguely drawn and cover a variety of terrains. Although
transcultural psychiatry is not clearly distinguished on the basis of its
subject matter or its methods, most professionals involved in this area
share certain preoccupations about the object of their study. That it has
something to do with 'cultural differences' in relation to psychiatry is
perhaps the most influential of such notions. From this point of view
it is often argued that transcultural psychiatry will inform us of the
pathoplastic effects of culture on mental illness, and from such a basis
we would even understand the aetiological nature of such conditions.
This approach is perhaps not all that dissimilar from other social or
epidemiological enquiries in relation to health and ill-health but it often
evokes larger social structures like 'culture' to explain differences and
similarities that exist between peoples or their experiences. Thus the concept of 'culture' is at the heart of this line of enquiry, although there
is no theoretical model that links this, specifically and directly, with the
dependent variable; furthermore, the delineation of transcultural

158

psychiatry from social or epidemiological psychiatry or anthropology is often vague and imprecise. In fact, attempts at specifying what is meant by transcultural psychiatry, while emphasising the central importance of culture, do not proceed beyond looking at definitions of culture to definitions of this special area of study.

It is, however, not just a problem of definition. There is a more important issue that is obscured by the semantic argument. This has to do with the ethnocentric and Eurocentric bias that has been built into transcultural psychiatry, and in such a context, words like 'culture' or 'ethnicity' take on a special, politically loaded meaning. From being mere concepts in the limited setting of a specialist theory or professional practice, their apparent neutrality of meaning becomes instrumental in signifying ideologies, preferences or norms which are subsequently imposed at all levels of understanding within this area. Invested with a new meaning these mere words or concepts suddenly become powerful tools with which the transcultural psychiatrist sets out to particularise social structures which are products of historical and political struggles. As a result, culture or aspects of people's lives and experience are reduced to mere but manageable problems falling within the clinical or professional competence of the culturally informed practitioner.

At its simplest and perhaps the most obvious level, transcultural psychiatry can be seen as something to do with white psychiatrists or mental health professionals and black patients or clients. Chakraborty (1974), for example, has drawn attention to the built-in ethnocentrism of the transcultural approach. Her observations would suggest that the effects of child-rearing on adult personality are considered as legitimately falling within the remit of transcultural psychiatry if it happened in Calcutta but not in Glasgow. Today, however, the boundaries of transcultural psychiatry are no longer congruent with geographical boundaries between countries but follow the divisions of race or ethnicity. Child-rearing practices in Glasgow or Bradford are legitimate transcultural concerns, but *only* among the Mirpuris, the Sikhs or the Afro-Caribbeans living in those cities. Such a demarcation of an area of study or clinical practice based on a common idea about race or ethnicity also transcends other divisions across class or gender. Since transcultural psychiatry has no special methods or a specified subject matter that distinguishes it from psychiatry in general, it must be the only specialty where the skin colour of the subject becomes its defining characteristic. Furthermore, it is the race or ethnicity of the practitioner/researcher that legitimises this demarcation: transculturalism is not just about black clients. Without its white practitioners it would have no reason to survive and no vested interest or political energy to sustain it. As there can be no servants if there are no masters, the survival of transcultural psychiatry is solely dependent on the interests of those who espouse its cause, and until recently such interests have coincided with those of the liberal traditions of Western medicine. The reification of culture and the investment of a new meaning to it and the adaptation of such a concept to a black-white paradigm have only recreated within psychiatry the larger, more general divisions that exist within our societies. What must be emphasised here, and used as a basis of relevant analysis, is the ethnocentric bias of psychiatry as such (or of much anthropology or sociology for that matter) and how psychiatric theories, like most scientific and humanistic theories, have played their part in reinforcing prevailing notions about race, culture and illness.

In the Whiggish history of psychiatry the emergence of transcultural psychiatry is usually seen as a scientific development consistent with the need for more information on various aspects and manifestations of mental disorders upon which new scientific theories could be built or old ones tested. However, a critical scrutiny of the historical antecedents of transcultural psychiatry will appraise us of the social and political context within which such a need was articulated, and of how economic and political considerations demanded that 'scientific activity' should include assiduous comparisons of Europeans with non-Europeans.[2] The emergence of this kind of scientific activity within psychiatry was not dissimilar to the evolution and the establishment of modern medicine within industrialised, capitalistic societies as part of a process that justified the detachment of the process of production and the individual involvement in it from the human consequences of labour exploitation.[3] Such a splitting could only be legitimised and made acceptable by the scientific explanations provided by medicine. The success of this approach was dependent on medicine providing a combination of naturalistic and individualistic theories of illness causation which concealed the social determinants of ill-health. The subsequent emergence of social medicine, which linked social conditions with ill health and thus implicitly argued for social reforms, although radical in its intentions, did not ever assume the revolutionary impact because of its transformation to a kind of turgid environmentalism. Social factors were thus abstracted and set aside from their social context and were reified as factors which were considered as somehow existing by themselves. Like diseases 'caused' by 'miasma' or 'germs' that could be treated, social diseases were the products of the social conditions that could be managed. The sole responsibility of acquiring such diseases, however, rested with the individuals suffering from them, and this abrogation of other influences was achieved by those in whom the responsibility for treating, studying and defining ill health was vested, namely the physicians (Stark, 1982).

The ascendancy of such a formulation about health and ill health found a ready echo in the study of mental illnesses as well. Scull (1982) has described the struggle of the alienists in the latter part of the nineteenth century to capture the domain of mental suffering and madness as a separate branch of specialisation and locate it within the burgeoning discipline of medicine. This proved to be a successful approach partly because the ideology of physical medicine was applied with great vigour and enthusiasm to the study and management of mental illnesses by those designated to run the asylums and other mental institutions. Their success was also due to the spectacular advances that were being made in the understanding of infectious diseases, although psychiatry was trailing in the wake of such medical 'breakthroughs'. Subsequently a variety of ideas, emanating from sociology to psychology, were adopted by psychiatrists, but the basic medical paradigm on which theories of ill-health were being formulated remained the same and continued to be defended with increasing vigour. The emergence of a sociology of medicine shows this amalgamation of novel, socially informed theories with the individualistic and naturalistic model of medicine. For example, in the field of psychiatry, an influential idea towards the end of the last century was the super-organic theory of culture as put forward by the French sociologist, Emil Durkheim. This suggested an association between societal factors or social structures and deviant behaviour. Subsequently, however, 'cultural' factors which Durkheim had used in a very limited sense came to account for a variety of economic, political and physical environmental factors, and a package of 'social pressures' was formulated, which was readily fitted into a simple linear relationship of 'things' causing disease in individuals. It has been argued that the departure from Durkheim's original theory was in ignoring his exposition of 'social malaise' resulting from the decline and disintegration of traditional society and supplanting it with a model that invoked 'individual distress' as the relevant consequence of experiencing certain social pressures (and the legitimate concern of medicine). Thus the relationship between societal factors and social malaise was restated as that between social pathology (like an infectious agent) causing distress and disease in individuals exposed or vulnerable to it. The level of understanding and explanation was thus shifted from the society at large to the individual in particular. As a result, socialisation of illness was achieved not as a refutation but as confirmation of individualisation of illness. Such reification of social factors which in turn suggests the possibility of intervention at the individual level at the expense of social or political action is a predominant theme among the environmentalist school of psychiatrists. The recoding of social reality in factors or 'things' like sex, social class and culture, and thus rendering them quantifiable or measurable as variables, abstracts them from the social relations or struggles in a larger context and minimises the possibility of abolishing the abnormal conditions, the task set aside for social medicine by the nineteenth-century radicals such as Rudolf Virchow. Transcultural psychiatry, similarly, succeeds in deconstructing and depoliticising culture in relation to mental illness and a new 'scientific' discipline is born. Cultural reductionism is the most important theoretical theme in this area. Culture, in a detached and reified manner, is the crucial mediating and explanatory variable in relation to the pathology that interests the transcultural psychiatrists. In the best traditions of social medicine, culture is easily and 'scientifically' invoked and the genesis and manifestations of clinical syndromes are conveniently located within it.

If it was a bourgeois ideology, emerging in a historically specific context and as a product of capitalism in Western Europe, that helped to refine and reinforce the premises of much of modern medicine and scientific psychiatry, it required another context, again determined by the political and economic priorities of the time, to detach cultural psychiatry from, say, social psychiatry and give the area a new meaning and a new purpose. The advancement and appeal of transcultural psychiatry owed a great deal to colonialism and scientific racism.

One important strand in the evolution of transcultural studies in psychiatry is the contribution of what has come to be known as 'comparative psychiatry'. Comparative psychiatry means the study of the relations between mental disorder and the psychological characteristics that differentiate nations, peoples or cultures (Murphy, 1982). Leaving aside the untested assumptions behind such a definition (e.g. certain psychological characteristics are inherent in certain cultures or that there could be a discontinuity in the distribution of certain psychological features across geographical or cultural boundaries), one could look at the need for such studies and how this type of comparison between nations and cultures differs from (and in many ways is set aside from) comparisons in, say, epidemiology.

Comparisons of disease rates (or its consequences) and certain kinds of behaviour (like smoking), living conditions, environmental differences, etc. across time, place and person are the essence of much of epidemiology. Within the available model of medicine such an approach is a useful way of elucidating the relationship between illnesses and conditions/agents that might be associated with its causation, maintenance or remission. Although the concepts and methods employed in this area were gradually refined over three centuries, one can trace the beginnings of such comparisons to the mid-seventeenth century with John Graunt's painstakingly detailed observations on the weekly bills of mortality returned by the parishes of London (Susser, 1973). As Murphy points out (1982), even in psychiatry, similar methods had been employed regularly before the advent of comparative psychiatry as a specifically designated area of study. In Western Europe, psychiatrists like Pinel, Morel and Bingham were interested in studying variations of psychopathology in foreign patients. Differences between Western European and Latin peoples were being articulated in terms of 'decadence and degeneracy'. But it was the advent of 'civilisation theory' which understood psychopathology as somehow causally related to 'civilisation' that gave a theoretical edge to comparative psychiatry which was subsequently used to cut itself free from other types of comparisons hitherto undertaken in studying mental illnesses.

The emergence of these ideas took place in a background of major political and economic upheavals in Europe. Theories about racial superiority were being articulated with increasing vigour by philosophers, political thinkers and scientists at this time, and the Franco-Prussian wars had fuelled the need for chauvinistic and nationalistic ideals. European colonisation of Africa was also gathering momentum, and the political and economic oppression of black people and their countries was being justified not just in political but also in scientific terms. Medicine or psychiatry reflected such tensions as existed in the political and military fields, although scientists and clinicians, themselves the products of an increasingly capitalistic society heady with nascent imperialism, took great pains to set up their ideas and observations under the cloak of scientific neutrality. Although the early work and intentions of these scientists could be seen as radical in that they were putting forward a materialistic and reductionistic ideology to challenge orthodox religion and superstition and in that they were instrumental in questioning the philosophical basis of inequality conceived as somehow preordained, (Rose *et al.*, 1984), they were at the same time legitimising bourgeois society that was in turn creating novel forms of exploitation including that of people from outside Western Europe for sustaining the growth of capitalism. The great ideological battle in the nineteenth century was to replace an outdated and 'non-scientific' view of the world with

'evidence' and theories derived from experimentation and ritual observations coded in essentially reductionistic and individualistic science.[4]
What emerged out of it was a bourgeois ideology which was, in its turn,
ruthlessly used to construct newer levels of oppression and exploitation.
It is the link between science (here clinical medicine or psychiatry as
a form of human activity) and the particular characteristics of the society
within which it is produced that is crucial to our understanding of how
'scientific' or 'medical' advancement takes place (Rose *et al.*, 1984).

It was, however, Emil Kraepelin, the famous German psychiatrist,
who first used the term 'comparative psychiatry' with the particular meaning it has today, i.e. systematic comparisons between Europeans and
non-Europeans. Kraepelin was an ardent advocate of scientific psychiatry,
and much of our current theories on psychiatric nosology and psychopathology owe a great deal to him. At the turn of the century the esteemed
professor, already renowned as the father of scientific psychiatry, undertook a long and somewhat arduous journey to the Far East, mainly to
Singapore and Java. His impressions (for they were nothing more than
that, given the short time he spent in Java) were subsequently elevated
to the level of clinical or scientific wisdom, although Kraepelin's own
interpretation of his findings were as a corollary or confirmation of his
painstakingly detailed descriptions of psychopathology among the
Volksart of urban Germany. However, much was made of his 'dispassion-
ate interest in facts for their own sake' and he, more than anyone else,
was seen as making it possible to carry out 'scientific' studies in this
area. Referring to Kraepelin's 'data' (collected by a European psychiatrist
who was visiting the mental asylums in the Far East and examining, ob-
serving, and presumably listening to and questioning the natives through
expatriate Europeans), Murphy (1982) noted that 'handled correctly, they
were quite legitimate grounds for carrying out comparative studies . . .'.

What is quite forgotten in the discussion of the emergence of new
ideas in medicine, or for that matter science in general, is the context,
both historical and political, within which such ideas are fashioned. It
is informative to seek some explanations for the emergence of Kraepeli-
nian comparative psychiatry at the time it did, and for its ready acceptance as a legitimate and fruitful area of enquiry. Towards the latter half
of the nineteenth century the Anglo-French domination of medical
psychology was being successfully challenged by the vigourous establishment of German medicine, rejuvenated by the Prussian victory over
France. Allied to the materialistic and individualistic notions of medicine
which helped to conceal and manage the social determinants of ill health,
psychiatry was also fashioning the ideology of hereditarian inequality

among people. Morel's idea of hereditarian degeneracy or decadence as a foundation for psychiatry was echoed in Cesare Lambroso's influential theories about criminality as a product of inherent, biological deficits based on his speculations on the inmates of prisons and asylums in Pavia. The dominance of concepts and ideas in science is such that they are often more crucial than facts or observations in determining modes of thought or choice of scientific enquiry (Susser, 1973). Towards the end of the century many of those ideas about the hereditarian basis of insanity (if not much of human behaviour) and the supremacy of one race over the other were not only finding ready echoes in the political thinking prevailing at that time but also were consonant with the ideology of a reductionist science. Thus going back to Kraepelin and his 'observations' in Java one can see the emergence of a certain kind of meaning that went beyond mere facts, which was not only consistent with the idea of a scientifically descriptive clinical psychiatry but which also echoed prevailing notions about mental illness, its causation and the 'natives of Java'. In his article on the patterns of mental disorder (note that Kraepelin's interest here was in describing variation in mental illness as a whole and thus making it accessible to further scientific scrutiny, and not in mental illness among the Javanese as such), he wrote:

Almost entirely uninvestigated to date is the relationship between race and the form madness takes, although such investigation would surely be a valuable source of information. Of course, it has often been said that Jews, in particular those from Eastern Europe, tend to display 'degenerate' and hysterical symptoms which are at variance with the usual clinical picture of the illness but a more exact demonstration of this peculiarity does not yet seem to be possible. It is however correct to say that there are differences in the behaviour pattern of mentally ill patients from different countries and races, but there is a dearth of research in this area which however is very difficult given the differing compositions of mental asylum populations.

We do know something about unusual forms of disease that have been observed here and there, and that most are classified as hysterical — but we know nothing about the connection between such symptoms and the psychological characteristics of the race involved. My experience in Java showed me that the study of comparative psychiatry can lead to important results. I was struck by the fact that in the native population, melancholia did not seem to exist at all, whereas manic states were by no means infrequent. This is in accordance with the observation that suicide in these patients is almost unknown.

Understandably one does not find delusions of guilt, as they of course, are rooted in our religious ideas; in fact I could find no emotion that could correspond to our pronounced guilt feelings or sense of responsibility. The most commonly occuring disease, namely dementia praecox, appears to manifest itself primarily as a confused, excited state, whereas the negativistic stupor that we see so often was scarcely found at all. Auditory hallucinations were low in evidence, perhaps on account of the smaller role that language plays in thinking among these patients. Delusions too were fewer and scantier in content, probably because the need to think deeply about one's life experience is low (Kraepelin, 1904).

In an earlier paper he had of course set out his observations in a more limited perspective — that of a curious investigator describing what he encountered in the Buitenzorg asylum in Java — and he was particularly at pains to emphasise the differences in frequency of clinical states between European and non-European patients. But it was not the data or the facts that formed the cornerstone of comparative psychiatry (or transcultural psychiatry) but the explanations largely unsubstantiated, and often no more than mere assertions that in the end became the sole concern of this new discipline. Comparisons of disease frequency or its association with other factors became of secondary importance, and what Kraepelin had offered as speculative explanations became the organising principles of comparative psychiatry. The professor himself had a singular vision and was clearly articulating the pervasive notions about non-European cultures that prevailed in his day when he wrote about 'racial characteristics' (lack of responsibility, linguistic poverty, the absence of deep self-reflection, etc.). For the scientific investigator the questions were straightforward and simple. For example, 'if racial characteristics are reflected in a nation's religion and its customs, in its spiritual and artistic achievements, in its political activity and historical development, they must also find expression in the frequency and clinical forms of its mental disorders, especially those which have no external cause' (Kraepelin, 1921). It was these racial characteristics, viewed exclusively from a Christian, European tradition, that subsequently excited the interest of transcultural psychiatry. Connections or comparisons between races or cultures when they were made were not of 'facts' or other empirical observations but of politically loaded notions about psychological and social characteristics. Again, to quote Kraepelin from his book, *Manic Depressive Insanity and Paranoia*, one can see the emergence of this particular kind of explanation. Discussing the form manic depressive insanity took, he called upon his observations among the natives of Java (Kraepelin, 1921a).

> These observations confirm the view, that for the form of the clinical picture, which our morbid process produces, the idiosyncrasy of the psychic personality in question is of great importance. A comparison might be made between the behaviour of the Javanese patients and that of our youthful patients, a *psychically undeveloped* population with the *immature* European youth.

What is not in doubt here is that the professor was drawing upon common notions of racial superiority and was in turn giving legitimacy to it. The doubts creep in only when we begin to ask how much of it was based on 'data' or 'impartial observations' that provided the grist to the scientific mill. Later, in discussing the causes of paranoia (Kraepelin, 1921b) a similar concept of psychic undevelopment is invoked again, not only to describe the psychopathology of insanity but to equate it with certain 'cultural and racial characteristics'. He wrote:

> if one will, one might say that the world of ideas of a savage, who sees himself surrounded by demons who lie in wait for him everywhere, and perceives innumerable signs protending disaster or good fortune, or of a medicine man who has at his command the magic powers of the fetish and produces supernatural powers by his incantations, does not fundamentally differ very much from paranoiac delusional systems. Only in the former cases it concerns stages of general culture, in the latter purely personal morbid development.

Kraepelin himself had no doubts about the usefulness of such studies, although the methodological pitfalls of scientific investigation into this question must have been obvious to him. But what was being fashioned by comparative psychiatry was a new area of investigation, not based on novel methods or a new theory but the delineation of a new line of enquiry which would (at least for Kraepelin) contribute to the growth of scientific psychiatry. This 'master builder' of psychiatry in his commitment to collect all available material to erect his edifice, to establish beyond doubt the somatic basis of mental disorder, was also making a major contribution to the evolution of scientific medicine based on naturalistic and individualist theories of illness causation. Comparative psychiatry for him was only part of the more important task of establishing psychiatry as a 'particularly developed branch of neuropathology'. Kraepelin's notion of 'comparative psychiatry', however, became detached from mainstream psychiatry over the next few decades and gradually reorientated itself around emerging ideas from anthropology and psychoanalysis.

The subsequent evolution of transcultural psychiatry was heavily influenced, if not made possible, by the emergence of psychoanalytic theory with its universal principles and the newly fledged 'science' of anthropology and its humanistic speculations. The concepts of the unconscious and its mechanisms, the primitive, malevolent and destructive forces which were equated with the way 'primitive people' actually thought and behaved and how the minds of the child, the neurotic and that of the 'primitive people' were at parallel stages of development, were, in a limited sense, reiteration of common notions about non-European people that were embedded in the cultural history of nineteenth-century Europe. Freud's serious attempts to incorporate anthropological speculations to substantiate his own theories, although challenged by some workers in the area, were further evidence of the scientific confirmation of such common themes, and these offered a theory on the basis of which 'primitive societies' were to be understood. The availability of another scientific paradigm, fashioned by anthropology with its exclusive interest in non-white and non-European populations and societies, was also instrumental in supplanting biological notions of race with a kind of cultural determinism, which was, however, equally reductionistic in its approach. This again located 'culture' or 'beliefs' as acting primarily through individual lives. Although the cultural relativism advocated by the early anthropologists was an attempt to get away from the normative and ethnocentric notions of the time, this new discipline in its turn was legitimating the study of 'primitive' people as a science. Thus such observations as made by the European and North American anthropologists were fragmented and distorted through the methods and theories which were in turn informed and influenced by their own professional background and historical context. It would be naive to suppose that the observations and interpretations brought back to Europe by the indefatigable investigators were 'value-free' in any sense, but the overriding question posed by such investigations was the legitimacy and relevance of this new science to the subjects under scrutiny. Another aspect of the predominance of a scientific or professional approach in understanding 'culture' in a political and economic vacuum was the tendency for such an approach to recreate itself by its own efforts. Vine Deloria (1970) in his book *Custer Died for your Sins* was berating social scientists for carrying out research that bore no relation to potential service. He wrote:

Anthropologists come out to Indian reservations to make observations. During the winter, these observations will become books by which future anthropologists will be trained so that they can come out to reservations years from now and verify the observations they have studied.

It was a measure of the scientific acceptance of anthropological observations that such questions were rarely raised, and these new facts, while questioning the universality of Western psychiatric (and in particular psychoanalytic) theories, posited in its place a new way of understanding or a kind of differentiation of the people and their 'culture'. This form of cultural pluralism further reinforced the relevance of anthropology while dissociating the science of anthropology from the political context within which it had developed.

The end of the nineteenth and the advent of the twentieth century saw not only the flowering of psychoanalytic theory and the increasing maturity of anthropology but also the subjugation and colonisation of black people in most of Asia and Africa by European nations. The white man's burden was not only to rule and 'civilise' but also to study and understand 'the natives'. Foreigners were not only different in their religion and their biology but also in their culture and their 'ethos'. Like the colonial invaders who wanted the people's land and their labour, the anthropologists and other 'ethnoscientists' arrived, unannounced and uninvited, to seek, study and 'understand' their culture. The pursuit of this knowledge was unrelenting and unchecked.[5]

Another significant development that occurred at this time in relation to the study of mental illness was the 'cultural debut' of the mental hygiene movement. Aided by the interpretations of psychoanalytic theory, the mental helath movement placed itself in a powerful position to incorporate all aspects of life within its 'relevant' subject matter, and the ideology that followed from it was to give priority and legitimacy to the psychiatric profession to pass 'scientific' judgement on whole areas of private and public life (Kovel, 1981). Dragged out of the 'organic doldrums' of the nineteenth century, psychiatric theory brought itself to bear upon ever-expanding and increasingly ill-defined areas of human activity. Comparative psychiatry, as seen by Kraepelin, was no longer concerned with variations in the manifestation of mental illness alone but took as part of its area of expertise the need and the legitimacy of 'culture', or ways of life reified as 'upbringing', 'family', 'childhood', 'adolescence', etc. This was, in many ways, a redefinition of 'the characteristics' (the racial characteristics referred to by Kraepelin, for example) that determined the production of illness. Although such characteristics were couched as 'mere descriptions', they clearly implied a kind of measurement against normative standards and were assumed to be contributing, in a causally significant way, to the genesis of mental illness. But it implied more than that. These aspects of life, of human activity/consciousness, were legitimate areas for investigation *in their own right*. The publicly declared justification for studying 'characteristics' as having some relationship to illness/distress which fell within the expertise of physicians and psychiatrists, was no longer necessary. Culture became the object of the study, and the emphasis in transcultural psychiatry became less about psychiatry and more about culture. As the organising principle in this area was increasingly specified as culture, it was invested with a meaning and direction that was specifically to do with 'their' (i.e. non-European) culture. As Haldipur (1980) points out, all that merits the appellation 'culture' in this context is abroad. Not that 'culture' is not deemed to be a useful variable in the study of mental illness as such: the so-called cultural factors or social factors are much emphasised in the environmentalist school of psychiatry, are incorporated in many of its theories and are subsumed in the mainstream of much of psychiatric thought and practice. But when 'culture' is signified in a reified and conditional manner, as in transcultural psychiatry, it means culture that is non-European or that of non-white people.

Science, especially a humanistic science, in its evolution and practice embodies a number of ideologies. As a form of human activity it reflects dominant ideologies in a way that is at the same time concealed and effective.[6] The purpose of scientific activity is detached from the direction of the ideology it embodies but it sustains the hegemony of the latter by constantly confirming it through 'the evidence', the 'facts' and a selective yet convincing view of reality (Rose *et al.*, 1984). As the biblical and ideological notions about inequality were being challenged with increasing vigour, it was necessary to seek out and substantiate other notions of human diversity that seemed to justify the more obvious political and economic inequality. The social and humanistic sciences were evolving rapidly at the same time as the entrenchment of capitalism and the emergence of colonialism, to provide new evidence and novel theories of scientific explanations. Such developments in the field of medicine and psychiatry were consistent with the colonialistic view of the world, and even found support among the increasingly powerful liberal circles among the colonisers. Carother's ethnopsychiatric studies in Africa (see for example, Carothers 1953, 1972) so extensively quoted in most accounts of transcultural psychiatry, although they were nothing more than reiterations of crude stereotypes, somehow signalled the need for a new kind of Fabian colonialsim.[7] This kind of academic racism not only achieved a limited and biased description of black people, but also provided a basis, a theory for intervention and action.[8]

Over the last few decades there have been major changes in transcultural psychiatry, at least as it is conceptualised and practised in the UK. With the liberation of the colonies, ethno-psychiatry has changed its preoccupations completely.[9]

In many ways, the concerns of transcultural psychiatry have changed over the last two or three decades. Although there is still a lingering fascination with exotic cultures in certain quarters, the heady days of grand explanations which invoked crude cultural stereotypes in relation to psychopathology appear to be over. There is now a renewed interest in the application of relevant epidemiological methods in the comparative study of mental disorders across national boundaries, and a more sober appraisal of the demonstrated differences and similarities in disease rates or illness presentation. The enthusiasm for seeking simplistic cultural explanations also appears to be waning. Through the work of a new generation of anthropologists/psychiatrists, Western biomedicine and its cultural embedding are beginning to be examined with critical vigour. Much of the ethnographic material in relation to psychopathology is being more formally examined, often drawing upon theories that go beyond merely functional explanations. However, as the study of the relationship between culture and psychopathology is thus increasingly adopted by the mainstream disciplines of anthropology and sociology as areas of legitimate enquiry (and not being set aside as exotic sub-specialities), the nineteenth-century model of cultural psychiatry with its reductionistic themes is making a comeback in a different context. In many ways this renaissance in cultural psychiatry has coincided with the end of the Empire and the arrival of a visible black minority in Western European countries. Ideas and strategies fashioned abroad by the assiduous study of colonised people are being reformulated and applied by professional psychiatrists and fellow mental health professionals in the context of responding to 'ethnic minority health problems in Europe'. The language and the approach of this new transcultural psychiatry may look different but the underlying assumptions and the professional intentions are the same as those that seduced the academic colonialists to seek scientific explanations at the outposts of the Empire at the turn of the century. With the liberation of much of Asia and Africa from colonial rule in the 1950s and 1960s, colonial psychiatry had been in the retreat for a few decades, but since the early 1970s we are again witnessing the emergence of a kind of medicine (and psychiatry) that embodies certain pernicious notions about black people and their lives and struggles. In the United Kingdom (and to a lesser extent in the rest of Western Europe), there has been a resurgence of interest in this whole area of health care of 'ethnic minorities', and perhaps not for the first time in recent history we are witnessing the harnessing of genuine professional concerns to a general political strategy. The 'coming of age' of transcultural psychiatry must be seen and understood against this background.

It was the arrival of increasing numbers of black people in European countries and the artificially constructed need for 'immigration control' that provided medicine and psychiatry with a new political role. Although the application of certain arbitrary 'healthy standards' of behaviour to potential immigrants was started by Dr Salmon of the US Public Health Service Department as far back as 1904, the mental health of immigrants became a political issue only after successive governments enacted racist immigration control to limit the number of black people arriving in the UK.[10] The laws that kept black people out of this country (even in spite of the fact that they had a legitimate right to come here) were a further affirmation of the undesirability of a black presence as articulated by politicians and echoed by many academics. However, it was the evolution of state racism over the last twenty years, shifting the focus of control of black people from limiting their entry to internal control and repression (culminating in the Nationality Act of 1981) that has allowed psychiatry and other welfare agencies to play their subtle yet crucial part in fashioning a new kind of academic racism (Black Health Workers and Patients Group, 1983).

It was the notion of black culture defined 'not as an organic aspect of the ongoing struggles of black people, but as something static and definable, providing easy, stereotyped formulae that the State could draw on for its strategies of control and pacification, coercion and consent' (BHWPG, 1983) that provided the basis for the resurgence of the transcultural approach in psychiatry. Once again, the political determinants of the growth of this home-brewed variety of transculturalism are clearly visible. The view that black people are a problem in a white society or that they have problems (because of their culture if not their biology) and thus demand a strategy and a corrective approach (firstly to protect the normative standards of the white society and then for their own sake) found much support in liberal professional circles. The deviance of Blacks or their culture could be articulated in depoliticised professional jargon that helped to sustain prevailing notions about the undesirability of a black presence in a white society and worked towards establishing a new kind of alliance between state powers, welfare, and law and order. Psychiatry in the form of transculturalism has proved to be a useful professional ally in providing new descriptions and explanations which have given a spurious scientific credibility to this racist ideology. The coercive powers invested in psychiatry and the profession's public role in setting arbitrary standards of normative behaviour and social functioning were instrumental in giving legitimacy to the transcultural approach. The liberal ethos embodied in the humanistic traditions of psychiatry offered a convenient framework within which the 'black problems' could be interpreted and professionalised. After all, black people in a racist society suffered great hardship and multiple deprivations, and evidence of their increased risk of psychiatric breakdown was beginning to be documented and discussed.[11] The much-discredited theories of genetic inferiority could not be invoked without risking the opprobrium of the liberal, humanistic cadres of modern practitioners. Hence, like the culture-of-poverty school of thought fashionable in sociology at one time, the inequalities and the patterns of deviance in ethnic minorities were understood as being propagated by purely cultural connections. This not only offered a scientifically legitimate explanation but further helped to locate the *cause* of the deviance within the individual or rather the package of culture in which he or she was partaking in a passive, static way. Out of this line of thinking arose the idea (again perceived and articulated by the professionals) of ethnic minority's special needs exclusively coded in and limited to their cultural background. Such objectification of black culture (or its further differentiation and segregation into Bengali, Muslim or Rasta cultures) and the reification of their lifestyles led to the emergence of a new cadre of transculturalists in education, psychiatry, social work and other related professions, who were fitted in the existing apparatus of state welfare as 'ethnic experts' and who argued the case for some kind of multiculturalism. Culture, defined in this simplistic and manageable way, not only was the most important explanatory variable in understanding black deviance (or psychopathology) but also helped to create a novel basis for defining normative standards and further marginalised the structural and political dimensions of inequalities in a racist society. The problems 'caused' by their culture could be in terms either of their illness (over-representation of black patients in psychiatric hospital, for example) or of diagnostic errors made by the clinician not acquainted with the pathoplastic effects of culture on illness.[12] All this provided transcultural psychiatry with a whole new area in which it could legitimise racist assumptions and impose strategies of therapeutic intervention. The professional interests in such an approach are obvious. Faced with a limited view or a selective understanding of how individual lives are inextricably linked to larger social structures the professional adopts the position that she/he is doing the best she/he could do. But underlying this professional enthusiasm is the anxiety that if technical solutions are not available or seen to be inadequate the very basis of professional competence or credibility could be at risk. However, a more powerful influence in this kind of amalgamation of partial intervention and professional tunnel-vision is the political basis of the professional ideology. Psychiatry, through transculturalism, is thus in one sense creating and responding to the problem of black deviance and in a more general way that of black people by adopting a strategy consistent with a general, more political, view of racial inequality. The determinants of much disadvantage and discrimination are conveniently ruled out of court by the adoption of this cultural strait-jacket. It is easier to respond to black people and their mental health by defining them (or their culture) as problem areas, and therefore requiring specialist, professional response. The advent of transculturalism has, as a result, provided a safe and easy opportunity for mental health professionals to conceptualise and deal with major social and political issues like institutional racism and inequality in supposedly neutral terms. The transcultural approach emphasises the cultural dependence of clinical problems (of genesis, presentation and management of mental ill-health among blacks) and by doing so the political and structural dimensions of contemporary racism are ignored and the model for welfare/treatment provisions is isolated from the day to day struggles of black people in this country.

There is no doubt that transcultural psychiatry raises important issues. But this importance does not refer to the possible solutions which this type of enquiry could provide for the mental health difficulties and disadvantages experienced by cultural or racial minorities in the West or in its declared commitment to elucidating the causation and manifestations of psychological disturbance through comparative studies. The significance of transcultural psychiatry should be in terms of understanding the political process of harnessing science or medicine to a repressive ideology and the responsibility of black people, professionals and non-professionals alike, in challenging its underlying assumptions and laying the framework for the emergence of a truly anti-racist psychiatry.

Notes

1. Also called ethnopsychiatry, cross-cultural psychiatry, comparative psychiatry, etc. The differences between these are often vague or even non-existent and there has been no attempt to specify what is meant by each term. For present purposes they are all seen as referring to the same area of professional activity.

2. For detailed accounts of how psychiatric theories and practice were influenced by racism see Thomas and Sillen (1972).

3. I variously draw upon the analysis put forward from the schools of radical health criticism (Ehrenreich, 1978) and the more orthodox Marxist approach, for example Stark (1982), in developing the arguments in relation to psychiatry. Such an analysis is argued from a poltically informed perspective and has been developed elegantly by a number of writers in relation to medicine in general. See, for example, Navarro (1976), Figlio (1977), Waitzkin (1978), and Doyal and Pennell (1979). The study of the historical context of the emergence of modern medicine is equally applicable to psychiatry. Its relevance is obvious given the biomedical emphasis in much of modern psychiatry.

4. For an excellent and detailed account of the emergence of science, scientific ideas and how they were influenced by social and political factors in their historical context, see Rose *et al.* (1984), especially Chapters 1 and 2.

5. See, for example, Margaret Mead's musings in 1932 (Mead, 1964), sitting on a hilltop in New Guinea, about the village which she 'did not leave for seven long months'. She was considering what to do with a huge sum of money — the possibility of 'a grant for a five-year field study to investigate the surviving, unstudied primitive cultures of the world'. She wrote, 'Here, from one standpoint, was a dream coming true; Franz Boas and Radcliffe-Brown had each made plan after plan for institutes which would undertake to explore whole regions systematically, each field worker's research dovetailed into each other's. The central responsibility of anthropologists to rescue and record and publish the information on these vanishing cultures and peoples would be discharged. But as I sat there . . . I realised sharply and acutely there were not enough of us. There were not enough anthropologists in the world to spend that money quickly, wisely and well. Either we would have to send young, untrained students into the field . . . or [we] would have to set to work with a frantic disregard of when and how anything would ever be published . . . Would it be possible to ask of disciplines . . . dealing with human behaviour — sociology, economics, psychology, political science, law — to choose one or two of their best trained and most promising students, give them extra, special training in anthropology, and then send them out, each free to follow his own special research interest but obligated also to bring back a respectable account of the whole culture?'

6. Not all that dissimilar to Marx's observation that the ruling ideas of any time are the ideas of the ruling classes. In this context, it is interesting to note that the transcultural approach, while enthusiastically embracing racist and oppressive notions about the colonised black people, has rarely concerned itself with overtly political and revolutionary position adopted by Franz Fanon, the most astute psychiatric observer of colonialism. Although Fanon's brilliant expositions of the *experience* of oppression by black people and the psychological consequences (Fanon, 1952) have found acceptance at least in certain quarters, his trenchant observations on the political aspects of psychiatry and his exhortations to psychiatrists and doctors to political commitment (Fanon, 1964) have found little space in accounts of transcultural psychiatry.

7. Carothers' 'study' was not only the first in a host of similar adventures by those indulging in 'colonial psychiatry' but also continued to hold sway in academic/governmental circles until quite recently. For an informed criticism of Carothers see Lumsden (1976).

8. The 'national character concept' served a similar function after the war in Europe (Roundtable, 1945). Partly to depoliticise aspects of the struggle against Nazism and as

a way of avoiding political conflict that was seen as inevitable, professional explanation and intervention was called for after the Second World War. American psychiatrists, psychologists and anthropologists concluded that German culture had a paranoid trend and German personality development encouraged the growth of paranoid individuals. The American psychiatrists and anthropologists even drew up a plan to transform the German culture and this was to be achieved by stressing the guilt of all Germans and by changing the family life patterns peculiar to Germany.

9. The independence of the colonies, an overtly political development, also had a dramatic effect on the substance or the evidence of scientific enquiries. Prince's study of depression in Sub-Saharan Africa (Prince, 1968) showed that all reports recorded the rarity of this condition up to 1956 but most of the subsequent studies came to the opposite conclusion. One of the explanations offered by Prince is that depression, a European disease — a manifestation of civilisation, was found with increasing frequency after 1956 because the European investigators were influenced by the fact that the first African country (Ghana) had achieved its independence in that year.

10. On average, two individuals a week are denied permission to enter the UK at the ports of entry for psychiatric reasons (Bluglass, 1985). Although no information about the ethnic status of this group is made available, the decision to bar entry is often the result of a combined decision by immigration officials and their medical staff.

11. There is conflicting and often confusing evidence in relation to the rates of mental illness among black people in the UK. From available data, all that can be said conclusively is that black people in the UK have an increased risk, when compared to native born Whites, of being admitted to psychiatric hospitals.

12. One of the tasks that colonial psychiatrists had assigned to themselves was the identification and descriptions of madness among the natives. Not unlike the 'discovery' of countries by illustrious explorers from the West, much excitement was generated within European psychiatry by the 'discovery' of newer kinds of madness. The so-called 'culture-bound syndromes' — signalling the incipient idea of culture as pathology while confirming culture-free and therefore value-free Western medical nosology — provided much scope for colonial psychiatry to set itself apart as a separate specialty. Much of the data related to these instances was speculative or based on hearsay, but the importance attached to these conditions was indicative of how certain kinds of behaviour were culturally stereotyped and even used as a way of understanding 'the culture' itself. The latter-day fetish among transcultural psychiatrists about the finer points of clinical diagnosis when faced with black patients has many parallels with the earlier preoccupation with exotic 'culture-bound' syndromes. Excursions into nosology in this context conceal and manage important issues rather than clarify concepts. For example, the profusion of diagnostic labels reserved for black clients like 'Caribbean psychosis', 'New Cross psychosis', 'Begum syndrome' not only signify the separation of clinical phenomena and their confirmation as different from other kinds of 'culture-free madness' that occur in more familiar settings but also are instrumental in focusing discusssion on culture or communication as the most significant locus of difficulties which are in turn blamed on the patients. Also there is a pernicious notion that all that we need to do is get our diagnosis right (by closer observation, better understanding of their culture, learning to speak Pushtu or Bengali, more research, etc.) and assign these disturbances among black people to some classificatory scheme; then it is suggested, the linear relationship between culture and pathology would open itself for investigation. This approach is also convenient in keeping the issues strictly 'professional' (i.e. diagnosis).

References

Black Health Workers and Patients Group (1983) 'Psychiatry and the Corporate State', *Race and Class, 25,* 49–64

Bluglass, R. (1985) 'Parliamentary News', *Bulletin of the Royal College of Psychiatrists, 9,* 116

Carothers, J.C. (1953) *The African Mind in Health and Disease. A Study in Ethno-psychiatry,* WHO Monograph Series, Geneva

Carothers, J.C. (1972) *The Mind of Man in Africa,* Stacey Press, London

Chakraborty, A. (1974) 'A Challenge to Transcultural Psychiatry. Whither Transcultural Psychiatry?', *Transcultural Psychiatry Research Review,* 102–7

Deloria, V. (Jr) (1970) *Custer Died for your Sins* Avon, New York

Doyal, L. and Pennell, I. (1979) *The Political Economy of Health,* Pluto Press, London

Ehrenreich, J. (ed.) (1978) *The Cultural Crisis of Modern Medicine,* Monthly Review Press, New York

Fanon, F. (1952) *Peau noire, masques blancs,* Editions du Seuil, Paris. Transl. Charles Lam Markmann, 1965 *Black Skin, White Masks,* Grove Press, New York

Fanon, F. (1961) *Les damnes de la terre* Maspero, Paris. Transl. Constance Farrington, 1965, *The Wretched of the Earth,* Grove Press, New York

Fanon, F. (1964) *Pour la Revolution Africaine, Ecrits politiques,* Maspero, Paris. Transl. Haakon Chevalier, 1967, *Toward the African Revolution,* Monthly Review Press, New York

Figlio, K. (1977) 'The Historiography of Scientific Medicine: an Invitation to the Human Sciences', *Comparative Studies in Society and History, 19,* 262–86

Haldipur, C.V. (1980) 'The Idea of "Cultural" Psychiatry: a Comment on the Foundations of Cultural Psychiatry', *Comprehensive Psychiatry, 21,* 206–11

Kovel, J. (1981) 'The American Mental Health Industry', in *Critical Psychiatry. The Politics of Mental Health,* D. Ingleby (ed.), Penguin, Harmondsworth

Kraepelin, E. (1904) 'Vergleichende Psychiatrie', *Zentbl. Nervenheilk Psychiat., 27,* 433–7. Translated as 'Comparative Psychiatry', in *Themes and Variations in European Psychiatry* S.R. Hirsch and M. Shepherd (eds), 1974, John Wright & Sons, Bristol

Kraepelin, E. (1921a) *Manic-depressive Insanity and Paranoia,* p. 171. Transl. R.M. Barclay and G.M. Robertson, Livingstone, Edinburgh

Kraepelin, E. (1921b) *Manic-depressive Insanity and Paranoia,* p. 261, Transl. R.M. Barclay and G.M. Robertson, Livingstone, Edinburgh

Lumsden, D.P. (1976) 'On "Transcultural Psychiatry", Africans, and Academic Racism', *American Anthropologist, 78* (1), 101–4

Mead, M. (1964) *Anthropology: a Human Science,* pp. 3–5, Van Nostrand, London

Murphy, H.B.M. (1982) *Comparative Psychiatry. The International and Intercultural Distribution of Mental Illness,* Springer, New York

Navarro, V. (1976) *Medicine under Capitalism,* Prodsit, New York

Prince, R. (1968) 'The Changing Pattern of Depressive Syndromes in Africa', *Canadian Journal of African Studies, 1,* 177–92

Rose, S., Kamin, L.J. and Lewontin, R.C. (1984) *Not in our Genes. Biology, Ideology and Human Nature,* Penguin, Harmondsworth

Roundtable, (1945) 'Germany after the War', *American Journal of Orthopsychiatry, 15,* 381–441

Scull, A.T. (1982) *Museums of Madness. The Social Organization of Insanity in Nineteenth-century England,* Penguin, Harmondsworth

Stark, E. (1982) 'What is Medicine?', *Radical Science Journal,* No. 12, 46–89

Susser, M. (1973) *Causal Thinking in the Health Sciences. Concepts and Strategies of*

Epidemiology, Oxford University Press, London

Thomas, A. and Sillen, S. (1972) *Racism and Psychiatry,* Brunner/Mazel, New York

Waitzkin, H. (1978) 'A Marxist View of Medical Care', *Annals of Internal Medicine,* 89, 264–78

11 THE MENTAL HEALTH IMPACT OF BRITISH CULTURAL TRADITIONS

H.B.M. Murphy

Introduction

Every worker in the mental health field should be trained to recognise the ways in which his own cultural upbringing is likely to have affected his perceptions of the problems which his clients bring, and to affect also the psychiatric vulnerability of those who share that cultural upbringing. At a more abstract level, moreover, there is a need for theorising and generalisations in psychiatry to take into consideration not just the possibility but the probability that the observations from which they start may have reflected, in biasing fashion, the cultural background of the investigator and his subjects. At the joint WHO/ADHAMA conference on Classification and Diagnosis in Psychiatry which took place in Copenhagen in 1982, one of the major papers was that presented by leading Asian psychiatrists criticising existing classifications as being too orientated towards European and North American practice while paying only superficial attention to numerically much more important syndromes afflicting the rest of the world. Part of the imbalance complained of may have arisen from a European genetic predisposition to certain rare but now well-researched conditions, and part has derived from earlier ignorance of the syndromes afflicting less developed societies; however, most of it must be considered to arise from cultural backgrounds biasing either the vulnerability of subjects to certain disorders or the ways in which our professionals perceive the latter. The time is now overdue for the world's psychiatric authorities, who are mainly of European origin, to confront the question of how far their writings and teachings are being distorted, unknowingly, by cultural factors.

In Britain that need is greater than in many other societies, in part because so many overseas psychiatrists still come there for training, and in part because so much of the psychiatric care of its general population is now in the hands of persons who do not have a British cultural upbringing. But what is a British cultural upbringing? What justification is there for separating this from, say, European cultural tradition, Anglo-Saxon cultural tradition (implicitly including the dominant North

179

American and Australian cultures), or more broadly still the cultural traditions of the 'Western World'? Is there a unity in British culture or should we more correctly be referring to Scottish, Irish, Cockney, Liverpudlian and a string of other local traditions? With the impact of international television, pop culture, immigrants, tourism and resurgent class conflict, are there still cultural features to which the label 'British' properly applies?

The answer to that depends on one's use of the term 'culture'. If one views culture as a society-wide teaching on how to adapt to a shared set of circumstances, as I do, then it is probable (but not inevitable) that societies which confront similar circumstances will develop similar patterns of adaptation which then become traditional cultural features, and sections of a society which have, over sufficient time, had to confront different circumstances will develop subcultural differences. But there is no reason to say that something is not 'British' because it is shared by some other culture or alternatively not shared by all groups within British society. The conditions to which today's British culture represents an adaptation are similar to those which the rest of Western Europe and North America have confronted, so that similarities are to be expected. However, since cultural attitudes, habits and beliefs are in large part automatic and unconscious, they tend to be slow to change as circumstances change, and hence the character of any contemporary culture depends as much or more on past circumstances and events as on present ones. Britain and France thus have easily distinguishable cultures as well as languages, but one can still classify them as both culturally European just as, in other chapters of this book, substantially different cultural groups can still be subsumed under the heading of African or Asian.

Historical Roots and Changes

Because we gain a better perspective when we include the past than when we consider only the present, and because one wishes to distinguish the more permanent from the more transient features when discussing cultural influences, I am starting here with a probable connection between clinical features and culture change which still has some relevance today. The connection relates to the symptomatology of what was then called melancholia and is now called depression. The time was the seventeenth and eighteenth centuries, and certain cultural features which developed at that time can still, I think, be recognised in Britain today.

From ancient Greek times until the seventeenth century, the symptoms of melancholia remained fairly stable throughout Europe and were predominantly somatic. In 1621 Robert Burton summarised that picture in his well-known book, *The Anatomy of Melancholy*, (Burton, 1621) and the physicians of his time did not depict it as in any way different. Psychological symptoms were certainly present and distinguishing, but somatic ones were equally so and the picture was very different from the common depressive syndromes in Europe today. In 1669, as I have described elsewhere (Murphy 1978a), Richard Baxter reported in great detail the clinical features of the many depressed persons he was then seeing, and his picture is very similar to what we think of as depression today. A further 60 years on, these new symptoms of depression were described by George Chyne (1733) as affecting '. . . almost a third of the people of condition (i.e. the educated class) in England'. Burton and Baxter were both clergymen, not physicians, and it was not inappropriate that they should write on melancholia since its symptoms were often thought more spiritual than mental. Cheyne was an Edinburgh-trained physician, and the statement which I have just cited should be taken as referring to a mixed bag of neuroses and psychoses rather than to depression alone; but what he called the 'English Malady' was dominated by depressive features and his claim that such disorders were disproportionately affecting the English ('of condition') is confirmed by other sources. However, the same rise in frequency and change in symptomatology were not taking place in the rest of Euorpe; rather, clinical descriptions from there continued until the end of the eighteenth century to repeat the older picture which Burton had summarised. Thus, that mouthpiece of the French Enlightenment intended to embody the newest ideas of the time, Diderot's *L'Encyclopedie*, describes melancholia as of abdominal origin with mainly abdominal symptoms and with the brain only secondarily affected (Diderot and D'Alembert, 1751–1772). The 'English Malady', meanwhile, was declining in frequency, and by the early nineteenth century England's mental health (as well as its psychiatric services) seems to have been above average.

One can hypothesise, as has been done for schizophrenia, that such a change in symptomatology and incidence must represent the spread of a new organic pathogen first in England and then elsewhere. However, there is no evidence that the lower classes in England had many cases of the same syndrome over the same years as one would expect if a virus were involved (although they did show excessive alcohol abuse at that time, in part due to the very low price of gin), and there is no independent evidence for an organic agent, whereas such evidence exists for important cultural changes. The 1730s, when Cheyne published his book, are thought by most historians to have witnessed the start of the Industrial Revolution, a revolution which began in England and spread to other countries only 50 to 100 years later. It is agreed that this occurred not just because of certain technological discoveries or even changes in social structure, but because of a gradual change in mentality over the previous century, as described by the great German sociologist Max Weber in his book, *The Protestant Ethic and the Rise of Capitalism* (1930). The type of Protestantism that came to prevail in Britain during that century, when combined with changes in child-rearing (Sommerville, 1982) and in geographic mobility, apparently led to a much greater internalisation of parental teachings than formerly, a greater sense of responsiblity for one's own welfare, and an increasing isolation from other people. Moreover, whereas the Puritan element in that Protestantism was initially likely to have been engendering a severe super-ego, there is evidence that from 1750 onwards the heavy burden of its teachings on the child relaxed (Trumbach, 1978), so that one might expect a decline in depressive symptomatology in consequence.

There are other available illustrations of a shift in British cultural teachings being followed by a shift in the incidence of symptomatology of a disease, for instance shifts that preceded first the rise of perforating peptic ulcer in females in the nineteenth century and then the marked surge in male peptic ulcer incidence in the early twentieth (Murphy, 1978b). However, even the first half of this century may not appear to most readers to have much pertinence for an understanding of the relationship between culture and psychopathology among the British today. To establish the latter link one needs more recent data and preferably of a comparative character, enabling us to see how far certain clinical features in persons of British cultural upbringing are present in members of other cultures. Such data can be found in Britain itself, but the possibility of a cultural bias on the part of the observer, as well as the problem of comparing groups of equivalent education and social class, make their interpretation difficult. It is easier, therefore, to compare British and other cultural groups of immigrants to some overseas country, and that is what I now propose to do.

Distinguishing Features: Hospitalisation Patterns

Impressions regarding the clinical features of immigrant patients from different parts of Europe can be found in American psychiatric literature from the 1860s onwards, and then in Canadian and Australian literature until the 1970s. The earliest reports do not make sufficient allowance for such matters as differences in the age distribution of the various immigrant groups, and hospitalisation data referring to the 1970s and later have not been able to allow for the increase in outpatient services. Between 1930 and 1970, however, hospitalisation patterns among immigrants and their descendants did provide fairly convincing comparisons, starting with the work of Benjamin Malzberg in New York State.

For the years 1929–31, Malzberg was able to calculate fairly reliable first-admission rates for five groups of West European origin: English, Irish, Scandinavian, German and Italian. Moreover, he was able to distinguish, both in the patients and in the general population, those born overseas from those born in the USA of immigrant parents. Of the five groups which he distinguished, the English clearly faced the fewest difficulties as immigrants, since they spoke the local language, shared numerous cultural traditions with the 'Old' Americans, were more likely to be familiar with city life (in New York State the immigrants were mainly in the city), and had the highest average level of education. Insofar as immigration constituted a strain conducive to mental disorder, therefore, they should have shown the best mental health. Malzberg's data as summarised in Figure 11.1, however, indicate that this was not significantly the case. The obvious feature in Figure 11.1 is the high rate curve for the immigrant Irish, something I will comment on later, but beyond that we see that those of English origin tend to be about average, slightly better than the others at the younger ages and worse above the age of 65. (Separating the sexes does not change the main picture.) This could be interpreted as indicating that cultural background and migrational experience are irrelevant, were it not for the fact that the rates for the second generation are nearly always lower than those for the first, and that the Irish do have significantly higher rates than the rest, in both generations. The easiest alternative explanation is that in the given situation some features in the background of the English group were counterbalancing the advantages they should have had.

Later US analyses cover a wider range of immigrant groups but give less satisfactory data on the British-origin group, as a result of certain changes in the census cross-tabulations. For 1961, however, I was able to undertake analyses of some 22 000 Canadian mental hospital admissions by culture of origin, cross-tabulated by a wide range of variables. Canadian administrative tradition did not differentiate the Irish origin from the Scots or English origin, as did the US, but it did differentiate religious affiliations. In consequence, I was able to distinguish British-origin Roman Catholics, who are mainly Irish in origin there, from the

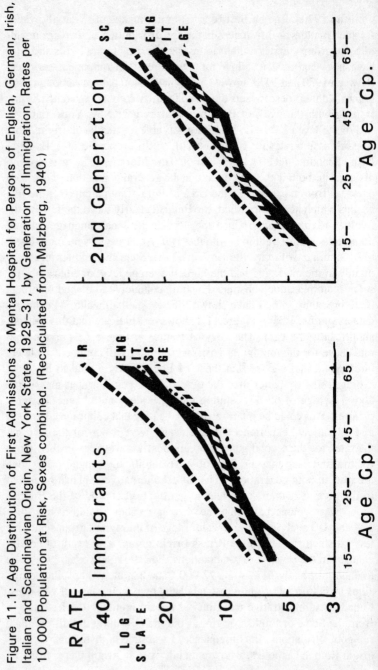

Figure 11.1: Age Distribution of First Admissions to Mental Hospital for Persons of English, German, Irish, Italian and Scandinavian Origin, New York State, 1929–31, by Generation of Immigration, Rates per 10 000 Population at Risk, Sexes combined. (Recalculated from Malzberg, 1940.)

remaining British origin on a number of variables, and the results from this are given in Table 11.1. When not otherwise specified, the findings relate not just to the first but also to the second and subsequent generations of immigration, but separate rates for the first generation (i.e. those born outside of Canada) were calculated. Use of standardised morbidity

Table 11.1: Standardised Morbidity Ratios of First Admission to Mental Hospital in Canada, 1961, by Sex and Religious Affiliation; Persons of British Origin Only (Murphy 1978c)

| | Canadians of British Origin | | | |
| | Males | | Females | |
	Catholic	Non-Catholic	Catholic	Non-Catholic
Age Group				
15–24	159[+]	91	157[+]	100
25–44	165[+]	106	136[+]	92[−]
45–64	145	90[−]	92	99
65 +	88	116[+]	71[−]	121[+]
Duration of first admission				
Under 6 months	131[+]	89[−]	92	84[−]
6–18 months	136[+]	96	125[+]	100
Over 18 months	138[+]	102	114	101
Diagnosis				
Schizophrenia	114	76[−]	123[+]	80[−]
Affective psychoses	80	100	81	98
Other depression	99	101	115	102
Other neuroses	130[+]	98	134[+]	68[−]
Senile and arteriosclerotic psychoses	82	112[+]	61[−]	126[+]
Alcoholic disorders	236[+]	107	163[+]	100
Character disorders	154[+]	97	133[+]	101
Marital status				
Single	110[+]		96	
Married	110[+]		97	
Widowed and divorced	118[+]		103	
Education				
Some university years	110		100	
High school	107		101	
Less than high school	121[+]		97	
Immigrant status				
Immigrant	111		109	
Born in Canada	115[+]		101	

Note: Standardisation is based on 100 representing the overall Canadian rate for each cell of the table, after allowance for provincial distribution and, except for the age groups and for the widowed and divorced, for age. Ratios marked [+] are significantly higher than for all Canadians; ratios marked [−] are significantly lower; ratios marked either way are not significantly different from the mean but may indicate a tendency. Non-Catholics are predominantly from England and carry greater numerical weight in the combined ratios than the Catholics, who are predominantly of Irish stock. Census data were not available in a form that permitted the combined origin and religious affiliation categories to be cross-tabulated by marital status, immigrant status or education.

ratios permit comparison both between the Catholic and non-Catholic of British origin, and with the Canadian population in general.

Compared with the Canadian population as a whole, the non-Catholic British origin are distinguished by:

(a)   a significantly higher first-admission rate for the senile and arteriosclerotic psychoses in both sexes;

(b)   a significantly lower first-admission rate in both sexes for schizophrenia;

(c)   signficantly fewer cases than average requiring less than 6 months in hospital;

(d)   significantly lower rates for female admissions with neurosis.

The excess of senile and arteriosclerotic psychoses had been remarked by Malzberg in New York, and subsequently reported from Australia (Krupinski and Stoller, 1965). The low schizophrenia rate has likewise been found in Australia (*op. cit.*), and a closer examination of the Canadian data suggests that it arises mainly through the British-origin unskilled labourer class producing less of an excess of this disorder than is usual (although they have a greater than usual excess of other disorders, notably alcoholism).

In Britain itself, the local born exhibit, as one would expect, substantially lower rates of mental hospitalisation than most groups of immigrants, and that is not something to attribute to culture; but there are exceptions. According to Cochrane's (1977) analysis of 1971 admissions, persons born in the UK have substantially higher admission rates for the senile and pre-senile psychoses than any immigrant group except the Irish-born, allowing for age; and they have more than usually low rates for schizophrenia. Hence although there is a problem of birthplace being inadequately recorded in British hospitals (Dean *et al.*, 1981b), these observations agree with the main ones from Canada, Australia and the USA, and thus give added support to linking certain features to the culture. Compared with the Canadian data, the main differrence in emphasis in Cochrane's data concerns alcoholism, which is unusually high in Scottish-origin persons residing in England and Wales but low in the English- and Welsh-born. This suggests that the slightly above average standardised morbidity ratio for the non-Catholic British-origin in Canada may be attributable to those of Scottish origin, with the remainder having a below-average rate.

Distinguishing Features: Other

Attribution to a cultural influence from such bare statistics, however, is an unsatisfactory and perhaps questionable business: one wants clinical details to flesh out these bones. More particularly, one would like to see some similarity between symptoms and cultural traits, and get an impression of the relationships between the patients and people of the same cultural background around them. At approximately the same time as the analysis of the Canadian hospitalisation data was going on, I was also studying mental patients and their milieux in 13 Canadian villages of British, French, German and Polish cultural origin, with the British group being divided into Irish Catholic, Irish Protestant and other Protestant. Later, some colleagues and I looked at the symptom patterns of British-Canadian and French-Canadian patients matched for age, sex, diagnosis and chronicity, and then at some responses to treatment. From such sources some fleshing-out becomes possible.

The most concrete and dramatic results from these other studies derived from the use of a very carefully translated diagnostic interview (the Mental Status Schedule of Spitzer *et al.,* 1966) with the matched samples of male schizophrenics. A single bilingual interviewer was used throughout, the patients had to have been ill for at least 6 months but not more than 5 years, and hospitals in both Quebec and Ontario were sampled to avoid possible bias as a result of admission or treatment policies. Despite this care in matching, however, there were very marked differences in the answers to certain of the items on the Mental Status Schedule, as Table 11.2 shows. Although French-Canadian schizophrenics tend to run an even more chronic course than British-Canadian ones, they do not at all show the social withdrawal which the latter show and which British textbooks, along with German and Scandinavian ones, have tended to teach as a primary feature of the disease. Accordingly, there is reason to think that this feature in British (but not only British) schizophrenics has a cultural origin, most plausibly linked to the isolation from others which has been described as developing in the culture from the seventeenth century onwards, and which my colleague Juan-Carlos Negrete (1973) found also to differentiate British-origin from French-origin alcoholics. His Anglo-Protestant sample had cut themselves off from their families and communities to a signficantly greater extent than his Franco-Catholic one, and the former's spouses were correspondingly readier to reject them than the latter's spouses were.

In the villages the differences respecting schizophrenics were less objectifiable (a more open-ended approach with fewer cases) but no less

Table 11.2: Selected Symptom Differences (%) between British-Canadian and French-Canadian Patients in Psychiatric Units (Murphy, 1974)

	Cultural Origin				
	British		French		
Provincial location of Hospitals	Quebec	Ontario	Quebec	Ontario	
Symptoms					
(a) *Schizophrenia sample*					
Complains abundantly of family, friends or associates	0	0	65	70	0.001
Feels friends avoid, reject or dislike him	12	10	50	70	0.01
Says people know of his guilt, faults or problems	12	10	60	60	0.01
Feels he has no friends	27		40		
(b) *Depression sample*					−0.02
Feels she has no friends	20		60		
Has difficulty in thinking or in expressing herself	45		0		0.005
Cannot concentrate	60		15		0.01
Has numerous somatic troubles	15		60		0.01

The schizophrenic sample comprised hospitalised young males with a duration of illness not less than 6 months or more than 5 years. The depression sample comprised middle-aged women entering into treatment at two general hospital psychiatric units and interviewed prior to commencing treatment. Statistical significance of the 'feels has no friends' symptom is based on the combined samples.

interesting. The British Protestant patients showed a markedly greater effort at retaining a working role and a greater tendency to clinical deterioration when that was lost, than was true of the schizophrenics of other origins. The formers' neighbours, similarly, showed considerable tolerance for deviant behaviour if a job was retained but intolerance if it was lost, whereas in other types of village the communities (particularly the more traditional French-Canadian) supported their patients regardless of whether they had jobs or not, but rejected them more quickly if they infringed certain other types of social expectation such as respect for the church. (The Irish Catholic patients' relationships with their communities tended to depend on their families; if the latter were respected, they were accorded wide latitude; if they were not, then the patients were teased.) Concerning chronicity, the main factors recognised in the villages seemed to relate to social variables other than culture, but on the other hand we know that schizophrenia tends to run a more chronic course in 'developed' than in 'developing' countries (Murphy and Raman, 1971; WHO, 1979), and a sociocultural explanation is the most likely although non-cultural factors may also be at play. (In the WHO study report it is noted regarding the London sample that 'A study of patients remaining in hospital more than six months showed that in many cases patients were free of symptoms but could not be discharged because of lack of suitable accomodation' (WHO, 1979, p. 108).) Because of the village findings, it would seem likely that rehabilitation calls for different strategies in different cultures, whether the basic disease has a more chronic tendency or not, and I recommended at that time that British-Canadian patients be found work, even in isolated locations, whereas the French-Canadian patients needed to be found communal support close to other people but not necessarily work.

Regarding other disorders, it became apparent in the villages that the older British-Canadian residents tended to get referred to mental hospital because they insisted in trying to live alone, resented feeling dependent, and either neglected themselves or became paranoid about visitors; whereas in other groups the aged accepted dependency and sought to live with others. The latter characteristic sometimes led to depression (particularly in traditional French-Canadian villages) when the respect and attention which the old people had looked forward to was not forthcoming; whereas that was not seen among the British Protestant group. At a younger age, as Table 11.2 shows, there are differences in the symptoms of depression in British- and French-Canadians, extending to their responses to treatment (Murphy, 1974). One can interpret these as indicating that depression has a more organic character in the former than in the latter, but an alternative explanation is that the one group is most sensitive to their own mental functioning whereas the other is more concerned with their relationship to their body and their society.

Possible Cultural Links

The most obvious feature in the foregoing observations concerns social dependency and isolation. Compared with French-Canadian and to a lesser degree most other Canadian subcultures, the British-origin patients loosen their social ties more easily, receive less communal support (but also less communal censure, if they can manage some form of self-sufficiency) and are more distrustful of social intervention in old age. These traits affect the more mentally vulnerable individual's activity to survive outside of hospital, but they are not exclusive to the vulnerable. I think most international observers would see a certain insistence on trying to manage alone, and an expectation that other people should also be able to manage alone, as typical of the British, at least in the recent past, and I suggest that this may have had its roots in the cultural change that took place in the seventeenth century. Psychiatrically, it is a trait which brings advantages as well as disadvantages. The greater internalisation of one's society which at least partly underlies this characteristic means that under most environmental difficulties the individual is more likely to be able to continue pursuing longer-term goals without the support of others, although it also means that his vulnerability greatly increases when the values of the internalised society are seriously called into question, and that he is less able to share in a communal response to the difficulty. Such an inference is supported by such data as we possess regarding the resilience of isolated colonial missionaries and administrators from various backgrounds earlier in this century, the British handling the cultural isolation better than many other groups but showing relatively high morbidity when their missionaries to China found not just their religion but also their culture challenged by one that was much older.

A second feature that stands out in the hospitalisation data from the different overseas locations is that, despite the advantages of mother tongue, shared customs and (usually) education, the British-origin group do not have particularly low admission rates. Krupinski (1975) has made the same observation regarding migrants to Australia, and has linked it to the British-origin group possessing excessive expectations regarding their new situation. This is an inference with which I agree, and which cannot be attributed to these immigrants being more ignorant of the receiving-country conditions than other immigrant groups are. It is a commonly heard complaint in Australia, some parts of Canada, and particularly New Zealand, that immigrants from Britain bring too high an opinion of themselves and of the culture that moulded them. They thus put less effort into self-advancement than many other cultural groups of immigrants and are less happy with the results obtained, so that one may infer that in some instances the conflict between expectation and reality brings on a mental disturbance. Whether this is something occuring mainly in those who choose to emigrate or is to be found in the homeland Briton's expectations and real social situation I leave to persons more knowledgeable than myself regarding present-day Britain to judge. The Canadian data suggest that the problem is mainly among those with above-average education (as may also be true with Dutch emigrants) and that one of the attempted defences is alcohol dependency.

The third, though much less definite, feature of mental disorder among the British-origin group, in my data, is the relative excess of compulsive, obsessional and guilt symptoms in their neuroses, balanced by a relative absence of simple anxiety states and somatisations. Judging by a general reading of papers on the neuroses from different countries, these features probably distinguish the British neurotics from those of most other countries, although not necessarily of North-Western Europe. A possible explanation is that the greater internalisation which was noted above leads to the neuroses assuming a less spontaneous and more convoluted character in North-West Europeans than in most other cultural groups. Regarding guilt feelings, however, the main difference may lie less in their presence than in what they relate to. Evidence from Egypt, Japan and most recently Korea indicates that peoples who had previously been thought not to show this symptom do in fact suffer from it, but feel it in relation to other people, particularly family, whereas in the British it is in relation to the self or God.

The Irish and Scots

The Irish should really have had a chapter to themselves in this volume. Failing that I must briefly summarise the considerable literature which has been written on their mental health problems. Readers seeking a fuller review of the subject are referred to my earlier paper (Murphy, 1975).

Both at home and abroad, the Irish rates of schizophrenia and of psychological alcoholism admissions are among the highest in the world. The latest report at time of writing (Dean *et al.*, 1981a) indicates that the Irish-born population living in South-East England had 2.4 times the expected number of first admissions for schizophrenia in both sexes, 5.3 times the expected male admissions for alcoholism, and 4.0 times the expected female admission for the latter disorder. In the Republic of Ireland the hospitalisation rates are still higher; in Northern Ireland they are high for the Catholic moiety but average for the non-Catholic; in North America they are high for alcoholism regardless of generation (as far as can be traced) but for schizophrenia their rate seems to drop back to normal as successive generations pass. (Incidentally, despite its high admission rate for psychological alcoholism, the Republic of Ireland has the second-lowest mortality rate from liver cirrhosis of the 53 countries reporting this statistic to the WHO, casting serious doubt on the usefulness of the unitary concept of alcoholism which the WHO itself supports.) Regarding the neuroses there are conflicting reports, with one survey having found Irish to have more symptoms than English (Kelleher, 1972) and another finding them to have fewer (Cochrane and Stopes-Roe,

1979); but the Canadian data in Table 11.1 favours the former view. On the other hand, as that table and some other sources indicate, they have below-average rates for the senile and arteriosclerotic psychoses after the first immigrant generation.

Both in the Republic and in Northern Ireland, hospitalisation rates are highest in the west and decline as one approaches the major eastern centres of Dublin and Belfast, that being true even when one considers the northern Catholics only, excluding the non-Catholics. An American anthropologist studying the subject in a west-coast population has suggested that some of the so-called schizophrenics in hospital might have been suffering from 'ontological insecurity' or 'problems of living' rather than from any definite disease (Scheper-Hughes, 1979); and I myself have formed a similar impression of some of the alcoholics seen in the Republic's hospitals. However, in Northern Ireland and in overseas countries where Irish patients are judged according to the same criteria as are applied to patients of other cultural origins, it is unlikely that such diagnostic biases would occur. In Northern Ireland, whereas alcoholic admissions are generally much higher among the Catholics than among the non-Catholics, this difference disappears in that part of the territory where Catholic attacks on non-Catholics have been most successful and free from retaliation (Murphy, in preparation), suggesting that the excess of alcoholism may only arise when there is lack of self-confidence. However, the distribution of schizophrenia is not related either to the same variable or to the more obvious measures of social disadvantage, but instead is related to the percentage celibacy in the local population, and the higher Catholic rates for this condition prove to be confined to the never-married (Murphy and Vega, 1982). A wide range of hypotheses have been explored to explain the undue vulnerability to schizophrenia and alcoholism — migration, social-class differences, genotypes, child-rearing, interpersonal relations outside of the family, etc. — but none has been confirmed. At time of writing my Northern Ireland data lead me to favour a child-rearing hypothesis with respect to schizophrenia, and a social insecurity one with respect to alcoholism, but not excluding some genetic factor in the latter case in view of the alcoholism patterns in north-west Scotland, the Celtic fringe in France, and the persistence of the problem in successive generations of Irish-Americans.

About the Scots there are only few comparative data to call on, since the US and Canadian sources do not differentiate them from other British, and a comparison of data from Scotland and from England is complicated by differences in service structure. However, one feature which seems to characterise them is alcohol abuse, not at as high a level as among the Irish but higher than in most other West-European cultures. This is shown in Cochrane's (1977) hospitalisation data for migrants to England and Wales, but is by no means confined to migrants, as successive hospital reports from Scotland itself show, plus Primrose's little community study (1962). There has been enough written about drinking patterns in Scotland and the possible effect of such factors as Presbyterian strictness and the belief in whisky as a medicine, but it is difficult to evaluate such opinions without comparative reports using the same criteria in appropriate other societies.

Regarding other conditions, the best-known local phenomenon is probably the high rate of attempted suicide in Edinburgh since the 1960s. I believe, however, that this relates to local conditions, notably the well publicised opening of the Poisons Treatment Centre there, rather than to particular cultural traditions. Certain mental health features reported from Glasgow also seem to relate to local circumstances. Concerning more longstanding differences, I remember D.K. Henderson teaching us that his psychiatric residents were prone to diagnose any Orcadian that reached their service as depressed, due to nothing more than the latter's weighty mode of communication, but I do not know if this is still true or if there was a substratum of pathology in the picture.

For the Welsh and smaller British subcultures I know of no distinguishing psychiatric features once one allows for occupation, e.g. mining. The descendents of Welsh settlers in Patagonia are reported to retain distinctive psychological characteristics, but I have been unable to get any psychiatric data on them.

Conclusion

Because it is easy to write too loosely on supposedly racial or cultural influences on mental health, I have chosen to focus this chapter rather drily on epidemiological statistics, most of them not even from Britain. These are only the bare bones of what one should be able to construct in the way of a picture of the mental health strengths and weaknesses which a culture such as the British one promotes. It is time that clinicians, particularly those with experience in several cultures, both European and non-European, added some flesh to these bones through accurate investigation and comparison. I hope that I have demonstrated that the subject is a legitimate one for study, even with relatively elementary tools, and that I therefore may have been able to persuade some readers to take it up.

References

Burton, R. (1621) *The Anatomy of Melancholy,* F. Dell and P. Jordan-Smith (eds) (1955), Tudor Press, New York

Cheyne, G. (1733) *The English Malady; or a Treatise of Nervous Diseases of all Kinds* . . . Strahan, London

Cochrane, R. (1977) 'Mental Illness in Immigrants to England and Wales: an Analysis of Mental Hospital Admissions, 1971', *Social Psychiatry, 12,* 25–35

Cochrane, R. and Stopes-Roe, M. (1979) 'Psychological Disturbance in Ireland, in England and in Irish Emigrants to England; a Comparative Study', *Economic and Social Review, 10,* 301–20

Cooper, J.E., Kendell, R.E., Gurland, B.J., Sharpe, L., Copeland, J.R.M. and Simon, R. (1972) *Psychiatric Diagnosis in New York and London,* Maudsley Monograph No. 20, Oxford University Press, London

Dean, G., Downing, H. and Shelley, E. (1981a) 'First Admissions to Psychiatric Hospitals in South-east England in 1976 among Immigrants from Ireland', *British Medical Journal, 282,* 1831–3

Dean, G., Walsh, D., Downing, H. and Shelley, E. (1981b) 'First Admissions of Native-born and Immigrants to Psychiatric Hospitals in South-east England, 1976', *British Journal of Psychiatry, 139,* 506–12

Diderot, D. and D'Alembert, J.L. (1751–1772) *L'Encyclopedie ou Dictionnaire raisonné des sciences, des arts et des métiers,* Breton, Paris

Kelleher, M.J. (1972) 'Cross-national (Anglo-Irish) Differences in Obsessional Symptoms and Traits of Personality', *Psychological Medicine, 2,* 33–41

Krupinski, J. (1975) 'Psychological Maladaptation in Ethnic Concentrations in Victoria, Australia', in I. Pilowsky (ed.), *Cultures in Collision,* pp. 49–58, Australian National Association for Mental Health, Adelaide

Krupinski, J. and Stoller, A. (1965) 'Incidence of Mental Disorders in Victoria, Australia, According to Country of Birth', *Medical Journal of Australia, 2,* 265–9

Malzberg, B. (1940) *Social and Biological Aspects of Mental Disease,* (a revision of previously published papers) State Hospitals Press, Utica

Murphy, H.B.M. (1974) 'Differences between Mental Disorders of French Canadians and British Canadians', *Canadian Psychiatric Association, 19,* 247–57

Murphy, H.B.M. (1975) 'Alcoholism and Schizophrenia in the Irish; a Review', *Transcultural Psychiatry Research Review, 12,* 116–39

Murphy, H.B.M. (1978a) 'The Advent of Guilt Feelings as a Common Depressive Symptom: a Historical Comparison on Two Continents', *Psychiatry, 118,* 229–42

Murphy, H.B.M. (1978b) 'Historic Changes in the Sex Ratios for Different Disorders', *Social Science and Medicine, 12 B,* 143–9

Murphy, H.B.M. (1978c) 'European Cultural Offshoots in the New World: Differences in their Mental Hospitalisation Patterns. Part I: British, French and Italian Influences', *Social Psychiatry, 13,* 1–9

Murphy, H.B.M. (in preparation) 'Minority Status, Civil Strife and the Major Mental Disorders: Hospitalisation Patterns in Northern Ireland'

Murphy, H.B.M. and Raman, A.C. (1971) 'The Chronicity of Schizophrenia in Indigenous Tropical Peoples', *British Journal of Psychiatry, 118,* 489–97

Murphy, H.B.M. and Vega, G. (1982) 'Schizophrenia and Religious Affiliation in Northern Ireland', *Psychological Medicine, 12,* 595–605

Negrete, J.C. (1973) 'Cultural Influences on the Social Performance of Chronic Alcoholics: a Comparative Study', *Quarterly Journal on Study of Alcoholism, 34,* 905–16

Primrose, E.J.R. (1962) *Psychological Illness: a Community Study,* Tavistock, London

Scheper-Hughes, N. (1979) *Saints, Scholars and Schizophrenics: Madness and Badness in Western Ireland,* University of California Press, Berkeley

Somerville, C.J. (1982) *The Rise and Fall of Childhood*, Sage, London

Spitzer, R.L., Burdock, E.I., Hardesty, A.S. (1966) *The Mental Status Schedule*, State Psychiatric Institute, New York

Trumbach, R. (1978) *The Rise of the Egalitarian Family*, Academic Press, London

Weber, M. (1930) *The Protestant Ethic and the Spirit of Capitalism*, transl. Talcott Parsons, Allen & Unwin, London

World Health Organization (1979) *Schizophrenia: an International Follow-up Study*, Wiley, New York

12 TRANSCULTURAL SOCIAL WORK

John Triseliotis

Equal but different. (Herodotus)

This chapter examines the response of the social-work services to the ethnic dimension in society and reviews the key issues currently confronting policy makers, administrators and practitioners. Some of the issues and approaches discussed here are of obvious relevance to other social services besides social work.

Background

Social workers, in common with others in the caring professions, took a long time to begin to recognise the emerging multi-ethnic nature of post-war British society and the challenge this posed to their practices. This failure was accompanied by a slowness to grasp and anticitpate the extensive disadvantages suffered mainly by the black and Asian communities. Not surprisingly, the underlying racism and discrimination went unchallenged. The youthfulness of the social-work profession can only partly account for this blindness and for the absence of a coherent approach to the issues. In this respect the strictures of Dr. Martin Luther King (1964), directed to the social scientists in the United States for playing little or no role in disclosing the truth about the plight of the minorities, could be applied here.

In the years that followed the main wave of post-war immigration, public attention was mostly focused on what were seen to be the weaknesses within the new 'immigrants' themselves. Their strengths and significant contribution to the British economy and way of life were largely ignored. A series of controlling Immigration Acts and the impact of racist propaganda created an atmosphere which sought to present minorities, mainly those of dark skins, as a homogeneous 'problem' group. The creation of such a stereotype and the labelling of whole cultures foreign to one's own as 'inferior' usually adds the missing respectability for the exploitation and opression of minorities. Inevitably some of those delegated to deliver services to minorities adopt these stereotypes, which are subsequently reflected in their planning and practices. The results of direct and indirect forms of discrimination have been very well documented by Little and Robins (1982), who concluded from their extensive review of the literature that 'ethnic minorities are disproportionately experiencing the worst that our society has to offer' (p. 8).

Social workers involved with ethnic minorities not only have to overcome their personal prejudices and gain an understanding of cultural backgrounds, but also have to face the problem of establishing their credibility among some of the most disadvantaged communities: all this in the knowledge that although large numbers of ethnic minority people are out of work or poorly housed, the social-work services are organised to provide at most relief from such ills, rather than to tackle them directly. If indigenous people find this circumscribed and ambiguous role hard to understand, it is even more so for members of ethnic minorities who are unfamiliar with the whole concept of 'social work'. Social work, being mainly the product of Western religious beliefs, of a capitalist economic system and of individualistic ideologies, is largely alien to cultures which have not gone through the same processes. Western culture, by focusing almost wholly on the individual, places unusual importance on such concepts as self-reliance, self-help, privacy, individual identity and independence. It is not surprising, therefore, that white social workers are more sensitive to the dangers of fostering client dependency than to failure to respond to need. In contrast, many of the attitudes and much of the behaviour of minorities have originated from cultural backgrounds which put the emphasis on group and family relationships. These in turn tend to foster greater interdependence. Behaviour fashioned by such influences imposes a different approach to living, the making of relationships, the seeking of help and the resolution of problems from that found in Western societies. Not surprisingly, these and other variations in cultural orientations tend to challenge white social workers, at both the personal and professional level.

The literature, both in Britain and in the USA, began to reflect some awareness of the ethnic dimension in social work only some twenty years ago. (See Triseliotis, 1963, 1965; Kent, 1965.) Real concern about the social-work needs of ethnic minorities led to a conference of Chairmen of Social Services Committees, of the Directors of Social Services and of members of the Commission for Racial Equality, at which social work's response to the ethnic dimension was the main theme. The report that followed (ADSS/CREE, 1978) outlined a framework within which the social services departments in multiracial areas were encouraged to set about assessing their local position and formulating policies. The document bravely admitted that the 'response of social service departments to the existence of multi-racial communities has been patchy, piecemeal and lacking in strategy' (p. 14).

Social Policy Considerations

The issues and dilemmas facing social workers and social service departments in the area of ethnicity cannot be divorced from wider social policy considerations. Concerns about the plight of the black population in the USA during the 1960s generated a number of interesting ideas about how to tackle racial disadvantage. Both in the US and Britain, the debate about choices polarised between the twin approaches of 'universalist provision' and 'positive discrimination', otherwise known as 'affirmative action'. At its most basic, the 'universalist' position views ethnic minorities as being oppressed and exploited similar to the indigenous disadvantaged groups. It tends to play down differences between what are seen to be groups of people with similar basic needs and considers the State as responsible for providing 'equality of opportunity' for all, and for making services easily available to all irrespective of creed or colour. Such an approach confirms a right and not a stigma on the recipient and furthermore avoids creating two classes of citizen. In contrast, 'positive discrimination' or 'affirmative action' towards a group can invoke, it is argued, stigma and racist envy. It can also lead to too many discretionary decisions. Universalist policies and services, it is again claimed, tend to promote a more integrative type of relationship in society, though it does not follow that such a society is also a 'good' one. The thrust of the universalist argument is that the attack on disadvantage can only come as part of a wider package which has a better chance of being accepted by the public, e.g. improved social-work services, schools, hospitals, housing for everybody. Rex (1983) criticises the positive discrimination approach, mainly for detracting from the fight against racial discrimination and the promotion of 'equality of opportunity'. He argues that the notion of 'positive discrimination' detracts from the development of independent political action by people themselves.

In contrast, Livingstone (1979), reflecting on the 1960s scene in the United States, argues that 'without affirmative action, the struggle for racial justice would be stalemated, at the price of both justice and social peace'. The case for positive discrimination or affirmative action in Britain is well argued by Little and Robins (1982) and it also featured in the Scarman report (1982). The supporters of affirmative action point to the failure of the 'equal opportunity' or 'equal treatment for all' concept, as shown by the continued disparities between the minorities and other groups. In addition, the universalist approach, by failing to acknowledge and respond to differences, indirectly appears to favour the assimilation of minorities. Though the universalist position has much to commend it, it fails to recognise that the minorities have special needs which are not readily accommodated by existing categories of need, and that special provision is indicated. There is also no serious reason, as we shall see later, why some universalist services should not respond to differences by being delivered separately. Attempts to deny differences, along with the 'subsidiary' role into which minorities have been relegated, have strengthened feelings of distinctiveness among the minorities themselves. For example, a recent study by Field (1984) found that a commitment to the culture of the minority group provides support for the black or Asian adolescent's self-respect, and is an explanation for the growing preference for friends of the same ethnic group.

Little and Robins (1982) make the point that a policy of positive discrimination would have to identify not just areas but also groups that require special provision. Scarman (1982), on the other hand, argues for positive discrimination by area only on the ground of the special problems faced by minorities in areas of acute deprivation. Group-based action would mean giving priority to people identified by ethnicity. In the case of individuals, they will be judged first on the basis of their ethnicity or racial group and then on merit. Some minority-group leaders maintain, though, that such a step would undermine the 'self-respect and dignity' of ethnic minority groups, and that they would rather see the emphasis being placed on 'equality of opportunity' and on 'rights'. To those who voice fears that positive discrimination by group might increase racial tensions and lead to a backlash, its proponents are at pains to explain that they are not advocating 'favourable advantage over white people' (Scarman, 1982). The USA is quoted as an example where projects directed mainly to black communities have not produced the anticipated fears. The threatened backlash usually occurs, it is argued, when resources made available are not extra but taken away from some other deprived group. Dwarkin, writing in *The Times* on 12 February 1981, justified positive action not because of past injustices, but 'rather for the future benefit to the community as a whole'. 'Any plan', he added, 'that might reduce racial tension and racial inequality is in general and not just in some sectarian interest'.

The arguments for affirmative action are too powerful to be ignored, especially in the face of repeated evidence of how far behind some minorities are. Affirmative action could help to bring them to a level from which they can compete on equal terms with Whites for jobs, housing, and social and health services. Ethnic minorities, though, should not be deluded. In the end they will obtain good social services only when these are improved for all rather than from fighting over the same cake. Affirmative action can only be a short-term option and not a long-term solution to the needs of both black and white. A testament to the limitations of positive discrimination by itself is the minor improvements effected in the position of blacks in the USA since the 1960s. Possibly this more than anything else explains the absence of any real backlash. It is unrealistic, of course, to expect that the personal social services, with their very limited role, can by themselves achieve goals of 'equality of opportunity' or the eradication of racial discrimination. What they can do is to ensure that they become more ethnically sensitive when delivering general or separate services to minorities.

Organisational Changes

The application of policies that aim at responding to differences in ethnicity necessitates a number of changes to existing organisational structures. However, short of providing for separate development in all areas of the minorities' lives, a viable alternative organisational set-up might be one that combines the adaptation of existing services with separate development. There are those who will say that organisational adaptation by itself is enough and that nothing more needs to be done. Such an argument fails again to recognise that it is unrealistic to expect agencies administered by whites, and with a long history of service delivery to a white indigenous population, suddenly to adapt sufficiently to meet the needs of those groups which are culturally different.

The Need for Adaptation of the Social-work Services

A number of recent studies demonstrate conclusively the failure of the personal social services to respond to the social-work needs of ethnic minorities (Jones, 1977; ADSS/CREE Report, 1978; Connelly, 1981; Cheetham, 1982; Griffiths, 1984). Connelly, like others, attributes this failure partly to the tendency within social service departments to treat everyone the same 'irrespective of race or sex'. This apparently liberal and 'neutral' approach tends to deny differences between ethnic groups and, as a result, does not even recognise the necessity for the adaptation of services. Although it is true that common human needs transcend racial and cultural differences, it is equally true that racial and cultural factors influence need, demanding a more distinctive approach. At the opposite end of treating everyone the same is the tendency to explain most phenomena of need among ethnic minorities as a 'manifestation of cultural differences', possibly not requiring attention. Either position sidesteps the real issues. A more worrying conclusion of the studies quoted above is the claim that the neglect they found is not a mere function of structure and organisation, but the result of ethnocentric beliefs and biases among some practitioners.

Awareness of the ethnic dimension in the personal social services varies from staff who are committed to cultural pluralism to those who have given no thought to the matter or who say that it 'almost isn't an issue'. In one area the senior heading a team in a part of the city whose population was 50 per cent Asian is quoted by Connelly (1981) as saying that, as only 15 per cent of the cases coming to them concerned Asians, ethnic minority considerations were of little significance for staff. As recently as 1983, Renate Olins, Director of the London Marriage Guidance Council, was reported in *New Society* (14 April, 1983) as saying that she did not 'think a counsellor needs special training in racial and cultural minorities. She only needs to know what's important for those people as individuals.' Yet the Vale conference in the United States (see Sue, 1973) declared it 'unethical' to try to counsel a person of a different culture without the counsellor being competent in understanding the central cultural characteristics of the respective group. On the positive side, Connelly found that in one area team the social workers saw the ethnic dimension as an inextricable part of the social-work task. Griffiths (1984), who carried out a survey into the adequacy of Derbyshire's social services for ethnic minorities, identified not only that the demand for social-work services in the area was low, but also that 'practices and policies relating to people of ethnic minorities have until now been improvisations, inadequate and largely uneducated attempts' (p. 80). The inappropriateness of the services extended to children, the mentally ill, the elderly and to families in general.

There is no evidence to support the view that the low uptake of services by Asians is because they prefer to contain their problems within the extended family. When members of ethnic minorities gave evidence to the Barclay Committee (Barclay Report, 1982, pp. 11–21), they pointed to the failure of the services to make themselves relevant to ethnic needs. These spokespeople indicated that they viewed social workers as representatives of authority, with which they preferred to have as few dealings as possible, or that they actively distrusted their authority. The Barclay Report went on to add that it was not just that social workers represented authority, but that the authority was seen as alien in understanding the cultural practices of particular groups. Similar criticisms have also been made about the Probation Service. For example, because of the way some probation officers' social enquiry reports are written, Afro-Caribbeans tend to be under-represented in non-custodial supervision, whereas Asian and white clients have comparable rates (for a summary of findings see Staplehurst, 1983). A recent study by Barker (1984) for Age Concern found that black and Asian old people in Britain are suffering cultural insensitivity, discrimination and outright racism in almost every area of life. On top of all this, it is now the practice of some DHSS officers and hospital staff to demand evidence from those with dark skin to prove their British citizenship before they can obtain services.

Any approach that seeks to take account of cultural differences is bound to pose a threat not only to structures but also to the workers' personal beliefs and values. The idea of increased responsiveness to ethnic minority need adds major new dimensions of responsibility to mostly indigenous workers who, in the main, are reared and trained in their own cultural traditions. Some workers may not only interpret minority-group intentions and behaviour wrongly, but they may also be ambivalent or downright hostile to the idea of taking initiatives to adapt their services. For example, one exasperated worker recently asked me, 'why should we share our resources with them?' Other social workers hope that under continued pressure ethnic minorities will eventually 'assimilate', and that therefore nothing needs to be done now. Connelly (1981) quotes one respondent who remarked, 'If we work at it long enough we will make them white.' Again, members of ethnic minorities, when speaking to the Barclay Committee, referred to 'prejudice on the part of individual social workers and a lack of concern for the difficulties of members of minority groups — and a failure to challenge the racial prejudices of other agencies' (§ 11.24). Farrar (1984), an ethnic adviser to the Bradford Social Services, is quoted as saying that he had been surprised to find that social workers 'have the same prejudices as the general population'. Husband (1978) also claims that there are many examples of racism in social work.

Forms of Adaptation

There is no shortage of prescriptive accounts of how social service departments can adapt their services to become more ethnically sensitive and relevant to the needs of ethnic minorities. A few departments have already started moving in this direction. The ADSS/CREE Report (1978), Cheetham (1982) and Griffiths (1984) set out a range of desirable adaptations. Considerable emphasis is placed on the recruitment, training and deployment of ethnic minority staff, the organisation of day and residential centres, the provision of domiciliary services, the training of interpreters, and the use of ethnic volunteers. The concept of adaptation goes well beyond the recruitment of ethnic minority staff to one that offers choices to minorities in such matters as day and residential services, with attention being paid to their health, religions and dietary requirements. More important, minorities should have a decision-making role at the policy and planning levels of the work of both statutory and voluntary agencies. This implies adequate representation on committees and panels, both at central and neighbourhood levels, and opportunities to assume management and leadership roles. Their participation, at all levels, is essential if they are to be offered the opportunity to express more coherently their ethnic and individual preferences, and to learn how to tackle indigenous organisations. If social work is about the 'individualisation' of service, then the field of ethnicity offers an ideal testing ground.

With few exceptions, the recruitment of ethnic minority social workers and social-care staff has been very slow. The main excuse offered is the unconvincing argument that there are no trained ethnic minority social workers to be recruited. Yet the same authorities which now frown on the idea of employing untrained ethnic staff and subsequently seconding them to training did exactly this in the 1970s with white staff. Voluntary agencies, according to a report from the National Council for Voluntary Organisations (1984), are trailing even further behind many statutory services in promoting racial harmony and looking after the interests of ethnic minorities. In contrast, the Huddersfield Citizens Advice Bureau in 1984 employed eight ethnic workers out of a staff of 25.

The involvement of ethnic minority people as volunteers has yet to be systematically explored. So far ethnic people have been used mostly as interpreters, and not always in a suitable manner. A more imaginative example of using volunteers is quoted in the Annual Report of the South Yorkshire Probation Service, 1978, p. 48. In Sheffield during 1978, five workers from a local Caribbean Centre run by Sheffield Youth Service were accredited as volunteers. Their purpose was to help form and maintain contact with young West Indians under supervision or in residential establishments. In another example, three black volunteers or 'probation aides' were appointed to work at Hindley Borstal with a group of 'recalcitrant' black trainees (Murphy, 1978, p. 9). Though there are other examples of successful efforts, the field is still wide open for further experimentation. It is one of a number of ways in which minorities are offered the opportunity to demonstrate their strengths. It would be a retrograde step, though, if the employment of ethnic staff and the use of ethnic volunteers were seen as a substitute for white staff engaging themselves with ethnic minorities, or as a reason for ethnic people to confine themselves to their own groups.

Separate Provision

The separate development of services for ethnic minorities could come about through the application of positive discrimination policies and the separate delivery of some universalist services. One way to achieve this is through the setting-up of voluntary agencies publicly funded, or based on a mixture of 'self-help' and public funding, and run by the minorities themselves. Obviously, as the ethnic minorities are not a homogeneous group, separate agencies would have to be set up for the different ethnic, religious and racial groups. A policy of pluralist provision, though, without substantial additional resources being made available, could lead to considerable tensions and antagonisms between the different groups. This is not unknown in areas where agencies are practising a policy of partial separate development. There is also no shortage of examples of minorities running their own 'self-help' groups. One of many is the Community Centre for Gujeratis in Harlesden, North-West London, whose main purpose is to provide company and support for older Asians who will not use Council facilities because of their own lack of English or the absence of ethnic meals. Another is the day centre for the Asian elderly set up by the Wembley District and Indian Association. There is also the North Lewisham Project funded by the British Council of Churches and the local council, which was established to improve the self-image of young black people and the services provided for them.

Examples from the USA also suggest that separate development as a route to cultural pluralism is a viable alternative. However, cautiousness is required when quoting from American experience because the history and structure of the British social services are very different from those in the United States. Like 'positive discrimination', separate development can be justified for specific needs, but the idea of separate development or separate resources in all or most areas of the minorities' lives could prove divisive. Such an idea conjures up images of segregation which would be abhorrent to most of us. Though the dividing line between separation and segregation is a thin one, it is a fact that a kind of segregation already operates from the way some minorities, confined to semi-ghettos in decaying urban areas, have few, if any, opportunities of getting out. We cannot talk of an integrated society which allows for diversity in culture and customs when broader social policies and racism are leading to a segregated experience. Irrespective of this, all-out separate development through grant-aiding, voluntarism and self-help is no substitute for comprehensive public social services. Desirable as such initiatives are, they can only be complementary to, rather than a substitute for, public provision. Failure to adapt existing services and develop some separately may simply result in ethnic minorities continuing not to use them and demanding the setting-up of their own, or to their using the services only as a very last resort.

Child-care Services

Some of the services suggested for separate devlopment include those for children in care, residential and day-care services for the elderly and perhaps for under-fives, and youth services. Cheetham (1982), for example, argues against mixed children's homes run by Whites and Blacks, because they do not approximate to the child's own environment. She cites one home, featured in her DHSS study (1981), where staff did not even know if Asian children were Hindu or Muslim. Ignorance by the staff of the children's customs, special needs, religious preferences, etc. was also found in the Griffiths' survey (1984). The urge for separate provision for ethnic children in care and for placing them with foster and adoptive parents of their respective groups is rightly argued on grounds of identity. The basic argument is that the identity of black children cared for or brought up by Whites will be impaired mainly because they will be brought up by people who are ignorant of the childrens' racial and ethnic backgrounds. Though available British studies suggest that transracial adoptions and long-term fostering work well, they also point out that black children brought up in white families are not clear about their racial or ethnic identity (Gill and Jackson, 1983; Rowe *et al.*, 1984). Chimezie (1975) also makes the point that in a racist society black children require 'survival strategies' and that these can only be learned through interaction with black people. But studies have equally found that 'matching' children and families by religion, social background, intelligence, etc. are largely irrelevant to the outcome of adoption (Witmer *et al.*, 1963; Jaffee and Fanshel, 1970; Shireman and

Johnson, 1980; Triseliotis and Russell, 1984).

The studies just quoted, albeit involving only white children, have also shown that though knowledge and understanding about origins and backgrounds are crucial to the adoptee's self-concept, they are subordinate to the quality of relationships pertaining within the family. In other words 'love' and 'good care' are very powerful attributes which not only can help heal earlier psychological traumas in children, but can also transcend certain differences and handicaps in the adoptee-adopter relationship. There is not enough space here for a full discussion of such a complex issue. It should not be impossible, however, to set up a study to examine and evaluate the issues surrounding this important controversy. It is my view based on my studies and those of others, that it is in the best interests of children to be placed with members of their respective ethnic group. Such an arrangement makes it easier for the child to base his developing personal and social identity not only on his psychological parents, but also on his family of origin, on his heritage and on his carers. Adoption allowances could also be used flexibly to encourage black families to adopt more black children. No matching, though, whether based on colour or otherwise, can make up for shortcomings in the adoptive or foster home. While agreeing that every effort should be made to place ethnic children with their respective ethnic group, the question still remains of what to do with those for whom no families can be found. A recent study of adults who experienced long periods in residential care found that children who grow up in institutions are signficantly more handicapped in a range of life-coping areas when compared with those who grow up adopted or in long-term foster care (Triseliotis and Russell, 1984). On the basis of this, and of other similar evidence, it would be irresponsible to deny children who cannot be matched with their respective ethnic group the opportunity to grow up with any suitable family of whatever colour. This should also include the fostering or adoption of white children by black families. In answer to a questionnaire, 71 per cent of black people said the overriding concern was that black children should be given a normal family life, whether in a black or white family (Bagley and Young, 1980). However, if black children have to be placed with white families, the latter should be in mixed neighbourhoods where the child can mix with other black children.

The knowledge, however, that black children can do reasonably well with white families could lead to continued inactivity on the part of local authorities in identifying, recruiting and preparing black and ethnic families for the fostering or adoptive role. It is not enough to say that black families do not come forward in sufficient numbers to act as foster or adoptive families. The Souls Kids Campaign (1976), though not spectacularly successful, still demonstrated that an active policy of recruitment is necessary for good results to be achieved. Only a tiny number of local authorities have picked up this challenge so far. The criteria used for approving foster and adoptive families have to be adapted to the circumstances of the ethnic minorities rather than applying those used for assessing white families. The lamentable fact remains that policies and programmes aimed at preventing children, of any colour, from coming into care at all are still in their infancy.

The Ethnic Elderly

A further area where separate development is inevitable is in the provision of day and residential care services for the ethnic elderly who may become isolated and lose their identity in a home or centre where the majority of residents are white. It is not simply a question of language, but the opportunity to exercise religious worship, to have food to one's liking, and not to be exposed to the hostility of white residents. Connelly (1981) found that the idea of providing ethnic meals produced a response of 'like it or lump it' from some managers in the social services. In contrast the Brent Social Service Department, which was possibly the first to introduce ethnic meals-on-wheels in 1976, has demonstrated the feasibility of delivering a gerneral service in a separate form to take account of ethnic preferences. In the case of Brent, not only are ethnic meals delivered but these are also prepared and cooked by ethnic staff. Ingrid Clements, meals orgainser with Brent social services, found that this necessary step required a very painful adaptation on her part and that of other white staff (I. Clements, pers. comm., 1984). Ethnic meals are not confined solely to Asians. Other minorities too have a preference for their own ethnic food.

Most separate development is likely to come through the use of Section 11 of the 1966 Local Government Act, which could help to stimulate the setting-up of voluntary agencies and of self-help groups among ethnic minorities. Such a step could encourage ethnic minorities to define and meet their needs in their own way. Self-achievement could also stimulate further the minorities' confidence in their ability to tackle at least some of their own problems. A service set up by those who need it becomes more local and avoids stigmatisation. The community-based approach of drop-in centres, such as the Melting Pot Foundation in Lambeth, has shown, for example, that black teenagers can be attracted to a facility which is informal and where they are not exposed to racial discrimination.

Other examples could be neighbourhood-based day-care facilities for the young and old, self-help groups for single parents, self-run hostels for black homeless youth, community centres for isolated Asian women, or shelters for women exposed to unacceptable violence within their homes.

Like affirmative action, separate development by itself is necessary but of limited value if not accompanied by concerted efforts to overcome racism and unfair inequality. Inevitably the achievement of cultural pluralism, which does not become a euphemism for segregation, plus equality of opportunity, presents real dilemmas.

Face to Face

In contrast to the initial writings, recent social-work literature on ethnicity has focused its attention more on policy and organisational issues and less on direct practice. Policy and organisational issues deserved a more serious analysis, but the fact still remains that little is known about the intricate aspects of transcultural face-to-face practice. One possible explanation of the dearth of material about the 'how' of practice is that writings arising from direct work with clients and client-groups require some speculating and generalising from specific situations. This stage in knowledge-building is necessary until research can either confirm or refute practice observations. Yet not many practitioners seem prepared to risk exposing themselves to retrospective 'insights' and 'wisdoms' in such a sensitive area.

There are many areas of practice about which much more knowledge is required than is currently available. Among others, these include the way different ethnic groups view external intervention and professional helpers; the needs which minorities bring to social workers, and under what circumstances; the process of building working-type relationships; meanings attributed to verbal and non-verbal forms of communication; and an identification of interventive approaches which take account of cultural differences. For example, a study carried out by the Citizens' Advice Bureau (1984) in West Yorkshire showed that most Asians find the idea of giving advice to people outside their own extended family groups to be unacceptable. They also said that they felt unable to trust workers without having more personal knowledge about them. Yet Western social work generally discourages the revelation of personal information on the part of the worker. West Indians, according to the same study, distrusted formality, preferring a free and easy environment.

Bang (1983), in an excellent monograph, also refers to relationships with Vietnamese refugees which need to be warmer and less formal.

The tasks facing social workers engaged in transcultural social work do not basically differ from those undertaken in ethnocentric-type work. They involve the collection, study and assessment of relevant information, and eventually the mutual exploration of possible solutions. What is different is the kind of cultural understanding and racial awareness that is brought to bear on this assessment, including the type of analysis the worker has arrived at concerning the position of minorities in Britain. A corollary to this is the worker's capacity to manage difference and to construe facts and feelings in the context of the minorities' culture and life situations. He also has to be prepared to move away from a solely person-focused approach to problems, to one that encompasses the impact of racism and of socioeconomic factors on the lives of minorities. Such an approach could go a long way to closing the gap in perspectives between minority clients and social workers.

The demonstration of empathy, warmth and respect, which have been found to contribute to the establishment of good working relationships with white clients, are equally valid in transcultural work. These attributes, however, are no substitute for technical know-how, and for adapting traditional Western-type interventive approaches to the needs of minorities. As a representative of the majority culture, the white worker also has to overcome the suspicions and mistrust of minorities, whose disadvantages are mostly the result of discrimination exercised by the majority culture. The commitment and affinity felt towards the minorities' predicament is usually tested through the worker's readiness to speak out about the way institutional racism or the possibly discriminatory policies and practices of his own or other organisations affect the minorities.

The social worker's main role *vis-à-vis* ethnic minorities is briefly to provide information or to link them to resources, including assistance in developing their own support systems and organisations, and to act as mediator/counsellor in situations of strained social or family relationships. It is true now, as it was almost twenty years ago, that because of the minorities' social and economic position, and of their cultural experiences, 'they are usually more accessible to measures intended to alleviate pressing social needs than to help aimed at resolving interpersonal problems' (Triseliotis, 1965). Research carried out since has supported a somewhat similar approach with white clients. For example, Sainsbury (1975) found from a study of 26 very disadvantaged white families that client satisfaction was associated with a progression of activity with material and practical needs tackled first, before other areas such as marital problems were explored. Intervention with resource agencies again tests the worker's resolve to help, and his advocacy skills on behalf of the minorities. This is not to suggest that minorities do not have personal problems. These may, however, have to wait while more pressing needs are attended to and until some form of trust has been established. There is no doubt that some minority clients do find it more acceptable to present themselves with practical and social problems rather than with family and personal ones.

Because a large part of a social worker's job is about making assessments, ignorance about cultural and ethnic factors can easily lead to inappropriate conclusions and actions, or to 'benign' neglect. This is not the same as explaining everything in cultural terms, as this could equally lead to a failure to act in the face of suffering, e.g. failing to provide a shelter to a harassed Asian woman on the grounds that Asian women are used to acts of harassment on the part of their husbands, or explaining the cruel treatment of a child as being within the cultural norms. A proper evaluation of cultural factors avoids the dangers of both exaggeration and 'turning a blind eye'. Commenting on the importance of cultural factors, Cooper (1973) remarked that 'white workers influenced by a culture rampant with racism and unfamiliar with the intricacies and nuances of the lives of ethnic people may, even with the best intentions, fail to recognise when social and cultural forces predominate'. She goes on to add that 'some workers may exaggerate the importance or impact of ethnic factors', a point also made by Ahmed (1978).

Transcultural social work is not solely about white workers involved with ethnic minorities. It is also relevant to minority social workers who happen to be responsible for delivering services to members of the majority culture. The minority worker, like his white counterpart, has an equivalent responsibility to understand the majority culture. (This is said in the knowledge that so little is known about many aspects of British life. Western anthropologists seem to find it easier to observe distant tribes then to study their own urban communities.) One of the challenges the minority worker is likly to face is the implicit or explicit hostility of those white clients who may resent him as their worker, either because of his colour or his ethnicity, calling into question his competence. The ethnic worker may himself come to feel inferior *vis-à-vis* white clients who, not long ago, were the colonial masters of his country of origin. He may equally nurture mixed feelings towards white people in general for past and current injustices.

If there are problems to be overcome by those engaged in transcultural social work, working with one's own ethnic or racial group is far from being an easy ride. Delivering social work services to one's own ethnic group overcomes the cultural gap, but it can also generate unusual over-identification, or feelings of 'shame' on the part of the client, and, depending on the circumstances, a 'sold-out' attitude towards the worker. Encounters of this type can sometimes lead to a kind of impasse from which cultural familiarity offers no escape route. There is no convincing evidence as to whether better working relationships can be obtained through matching clients and workers by colour, ethnicity and sex, or simply by shared attitudes and beliefs. Bang (1983), talking about the Vietnamese, claims that they prefer English workers when wanting something concrete, but that they prefer one of their own workers for help with personal problems.

Cross-cultural Communication

The painful reality of transcultural communication is that words and phrases inteded to convey a certain thought, feeling or reaction may easily be misunderstood and viewed either as over- or under- statements, or as too vague, too direct or too hostile. Yet a similar explanation might not have been given by others sharing the same cultural background. Some verbal and non-verbal forms of communication, such as the display of feeling, gestures, eye contact or mood, can only be understood in their cultural context. Similarly, notions about directness or evasiveness, passivity or aggressivity, exuberance or withdrawal, can be misleading if viewed from an ethnocentric perspective. For example, some minorities express familial and other conflicts much more strongly than the British. Equally, whereas some are only too open, clear and direct about what they wish to convey, others are less so and may appear to agree with what has been said whereas in fact they feel the opposite.

Decisions made without cultural understanding may make the difference between, for example, community care or incarceration, or permission or denial of access to one's child in care. The risk always exists of labelling unfamiliar behaviour as 'aggressive', 'paranoid', 'hostile' or 'depressive'.

In previous writings I pointed out that the process of understanding how people from other cultures express and deal with their feelings, and how they display their moods, is like learning a new language (Triseliotis, 1965, 1972). A fair amount of negative discrimination towards minorities usually results from inappropriate interpretations of their behaviour and attitudes. Being wrongly understood is a source of continued anxiety for many minority people because it can lead to the denial of jobs, promotions, services, etc. Verbal and non-verbal forms of communication are part of the minorities' personal and social identity, and though they are likely to be modified by new experiences, it should not be expected that they will be shed out of preference for the ways of the majority culture.

Western social work and psychiatric literature have traditionally linked the inhibition or over-control of feeling with tension leading to 'neurotic' symptoms or behaviour. Because of this, considerable time is usually spent during the training of social workers on how they can help their clients towards more open forms of communication, increased sharing of feelings, and the giving of feedback in relationships. Overall there is encouragement towards the open display and sharing of feelings and emotions, particularly those of 'extremes of anger or love'. Yet in my work with some minorities I often found myself doing exactly the opposite: that is, encouraging them to limit or control feedback and the display of very negative feelings. Their problem was not usually one of lack of feedback but of too much. Similarly, when running groups composed of members of certain minorities, a frequent task was finding ways of limiting members' contributions and encouraging more listening. This was in contrast to the long silences endured in groups of whites. Paradoxically, and because of cultural taboos operating among some of the minorities, the disclosure of intimate, personal and family relationships to outsiders is generally discouraged. The worker needs to recognise and respect these boundaries.

Counselling Techniques

Western-type counselling requires considerable modification if it is to be of relevance to minorities. For example, because of cultural factors, some ethnic minority clients respond better to more active, more open and clear approaches, which include suggestions, as compared with the mostly reflective, rather introspective and almost totally permissive forms of counselling used by white counsellors. Smith (1981) points out that black people tend to view the role of counsellor as quite alien, and that they often use the family and the Church as places for dealing with the inner self and for searching for understanding. When they visit counsellors "they frequently go with the belief that they will be able to obtain advice about a specific matter" (p. 165). Harper (1973), referring to black people, argues that effective counselling requires techniques that bring a client to a level of awareness and action: 'directive, confrontive and persuasive approaches are most compatible'. Like Harper, Fitch (1975) agrees that West Indians may in some circumstances require 'a direct response'. Atkinson *et al.* (1978) comment that people of different cultural backgrounds respond differently to the use of different counselling skills, and adds, for example, that Asians 'prefer a logical, rational, structured counselling approach over an affective, reflective, ambiguous one'. Also, an approach that focuses on behaviour and action rather than on moods and feelings seems to be nearer the experiences of minorities, particularly those from the New Commonwealth. Sue (1981), commenting generally on counselling, adds that the unstructured nature of counselling may generate anxiety among minorities who have been reared in an environment that actively structures social relationships and patterns of interaction.

In societies where roles and relationships are culturally sanctioned, with well-defined rights and obligations (e.g. between husband and wife, parents and children), the role of mediator rather than that of counsellor seems to be more responsive to the experiences and traditions of minorites. For example, work with families suggests that Western-style 'family therapy' is inappropriate with Asian families. Hitch (1981) points out that in contrast to Asian families, the Western view of the family is of a system which is open to restructuring, and to a redefinition of the roles and power structures. He adds that within Asian families:

> conflicts are often about the use and style of power, not about the structure itself; thus the conflicts are both personal and political, and the resolution is by bargaining with resources. As strategy and tactics require some degree of secrecy, it is likely that this is the reason why attempts to get open communication in work with Asian families frequently fail.

Mediation, arbitration, bargaining and conciliation aimed at helping families to settle internal conflicts or disputes with outside institutions are more familiar methods to both Asian and black people than the Western-style counselling which conveys notions of therapy and pathology. The mediation approach can encompass marital disputes, instances of suspected child abuse, the struggles of Asian adolescents for greater independence, or the disagreements between West Indian teenagers and their families. It is also appropriate, within this model, for the worker sometimes to see separately, even for a few minutes, family members who carry culturally sanctioned authority, either to make a point or to reach an agreement. The approach avoids the danger of 'shaming' or of anyone 'losing face', and it also conveys respect for patterns of authority and traditional roles. Responsibility is kept firmly within the family. When working with black or Asian families the worker should also partly set aside Western ideas about privacy and confidentiality, and be prepared to see whoever is present and whoever drops in, without isolating individuals and families from their support systems. Workers at the Asian resource centre at Handsworth, Birmingham, deal with individual problems except very personal ones, in an open office and in the form of an open debate.

The methods described here are meant only as a general rather than a specific guide when dealing with the diverse needs of ethnic minorities. Subtle differences and sometimes contradictions are inevitable: hence the need for more detailed studies. For example, though some writers referred to earlier argue for 'clarity and lack of ambiguity' when dealing with Asians, Bang (1983, p. 16), referring to the Vietnamese, suggests that the worker approach the problems 'indirectly' and talk in 'allegories', 'sometimes for as long as an hour' and make 'pretexts' for the visit.

The preoccupations of many Western social workers and 'therapists' with the past, requiring detailed developmental histories of individual clients or patients, often leaves members of minorities perplexed. Whereas most Western 'therapists' tend to attribute current personal ills to childhood experiences, this is not a familiar idea among minorities. The past does not dominate their thinking in the same way that it does with Western people. More meaningful, and nearer to the minorities' experiences, are their concerns about their current life situations and about the future. Closely related to this outlook is also the orientation of some minorities towards a philosophy of life which accepts the 'fatality' of life and the considerable influence of external factors in shaping their destinies. Such an outlook tends to discourage self-examination when faced with troubles or conflict. Western culture, on the other hand, places the emphasis on the individual being responsible for his destiny, and in the face of adversity it encourages a rather introspective approach requiring a detailed examination of one's attitudes and behaviour.

The Training of Social Workers

The Central Council for Education and Training in Social Work (CCETSW) requires institutions running social-work courses to prepare student for cross-cultural social work. The amount of time allocated to the subject is left to the institutions themselves. Not surprisingly, the length and content of such courses vary. In 1982, the Council published a useful handbook making suggestions about content, and providing a wide-ranging bibliography. The main problem is how to present the subject in a way that goes well beyond theoretical teaching about cultural backgrounds and social-policy and social work issues. Although intellectual understanding is important, opportunities are also necessary to examine personal attitudes with the aim of developing racial awareness and sensitivity towards ethnic minorities. Sadly, no satisfactory exercises are available to facilitate the process of 'attitudinal training' or 'consciousness raising'. The problem is compounded in those areas where students have no opportunities for transcultural practice to use as a medium for the examination of attitudes.

Our own teaching on the subject gained considerably in student popularity after it was arranged in the form of a conference with the students being involved in the planning. A variety of teaching methods were used, such as direct input, exercises, group discussions and films. The most interesting part proved to be the participation, with the help of the local Community Relations office, of members of different ethnic groups, such as Pakistani, Indian, Chinese, West Indian and Vietnamese. To avoid the danger of viewing this part of the course in isolation, a conscious effort is made to identify the implications of cultural factors in the rest of the teaching. Inevitably, with a crowded timetable which restricts the amount of time available, only very modest goals can be attained. It is our expectation that training for transcultural social work will continue as part of in-service training after the students are in employment.

Conclusion

Transcultural social work goes well beyond the face-to-face interaction between social workers and people who do not share the same cultural background. It involves getting the policies right and developing organisational structures that are sensitive to cultural diversity and provide for separate development in specific areas of need. Direct service requires a good grasp of cultural backgrounds, the adaptation of Western-type methods, and advocacy skills based on a commitment to the needs of some of the most disadvantaged groups in British society. It would be misleading, though, to conclude from what has been said that transcultural social work is an esoteric activity open only to a selected few. This is far from being the case: the field is wide open to anyone prepared to shed stereotypes and abandon an ethnocentric approach to social-work practice.

References

Ahmed, S. (1978) 'Asian Girls and Culture Conflict', *Social Work Today, 9* (47), 14–16

Association of Directors of Social Services and the Commission for Racial Equality (1978) *Multi-racial Britain: the Social Services Response*, Commission for Racial Equality, London

Atkinson, D..R., Maruyama, M. and Matsui, S. (1978) 'The Effects of the Counsellor Race and Counselling Approach to Asian Americans' Perceptions of Counsellor Credibility and Utility', *Journal of Counselling Psychology, 25,* 76–83

Bagley,C. and Young, L. (1980) 'Transracial Adoption: Views of a Black Community Sample', *London, Community Care, 304,* 16–18

Bang, S. (1983) *We come as a Friend: Towards a Vietnamese Model of Social Work,* Leeds Refugee Action, Leeds

Barclay Report (1982) *Social Workers: their Role and Tasks,* Bedford Square Press for the NISW, London

Barker, J. (1984) *Black and Asian Old People in Britain,* Age Concern, London

Central Council for Education and Training in Social Work (1982) *Teaching Social Work in a Multi-racial Society: The report of a working group,* 52 (2) pp. 76–84

Cheetham, J. (1981) *Social Work Services for Ethnic Minorities in Britain and the USA,* Department of Health and Social Security, London

Cheetham, J. (ed.) (1982) *Social Work and Ethnicity,* Allen & Unwin, London

Chimezie, A. (1975) 'Transcultural Adoption of Black Children', *Social Work, 20,* (4), 296–301

Citizens Advice Bureau (1984) *The Kirklees Ethnic Minorities Advice Project,* National Association of Citizens Advice Bureaux, London

Connelly, N. (1981) *Social Services Provision in Multi-racial Areas,* Policy Studies Institute, London

Cooper, S. (1973) 'A Look at the Effect of Racism on Clinical Work', *Social Casework, 54* (3), 67–76

Farrar, N. (1984) Quoted by Sharron, H. 'Meeting the Ethnic Challenge', *Social Work Today,* 6 August 1984

Field, S. (1984) *The Attitudes of Ethnic Minorities,* Home Office Research Studies, Report No. 80, HMSO, London

Fitch, D. (1975) *Counselling the Carribean Family,*Commission for Racial Equality, London

Gill, O. and Jackson, B. (1983) *Adoption and Race,* Batsford, London

Griffiths, J. (1984) *Study of Social Service Provision to Ethnic Minority Groups,* Derbyshire County Council, Matlock

Harper,R. (1973) 'What Counsellors Must Know about the Social Sciences of Black Americans', *Journal of Negro Education, 3,* 16–19

Hitch, P.J. (1981) 'The Politics of Intervention in Asian Families', *Bulletin of the Transcultural Psychiatry Society (U.K.),* Spring issue (no paging)

Husband, C. (1978) 'Racism in Social Work', *Community Care,* No. 241, pp. 39–40

Jaffee, B. and Fanshel, D. (1970) *How they Fared in Adoption: a Follow-up Study,* Columbia University Press, New York

Jones, C. (1977) *Immigration and Social Policy in Britain,* Tavistock, London

Kent, B. (1965) 'The Social Worker's Cultural Pattern as it Affects Casework with Immigrants', *Social Work, 22,* No. 4

King, M.L. (1968) 'The Role of the Behavioural Scientist in the Civil Rights Movement', *American Psychologist, 23,* 180–6

Little, A. and Robins, D. (1982) *Loading the Law,* Commission for Racial Equality, London

Livingstone, J.C. (1979) 'Fast Game? Inequality and Affirmative Action', quoted by Little and Robins (1982)

Murphy, G. (1978) 'Merseyside Probation and After-Care Service and the Black Community', internal paper, SPO, Liverpool

National Council for Voluntary Organisations (1984) *A Multi-Racial Society: the Role of National Voluntary Organisations,* Bedford Square Press, London

Rex, J. (1983) 'The Segregation or Integration of Britain's Black Minorities', the James Seth Memorial Lecture given at the University of Edinburgh, November

Rowe, J., Cain, H., Hundleby, M. and Keane, A (1984), *Long-Term Foster Care,* Batsford, London

Sainsbury, E. (1975) *Social Work with Families,* Routledge and Kegan Paul, London

Scarman, Lord (1982) *The Scarman Report The Brixton Disorders, 10–12 April 1981,* Pelican Books, London

Shireman, J.F. and Johnson, P.R. (1980) *Adoption: Three Alternatives,* Part II, Child Care Society, Chicago

Smith, E.J. (1981) 'Cultural and Historical Perspectives in Counselling Blacks', in D.W. Sue, *Counselling the Culturally Different,* Wiley, New York

'Soul Kids Campaign' (1976) Association of British Adoption and Fostering Agencies, London

South Yorkshire Probation and After-Care Service (1978) Annual Report, Sheffield

Staplehurst, A. (1983) *Working with Young Afro-Caribbean Offenders,* Monograph published by the University of East Anglia and *Social Work Today*

Sue, D.W. (ed.) (1981) *Counselling the Culturally Different,* Wiley, New York

Triseliotis, J. (1963) 'Immigrant Schoolchildren and their Problems of Adjustment', *Case Conference, 9,* (7), 187–92

Triseliotis, J. (1965) 'Casework with Immigrants: the Implications of Cultural Factors', *British Journal of Psychiatric Social Work, 8,* (1) 15–27

Triseliotis, J. (ed.) (1972) *Social Work with Coloured Immigrants and their Families,* Oxford University Press, London

Triseliotis, J. and Russell, J. (1984) *Hard to Place: the Outcome of Adoption and Residential Care,* Heinemann, London

Witmer, L. H., Herzog, E., Weinstein, E.A. and Sullivan, M.E. (1963) *Independent Adoption: a Follow-up Study,* Russell Sage Foundation, New York

13 CULTURE AND PSYCHIATRIC NURSING: IMPLICATIONS FOR TRAINING

Bryn D. Davis

Introduction

In any aspect of health care it is today's premise that we deal with the whole person, and not only that but the whole person in his/her social context. The boundaries have extended from the body, to the body and mind, and thence to the groups and culture within which the individual is located. With respect to these developments there have been or should be similar moves concerning the multidisciplinary base for health care, and in particular for nursing care.

Nurses, it is frequently acknowledged, are the professional group that has most dealings with and for patients, mainly on a face-to-face basis. Nurses as a professional group are also claiming to deal with the whole person in their social context, and to apply models of nursing which make the assessment of the patient's needs the basis of care. Physiology, psychology and sociology are usually the informing disciplines which are drawn on in the assessment of patient needs and the planning of care. However, there is now much support for the argument that ethnographic perspectives should be included in the preparation of nurses.

In the UK recently there have been various articles in the nursing journals calling for an ethnographic approach (e.g. Burrows, 1982; Dobson, 1983). Burrows argues that 'in this country . . . nursing is taught and practised as if all patients were members of the dominant Christian, Caucasian group', (p. 478). She warns that ethnocentric beliefs may deny the importance of other belief systems. Dobson recognises the all-pervasive nature of cultural influences into all aspects of life, since they are socialised into our behaviour, attitudes and beliefs from infancy. This can lead to culture shock when an individual is confronted by an alternative, insensitive culture. Such confrontation is all too frequently experienced in contact with the health services, hospital as well as community, and at the hands of nurses, who are usually caring in other respects.

These two pleas for ethnographic approaches claim that, in order to achieve this, changes need to be made in the nurse education curriculum.

218

Attempts have been made in the USA and in Canada to develop such curricula, some of which will be discussed further below.

However, it is first necessary to relate the concern for an ethnographic approach to psychiatric nurses in particular — the main focus of this chapter. As indicated above, we are also concerned here with patients' identified needs as the basis of care. We therefore propose to consider the implications of culture for nursing, and to apply these to psychiatric nursing. As Leininger has argued (1967), the Western criteria used in separating the 'normal' from the 'abnormal' in medicine may not be those used by other cultures. Health and illness are important, active components of any culture, and relate intimately to religious, social, political and economic beliefs.

The development of a transcultural approach to nursing owes a great deal to Leininger, who has been researching, teaching and publishing in the field for some twenty years. Unfortunately her articles tend to be somewhat repetitive, and yet it is possible to extract from her writings, such as those collected in Leininger (1978a), nuggets of wisdom which illustrate the progress of her work and offer a theoretical formulation and model as a basis for further exploration and application.

Anthropological studies have contributed much to the health field, and Leininger (1968) has identified six major areas: first, a holistic approach to the study of man; secondly, the knowledge base of different cultures provides a rich comparative viewpoint; thirdly, the longitudinal view of cultural development gives us a deeper appreciation of man's behaviour; fourthly, the cultural patterns identified provide important data for health professionals; fifthly, the research technique of participant observation developed by anthropologists is a useful tool for the study of health problems; and sixthly, anthropologists see health and illness as integral parts of culture. Applying these contributions from anthropology, Leininger has generated various perspectives on transcultural nursing care from her own and others' explorations (1978b). A summary of these is given here.

Culturological Assessment

Identifiable differences in caring values and behaviour between cultures lead to differences in care expectations of care seekers, particularly with regard to technological aspects of care, which can lead to poor interpersonal relationships and low satisfaction. These can lead to cultural conflict and stresses in caring contexts. Cultures based on kinship and group care expect more humanistic approaches to nursing care and less technological care. There is also less desire for self-care.

From these observations Leininger has developed a paradigm for a 'culturological nursing assessment' as a basis for nursing practice (1978c):

(1) Cultural life patterns
(2) Cultural values, norms and expressions
(3) Cultural taboos and myths
(4) World view and ethnocentric tendencies
(5) Cultural diversities
(6) Life-caring rituals and rites of passage
(7) Folk and professional health-illness systems
(8) Specific caring behaviours, and nursing care, values, beliefs and practices
(9) Cultural changes and acculturation.

This form of assessment can be applied to individuals, groups or societies.

Relationships between Nurses and Patients

The points made so far relate to nurses' attitudes to patient care, and to the overall nursing situation, although their application to psychiatric nursing can be seen. Another important aspect not covered so far is that of the nurses themselves. Many nurses training and working in this country are from different cultures, intending either to remain here working in the British culture or to return to their own people with a British approach to health and health care.

With the first group, immigrants intending to stay in the UK, the new recruits must be introduced to the new culture in terms of everyday living for themselves as well as in terms of their role in health care. The second group, visitors to this country intending to return to their own after their course, must be introduced to the British culture for their everyday living, and for their role in health care. However, they should also have their own cultural health-care role catered for. In this way they would be prepared to return to their own people, values, beliefs and practices without necessarily imposing a Western-style approach to health care. This would allow them to take ideas and insights from their experience in this country home with them for consideration and, perhaps, implementation.

The question of relationships between cultural groups of nurses and

Figure 13.1: Illustration of the Cultural Relationships between Nurses and Patients

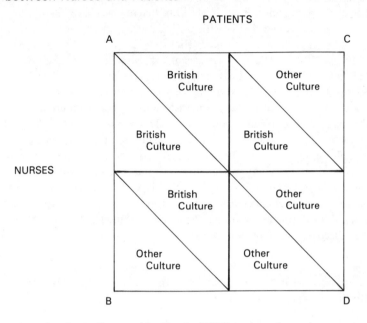

PATIENTS

NURSES

patients has been discussed by Davis (1980) and a schematic representation has been suggested. Figure 13.1 shows this schema of the complex relationships involved between immigrant and indigenous groups. It offers four combinations but in reality these four basic relationships may appear in mixed format. For example, a team of nurses may consist of British and other cultures, as in boxes A and B, caring for patients of British culture. We may also find a team of British nurses caring for a mixed group of British and other culture patients as in boxes A and C combined. It may also occur that the situation as represented by boxes A, B and C is found, nurses from a variety of cultures caring for a group of patients from a variety of cultures.

Added to these complex relationships is the factor that nurses and patients may be drawn from resident immigrant populations, e.g. Afro-Caribbean, Asian, European. Having adapted to a certain extent to the British way of life, they may very well feel that it is important that they try to retain some of their generic culture, even though born and bred in the UK. However, they may also feel that because of the physical differences between them and the indigenous population, as well as the cultural ones, as an underprivileged group they suffer, prejudice and discrimination. The attitudes and reactions engendered by such experiences may well be reflected in their behaviour as patients and nurses. The question of racism in the NHS is one that has been aired in the nursing press and is one that is still causing much concern as is revealed in the correspondence generated (Hicks, 1982; *Nursing Times*, 1982).

In the USA, similar experiences and discussions have taken place. Tallmer *et al.* (1977), for example, describe the reactions of black and Puerto Rican nursing aides in long-stay nursing homes for the elderly. They observe that 'it has been established that minority group membership exposes one to innumerable psychological assaults' (p. 177), and they consider the implications in the socialisation process that follows an upbringing in imposed lower social class status and poverty with associated prejudice. Aggression or over-protective responses can occur which cannot be helpful for the elderly, dependent patient, nor for the professional development of the nursing aide. The authors argue for a culturally informed curriculum. This aspect of their paper will be further discussed later in this chapter.

Transcultural Psychiatric Nursing: the Expression of Mental Illness in Different Cultures

Nursing in the United States of America has been more aware of cultural aspects of mental illness, and the importance of anthropology in the knowledge base of nursing in general has been noted earlier in this chapter. Brown (1974) has highlighted some of the differences in mental illness as expressed by American Indian patients. However, her argument is that these differences are superficial, and that the illnesses can be fitted into the internationally accepted classifications. Nevertheless, the variety of symptoms associated with particular disorders can make the planning of nursing care confusing. She describes some of the findings of a survey by the McGill Transcultural Psychiatric Study Group with reference to depression and schizophrenia (Murphy *et al.*, 1963, 1964). These showed a wide variety of symptoms, only four universal ones being identified for depression: insomnia and early-morning wakening; a mood of dejection; withdrawal from emotional and social relationships; and fatigue. One symptom, usually a predominant one in Western cultures, intrapunitiveness, was totally lacking in many other cultures.

Equally varied patterns of symptoms were found regarding schizophrenia. Religion (as a cultural phenomenon) was an important factor, associated with delusions of destruction and religion in Muslim and Christian cultures. Christian culture was strongly associated with intrapunitiveness in depression, which was rare in Muslim cultures. Röscher (1974) reports how an African woman was diagnosed as schizophrenic after she described herself as coming from the Moon four months previously. She was now trying to return to the Moon. In her cultural idiom she had been describing her amenorrhoea, and had been wanting treatment for it. A nurse sensitive to this idiom was able to change the diagnosis and obtain referral to a gynaecologist. The McGill survey (Murphy *et al.*, 1963, 1964), also indicated that culture influenced or was related to the incidence and prevalence of particular mental disorders. For example, Eskimo and African cultures had low incidences of depression, whereas the former had a high incidence of hysteria.

Britain nowadays contains a very varied mixture of cultures, and practitioners working in the field of mental health can encounter a wide variety of mental health problems. This applies particularly to nurses. Variations in symptomatology as identified and discussed by psychiatrists such as Rack (1982) and Littlewood and Lipsedge (1982) have importance for nursing practice. Nurses sensitive to cultural factors in a particular patient profile can be a major influence on the care that that patient receives. Nurses are also important in the collection of case material. Spending much more time in contact with patients than other health-care professionals, they are well placed to observe details of the patient's lifestyle. This can be most valuable in providing a culturally valid picture of the patient's needs.

Thus at two levels nurses must be culturally aware. In helping to deliver care and treatment, they have a role in ensuring that these are presented in a format and context that will make them acceptable to patients. Secondly, in their observations and interactions with patients, nurses are particularly well placed to collect information that will help in the correct identification of each patient's cultural niche. From this information a picture can be obtained of the interpretation and explanation of the clinical situation by the patient and/or his family.

Notes made by nurses of their observation and conversations with patients can provide a rich source of information from which culturally valid assessments can be made, and on which culturally valid plans of care can be based. In the USA and Canada there has been a relatively long history of involvement by nurses in making cultural assessments in both general and psychiatric settings (Brown, 1974; Brink, 1976; Leininger, 1978a). Many of these nurses have undertaken fieldwork with ethnic minority groups in their countries or in other regions such as India or South America. This reflects the education and training they have in knowledge and techniques.

Very few such studies have been reported in the British literature. Of the few that can be discussed, those of Fosdike (1980), Webb (1981), Schofield (1981), Dobson (1983) and Mayor (1984) are the more recent. Most have been concerned with the Asian communities in Britain, although that of Fosdike was concerned with a Moroccan community and that of Webb with both Asian and Afro-Caribbean. The main concern of these studies was with cultural aspects of general health, and in particular the role of the health visitor. However, Webb emphasised the importance of health education, and Schofield was the only researcher to be specifically concerned with mental health, although as a health visitor and not as a psychiatric nurse.

Nevertheless these reports provide very useful resource material of which psychiatric nurses in general and community psychiatric nurses in particular should be making use. Important points raised are kinship and its part in the social structure of ethnic communities, and its impact on attitudes to health, illness, treatment and care. In many immigrant groups the traditional extended family may be lost and yet traditional roles and levels of status are still expected and enforced. This can put individuals in these immigrant communities under stress without the usual support from the extended family (Fosdike, 1980; Schofield, 1981).

Religion is another point raised by the British studies, and in many cultures, particularly these embracing the Muslim religion, it can have a much more potent influence on lifestyle and interpersonal relationships. This can be reflected in concepts and practices of punishment, for example. Attitudes to diet, hygiene and health also reflect the importance of religion (Fosdike, 1980). As Schofield points out, ignorance of anatomy and physiology fostered by strict religious laws can lead to many superstitious beliefs about health and to a reliance on folk medicine and folk medical experts such as the hakim.

Another major factor emphasised by all the studies is that of language. Mental illness in particular is expressed verbally, with, usually, very few physical signs. Even in general health, however, the report of symptoms is a major source of clinical information. Adequate interpretation of the patient's problems would seem to be of major importance, yet pidgin English and non-verbal communication seem to be used with all too great frequency. The elderly members of these ethnic minority groups seem to experience the greatest difficulty in adapting linguistically. Describing the introduction of a telephone service in association with local radio. Webb (1981) found that 11 per cent of telephone enquiries about health-related matters were about mental health problems. The telephones were manned by volunteers most of whom could speak the languages involved. The volunteers were health-care professionals covering most of the specialist areas expected. However, virtually no Asian or Afro-Caribbean specialists in gynaecology, family planning and obstetrics could be found in London. An evaluation of the advice given was undertaken via follow-up calls. Ninety-nine people felt the advice was useful and followed it; 34 felt it was useless. Of these a high proportion referred back to their GP reported that they found the GP unhelpful. With particular reference to the mental health of Asian women, Schofield (1981) has reviewed the major problems that have been identified. Depression figures as a frequent and distressing feature for many women (Wilson, 1977; Knight, 1978), and Burrows (1983) has pointed out the possibility of psychotic reactions. The Community Relations Commission (1976) has highlighted the importance of hysterical conversion reaction and paranoid reactions.

In the USA, Osborne (1976) has discussed the unique needs of ethnic minority clients. He identifies two major errors in the approaches of nurses in their dealings with these patients. The first is that the nurse ignores the racial and cultural identity of the client in an attempt at a liberal attitude, assuming that in treating him as a generic human being (white middle-class American in Osborne's setting) adequate care will be given. The second error pointed out by Osborne is that of being overwhelmed by the racial characteristics and of dealing with the client as a cultural stereotype, ignoring the individual social and interpersonal factors that are relevant to the assessment of his needs.

Although such errors have been reported in Britain (Wilson, 1978) involving the attitudes of health visitors to Asian women, the evidence on which these reports were based is not clearly established, and is challenged by Schofield (1981). Nevertheless, these are errors of approach that can all too easily occur (Webb, 1981). Misguided attempts at a 'liberal' approach based on a strategy of treating all clients or patients alike, and thus hoping to prevent either favouritism or prejudice, can lead to the loss of individuality and the 'whole' patient/client, and thus render ineffective the care that is given.

Osborne (1976) recognises that many health-care workers feel that it is an overwhelming task to take in all there is to know about other cultures one might come across. He points out, though, that there is now much resource material in books, journals and through colleagues. This may not be quite the case in the UK, but it is, however, possible to use the client as a primary cultural resource from which a personal idiographic perception of the cultural relevancies can be taken. In this way the simplistic racial stereotype can be lost and the human being with his unique ethnic persona can be met.

If we are sensitised to the concepts behind a cultural approach to health care, we can identify defensive strategies employed by the member of a minority group when feeling disadvantaged or stressed by or in the larger culture. It is important to appreciate the influence of feelings of inferiority, inadequacy and perceived incompetence in the dynamic client-therapist relationship. Anger is another reaction often felt but not so frequently expressed, leading to hostile responses. Although usually this suppression can be maintained, occasionally it may escape and be directed against those who cannot retaliate or against inanimate objects. In an extreme situation the suppression may lead to ideas of reference or to paranoid ideas (Osborne, 1976). Clients with these suppressed or expressed feelings may withhold themselves from sharing in the therapeutic relationship. They may even withdraw from it physically, or psychologically by cognitive screening or overcompensation.

Of major importance for the psychiatric nurse is the relationship between culture, stress and the various methods of coping with illness, as pointed out by Brown (1974). The balancing methods within a culture, whereby stresses are matched by rituals and processes often supported by or couched in religious or spiritual contexts, may be lost when groups or communities of one culture are trying to integrate or at least interact with a host culture. The stresses in the immigrant culture may not be recognised or acknowledged; the balancing mechanisms may not be recognised or may be destroyed in the integration. The methods of coping or treatment offered by the host culture may be unrecognisable as ways of balancing the stresses by the immigrants.

Examples of this were found by Webb (1981) in her report of the phone-in exercise. A small but significant proportion of those followed up claimed that the advice offered was useless. It was not seen as a valid way of coping with respect to the individual's cultural mores.

Much can also be learnt by Western nurses from a study of ways in which other cultures do cope with, absorb or care for their mentally ill. The problem of social isolation or institutionalisation does not occur in many non-Western cultures. Consequently there are not the associated problems of apathy, social withdrawal and antisocial behaviour (Brown, 1974).

Preparation for Transcultural Psychiatric Nursing

Is it possible to educate nurses in such a way that they will be sensitised to cultural concepts and able to practise in a multiracial society? The preparation of health-care workers, particularly psychiatric nurses, must take into account the cultural needs of the patient/client if problems such as those identified earlier are to be alleviated. Many programmes have been developed, in the USA in particular, to do just this.

Although a variety of cultural relationships between nurses and patients have been identified (Figure 13.1), the main approach to the transcultural preparation of nurses has been for indigenous nurses to be made aware of and to become skilled in cultural aspects of their multicultural society and patient group. Those programmes that have been offered at this level are those that will be considered here. The needs of immigrant groups of nurses in facing the indigenous patient group and the multicultural patient group will be dealt with below.

A workshop consisting of a three-session course for nurses' aides was mounted in New York (Tallmer *et al.*, 1977). This is considered by the authors to be the basic minimum preparation for transcultural nursing. The aides in question were working in nursing homes for the elderly. They were mainly Puerto Rican or black American, and the elderly residents were white middle-class Americans.

The course focused on the psychosocial role of the aide, 'with particular emphasis on an understanding of how attitudes are formed and reinforced by cultural differences' (p. 182). Evaluation of this short course was undertaken using a specially developed questionnaire which incorporated items from the Kogan OP Scale (Kogan, 1961). The administration and discussion of the questionnaire items formed the first activity of the course, and the final activity of the third and final session. A major finding of the evaluation was that, even for such a short course, 83 per cent of the aides reported that the course had helped them to understand the role cultural differences play in creating differences between people. However, although acknowledging the increased knowledge, fewer aides reported changes in their feelings about cultural differences for old people. No assessment of the aides' performance was made, and although a follow-up at 6–12 months was suggested, none was reported.

This exercise was an attempt to cope with an identified cultural problem, and though concerned with the preparation of nursing aides (who did not have any substantive training anyway) it at least demonstrated the importance of recognising the cultural dynamics of a care situation.

The problems involved in planning for change, such as the introduction of a cultural component into the nursing curriculum, have been discussed by Garner and Merrill (1976). They based their approach on the work of Benne and Birnbaum (1969). Major factors in their strategy involved the policy-making body, both the formal and informal organisation of the institution, and as wide as involvement by members of the institution as possible. In the School of Nursing concerned, Garner and Merrill elected to begin with the end product, the graduate nurse, and the expectations with particular reference to cultural sensitivity, awareness and skills. Working backwards, they then made an analysis of the school and staff, and finally considered the curriculum itself.

Cultural-content modules were developed with the help of ethnic minority staff and recent graduates from the School, with the following titles:

philosophical appreciation of various ethnic cultures;
psychosocial considerations;
maternal-child considerations;
physiological considerations;
familial considerations.

Each module consisted of instructor's guide; students' instructions; terminal objectives; specific behavioural objectives; a pre-test to determine what knowledge and/or skills the student already possessed; learning activities; a post-test; and an evaluation sheet.

In this brief but instructive paper, Garner and Merrill (1976) provide succinct guidelines for any process of change with reference to a curriculum, and especially for the introduction of cultural content. They emphasise the importance of the process of change beginning at a point of stress (not greatest stress, though), for there, change will be most appreciated. Identifying the point of stress and getting consensus acknowledgement depend to a large extent on the skill and degree of commitment of those working for change.

In an exercise which was on a much larger scale, the Western Interstate Commission for Higher Education set up a project concerned with models introducing cultural diversity in nursing curricula (Branch, 1976). This project involved some 39 Schools of Nursing. The curriculum innovation included specific information input about major ethnic groups (mainly those groups encountered by nurses in the USA). Examples of the topics covered by the multicultural curriculum are:

historical perspectives;
communication styles;
nutritional preferences and taboos;
religion;
family dynamics;
health/illness beliefs and practices;
physical assessment;
mental health assessment;
community structure and dynamics.

In an initial survey it was found that many schools were ill prepared administratively to provide nurses with the knowledge, skills and sensitivity required (Branch, 1976). Before programmes could start, teaching staff were in need of development and curricula were in need of review. Similar problems have faced others in their attempts to bring about the introduction of cultural content into nursing education (see also Leininger, 1978a). Spratlen (1976) has recognised some of these issues and argues that innovation in the clinical area is one way to achieve the overall goal of a culturally sensitive approach to health care. Her efforts were in the field of mental health and involved the inclusion in the therapeutic team of members of the ethnic/cultural group to which the client/patient belonged. Spratlen also argues that interpersonal relationships in the therapeutic milieu that are more open, honest and tolerant are likely to be more culturally sensitive. The structure of the clinical setting should be such as to facilitate and encourage interactions and readjustments. Such innovations in the clinical setting, supporting by relevant curriculum development in the educational system, are the way forward, claims Spratlen (1976).

The discrepancies that all too frequently occur between educational models/ideals and clinical practice are a possible major stumbling block to cultural curriculum development. If the innovations are only concerned with class work, even though embracing knowledge, affect and skills, reality shock as described by Kramer (1974) and others will prevent the transfer of these acquisitions into the clinical practice. Kramer herself has given details of ways to decrease the likelihood of such 'shock' occurring, and her suggestions could also form the basis of cultural content innovation.

Although in the proposals for curriculum development considered here, and in those of others such as Baker and Mayer (1982) there has been a major emphasis on information input, and although the nature of this input has been specified in some detail by the authors, relatively little emphasis has been put on experiential aspects of the curriculum and the associated development of skills. The proposal of Baker and Mayer does involve participation in multicultural groups, and the utilisation of local resources such as people and facilities. Nevertheless, it is argued here that only through experience and practice can the sensitivities, empathies and skills needed for transcultural nursing practice be acquired.

As has been noted previously in this chapter, many mental health workers, realising the importance of cultural sensitivity, feel that there is just too much to learn about the different cultures involved. Osborne's suggestion that clients/patients can act as a primary resource of relevant information, links with the proposal of Spratlen that interaction in culturally diverse teams with culturally diverse client groups is an effective way of developing transcultural nursing skills. In the situation described by Baker and Mayer, interaction with the various ethnic groups in the local community was encouraged. The importance of social and interpersonal skills in transcultural nursing was noted earlier. In the development of these skills, experiential methods are usually preferred. In many ways the development and acquisition of social and interpersonal skills can be seen as an avenue for the facilitation of increased cultural sensitivity.

By extending the bounds of experiential social skills training to include cultural dimensions, a base would be created on which to attach the knowledge and attitudes acquired in more academic ways, as well as by interaction. The skills of listening, reflecting and questioning, for example, in an atmosphere of empathy, trust and unconditional regard — essential in dealing with patients of one's own culture — would then provide the basis for dealings with patients of any culture.

This social and interpersonal skills approach, emphasising experiential aspects of training and involving the clinical setting as much if not more than the classroom, is also an important way of helping nurses from different cultures to settle and work in a meaningful way with, say, the indigenous culture, or with other immigrant cultures.

Problems experienced by overseas and ethnic minority students as reported and discussed by, for example, Stones (1972), Clarke and Lee (1976), and Lee (1976), in Britian; Wong and Wong (1982) in Canada, and Abu-Saad and Kayser-Jones (1981) in the USA fall into a wide range of categories. Nevertheless the support systems proposed for them (e.g. Lee, 1976; Wong and Wong, 1982) include counselling and the development of interpersonal relationships with indigenous nurses. What has not been emphasised has been the cultural relationships between the immigrant or ethnic minority students and their indigenous peers. Acting as cultural resources for each other in experiential interpersonal settings would provide a most useful platform on which to build a transcultural approach to psychiatric nursing practice.

Conclusion

This chapter has been concerned with transcultural aspects of psychiatric nursing, and in particular with the preparation of psychiatric nurses for a culturally sensitive role. Nurses, of course, do not work in isolation, but as part of a mental health care team, alongside doctors, psychologists and social workers among others. They must align their nursing strategies with those of their colleagues, and it can be difficult for them to effect innovations in nursing care because of this. However, there is an increasing awareness of the cultural context in psychiatry generally, and within this movement nurses can demonstrate a willingness to adjust their practice, or even to take the initiative.

Anthropological and ethnographic studies have contributed much to our insights into cultural diversity, and continue to do so. It is not being argued here that nurses should somehow learn all about the different cultures they may meet, or about the way mental illness is or may be presented in different cultures. Evidence that health beliefs and practices do vary from culture to culture, in particular mental health beliefs, provides argument for developing cultural sensitivity. Individuals within each culture have their own perception of and commitment to the attitudes and practices associated with that culture. Nurses are required to care for individuals and not for clinical or cultural stereotypes.

There is evidence that nurses have tended in the past to care more for the 'average' patient than for particular individuals (Davis, 1981). Increasingly it is the aim of nursing education to prepare nurses for an approach to the whole patient whose nursing needs are assessed on an individual basis, prior to the planning of an individual programme of care. This approach depends on the development of communication and interpersonal skills which facilitate the assessment process and the implementation of care.

It is therefore the emphasis of this chapter that nurses should know about cultural diversity, and about its relevance to mental health care, but that their cultural sensitivity should be seen as an adjunct to their general interpersonal skills, and that their knowledge of and skills in transcultural nursing should mainly be acquired through interaction with people from other cultures. This interaction should occur professionally in the clinical setting and also in the local community. It should be supervised and supported in the classroom. There the experiences of individual students can be compared, contrasted and considered in the light of cultural or ethnic models.

The analysis of cultural nursing problems, as with the analysis of nursing problems in general, requires a multidisciplinary knowledge base. Principles from biology, psychology, sociology, anthropology, for example, inform the practice. They facilitate both the assessment of need and the planning of care, but they do not determine them. Culturally sensitive nursing is nursing that is related to individuals and is determined by the interaction between the nurse and the patient, in association with the other members of the mental health care team. Culturally sensitive nursing is therefore good nursing.

References

Abu-Saad, H. and Kayser-Jones, J. (1981) 'Foreign Nursing Students in the USA: Problems in their Education Experiences', *Journal of Advanced Nursing, 6*, 397–403

Baker, C.M. and Mayer, G.G. (1982) 'One Approach to Teaching Cultural Similarities and Differences', *Journal of Nursing Education, 21* (4), 17–22

Benne, K. and Birnbaum, M. (1969) 'Principles of Changing', in W.G. Bennis, K. Benne and R. Chinn (eds), *Planning for Change*, Holt Rinehart, New York

Branch, M. (1976) 'Models for Introducing Cultural Diversity in Nursing Curricula', *Journal of Nursing Education, 15* (2), 7–13

Brink, P.J. (1976) *Transcultural Nursing: a Book of Readings*, Prentice Hall, London

Brown, M.S. (1974) 'Anthropology, Nursing and Mental Health', *Journal of Psychiatric Nursing and Mental Health Services, 12* (1), 7–11

Burrows, A. (1983) 'Patient-centred Nursing Care in a Multi-racial Society: the Relevance of Ethnographic Perspectives in Nursing Curricula', *Journal of Advanced Nursing, 8*, 477–85

Clarke, M. and Lee, T.R. (1976) 'The Impressions of a Sample of British and Overseas Student Nurses of Some Social Aspects of their Training', *Journal of Advanced Nursing, 1*, 37–49

Community Relations Commission (1976) *Aspects of Mental Health in a Multi-racial Society*, Community Relations Commission, London

Davis, B.D. (1980) 'Nursing Training and Transcultural Psychiatry', paper read at Transcultural Psychiatry Society Conference, Bradford

Davis, B.D. (1981) 'Social skills in Nursing', in M. Argyle (ed.), *Social Skills and Health*, Methuen, London

Dobson, S. (1983) 'Bringing Culture into Care', *Nursing Times, 79*, 53–7

Fosdike, H. (1980) 'Assessing the Needs of an Ethnic Community', *Midwife, Health Visitor and Community Nurse, 16*, 148–54

Garner, V.M. and Merrill, E. (1976) 'A Model for Development and Implementation of Cultural Content in the Nursing Curriculum', *Journal of Nursing Education, 15* (2), 30–4

Hicks, C. (1982) 'Racism in Nursing', *Nursing Times, 78*, 789–91

Knight, L. (1977) 'Brides Who Run Away', *Community Care,,* 27 April

Kogan, N. (1961) 'Attitudes towards Old People: the Development of a Scale and an Examination of Correlates', *Journal of Abnormal and Social Psychology, 62*, 44–54

Kramer, M. (1974) *Reality Shock*, C.V. Mosby, St. Louis

Lee, H. (1976) 'Overseas Nursing Trainees: a Series of Five Articles', *Nursing Times,* 72, 21 and 28 October; 4, 11 and 18 November

Leininger, M. (1967) 'The Culture Concept and its Relevance to Nursing', *Journal of Nursing Education, 6,* 27–37

Leininger, M. (1968) 'The Significance of Cultural Concepts in Nursing', *Minnesota League for Nursing Bulletin, 16* (3), 3–12

Leininger, M. (ed.) (1978a) *Transcultural Nursing: Theories, Concepts, Practices,* Wiley, New York

Leininger, M. (1978b) 'Transcultural Nursing: Theories and Research Approaches', in M. Leininger (ed.), *Transcultural Nursing: Theories, Concepts, Practices,* Wiley, New York

Leininger, M. (1978c) 'Culturological Assessment Domains for Nursing Practices', in M. Leininger (ed.), *Transcultural Nursing: Theories, Concepts, Practices,* Wiley, New York

Littlewood, R. and Lipsedge, M. (1982) *Aliens and Alienists: Ethnic Minorities and Psychiatry,* Penguin, London

Mayor, V. (1984) 'The Asian Community, a Series of Two Articles', *Nursing Times, 80,* 40–2, 57–8

Murphy, H.B.M., Wittkower, E.D. and Chance, N.W. (1963) 'A Cross-cultural Survey of Schizophrenic Symptomatology', *International Journal of Social Psychology, 9,* 237–49

Murphy, H.B.M., Wittkower, E.D. and Chance, N.W. (1964) 'A Cross-cultural Enquiry into the Symptomatology of Depression', *Transcultural Psychiatry Research Review, 1* (15), 5–18

Nursing Times (1982) 'Racism in Nursing' (Correspondence), *Nursing Times, 78,* 868–9

Osborne, O.H. (1976) 'Unique Needs of Ethnic Minority Clients in a Multiracial Society: a Psychological Perspective', in *American Nursing Association, Affirmative Action towards Quality Nursing Care in a Multiracial Society,* Publication M-24 2500, American Nursing Association, Kansas City

Rack, P. (1982) *Race, Culture and Mental Disorder,* Tavistock, London

Röscher, C.I. (1974) 'Preparing Psychiatric Nurses for Serving the Needs of a Multicultural Society', *South African Nursing Journal, 41* (4), 13–15

Schofield, J. (1981) 'Behind the Veil: the Mental Health of Asian Women in Britain' (Series), *Health Visitor, 54;* (4), 138–41; (5), 183–6; (6), 248–51

Spratlen, L.P. (1976) 'Introducing Ethnic-Cultural Factors in Models of Nursing: Some Mental Health Care Applications', *Journal of Nursing Education, 15* (2), 25–9

Stone, R.W.H. (1972) 'Overseas Nurses in Britain: a Study of Male Recruits', Occasional Paper, *Nursing Times, 68,* 141–1

Taller, M., Mayer, M. and Hill, G. (1977) 'Educational Consultation on Mental Health in Long-term Care Facilities: Problems, Pitfalls and Solutions, Cross-cultural Issues in Nursing Home Settings', *Journal of Geriatric Psychiatry, 10* (2), 173–89

Webb, P. (1981) 'Report of an Ethnic Health Project, 1979/1980', *The Health Education Journal, 40* (3), 69–74

Wilson, A. (1977) 'A Burning Fever: the Isolation of Asian Women in Britain', *Race and Class,* Autumn

Wilson, A. (1978) *Finding a Voice,* Virago, London

Wong, S. and Wong, J. (1982) 'Problems in Teaching Ethnic Minority Nursing Students', *Journal of Advanced Nursing, 7,* 255–9

14 FAMILY THERAPY ACROSS CULTURES

Annie Lau

Introduction

Family therapy is practised today in a wide variety of social settings and, despite the diversity of ideas and approaches in current practice, is firmly based on the concept that an individual's problems can be helped by treating the entire family as a unit. In doing so, the family therapist will generally reinforce what is considered to be competent family functioning and discourage patterns of behaviour that are dysfunctional. The therapist may, however, assess a patient using norms that stem from the Western European cultural matrix, and needs to recognise that the definition of a family is itself a cultural construction. Although the literature relating to cultural aspects of family therapy is sparse (see Lau, 1984), most authors emphasise the importance of clarifying the cultural assumptions on which therapeutic strategies are based (Kinzie *et al.*, 1972).

In this chapter I shall examine, using clinical examples, the nature and the extent of congruence in the therapeutic models used with ethnic families. First however, a note with regard to my own ethnic presuppositions; my background being one of cultural and racial diversity.

I grew up in a traditional Chinese family in Malaya and after taking 'A' levels went to Canada to study medicine, where I eventually trained as a psychiatrist. With my English husband I came to live in the United Kingdom. I am therefore familiar with the cultural assumptions of Chinese family life, as well as with specific issues involved in migration and inter-ethnic marriage (McGoldrick *et al.*, 1982).

The relevance of cultural values to family relationship was vividly illustrated for me by a stone tableau in a public park in Singapore. Haw Par Villa was built by a rich Chinese philanthropist who felt the people needed a public park in which moral parables could be portrayed in stone. One such stone tableau illustrated the cardinal virtue of filial piety. At a time of famine in China, a young woman is confronted with a moral dilemma: does she offer her breast-milk to her old mother, who is starving — or does she save her remaining child, given her other child is already dead on the ground? (Figure 14.1). Despite her maternal instincts, she turns away from her crying baby and offers her breast to her mother.

234

Figure 14.1: Stone Tableau in Singapore

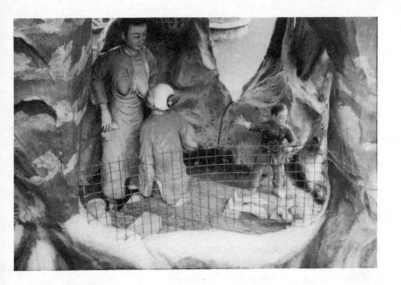

Thus, for traditional Chinese, the prescriptive rule is one of unquestioning filial piety, where responsibility to one's parents is paramount and transcends responsibilities to spouse and children. The story of this filial daughter represents a mythic personification of the ideal prototypes presented to all traditional Chinese children.

I have reproduced the above parable in the form of a sculpt in a variety of social-work and mental health settings in the UK, and invariably members of the audience, with the exception of Orientals and Asians, have felt acutely uncomfortable with the young mother's choice. In discussion, however, the point would usually be accepted that we were all bound by the cultural patternings of our group, and are not freely acting, but are culturally constrained individuals.

As shown in Table 14.1, we are confronted with five transcultural interfaces between the therapist and the family system. In all the situations described, apart from (A) where the therapist comes from the same ethnic group as his client family, the therapist may be handicapped by many factors that will mitigate against successful entry into the family system. The therapist may not possess the same world view as his clients; and so not be aware of how normality and pathology are culturally defined, what belief systems are sanctioned by the group, what is idiosyncratic,

Table 14.1: Transcultural Interfaces between Therapist and Family System

(A)	There is congruence between basic cultural positions of therapist and family where both belong to the same cultural group
(B)	There is dissonance between basic cultural positions of therapist and family where the family is non-Western or from extended family traditions.
(C)	There is dissonance between basic cultural positions of therapist and family where the therapist is non-Western or from extended family traditions.
(D)	There is cultural dissonance *within* the presenting family, and also with the therapist from a dominant culture: (a) families with first-generation British-born children (b) cross-cultural marriages
(E)	Therapist from minority culture interacts with family from a different minority culture

and what may possibly be indicative of psychopathology. Furthermore, the family therapist is likely to be unfamiliar with the norms governing appropriate behaviours for sex role and family role adaptations that are prescribed by the cultural group; and what interactive patterns and styles of communication are 'normal' for the group. What are typical family patterns? What are the normal expectations of sons and daughters? Is the eldest son expected to have special responsibilities for the family group, including the care of his aged parents? Or are daughters socialised to accept the importance of correct and demure behaviour in public, so as not to bring dishonour to the family name? How do people in that culture handle life-cycle transitions, and how do they maintain continuities with the past? In short, how does the group's culture organise the family's experience of itself and how do these differ from the therapist's own cultural perspective? Let us look briefly at some basic expectations of British family therapists.

The British family therapist, whichever theoretical model he espouses, will first decide on the relevant network that he will call 'family', convene a meeting of the family group and observe family behaviour around the presenting problem (e.g. a suicidal adolescent) in order to elicit a working hypothesis and a strategy for action. He will be interested in looking at how effectively the family is functioning as a system in the present, by assessing current family interactions, e.g. he will look at such behavioural items as the capacity for clear and direct communication, and control of deviant behaviour; he will be aware of life-cycle stresses in the present, and will probably look for emotional themes influencing intergenerational expectations; and he will also want to explore the inner experiential life of the family (Skynner, 1982). All of this, however, will be influenced by the moral imperatives he carries about the nature of a healthy family. One definition of healthy family structure is described in nuclear family terms by Aponte and Hoffman (1973):

> Family Therapists who think along structural lines see a healthy family as one where there are clear demarcations between the generations. Within each generational level, there will be strong ties, as well as adequate differentiation between individuals. The pair that is the governing unit, the parents, have to have a particularly strong alliance, and clearly worked out areas of functioning special to each. The same is true of children, except that differentiation with them should be appropriate to age. Of course, much of this will be defined by the culture, but the general rule of clear generation lines and adequate differentiation will hold. In an unhealthy family, or what Minuchin calls an enmeshed family, there is a blurring of the generation lines and a lack of differentiation.

How congruent is this description of a healthy family with a West Indian family, an Asian family, a Vietnamese family? I would suggest that this model — that of adequate differentiation and clear generational lines — denies the validity of other forms of family organisation as it is based on Western European norms. The therapist who believes that the governing unit in a family should always be the parents will have tremendous difficulty working within a situation where the grandparents have the final say on all important decisions within the family, from the grand-daughter's marriage to a son's place of residence. The psychiatrist who holds that the individuals's right to self-determination takes precedence over all other rights may act inappropriately with marginal adolescents caught in culture and identity conflict. I am convinced that in order to be able to mobilise the strengths inherent in family systems different from those in which we ourselves were socialised, or to identify important sources of competence, we need to be able to know what they are. We have to recognise that very real differences do, in fact, exist and that ethnic values constitute an active dynamic in family treatment (McGoldrick *et al.*, 1982).

The problems of taking cultural and ethnic factors into acount are further magnified in brief, problem-focused therapy. Here the therapist must work quickly. He often dispenses with a traditional case history with its laborious, time-consuming details, and is used to formulating quickly, often in the first fifteen minutes of the interview, a hypothesis of the nature of the dysfunctional family system. He then designs, sometimes with the help of a supervision group behind the one-way screen, an appropriate intervention. This is often extremely effective where everyone operates on the same set of cultural imperatives, but not when the meaning of often central and crucial events does not carry the same weight for the therapist and his client family. The therapist cannot then take the same short cuts, and make the conceptual leaps, required to direct his explorations into the real areas of concern. An example at this point may be useful.

A social worker reported, as evidence of an Asian (Hindu) father's 'disinterest' in his difficult and mildly deliquent fifteen-year-old son, the fact that father wanted him disposed of by being placed in care so that he could go home to India. Further exploration with the family revealed that the father was the eldest son in his family and his presence in India was needed in order to provide his own father, who had just died, with a proper funeral. The delinquent son felt disowned by his family and was testing this by saying he wanted to change his religion and become a Muslim like his mates. To the family this represented a total abnegation of his duties as a son as this would disqualify him from performing proper burial rites on his own father. The social worker's failure to recognise the significance of the son's role in this family, particularly around the time of the grandfather's death, meant he was not in touch with issues crucial to the understanding of this family's difficulties, which would have enabled him to feel usefully engaged with the family.

In reviewing the points of tension in the interface between the Western-trained family therapist and the client 'ethnic' family, one would need to consider the following areas:

(1) differences in systems of symbolic meaning;
(2) differences in family structure and organisation;
(3) language and communication.

Differences in Symbolic Meaning Systems

The data we collect on our patients derives largely from directly observable phenomena — i.e. signs and symptoms, patient self-reports, and reports from observers. In order to organise these data meaningfully, we have to be in touch with a level of functioning that is not readily observable but is none the less crucial; that is, the ideational, symbolic plane of functioning characteristic of the culture. It is the ideas, myths and beliefs of the culture (Seltzer and Seltzer, 1983) that determine the psychosocial identity of the individual and the moral imperatives he carries, through presenting the growing child and adolescent with both ideal and evil prototypes (Erickson, 1968). This ideational plane influences the perception, explanation and experience of health and illness, normality and deviance; determines what impulses and fantasies can become conscious, and which must be suppressed (Devereux, 1980). Culture also provides rules for how one is to be acceptably deviant; Linton (1936) calls these cultural 'patterns of misconduct'. For example, among traditional Chinese of all social classes, dysphoric affects are frequently somatised, and depressed individuals present usually with the biological concomitants of depression (Kleinman, 1980). Attitudes and beliefs about illness, illness behaviour, treatment expectations, doctor/patient transactions, and healing activities, are all cultural constructions.

The therapist needs to be familiar with the role of cultural materials in symptoms in order to know how to manage them. It is important to know when particular items of behaviour or symptomatology are maladaptive despite the fact that they conform to group norms or beliefs. Devereux (1980), in his discussion of the boundary between normality and psychopathology in different cultures, distinguishes between these behaviours that are sanctioned by a culture, though marginally deviant (e.g. the role of the shaman), and those behaviours that are idiosyncratic and indicative of psychopathology. The following case illustrates the cultural patterning of symptoms in the identified patient.

M-S (Chinese-Vietnamese)

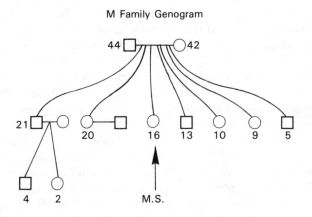

M Family Genogram

A sixteen-year-old Chinese-Vietnamese girl, M-S, was admitted to a hospital in Britain in February 1982 after reports of bizarre behaviour in secondary school. A similar episode of bizarre behaviour in 1979 a month after arrival in Hong Kong on a refugee boat from Vietnam was treated sucessfully by a Chinese exorcist/healer. Two days after admission she exhibited 'catatonic behaviour with waxy inflexibility' and was started on Haldol, a major tranquilliser. The purpose of the referral was to determine whether or not she was mentally ill.

The parents, in their forties, were demoralised and preoccupied with their poor adjustment to England. Married for over twenty years, they had seven children, all of whom came with them to this country. The older two children are married with children and live close by. M-S is the eldest of the group of five left at home. Father is unemployed and had been a security guard in Vietnam. They had been attending English classes unsuccessfully for the past two years since arrival in this country. In their youth they had moved to Vietnam from Hong Kong and had already once undergone the process of acculturation and learning a foreign language (Vietnamese).

I interviewed M-S with her parents in Chinese on the ward. M-S was fully orientated and there were no abnormal movements or gestures. Her speech was slurred, making it sometimes difficult to understand her, and she had some difficulty with articulation since Haldol was started. There was no evidence of formal thought disorder and no delusional thinking. There was some evidence of depressive affect: she told me she very much missed her two-year-old niece, who died suddenly last year. Also, she had, together with 25 other Vietnamese children, been subjected to intense bullying in school from a black group. She had bruises on her legs, and a younger sister had recently been transferred to another school. She described seeing figures, for example a female Chinese ghost (a beautiful lady with long hair) while in bed just prior to falling asleep at night (pseudo-hallucinations). The 'voices in her head' say things like, 'I am going to hit you', which suggests these were daily residues from the threats she received in school. She said she often lay awake at night worrying about school. She had also been attached to the Chinese healer in Hong Kong, who is now dead: as M-S put it, 'His ghost wanted the little one, so she died.' There is a marked cultural patterning in the content of the materials she described, and a naive belief in ghosts, the spirit world, charms and exorcism is common in her family and cultural group.

M-S seemed quite unsupported by her parents who were preoccupied with their own losses and poor adjustment to life in England, and were anxious not to draw too much attention to their family. When she wanted to talk about her niece's death, Mother interrupted several times to ask her to 'Try to forget it; it would be of no use to keep bringing it up.'

The class teacher confirmed the school situation to be a particularly stressful one: as well as herself, her four younger siblings (whose ages ranged from thirteen to five, and for whom, as the oldest sister, she felt responsible) were being severely harrassed in school. She was also reported to be more out-going compared with the other Vietnamese girls, and so encountered more rejection.

We looked at the network of relationships that maintained the problem and focused on two areas: the scapegoating of M-S in school by both her Vietnamese peers *and* the feared black aggressor group, and also the unresolved grief in the family about the recent death of the two-year-old child. Benign medical authority was used to reframe M-S's 'catatonic symptoms', which we felt were really of a hysterical dissociative nature. They were a normal and intelligible response to the unusual and overwhelming stresses in school, and to her particular role in the family in which she had to take responsibility for her younger siblings. In addition the symptoms provided a solution to the family depression, as they enabled family members to avoid confrontation with their own grief.

We said M-S was being a good daughter and a good elder sister in her use of non-verbal symbolic communication. She was literally 'stuck' and immobilised, unable to function as a responsible elder sibling. The medication was stopped immediately and M-S improved rapidly in hospital.

Differences in Family Structure and Organisation

There are differences in rules with regard to authority, continuity and interdependence in nuclear-family systems as compared with the extended family systems of Asia and the Far East (West Indian family organisation is excluded from this part of the discussion and will be considered separately).

Authority

Authority systems are clearly defined in the extended family, with age and rank conferring most authority. In patriarchal families, paternal grandfather is usually recognised as the head of the household, and all important decisions, including a grand-daughter's marriage (as in a Pakistani family), need to be referred to him. Where authority functions are exercised effectively by the head of the household, the family's continuity is ensured through the interdependence of its members. Also the family's capacity to control deviance in its members is maintained. Deviance is here defined as any behaviour that threatens the integrity of the family unit, be this child abuse, domestic conflict or violence, or adolescent rebellion. This has obvious clinical implications for the therapist who wants to help the family mobilise its authority; the authority structures need to be clearly identified.

Kinship Ties

In extended family systems, highly structured kinship ties define the individual's role, duties and obligations within the larger family (Ballard, 1982). Formal kinship terms are often used, as in Chinese and Indian families. For example, in an Asian (Indian), Japanese or Chinese family, elder siblings are expected to assume responsibility for their younger siblings' welfare, including, if cirucumstances permit, a good education. In return their younger siblings are expected to render to their older siblings a measure of respect and obedience. It is not uncommon for parents to punish an older brother more severely for fighting with a younger brother, as the older brother knows he should have set a good example and should not have allowed the fight to take place. Conflict with regard to family obligations is frequently an issue in mixed marriages, particularly where the individuals involved find it difficult to cope with intimacy. Elsewhere (Lau, 1984) I have described work with a family in which the parents were each preoccupied with their own losses and unable to share them with each other. The cultural issues as well as the couple's fear and avoidance of intimacy needed to be simultaneously engaged in therapy (Cohen, 1982; McGoldrick and Preto, 1984).

Parenting Functions

Shared or multiple parenting is common, and parenting functions are not restricted to the child's biological parents. Strong attachment bonds are formed from early childhood with grandparents, uncles and aunts. There is a wider variety of parental figures for sex-role identification and for the child to share his worries. A model of the son's obligation to provide for his parents in old age is provided by the following story, usually depicted visually. First, mother and father crow bring worms (food) to their helpless offspring in the nest where they wait with mouths gaping; this continues with the birds reaching maturity and flying away; in the final sequence, the positions are reversed. Mother and father crow wait with gaping mouths while their children return with worms to feed their parents as they themselves had been fed. It is interesting to note that in the Chinese People's Republic this principle of filial obligations is enshrined in the 1981 Marriage Law, where penalties are laid down for individuals with 'the capacity to bear relevant costs' who do not honour their obligations to needy family members, e.g. grandparents, grandchildren whose parents are deceased and minor young siblings (Hare-Mustin, 1982).

Adolescence

Adolescents are not expected to be as independent as their Western counterparts and more conformity to family norms of 'correct' behaviour is expected. Prevailing models for how the adolescent structures his life are still firmly rooted in the examples and precepts laid down by the family elders, who wield clear authority and will not tolerate behaviour that brings dishonour to the family name. They are not expected, for example to undergo the experience of 'leaving home' (Haley, 1980), which for the Western adolescent is often a highly traumatic though important developmental task that needs to be faced. However, where adolescents are caught in culture conflict, 'leaving home' issues can become explosive, with extremely serious consequences. Adolescents from traditional ethnic families may face other stresses not encountered by their Western counterparts. For example, religious mores in a Pakistani girl's family may discourage intermingling of the sexes, but her school environment will offer opportunities for experimentation in a way that may bring her into direct conflict with the family elders.

Marriage

The young woman enters marriage knowing it is a union of two families, that her own kinship system provides for her an important source of strength and support. It is not uncommon for young wives to go home to their mothers in the first year of an arranged marriage when adjustment problems in the marriage and to the husband's family become acute. This is a well-known traditional solution and a common tactical move (Ballard, 1982). It usually signals a brief period in which the wider family on both sides can help guide the couple over early marital stress. The family then provides a measure of control for aggression and violence within the marriage and towards children. The absence of this buffering network, as is often the case in Britain, often causes stress and tension, particularly in arranged marriages.

An important relationship in this buffering system to which we need to pay attention clinically is the mother-in-law/daughter-in-law relationship. This is a key relationship which has important influences on the integrity of the marriage to an extent not found in Western, free-choice marriages. This is especially important where women live together and the men go out to work. The young wife, I must stress, is unable to escape from her mother-in-law's authority and power; in many joint families it is mother-in-law who handles the budget, determines the meals and supervises the domestic routines. The daily tensions and struggles of the two women, and their ability or lack of it to resolve conflicts and negotiate compromises, determine the emotional climate affecting the three generations, including the children. The Old Testament story of Ruth and Naomi provides archetypal images of the loyalty of a daughter-in-law for the mother-in-law, where Ruth refuses to leave Naomi, her mother-in-law, following her husband's death. As a daughter-in-law the young woman curbs her aggressive impulses and waits for the day when, as mother-in-law and grandmother, she becomes the final authority on domestic decisions (Ballard, 1982). To a lesser extent, the young wife's relations with her sisters-in-law are also crucial: it is this subsystem in the female network that must devise mutually supportive strategies for 'containing' mother-in-law.

A Bereaved Family (Pakistani)

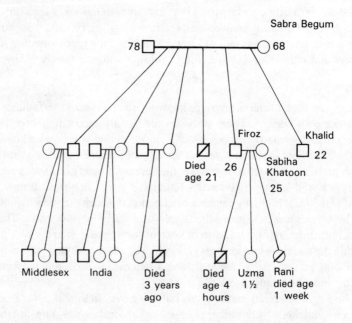

The neonatal unit was concerned about recently bereaved Pakistani parents, Firoz Ahmed, aged 26, and Sabiha Khatoon, aged 25. Their week-old child, Rani, had just died with a host of congenital anomalies. Two years before, a similar bereavement had occurred, the child dying a few hours after birth. There was a live child, aged one-and-a-half years old. In discussing the case we felt Sabiha's position in her family could be an extremely vulnerable one, given that she had produced two defective children. We were aware that in similar circumstances many Pakistani wives faced the risk of scapegoating and divorce, with the sons under pressure from their mothers to divorce their wives. Accordingly, we felt it was worth while to see the whole family in order to assess their capacity to mourn their recent loss and to offer support to the bereaved parents. An evening domiciliary visit was chosen a few days after Mrs Ahmed came home from hospital as the best method of assessing the whole family. I went accompanied by my Registrar, Dr Ruhi, who is of Pakistani origin.

As Sabra Begum, the mother-in-law, did not speak English, the session was conducted in a mixture of languages. When Sarba Begum was very involved, Urdu was the main language of communication, and at an appropriate moment Dr Ruhi would summarise for me what had happened. Prior to the session we were in agreement about the main areas that were to be explored with the family. We had also worked together for eight months in joint family interviews so that there was sufficient consensus about goals and techniques.

The family lived on the eleventh floor of a high-rise block of flats. The session was held in the family's living room, which was tidy and well kept. Initially the mother-in-law, Sabra Begum, stayed in the kitchen, but we asked that she join us. The following were present: mother-in-law, Mr and Mrs Ahmed, their one-and-a-half-year old daughter (Uzma), and Mr Ahmed's younger brother, Khalid, age 22. Mr and Mrs Ahmed lived with Mr Ahmed's parents. Khalid was single, a student at the technical college. He lived nearby but had evening meals with the family.

We elicited a genogram. Firoz Ahmed was the oldest surviving son in the family. There were three older sisters who lived some distance away (in India and in Middlesex). An older brother had died some four years previously of aplastic anaemia, and his picture, surrounded by a garland, graced the living-room wall. Three years previously, one sister had lost a child. A year later Mr and Mrs Ahmed's first-born child died at a few hours old. We found out that father-in-law, aged 78, was in a long-stay ward following a stroke, and this was a continuing source concern and stress in the family. We noticed that Sabiha looked sad and tired. She sat listlessly on the sofa next to her husband and made few attempts to touch or play with her pretty, well-dressed, one-and-a-half-year-old daughter, Uzma, who seemed to interact mainly with Khalid. He, however, often seemed impatient with the child and frequently shouted at her to behave. Firoz and his brother did most of the talking; with a bit of encouragement Sabra Begum, the mother-in-law, poured out to us her anxieties about the family; Sabiha was less spontaneous but there was good eye contact between her and her mother-in-law. They smiled often at each other and also touched. There was frequent non-verbal communication between Sabiha and her husband.

We looked at how the family was responding to the death of the newborn child. Sabra Begum said she was worried about her daughter-in-law who was still not eating or sleeping well. They also admitted readily to their own grief, and the uncle agreed that his impatience with his niece had to do with his difficulty in accepting the family's loss. Dr Ruhi asked what was usual family custom when a daughter-in-law returns home following childbirth: what ritual foods were prescribed and who organised these activities. (We felt we needed to find out if symbolic caretaking activities were being performed by the mother-in-law.) Sabra Begum said it was usual for the senior women in the family (i.e. mother-in-law and elder sisters-in-law) to prepare special foods in the post-partum period, and for the new mother to be excused all household tasks while she recuperates and attends to the needs of the newborn child. In this case, Sabiha was being given the foods prescribed by tradition and encouraged to rest. Sabiha came in and reinforced this: 'My mother-in-law is very kind and considerate to me', she said. 'She is doing all the cooking. Brother-in-law has taken over hoovering the house.'

As numerous references were made to God in the course of the interview, I asked Dr Ruhi to check out the strength of the religious support system. What did the family think was responsible for the baby's death? Sabra Begum here answered 'Children are a gift from God. It is His will if he decides to take them away. We cannot blame anyone.' We asked Sabiha directly if she felt blamed. She said no, but was interested in finding out whether there was a pattern in these deaths and if she and her husband should have more children. Firoz then said he really should not have allowed his wife to get pregnant so soon after the last child, and certainly there would not be any more pregnancies for the next year or so. He also stated that they wanted us to arrange for them to have genetic counselling.

West Indian Extended Family

The West Indian extended family functions by different rules compared with the extended family of Asia and Africa. In working-class families, blood relationships of either father or mother, more commonly mother, are stressed rather than the husband/wife relationship (Henriques, 1949). In the West Indies these consanguineous family groupings exhibit a high degree of stability and continuity over a long period. There is a strong sense of kin beyond that of the immediate family; and unlike Asian and African families, functional relationships are not necessarily defined by kinship, i.e. biological ties. Informal living arrangements, (Littlewood and Lipsedge, 1982), e.g. long-standing common-law relationships can and often do, confer onto individuals rights, responsibilities and the attendant authority one associates with formal relationships in white or Asian families. For example, the most senior woman in a black extended family may be grandfather's longstanding cohabitee, who is regarded as the matriarch of the family. Next to her in the hierarchy may follow several godmothers, who will strongly influence executive decisions made by parents about their children.

In the following case of a black mother/daughter dyad an attmept was made to mobilise the family's strengths by reaffirming intergenerational links.

A fifteen-year-old black girl was admitted to a residential unit after her mother complained she was beyond her control. The white social worker felt the girl's mother was not sufficiently connected with her daughter as she kept saying she wanted to go back to Jamaica to see her own mother. It turned out that the mother and daughter had violent arguments over the girl's adherence to Rastafarian beliefs, lifestyle and friends. For this rather rigid Pentecostal mother it represented a wholesale rejection of herself and her values as a mother. In working with the mother I found that at other periods of her life when things had been difficult, as when her husband had left her with a young baby, she had gone back to Jamaica for a holiday to see her mother and aunts and family. This contact with her roots had been sustaining, and had restored her faith in her ability to cope: in fact, it had enabled her to do so. Work with this mother and daughter was directed at exploring what it meant for each of them to be a daughter in Jamaica and in England. The girl eventually admitted her own need for emotional links with her mother and grandmother, and just as it was important for mother to be a good daughter and gain maternal grandmother's approval, it was equally important for her to gain approval from her mother. We were able to move from that position to negotiate acceptable standards of behaviour for the daughter which would still involve her achieving a stage-appropriate sense of autonomy. On working on this case we emphasised the importance for mother maintaining a sense of continuity with both her own mother in Jamaica and her daughter in England, and pointed out the strengths she had shown that had so far sustained her and her family.

Language and Communication

Obviously, where language is a difficulty, a proper assessment of the family's needs and strengths then becomes very difficult. Trained interpreters are rare; often, family members are asked to act as interpreters but the therapist then misses important nuances and subtleties in communication. Also an untrained interpreter often screens out vital information in the interchange between therapist and family (Schackman, 1983). I must confess I will not attempt to assess a family whose language I do not speak unless I am working with a colleague, e.g. a psychiatric registrar, who has worked with me over a period of time and with whom I can proceed from the same theoretical and conceptual base.

Some strategies are particularly difficult to carry out through an interpreter, for example those involving experimental techniques and where feelings need to be identified. Sometimes it is important to allow tension to build up in therapy sessions, and the therapist needs to be able to monitor directly the emotional experience of the family. Structural family therapy, as described by Minuchin (1974) often attempts to take family members beyond their normal thresholds, to keep them task-focused and unable to defuse the tension through using the usual homeostatic mechanisms. This sort of work, I feel, is not possible through an interpreter.

There are also difficulties in modes of communication. The Western-trained therapist tends to expect feelings to be expressed openly, clearly and directly. This is often done at variance with communicational styles in particular ethnic groups where direct communication and confrontation are avoided as this leads to 'loss of face within the group' (McGoldrick *et al.*, 1982). Instead more indirect means may be used, for example a reference to a folk parable or saying. This is particularly common in Malay and Chinese groups. In the negotiations around an arranged marriage, for example, it is important to be able to back off with grace and dignity in order to preserve the honour of families on both sides. Thus the unsuitability of a potential match may be hinted at through symbolic gestures that convey shared meaning, giving the other side the opportunity to withdraw.

Intervention Strategies for Working with Ethnic Minority Families

The family therapist must first know the family's cultural and religious background in sufficient detail in order to assess the content of the clinical materials. If necessary, the services of a cultural interpreter should be obtained. The therapist must be aware of the stresses, both present and historical, of the particular ethnic group to which his client family belongs. For example, Vietnamese refugees in Britain are still not in a position to form self-help organisations, unlike other groups, and many still live with recent memories of severe trauma, including torture. The therapist must also know the cultural rules to do with authority structures, differentiation and boundaries, so that he can avoid incongruent messages to the family. He has to clarify what the authority structures and networks are. An assessment needs to be made of existing cultural defences and the network and support systems most natural for the family, e.g. the church, neighbourhood and community associations. Where links with extended family are weak, the family unit may be more vulnerable to stresses in the life cycle than the comparative English family. Stagoll (1981) stresses, in work with Greek-Cypriot families in Melbourne, that the therapist needs to be sensitive to the tendency for immigrant parents to feel de-skilled by the therapist, and that it is important that he confirm, where appropriate, the parents' authority role with respect to the children. The family's sense of power needs to be mobilised and used effectively; where possible, the maladaptive response in the symptomatic family member needs to be stressed as normal and intelligible (rather than crazy) in the context of family worries, and the behaviour framed positively. This is illustrated by the case study of the Chinese-Vietnamese girl for whom it was particularly important that her 'mad' label be removed. Formulation of the problem and feedback to the family could also be enhanced using familiar cultural metaphors. For example, in working with an Asian family I once compared the role stereotyping in the family (good son/bad son) to those found in Indian films. This enabled the family to relax and laugh, and I felt I had managed to bridge the cultural gap.

Experiential family work aims to help family members experience feelings in their interpersonal context (Byng-Hall, 1982) and often introduces new experiences within the session (Madanes and Haley, 1977).

Elsewhere I have reported a case in which sculpting was used successfully with an Asian family to mobilise family members to more effective ways of communication around important affective themes (Lau, 1984). In transcultural family work, the use of rituals in order to facilitate affective expression has been reported by a number of authors (Scheff, 1979; Levick *et al.*, 1981). For example, Seltzer and Seltzer (1983) present successful work with Norwegian families using ritualistic interventions, e.g. funeral and coronation ceremonies, a binding ritual, 'the masking of the witch': rituals that both concretised and exposed an embedded theme in the family's culture into which they were 'frozen'.

It is important to stress that interventions with extended families must respect the pre-eminence of the family (Palazzoli *et al.*, 1977; Pearce, 1980). If necessary, interventions need to be reframed in order to reflect this all-important principle. Spiegel (1968), in comparing value systems between therapists and ethnic families, points out that Western therapists emphasise 'the importance of individual relationships and responsibilites instead of collateral or lineal relationships'. Work on Chinese families identifies that interpersonal (especially family) problems come higher on a hierarchy of perceived stress than intrapsychic problems (Kleinman, 1980). The following case illustrates an example of successful 'reframing' of an intervention.

An Indian boy had spent some time at an observation and assessment centre away from his family, and the field social worker and residential social worker had been working with the goal of eventually sending the boy home. This boy had been in a great deal of trouble prior to his admission to the centre but was settling down. During a supervision session with me, the social workers reported that, in a meeting with the boy's father, attempts to interest him in what was best for the boy in the way of vocational choice seemed to fall flat. The father seemed to think the staff were indulging his errant son's 'selfish interests'. When I explored this further, it emerged that they had been talking with the father purely on the level of what was best for the boy, i.e. where his interests and skills seemed to lie. I suggested they try again, this time to acknowledge first what we had previously agreed in a therapy session: that the boy needed to work on being a fully contributing member of the family. He had demonstrated his commitment to that goal by attending school at the centre in a satisfactory manner over the past three months. To move on he now needed family support in enabling him to choose the right job. The social workers agreed to try the 'family first' line and reported surprise at how much more effective it was in engaging the parent's interest and co-operation.

References

Aponte, H. and Hoffman, L. (1973) 'The Open Door; a Structural Approach to a Family with an Anorectic Child', *Family Process, 12*, 1–44

Ballard, R. (1982) 'South Asian Famliies', in R.H. Rapaport, M.P. Fogarty and R. Rapaport (eds), *Families in Britain*, Routledge and Kegan Paul, London

Byng-Hall, J. (1982) 'Dysfunctions of Feeling; Experiential Life of the Family', in A. Bentovim, G. Gorell Barnes and A. Cooklin (eds), *Family Therapy, Complementary Frameworks of Theory and Practice*, Vol. 1, pp. 111–30, Academic Press, London

Cohen, N. (1982) 'Same or Different? A Problem of Identity in Cross-cultural Marriages', *Journal of Family Therapy, 4*, 177–99

Devereux, G. (1980) *Basic Problems of Ethnopsychiatry*, transl. B. Miller Gulati and G. Devereux, University of Chicago Press, Chicago

Erickson, E.. (1968) *Identity, Youth and Crisis*, Norton, New York

Haley, J. (1980) *Leaving Home: the Therapy of Disturbed Young People*, McGraw-Hill, New York

Hare-Mustin, R.T. (1982) 'China's Marriage Law; a Model for Family Responsibilities and Relationships', *Family Process, 21* (4)

Henriques, F. (1949) 'West Indian Family Organisation', *The American Journal of Sociology, 55*, 30–7

Kinzie, D., Sushama, P.C. and Lee, M. (1972) 'Cross-cultural Family Therapy — a Malaysian Experience', *Family Process, 11*, 59–67

Kleinman, A. (1980) *Patients and Healers in the Context of Culture*, University of California Press, Berkeley

Lau, A. (1984) 'Transcultural Issues in Family Therapy', *Journal of Family Therapy, 6*, 91–112

Levick, S.E., Jalali, B. and Strauss, J.S. (1981) 'Onions and Tears: a Multi-dimensional Analyses of a Counter-ritual', *Family Process, 20*, 77–83

Linton, R.N. (1937) *The Study of Man*, Appleton-Century, New York

Littlewood, R. and Lipsedge, M. (1982) *Aliens and Alienists, Ethnic Minorities and Psychiatry*, Penguin, London

McGoldrick, M. and Preto, N.B. (1984) 'Ethnic Intermarriage — Implications for Therapy', *Family Process, 23*, 347–64

McGoldrick, M., Pearce, J.K. and Giordano, J. (eds) (1982) *Ethnicity and Family Therapy*, The Guildford Press, New York

Madanes, C. and Haley, J. (1977) 'Dimensions of Family Therapy', *Journal of Nervous and Mental Disease, 165* (2), 88–98

Minuchin, S. (1974) *Families and Family Therapy*, Tavistock, London

Palazzoli, M.S., Boscolo, L., Cecchin, G.F. and Prata, G. (1977) 'Family Rituals a Powerful Tool in Family Therapy', *Family Process, 16*, 445–53

Pearce, J.K. (1980) (in book review of *Blood of my Blood: the Dilemma of the Italian Americans*, by Richard Gambino, 1974, Doubleday, Anchor Books, Garden City), *Family Process, 19*, 93–4

Scheff, T.J. (1979) *Catharsis in Healing, Ritual and Drama*, University of California Press, Berkeley

Seltzer, W.J. and Seltzer, M.R. (1983) 'Material, Myth, and Magic. A Cultural Approach to Family Therapy', *Family Process, 22*, 3–14

Shackman, J. (1983) *The Right to be Understood. A Handbook on Working with, Employing and Training Community Interpreters*, National Extension College, Cambridge

Skynner, R. (1982) 'Frameworks for Viewing the Family as a System' in A. Bentovim, G. Gorell Barnes and A. Cooklin (eds), *Family Therapy, Complementary Frameworks of Theory and Practice*, Vol. 1, pp. 3–35, Academic Press, New York

Spiegel, J.P. (1968) 'Cultural Strain, Family Role Patterns and Intrapsychic Conflict', in J.G. Howelles (ed.), *Theory and Practice of Family Psychiatry*, Oliver and Boyd, London

Stagoll, B. (1981) 'Therapy with Greek Families Living in Australia', *International Journal of Family Therapy*, *3*, 167–79

15 THE 'CULTURE-BOUND SYNDROMES' OF THE DOMINANT CULTURE: CULTURE, PSYCHOPATHOLOGY AND BIOMEDICINE[†]

Roland Littlewood and Maurice Lipsedge

Data from a New Guinea tribe and the superficially very different data of psychiatry can be approached in terms of a single epistemology. (Bateson, 1958)

Theories of the relationship between culture and psychopathology have assumed that the notion of 'culture' and the domain of 'psychopathology' are distinct despite many studies of small-scale 'tribal' communities which do not make our Western separation between these two notions. Thus, given the clear theoretical distinction between these concepts in industrialised societies, Western psychopathology is often regarded as if it were culture-free (Chapter 4). However, Murphy (1977) has emphasised that the time is overdue for the relationship between cultural background and psychopathology to be more formally examined, and that 'we should cease thinking that *our* behavioural expectations are all "natural", not requiring re-examination'. As Gaines (1982) has pointed out, Western psychiatry can be studied in the same way as we might study a traditional theory of disease, 'one no less constructed, informed and communicated than another'.

We shall argue in this chapter that contemporary biomedical (scientific) conceptualisations of illness are closely tied to implicit cultural and political assumptions, particularly those concerning sex roles and notions of personal identity and the attribution of causality.

Some symptoms of schizophrenia and depression have been considered to be specifically Western (Murphy, 1978; Fabrega, 1982). Here we shall concentrate on reactions that appear to be particularly associated with industrialised cultures. We have taken the term 'culture-bound syndrome' to refer to (i) local patterns of time-limited behaviour, specific to a particular culture, and recognised as discrete by informants and observers alike; (ii) few instances of which have a biological cause;

† This chapter is an amended version of the paper 'The Butterfly and the Serpent', *Culture, Medicine and Psychiatry* (in press)

(iii) the individual is not held to be aware or responsible in the everyday sense; and (iv) the behaviour usually has a 'dramatic' quality (Littlewood and Lipsedge, 1985).

Rather than look in Western psychopathology for superficial similarities to the 'classic' culture-bound reactions (genital retraction — Barrett, 1978; possession states — Pattison and Wintrob, 1981), it will be more appropriate to consider how applicable to Britain are the models developed for small-scale societies.

Many classic culture-bound reactions follow a triphasic pattern; *dislocation* of the individual is followed by behaviour ('symptoms') which represent an *exaggeration* of this dislocation (frequently suggesting a direct contravention or 'inversion' of normative behaviour), followed by *restitution* of the individual back into everyday relationships (Littlewood and Lipsedge, 1985).

Culture-bound syndromes articulate not only personal predicament but also public concerns about core structural oppositions between age groups or the sexes. They have a shared meaning as public and dramatic representations in an individual whose personal situation demonstrates these oppositions, and they thus occur in certain well-defined situations. At the same time they have a personal expressive meaning for the particular individual and are functional ('instrumental'): 'in situations of deprivation or frustration where recourse to personal jural power is not available, the principal is able to adjust his or her situation by recourse to "mystical pressure" ' (Lewis, 1971). They appeal to values and beliefs which cannot be questioned because they are tied up with the most fundamental concerns of the community. Turner (1969) aptly calls this sideways recourse to mystical sanction 'the power of the weak' — what psychiatrists term 'manipulation'.

To consider some examples more fully described elsewhere (Littlewood and Lipsedge, 1985), *Negi Negi* in the New Guinea Highlands is the public destruction of property and threatened violence by young men who cannot perform their normal adult role when faced with enormous bride-price debts; the reaction exaggerates this social dislocation to the point where the young man dramatically declines membership of the social community altogether. *Sar* possession in Somalia legitimates outrageous behaviour for women in a patriarchal Islamic society when they are offended or neglected by their husbands. *Sar* diagnosis and treatment are in the hands of women's therapy groups which provide the only form of communal female organisation in opposition to the public ritual of Islam which is controlled by men; not surprisingly 'the sar spirits are said to hate men' (Lewis, 1971). In Tikopia aggrieved or rejected women threaten suicide by swimming out to sea; like overdoses they are 'successful' when no one is hurt. These reactions, then, are flexible and adaptive. Although at times the community may suspect personal advantage, this is not publicly expressed unless the reaction occurs 'excessively' or 'inappropriately'.

Culture-bound reactions are conservative because the 'mystical pressure' is still a part of the established order. They legitimate the *status quo* rather than question it; social contradictions are displayed but not ultimately resolved. They permit a constrained display of deviance, often glossed by a local notion of catharsis ('letting off steam'; Littlewood, 1984).

Our attempt to look for equivalent 'Western' reactions would appear quite straightforward apart from the notion of 'mystical pressure'. What is the unquestionable 'other-worldly authority', standing outside everyday personal relations, which might serve to explain and to legitimate Western culture-bound disorders?

In small-scale traditional communities, social organisation and normative principles, the categorisation of the natural world and human relations to it, are articulated through an intellectually tight system of supernatural beliefs which we usually refer to as religion. Religion in these communities therefore is an ideology. It both describes and prescribes, binding the individual into society and into the natural order; through its other-worldly authority it legitimates personal experience and the social order. By contrast, in the secularised West, Christianity has lost this power of social regulation and competes both with other religions and, more significantly, with a variety of alternative moral and political ideologies. Where then can we find an equivalent 'mystical' sanction which integrates personal distress into a shared conceptualisation of the world?

We would suggest that this legitimation of our present world view lies in contemporary science, which offers core notions of individual identity, responsibility and action. In its everyday context as it relates to our personal experience, science is most salient in the form of medicine. In all societies illness is experienced through an expressive system encoding indigenous notions of social order (Comaroff, 1978). While serious illness 'is an event that challenges meaning in this world . . . medical beliefs and practices organise the event into an episode which gives form and meaning' (Young, 1976). Professional intervention in sickness involves incorporating the patient into an overarching system of explanation, a common structural pattern which manifests itself in the bodily economy of every human being (Willis, 1978; Turner, 1984).

Social accountability is transferred on to an agency beyond the patient's control. Becoming ill is part of a social process leading to communal recognition of an abnormal state and a consequent readjustment of patterns of behaviour and expectations, and thence to changed roles and altered responsibility. Expectations of the sick person include exemption from discharging some social obligations, and from responsibility for the condition itself, together with a shared recognition that it is undesirable and involves an obligation to seek help and co-operate with treatment (Parsons, 1951). Withdrawal from everyday social responsibilities is made socially acceptable through some means of exculpation, usually through mechanisms of biophysical determinism (Young, 1976). To question the biomedical schema itself involves questioning some of our most fundamental assumptions about human nature and agency.

Biomedicine offers a powerful and unquestionable legitimate inversion of everyday behaviour. It will not be surprising, therefore, to find that many of our 'culture-bound syndromes' are already included in psychiatric nosologies and that others lie hidden in the fringes of general medicine.

Butterflies and Serpents: the Medicalisation of Women

In all societies women are 'excluded from participation in or contact with some realm in which the highest powers of the society are felt to reside' (Ortner, 1974). They are excluded by the dominant ideology which reflects men's experiences and interests. The facts of female physiology are transformed in almost all societies into a cultural rationale which assigns women to nature and the domestic sphere, and thus ensures their general inferiority to men (La Fontaine, 1981). Jordanovna (1980) suggests that medicine and science are characterised by the action of men on women; women are regarded as more 'natural', passive, awaiting male (cultural) organisation. In the heraldry of the Royal College of Psychiatrists, as sported on the ties of its members, this tradition is continued as the Butterflies of Psyche awaiting the Serpents of Asclepius. Serpent and Butterfly are in an opposed but complementary relationship: action by one engenders the opposed complement in the other (Bateson, 1958). Ingleby (1982) has argued that there is a close historical relationship between the psychiatric notions of 'woman' and 'patient', and both Chesler (1974) and Jordanovna (1981) have pointed out the similarity between neurotic symptom patterns and normative expectations of female behaviour. Thus, we may summarise the Serpent/Butterfly relationship as:

$$\frac{\text{Culture}}{\text{Nature}} = \frac{\text{Male}}{\text{Female}} = \frac{\text{Active}}{\text{Passive}} = \frac{\text{Cognition}}{\text{Affect}} = \frac{\text{Doctor}}{\text{Patient}}$$

(modified from Jordanovna, 1980).

To this Turner (1984) adds:

$$\frac{\text{Public}}{\text{Private}} = \frac{\text{Production}}{\text{Consumption}} = \frac{\text{Desire}}{\text{Need}}$$

A polythetic classification of this type stresses that the *relationship* between paired elements remains constant, not that there is equality between the superordinate or subordinate elements (Littlewood, 1984). Although the culture/nature distinction is commonly used in many societies to explain differences between men and women, it is not universal (Jordanovna, 1980). As we have seen in Chapter 4, the contemporary position in psychiatry is that mental illnesses take the complementary form: Whites (culture) have 'real' (natural) mental illness, whereas Blacks (nature) have culture-bound psychopathology. The culture/nature distinction is of course itself historically and politically determined: it is itself 'cultural'. The actual existing relationship remains the same; thus whereas an explanation of Black society in terms of nature (biological racism) is no longer acceptable, the same is not true for women.

Keller (1974) suggests that the core aspect of the female role in Western society is reflected in the ideals still held out to women: concentration on marriage, home and children as the primary focus of concern, with reliance on a male provider for sustenance and status. There is an expectation that women will emphasise nurturance and life-preserving activities, and that they live through and for others rather than for themselves. Women are expected to give up their occupation and place of residence when they marry and are banned from direct assertion and expression of aggression. The historical origin of this contemporary role lies in the Industrial Revolution, with the division of work by gender, arising from a physical separation between home and workplace which exaggerated the existing physical and emotional isolation of women (Turner, 1984) and produced a close relationship between the woman and her doctor which, to an extent, replaced aspects of the wife/husband relationship (Donzelot, 1980). The move away from the household as a focus for productive work has also diminished its responsibilities for religion, education and recreation, reducing its social significance, contracting women's responsibilities and isolating them from significant areas of public production.

Women's lack of power is attributed to their greater emotionality and their inability to cope with wider social responsibilities. A group of American therapists was asked to describe separately a healthy mature socially competent adult (sex unspecified), a man, and a woman (Broverman *et al.*, 1970). The behaviour and characteristics offered for 'a healthy adult' were similar to those for healthy men but opposite to those for healthy women: normative expectations of women included excitability in minor crises, vulnerability, sensitivity, emotionality and concern about their appearance. Dependency and passivity are expected of a woman; her image is of a person with a childish incapacity to govern herself and a need for male protection and direction (Broverman *et al.*, 1970).

Women report more illnesses than do men and utilise health services more frequently. The consulting rate for minor psychiatric disorders in general practice is more than twice as high for women as it is for men (Logan and Cushion, 1958). Married women are more likely than the unmarried to seek psychiatric help (Gove and Tudor, 1973), to attempt suicide and to report 'somatic symptoms indicative of psychological distress' (Dohrenwend and Dohrenwend, 1974).

It has been suggested that women report more illnesses because it is culturally acceptable for them to be ill (Weissman and Klerman, 1977). Contemporary Western women are permitted greater freedom than men to 'express feelings' and to recognise emotional difficulties (Phillips and Segal, 1969), enabling the woman to define her difficulties within a medical framework and bring them to the attention of her doctor (Horwitz, 1977). Widely used symptom scales are more representative of female than male patterns of expressing distress (Dohrenwend and Dohrenwend, 1974). Illness is more stigmatising for men, and women are rejected less strongly than men for exhibiting emotional symptoms (Phillips, 1966). Women's greater readiness to seek medical treatment reflects the general process of subordinates being more self-disclosing than superiors (Horwitz, 1977).

Doctors tend to locate the housewife's problems within the family and attribute her frustration and anxiety to the marriage, the menopause or the 'emptying of the nest' (Barrett and Roberts, 1978). They have certain assumptions about the nature of men and women: men have a primary natural 'drive' to work to support their wife and family, whereas women have an opposing but complementary 'drive' to nourish and cherish their husband and family. Men, then, are located in terms of their occupations, women in terms of their families. Women are considered to have vague and spurious worries, whereas men have specific physical or occupational problems; women seem to 'worry about nothing'. Barrett and Roberts comment that doctors do not accept that an underlying problem could be an enforced lack of meaning, independence and identity, and found more than one case of the woman's refusal to do housework resulting directly in hospitalisation and ECT.

Perverse Femininity: Conversion Hysteria in the Nineteenth Century

In the nineteenth century, hysteria was a socially recognised behaviour pattern mainly affecting women. The middle-class woman was taught that aggression, independence, assertion and curiosity were male traits inappropriate for women, whose nature was emotional, powerless, passive and nurturant and who were not expected to make achievements in any public area. Hysteria offered a solution to the onerous task of running a household, and of adjusting husband/wife or father/daughter relations, and one which did not challenge these core values. The development from simple conversion symptoms to a recognised discrete role as a 'hysteric' provided a parody of the core social values: women's expected dependency and restricted social role. The hysteric was characteristically female, the hysterical woman being perceived as the very embodiment of perverse femininity, an inversion of dominant male behaviour (Smith-Rosenberg, 1972). What Freud was to term the 'secondary gain' conferred by the hysterical role allowed a limited adjustment of husband/wife power relations in the family. 'Ill health will be her one weapon for maintaining her position. It will compel him to treat her with solicitude if she recovers; otherwise a relapse will threaten' (Freud, 1946).

The role of 'the hysteric' before Freud did not involve acceptance of individual responsibility for the illness; male physicians, and men in general, employed biological arguments to rationalise this exaggeration of traditional sex role as immutably rooted in anatomy and pathophysiology (Smith-Rosenberg, 1973). Thus the nineteenth-century view of women, or at least of middle-class women, was as frail and decorative creatures whose temperamental excesses were a result of a peculiar functioning of their sexual organs and whose very physical nature limited their activities to family roles.

The dominant male/passive female notion which embodied the hysterical reaction was of course mirrored in the therapy: the rational physician actively treating his passive patient in the grip of her nature.

The pattern of symptoms of Charcot's patients has been described as 'a folie à deux . . . a culture-bound syndrome emerging from the interaction between the professor and his clientele', to be replaced later by a less dramatic pattern of diffuse somatic complaints (Eisenberg, 1977). Female identity *vis-à-vis* men is particularly reinforced in collective and passive settings such as nurses' training schools and boarding schools, and these are the contemporary situations in which doctors continue to diagnose hysteria.

'Function for' or 'Function of': Overdoses

A contemporary reaction which offers parallels with the doctor/patient relation in hysteria in parasuicide with medically prescribed drugs. As in hysteria, the normative situation of active male (husband, doctor) and passive female (wife, patient) is mirrored in the drama of the hospital casualty department. The unease and anger which it evokes in the medical profession reflects its 'perverse' transformation of the clinical paradigm.

Women are closely identified with psychotropic medication. More women than men go to physicians and receive prescriptions, and there is an even greater disproportion in the number of women receiving psychotropic drugs. Physicians expect female patients to require them (Cooperstock, 1971). These are perhaps the 'attractive healthy women who thoroughly enjoy being ill' (*Daily Express*, 27 March 1984).

That we are not dealing simply with a 'real' gender disparity in psychological distress is suggested by the symbolism of medical advertising. Stimson (1975) found that women outnumbered men by 15 to 1 in medical advertisements for tranquillisers and antidepressants. Employed women are rare in drug advertisements, and women are usually shown as dependent housewives and child rearers: the world acts on them, they do not act on the world. Seidenberg (1974) too found that psychotropic drug advertisements emphasised women as the patients; they were represented as discontented with their role in life, dissatisfied with marriage, with washing dishes or attending parent-teacher association meetings. The treating physician was never depicted as a woman, and all the female patients appeared as helpless and anxious.

Overdoses of medical drugs are up to five times as common among women, especially in the age group 15–19. A study of fifty adolescent overdosers suggested they viewed their act as a means of gaining relief from a stressful situation or as a way of showing other people how desperate they felt; clinical staff who assessed their motives perceived an expressive intent but also noted that adolescents took overdoses in order to punish other people or change their behaviour (Hawton *et al.*, 1982). Many patients admitted that the induction of guilt in those whom they blamed for their distress was a predominant motive for the act (Bancroft *et al.*, 1979). Thus, whereas overdoses can be seen as pragmatic strategies designed to avoid or to adjust certain specific situations, the self-perception of the principal is of social dislocation or extrusion: the reaction exaggerates this extrusion, offering a threat of refusing membership in the human community altogether — an inversion of normal life-seeking norms.

The successful resolution of the inversion involves its complement: medical intervention returns the patient into everyday relationships. Not surprisingly, the overdose meets with little professional sympathy, particularly when it is recognised as an instrumental social mechanism rather than the sign of underlying individual hopelessness or psychiatric illness (Ramon *et al.*, 1975). Nurses are generally more sympathetic than are doctors to instrumental motives, perhaps because of their ambiguous position in the serpent : butterfly (doctor : patient :: male : female) equation (Littlewood and Littlewood, 1986); nurses are more likely to perceive overdoses as legitimate attempts to escape from distress (Ramon *et al.*, 1975).

Women who take overdoses gain access to medical facilities as the popular conception of suicidal behaviour is that it is a discrete event, 'something that happens to one', rather than something one intentionally brings about (Ginsburg, 1971). Relatives thus accept that the patient is not responsible for herself, and that her problems are outside her direct personal control, and responsibility for out-of-the-ordinary behaviour is thereby transferred to some agency beyond the patient's volition. That this is medical rather than jural is suggested by the continuing use of the popular term 'overdose' as opposed to 'self-poisoning'. The official translation of the behaviour into 'symptoms' takes place under socially prescribed conditions by the physician, who alone has the power to legitimate exculpating circumstances (Young, 1980). As with nineteenth-century hysteria, the resolution of the reaction involves a 'mystical pressure' which replicates the social structure in which the reaction occurs. Like other culture-bound syndromes it is fundamentally conservative; it displays core structural antagonisms but shows they are solvable within the existing political and symbolic framework. The drama of the scene in the casualty department replays the male doctor/female patient theme without questioning it, but it affords a degree of negotiation for the principal.

The Housewives' Disease: Agoraphobia

Agoraphobia is the inability or reluctance to leave home or to enter public places unaccompanied. Attempts to do so result in anxiety or other unpleasant symptoms, a fear of falling, fainting or otherwise losing control. Agoraphobics fear any situation in which escape to a safe place or dependable companion might be impeded. The majority are married women (Marks, 1970), hence the popular term 'housewives disease'. Physical space replicates social space (Ardener, 1981) and Bell and Newby (1976) point out that the home represents core social value: it is

> the framework within which the deference of wife to husband operates. Encouragement of ideologies of the home and home-centredness enables the identification of the wife with her husband's superordinate position to increase by emphasising a common adherence to territory, a solidarity of place. A woman's 'place' is therefore in the home, partly because to seek fulfilment outside the home could threaten to break down the ideological control which confinement within it promotes.

The agoraphobic reaction employs an exaggeration or caricature of the female role with its lack of control or power, mirroring the situation of Western European and American women in many areas of their lives with their extreme dependence on men (Symonds, 1971). In one study (Goldstein, 1973) 16 out of 20 female agoraphobic patients had felt strong urges to escape from their marriage and home at the time of the onset of the phobia, but were unable to do so because of realistic fears of isolation and the loss of economic support. Goldstein (1970) finds that agoraphobic symptoms develop concurrently with a sense of dislocation: a wish to end the marriage or to 'violate' the marital contract. The agoraphobic is often an unhappily married woman, low in self-sufficiency, in whom the fear evoked by physical isolation accompanies a persistent but unrealistic fantasy of liberation from the marraige — unrealistic because it is seen as leading to a social abyss (Wolpe, 1970). The agoraphobic woman conforms even more to the stereotypic role, but she gains a strategy which, without open defiance of the husband (Andrews, 1966), requires him to make sacrifices and gives her a veto over proposed joint activities (Buglass *et al.*, 1977). The very nature of a woman's household responsibility makes her illness the most potentially disturbing of all to family equilibrium, and agoraphobia is thus a particularly adaptive strategy (Parsons and Fox, 1952; Lazarus, 1972).

On occasion it is able to severely restrict the husband's activities to the point where he is virtually unable to leave the home (Fry, 1962). 'Husband and wife are compelled to live together in mutual distress, consoling themselves for all their differences with the mutual idea that this thing has been imposed upon them, beyond their control, and they can do nothing about it' (Fry, 1962).

At the age of thirteen, girls have five times as many 'fears' as have boys (Macfarlane *et al.*, 1954). There is ample documentary evidence of the way girls and women are presented in the media, which points to a relationship between fearfulness and dependency in women's social roles, providing the basis for the later development of agoraphobia. In a study of sex roles in school textbooks, the illustrations portray girls and adult women as if agoraphobic, pictured behind fences or windows, immobilised, helpless and watching (National Organisation for Women Task Force, 1974). As Durkheim (1951) wrote: 'The two sexes do not share equally in social life. Man is actively involved in it, while woman does little more than look on from a distance.'

The Sexual Body: Anorexia Nervosa

Anorexia nervosa was first described in France, Britain and Russia in the nineteenth century, and is now taking on epidemic proportions in countries undergoing rapid industrialisation. It is particularly common in middle-class Western adolescent girls. Although Prince (1983) suggests it is a culture-bound syndrome, it differs from the reactions we have described in having a 'biological component'; this, however, is likely to be secondary to a socially determined weight loss, for its occurrence parallels certain culture-bound (and class-bound) notions of female body imagery.

Dieting is encouraged by an industry that provides an extensive range of low-energy food products to facilitate slimming, reinforced by extensive medical publicity (Ritenbaugh, 1982). The top four British slimming magazines have a joint circulation of over 650 000. In a Swedish study (Nylander, 1971), 72 per cent of 21-year-old women felt that they had been fat at some time compared with 34 per cent of the men; twice as many women attributed their excess of weight to 'weak character'. In a similar study of over 6000 Americans, twice as many girls as boys perceived themselves as overweight; the girls were dissatisfied with their weight because they equated slimness with beauty. Excessive weight is more of a professional handicap to women than men; successful business women (and the wives of successful men!) are rarely overweight, and women's concepts of themselves in general are more closely tied to their appearance than are men's (Stuart and Jacobson, 1979). Women are more harshly penalised for failure to achieve slenderness as they are more often denied or granted access to social privilege on the basis of physical appearance (Elder, 1969): obese schoolgirls are less likely than their slender peers to be accepted for college despite comparable qualifications (Canning and Myer, 1966). British women can lose their jobs for being 'overweight' (*Daily Telegraph*, 1984): 'A woman increases her market value by being slender' (Millman, 1974). Whereas thinness is associated with upward social mobility, fatness is often the sign of 'ethnic minority status' (Millman, 1974).

Is anorexia an exaggeration or a rejection of the dominant cultural norm? Its exact relation to core social values is unclear, perhaps because it articulates current uncertainty about women's sexuality. Although the preferred sex object for men is slender (Garner and Garfinkel, 1980), a fuller figure implies sexuality through pregnancy; at the same time contemporary men appear to value the state of pregnancy less. Millman (1974) suggests that fat women are seen as unfeminine, in flight from sexuality, or alternatively as sexual in some perverse forbidden way, incestuous, out of control, dominant. Anorexia nervosa may be an attempt to emulate a valued youthful body form (Ritenbaugh, 1982) rather than an inversion of the dominant mode; the incidence in modelling students has been estimated to be 7 per cent (Garner and Garfinkel, 1980). If plumper girls are seen as more sexually mature (Millman, 1974), the male choice of sex object has become increasingly infantile — baby-faced and long-legged with shaven armpits (Cranshaw, 1983).

Boskind-Lodahl (1976) takes issue with the standard psychoanalytic interpretation of anorexia as simply a rejection of adult femininity, manifesting as fear of oral impregnation. She suggests that the determined pursuit of thinness by adolescent girls constitutes an exaggerated striving to achieve this norm, and that attempts to control her physical appearance demonstrate a concern with pleasing others. Crisp (1980) suggests the reaction involves the patient remaining a child and describes a typical anorexic:

> Within the context of her mounting panic at the prospect of her parents' marriage breaking up, her dieting quickly escalated, seeming suddenly easy and relieving to her and, as anorexia nervosa supervened, her father and mother were reunited in their unwritten contract together to care for her until she 'grew up'.

Other Reactions

Shoplifting

One form of shoplifting is that by middle-aged women who steal although they can apparently afford to buy what they take. The characteristic principal is a 50-year-old woman with non-specific physical and psychological symptoms who is neglected by her husband and children (Gibbens and Prince, 1962). Shopping is the occupation of women; whereas agoraphobia is a parody of the 'woman's place is in the home' notion, shoplifting is a public parody of the ideal woman as consumer and an affirmation of woman's asocial or irrational nature. As with bingeing, observers frequently discern an element of revenge, of personal assertion, in highly constrained circumstances. Thus a patient of ours, unhappily married, stole very publicly from a department store on the very day that her husband was appointed as its manager. A successful reaction involves public recognition of problems and enhanced domestic interest and concern. The woman herself is not held responsible in the usual way, as she would be if she were stealing for monetary gain, for the reaction is 'irrational' and is often attributed to 'depression' or the 'menopause'.

Domestic Sieges

Agoraphobia and anorexia nervosa are characteristic of women and only a minority of parasuicides are men. In certain situations it is men who are socially extruded and who employ adaptive culture-bound mechanisms to adjust their situation. In domestic sieges the typical principal is a divorced or separated man who has lost the custody of his child. Traditionally fathers have readily accepted the common practice of courts awarding custody of children to the mother; enormous value was placed on the powers of maternal instinct which justified denial of custody to fathers. Occasionally the father responds by seizing or abducting the child from the mother or guardian in violation of a custody ruling and threatens homicide, suicide or both. The legal outcome of domestic sieges is variable but at times the father secures more generous access (Lipsedge and Littlewood, 1985). He might be treated leniently by the courts, frequently with the aid of medical reports.

Flashing (Exhibitionism)

Like anorexia nervosa, *flashing* (exhibitionism) employs core cultural notions of body image and sexual identity (see Polhemus, 1978). In a society that condemns the overt display of male sexual arousal and which is, at the same time, intensely preoccupied with avoidance of effeminacy, the flasher is frequently a young adult male, 'passive and lacking in self-assertion', with poor social skills, who believes he has a small penis (Rooth, 1971). Like the Ḥamadsha principal (Littlewood and Lipsedge, 1985) he fails to live up to cultural norms of male activity. As with sieges, flashing is a dramatic time-limited public performance with a contravention of conventional behaviour: a caricature of rape rather than of paternal authority. 'A common theme is one of dominance and mastery: the exhibitionist, usually timid and unassertive with women, suddenly challenges one with his penis, briefly occupies her full attention and conjures up in her some powerful emotion, such as fear and disgust, or sexual curiosity and arousal. For a fleeting instant he experiences a moment of intense involvement in a situation where he is in control' (Rooth, 1971). The principal is frequently not held responsible; Magnan suggested in 1890 that the irresistible urge to exhibit 'annihilated the will' and should therefore carry exemption from legal sanction. If the dislocation is seen purely in terms of physical sex, flashing does not seem immediately adaptive: the performance seldom ends in coitus. Taking the longer view (and exhibitionism as a syndrome has probably developed in relation to a biomedical ethos), treatment involves encouragement and facilitation of sexual relationships. As with shoplifting, the immediate result of the drama is the ceding of control to others: 'discretion is not always the rule' (Rooth, 1971).

The Psychopolitics of the Culture-bound Syndromes: Inversion and Reflexivity

The reactions we have described are not phenomenologically discrete. Many similar patterns occur in non-Western societies. Thus, variants of male genital display are found elsewhere, although the flashing variant is most common in industrialised societies, particularly Anglo-Saxon ones (Rooth, 1974). Murphy (1982) suggests that Japanese *taijin kyok* (interpersonal phobia) and Eskimo 'kayak angst' bear a close relationship to agoraphobia. Similarly parasuicide in Singapore with caustic soda offers parallels with overdoses: it is carried out by isolated women faced with the threat of complete abandonment by husband or parents (Murphy, 1982).

Though social meanings and behaviour can be superimposed on a variety of existing biological patterns, e.g. kuru, premenstrual tension, adolescence, the symptomatic psychoses, drug intoxications (and perhaps

Table 15.1: Defining Criteria (? = Doubtful or unknown)

	Overdose	Shoplifting	Baby-snatching	Agoraphobia	Domestic sieges	Conversion hysteria	Anorexia	Chronic pain/Briquet's syndrome	Exhibitionism	Obesity	Reactive depression	Menopause	Trans-sexualism
Time-limited	+	+	+	?	+	?	0	0	+	0	0	0	0
Culture-specific	+	+	+	+	+	0	+	0	0	?	0	?	0
Discrete (locals)	+	+	+	?	+	?	+	0	+	0	+	+	+
Discrete (observer)	+	+	+	+	+	+	+	+	+	+	+	?	+
No major biological aetiology	+	+	+	+	+	+	?	+	+	?	+	+	+
Individual not aware/responsible	+	+	+	+	+	+	+	+	?	+	+	+	+
Dramatic	+	+	+	+	+	+	+	?	+	0	0	0	0
Dislocation	+	+	+	+	+	+	+	+	+	?	+	+	0
Inversion/exaggeration	+	+	+	+	?	+	+	+	+	?	?	?	0
Restitution	+	+	?	+	+	+	+	+	0	?	?	0	?
Symbolises core values	+	+	+	+	+	+	+	+	+	+	0	?	0
Situations of frustration	+	+	+	+	+	+	+	+	+	+	+	?	?
Non-dominant individuals	+	+	+	+	+	+	+	+	+	+	?	+	0
'Mystical pressure'	+	+	+	+	+	+	+	+	?	+	+	+	?

autism: Sanua, 1984), we have restricted our discussion to reactions not primarily associated with human physiology and which are public and dramatic presentations of core social issues. In a word, *theatre*: but a theatre that has a specific functional mechanism for the principal actor and one which may at times end in her death.

Table 15.1 sets out these reactions in relation to our defining criteria, together with four less likely candidates for comparison: obesity, menopause, trans-sexualism and reactive depression. The paradigms appear to be overdosing, shoplifting, baby-snatching, agoraphobia and domestic sieges. Many of the reactions show an inversion of the dominant symbolism. How helpful is the notion of 'inversion'? In the case of the male reactions, sieges and flashing, the pattern is an exaggerated reassertion or parody of dominant norms rather than their obvious inversion. Although clearly extraordinary behaviour relative to everyday articulation of the same symbolism, it would extend the notion of 'inversion' too far to include them. Like obesity, *amok* or suicide, it is the threat that provides bargaining power. Sieges certainly take place in situations in which the principal is excluded from fully participating in dominant values, but the performance is an assertion of such values. We have, however, seen recently a number of husbands who became agoraphobic after a period of compulsory redundancy during which the wife continued as the wage-earner. The female reactions also appear to be a parody or *reductio ad absurdum* of normal sex roles but in certain cases (agoraphobia, overdosing), women are, as we have seen, already in an inverted and socially extruded position and the reaction is an extension of this. In anorexia nervosa the relation is more complex but both anorexia and obesity (its apparent reverse) have a close subjective relationship to male/female relations: for many participants they are of course phases in the same reaction. The ambiguity and 'overdetermination' of anorexia reflects a current ambiguity over female sexuality and child-rearing which is not characteristic of the role of the woman as housekeeper (agoraphobia) or patient (overdoser).

Particular elements of the Serpent/Butterfly relation appear to be employed differentially in the different reactions: doctor/patient in overdoses; public/private in agoraphobia; production/consumption in shoplifting. They are not discretely related, however, and each reaction articulates the total complex out of which other situation-specific patterns can be generated. Thus a bank manager's widow faced with insoluble debts recently attempted undisguised to rob a bank where she was a customer, using her perfume spray as a gun: after a suspended court sentence facilitated the adjustment of her finances she commented 'I must have had a brain storm' (*The Times*, 1984). The popular notion of a 'brain storm' affords exculpation as an overriding and irrational but excusable impulse, clearly aligned with the medico-legal concept of 'diminished responsibility'. This coexists with the idea that at some unconscious level the reaction is 'understandable'.

The mystical power of biomedicine as 'external' justification for individual action, and the negotiating 'space' it affords seem relevant to those other reactions in which patient enacts a *pas de deux* with the doctor: Ganser syndrome, compensation neurosis, irritable bowel, Munchhausen's syndrome and chronic pain syndromes, apart from the many situations (such as non-compliance) where different explanatory models employed by doctor and patient afford the latter some control over the social drama. Mystical sanction seems less relevant to our two specifically male reactions, presumably because of the Serpent/Butterfly relationship (culture : nature :: male : female :: active : passive :: doctor : patient). For medical professionals themselves, whether male or female, the biomedical 'mystical pleasure' is difficult to employ personally; whereas student nurses frequently take overdoses, the reaction is rare among qualified nursing staff. The recourse to biomedical sanction has to be more complex and more 'dissociated' than overdosing. To determine the extent to which the reactions are 'conscious' attempts at adjustment is not helpful; though there is an element of parody in all of them, the irony is only partially perceived by principal and audience. Participants certainly experience despair and self-hatred.

All the reactions we have described are likely to be found as part of an endogenous depressive illness; we suggest the mediating factor is the sense of extrusion and isolation which is so characteristic of depression. Our emphasis on semiotic rather than psychological or physiological antecedents should thus not be taken to mean that individual personality or biology are irrelevant in the choice of reaction. It is not surprising that agoraphobic patients have 'phobic personalities' or that anorexics were overweight as children. The final path is overdetermined. Nevertheless the individual reaction is socially embedded: the male who takes an overdose or who develops anorexia is inevitably 'feminised'. Another patient of ours shoplifted from a London store where her domineering mother was well known, ostensibly to purchase her own birthday present to be given by her mother later in the week; in this setting her mother stood in a relationship to her analogous to that of husband to wife (we would be surprised to find a man engaging in shoplifting in a similar relationship with his wife or even a son with his mother).

We have previously outlined the interrelations between social, psychological and symbolic inversion (Littlewood, 1984). Reversal theory suggests that inversions occur in a universal non-rational 'ludic' mode (Apter, 1982), and Chesler (1974) emphasises that it is women who are 'conditioned to lose in order to win'. Devereux (1970) characterises this passive 'appeal of helplessness' (Symonds, 1971) as *chantage masochiste* (masochistic blackmail) and illustrates it with an agoraphobic case history and the 'psychology of cargo cults'. Rather than characterise such life-threatening and constricting situations as simply 'self-punitive' or 'manipulative', we would prefer to see the powerless individual as enmeshed in a situation which she cannot control, one which neither reflects her interests nor her perspective but which does afford room for manoeuvre by employing the dominant symbolism itself. If it was not a dangerous game, it would not work: physiological integrity is temporarily sacrificed to semiology.

The dominant structures are only adjusted, not challenged. Whether self-help groups or women's therapy groups can, like women's groups in the Third World (Lewis, 1971; Janzen, 1979), actually develop into alternative political structures ('counter-structures': Turner, 1969) is unlikely. It is interesting that these reactions are often 'resolved' through psychiatry: the psychiatrist, relative to other doctors, is more passive, more empathic, more 'feminine'.

'Culture-bound syndromes of the dominant culture' is perhaps a misnomer, for we have found them largely among women. Women and non-Europeans, as Engels (1884) pointed out, share similar historical experiences. In our Serpent/Butterfly schema both have a similar relationship to the dominant norms, collected, classified and controlled by modern medicine. If the practice of psychiatric diagnosis is associated with the dominant culture, we will be unlikely to find psychopathologies specific to *that* culture.

References and Further Reading

Andrews, J.D.W. (1966) 'Psychotherapy of Phobias', *Psychological Bulletin, 66*, 455–80

Apter, M.J. (1982) *The Experience of Motivation: the Theory of Psychological Reversals*, Academic Press, London

Ardener, S. (ed.) (1981) *Women and Space: Ground Rules and Social Maps*, Croom Helm, London

Bancroft, J., Hawton, K., Simpkins, S., Kingston, B., Cumming, C. and Whitwell, D. (1979) 'The Reasons People Give for Taking Overdoses: a Further Enquiry', *British Journal of Medical Psychology, 52*, 353–65

Barrett, K. (1978) 'Koro in a Londoner', *Lancet, ii*, 1319

Barrett, M. and Roberts, H. (1978) 'Doctors and their Patients: the Social Control of Women in General Practice', in C. Smart and B. Smart (eds), *Women, Sexuality and Social Control*, Routledge and Kegan Paul, London

Bateson, G. (1958) *Naven*, 2nd edn, Stanford University Press, Stanford

Bell, C. and Newby, H. (1976) 'Husbands and Wives: the Dynamics of the Differential Dialect', in D.L. Barker and S. Allen (eds), *Dependence and Exploitation in Work and Marriage*, Longman, London

Boskind-Lodahl, M. (1976) 'Cinderella's Stepsisters: Feminist Perspective on Anorexia Nervosa and Bulimia', *Signs: Journal of Women, Culture and Society, 2*, 342–56

Broverman, I.D., Broverman, D.M., Clarkson, F.E., Rosenkrantz, P.S. and Vogel, S.R. (1970) 'Sex Role Stereotypes and Clinical Judgements of Mental Health', *Journal of Consulting and Clinical Psychology, 34*, 1–7

Buglass, D.D., Clarke, J., Henderson, A.S., Kreitman, N. and Priestly, A.S. (1977) 'A Study of Agoraphobic Housewives', *Psychological Medicine, 7*, 73–86

Canning, H. and Myer, J. (1966) 'Obesity — its Possible Effect on College Acceptance', *New England Journal of Medicine, 275*, 1172–4

Chesler, P. (1974) *Women and Madness*, Allen Lane, London

Comaroff, J. (1978) 'Medicine and Culture: Some Anthropological Perspectives', *Social Science and Medicine, 12*, 247–54

Cooperstock, R. (1971) 'Sex Differences in the Use of Mood-modifying Drugs: an Explanatory Model', *Journal of Health and Social Behaviour, 12*, 238–44

Cranshaw, R. (1983) 'The Object of the Centrefold', *Block*, No. 9, 26–33

Crapanzano, V. (1973) *The Hamadsha: a Study in Moroccan Ethnopsychiatry*, University of California Press, Berkeley

Crisp, A.H. (1980) *Anorexia Nervosa*, Academic Press, London

Daily Express (1984) 'Wives Hooked on Illness are Giving GPs Headache', 27 March, London

Daily Telegraph (1984) 'Waitresses Told: "Slim or Lose Jobs" ', 13 August, London

Devereux, G. (1970) *Essais d'Ethnopsychiatrie Generale*, Gallimard, Paris

Dohrenwend, B.P. and Dohrenwend, B.S. (1974) 'Sex Differences and Psychiatric Disorders', *American Journal of Sociology, 81*, 1447–54

Donzelot, J. (1980) *The Policing of Families*, Hutchinson, London

Durkheim, E. (1951) *Suicide*, Free Press, New York

Eisenberg, L. (1977) 'Disease and Illness: Distinctions between Professional and Popular Ideas of Sickness', *Culture, Medicine and Psychiatry, 1*, 9–23

Elder, G.H. (1969) 'Appearance and Education in Marriage Mobility', *American Sociological Review, 34*, 516–33

Engels, F. (1884) *The Origin of the Family, Private Property and the State*, publ. 1942, International Publishers, New York

Fabrega, H. (1982) 'Culture and Psychiatric Illness', in A.J. Marsella and S.M. White (eds), *Cultural Conceptions of Mental Health and Therapy*, Reidel, Dordrecht

Freud, S. (1946) 'Fragment of an Analysis of a Case of Hysteria', *Collected Works*, Vols 55–56, Hogarth, London

Fry, W.F. (1962) 'The Marital Context of an Anxiety Syndrome', *Family Process, 14*, 245–52

Gaines, A.D. (1982) 'Cultural Definitions, Behaviour and the Person in American Psychiatry' in A.J. Marsella and G. White (eds), *Cultural Conceptions of Mental Health and Therapy*, Reidel, Dordrecht

Garner, D.M. and Garfinkel, P.E. (1980) 'Socio-cultural Factors in the Development of Anorexia Nervosa', *Psychological Medicine, 10*, 747–56

Gibbens, T.C.N. and Prince, J. (1962) *Shoplifting*, Institute for Study and Treatment of Delinquency, London

Ginsburg, G.P. (1971) 'Public Conceptions and Attitudes about Suicide', *Journal of Health and Social Behaviour, 12*, 200–1

Goldstein, A.J. (1970) 'Case Conference: Some Aspects of Agoraphobia', *Journal of Behavioural Therapy and Experimental Psychiatry, 1*, 305–13

Goldstein, A.J. (1973) 'Learning Theory Insufficiency in Understanding Agoraphobia — A Plea for Empiricism', *Proceedings of the European Association for Behaviour Therapy and Modification Meeting, 1971*, Urban and Schwarzenberg, Munich

Gove, W.R. and Tudor, J.F. (1973) 'Adult Sex Roles and Mental Illness', *American Journal of Sociology, 78*, 812–35

Hawton, K., O'Grady, J., Osborne, M. and Cole, D. (1982) 'Adolescents who Take Overdoses: their Characteristics, Problems and Contacts with Helping Agencies', *British Journal of Psychiatry, 140*, 118–23

Horwitz, A. (1977) 'The Pathways into Psychiatric Treatment: Some Differences between Men and Women', *Journal of Health and Social Behaviour, 18*, 169–78

Ingleby, D. (1982) 'The Social Construction of Mental Illness', in P. Wright and A. Treacher (eds), *The Problem of Medical Knowledge*, Edinburgh University Press, Edinburgh

Janzen, J.M. (1979) 'Drums Anonymous: towards an Understanding of Structures of Therapeutic Maintenance', in M.W. De Vries, R.L. Berg and M. Lipkin (eds), *The Use and Abuse of Medicine*, Praeger, New York

Jordanovna, L.J. (1980) 'Natural Facts: a Historical Perspective on Science and Sexuality', in C. MacCormack and M. Strathern (eds), *Nature, Culture and Gender*, Cambridge University Press, Cambridge

Jordanovna, L.J. (1981) 'Mental Illness, Mental Health', in Cambridge Women's Studies Collective (eds), *Women in Society*, Virago, London

Keller, S. (1974) 'The Female Role: Constants and Change', in V. Franks and V. Burtle (eds), *Women in Therapy*, Brunner/Mazel, New York

La Fontaine, J. (1981) 'The Domestication of the Savage Male', *Man, 16*, 333–49

Lazarus, A. (1972) 'Phobias: Broad Spectrum Behavioural Views', *Seminars in Psychiatry, 4*, 85–90

Lewis, I.M. (1971) *Ecstatic Religion*, Penguin, Harmondsworth

Lipsedge, M. and Littlewood, R. (1985) 'Domestic Sieges', (unpublished MS)

Littlewood, J. and Littlewood, R. (1986) 'Nurses and Excreta: the Structural Ambiguity of Morphological Discontinuity', submitted for publication

Littlewood, R. (1984) 'The Individual Articulation of Shared Symbols', *Journal of Operational Psychiatry, 15*, 17–24

Littlewood, R. and Lipsedge, M. (1985) 'Culture-bound Syndromes', in K. Granville-Grossman (ed.), *Recent Advances in Psychiatry — 5*, Churchill-Livingstone, Edinburgh

Logan, W.P.D. and Cushion, A.A. (1958) *Morbidity Statistics from General Practice*, Vol. 1 (General), H.M.S.O., London

Macfarlane, J., Allen, L. and Honzik, M. (1954) *A Developmental Study of the Problems of Normal Children*, University of California Press, Berkeley

Marks, I.M. (1970) 'Agoraphobic Syndrome (Phobic Anxiety State)', *Archives of General Psychiatry, 23*, 538–53

Millman, M. (1974) *Such a Pretty Face: Being Fat in America*, Norton, New York

Murphy, H.B.M. (1977) 'Transcultural Psychiatry Should Begin at Home', *Psychological Medicine, 7*, 369–71

Murphy, H.B.M. (1978) 'The Advent of Guilt Feelings as a Common Depressive Symptom', *Psychiatry, 41*, 229–43

Murphy, H.B.M. (1982) *Comparative Psychiatry*, Springer, Berlin

National Organisation for Women Task Force (1974) *Dick and Jane as Victims: a Survey of 134 Elementary School Readers*, Blackstock, London

Nylander, I. (1971) 'The Feeling of Being Fat and Dieting in the School Population', *Acta Sociomedica Scandinavica, 3*, 17–26

Ortner, S.B. (1974) 'Is Female to Male as Nature is to Culture?', in M.Z. Rosaldo and L. Lamphere (eds), *Women, Culture and Society*, Stanford University Press, Stanford

Parsons, T. (1951) 'Illness and the Role of the Physician: a Sociological Perspective', *American Journal of Othopsychiatry, 21*, 452–60

Parsons, P. and Fox, R. (1952) 'Illness, Therapy and the Modern Urban American Family', *Journal of Social Issues, 8*, 31–44

Pattison, E.M. and Wintrob, R.M. (1981) 'Possession and Exorcism in Contemporary America', *Journal of Operational Psychiatry, 12*, 12–30

Phillips, D.L. (1966) 'Rejection of the Mentally Ill: the Influence of Behavior and Sex', *American Sociology Review, 26*, 679–87

Phillips, D.L. and Segal, B. (1969) 'Sexual Status and Psychiatric Symptoms', *American Sociology Review, 29*, 678–87

Polhemus, T. (1978) *Social Aspects of the Human Body*, Penguin, Harmondsworth

Prince, R. (1983) 'Is Anorexia Nervosa a Culture-bound Syndrome', *Transcultural Psychiatry Research Review, 20*, 299–300

Ramon, S., Bancroft, J.H.J. and Skrimshire, A.M. (1975) 'Attitudes towards Self-poisoning among Physicians and Nurses in a General Hospital', *British Journal of Psychiatry, 127*, 257–64

Ritenbaugh, C. (1982) 'New Approaches to Old Problems: Interactions of Culture and Nutrition', in N.J. Chrisman and T.W. Maretzki (eds), *Clinically Applied Anthropology*,

Reidel, Dordrecht

Rooth, F.G. (1971) 'Indecent Exposure and Exhibitionism', *British Journal of Hospital Medicine,*, April, 521–33

Rooth, G. (1974) 'Exhibitionism outside Europe and America', *Archives of Sexual Behaviour, 2*, 351–63

Sanua, V.D. (1984) 'Is Infantile Autism a Universal Phenomenon? An Open Question', *International Journal of Social Psychiatry, 30*, 163–77

Seidenberg, R. (1974) 'Images of Health, Illness and Women in Drug Advertising', *Journal on Drug Issues, 4*, 264–7

Smith-Rosenberg, C. (1972) 'The Hysterical Woman: Sex Roles and Role Conflict in 19th-Century America', *Social Research, 39*, 652–78

Smith-Rosenberg, C. (1973) 'Puberty to Menopause: The Cycle of Femininity in 19th-Century America', *Feminist Studies, 1*, 58–72

Stimson, G. (1975) 'Women in a Doctored World', *New Society, 32*, 265–6

Stuart, R.B. and Jacobson, B. (1979) 'Sex Differences in Obesity', in E.S. Gomberg and V. Franks (eds), *Gender and Disordered Behaviour: Sex Differences in Psychopathology*, Brunner/Mazel, New York

Symonds, A. (1971) 'Phobias after Marriage: Women's Declaration of Independence', *American Journal of Psychoanalysis, 31*, 144–52

The Times (1984) 'The Kind and Gentle Bank Robber — aged 70', 6 October, London

Turner, B. (1984) *The Body and Society: Explorations in Social Theory*, Blackwell, Oxford

Turner, V. (1969) *The Ritual Process*, Routledge and Kegan Paul, London

Weissman, M.M. and Klerman, A.L. (1977) 'Sex Differences in the Epidemiology of Depression', *Archives of General Psychiatry, 34*, 98–111

Willis, R.G. (1978) 'Magic and Medicine in Ufipa', in P. Morley and R. Wallis (eds), *Culture and Curing*, Daedalus Press, Kings Lynn

Wolpe, J. (1970) 'Identifying the Antecedents of an Agoraphobic Reaction', *Behaviour Therapy and Experimental Psychiatry, 1*, 299

Young, A. (1976) 'Some Implications of Medical Beliefs and Practices for Social Anthropology', *American Anthropologist, 78*, 5–24

Young, A. (1980) 'An Anthropological Perspective on Medical Knowledge', *Journal of Medicine and Philosophy, 5*, 102–11

16 CHINESE PSYCHIATRY: DEVELOPMENT AND CHARACTERISTICS

Wen-Shing Tseng

Introduction

The development of psychiatry and the direction and progress of such a clinical science may be due to the influence of many variable factors. These factors include the stage of the progress in both medical theory and practice in the particular society, the general understanding of and attitude towards mental health and illness by the general public, and the social system and environment, as well as the historical background of the cultural group in which the discipline of psychiatry has been developed. With this orientation, a description of the development of psychiatry in China with reference to that in the West follows.

Psychiatric Concepts in Traditional Chinese Medicine

Although Chinese traditional medicine has been developed over the past 3000 years and was already documented in written medical texts as early as 200 BC, psychiatry as a medical subfield was not recognised, nor did psychiatrists exist as medical specialists. However, because abundant descriptions of psychiatric maladies and their treatments can be reviewed in the medical documents, we are able to trace the development of psychiatric conceptualisation in traditional Chinese medicine (Xu, 1955; Tseng, 1973).

Among all the psychiatric maladies, organic mental illness, such as febrile delirium and epilepsy, was the first neuropsychiatric complex recognised as 'illness'. Psychosis with excitement has also been recognised since early times. In contrast, minor psychiatric illness, such as neurosis, was not recognised as mental illness until recently. The relative order in which these maladies have been recognised in medical literature is very similar in both the Eastern and the Western traditions (Tseng, 1973). However, Chinese medicine, especially psychiatry, has been relatively less influenced by religious thoughts and movements throughout the course of history.

274

The study of medical textbooks reveals that the theoretical system of Chinese medicine as a whole is 'nature'-oriented and is based primarily on the concept of Yin and Yang, the theory of five elements, and the idea of correspondence between microcosm and macrocosm. Such a theoretical orientation also applies to psychiatry. The cause of mental disorders is attributed to natural factors, psychological stimulation, and the individual's own attributes (Xu, 1955).

Although the influence of emotional factors upon the occurrence of physical illness has been recognised in Chinese medicine since the beginning, and the improvement of the emotional condition was emphasised as a way of encouraging recovery (Chen, 1963), Chinese medicine in actual practice is very much oriented to the prescription of herbal medicines. More than 400 types of material from vegetable, animal and mineral sources are frequently used in traditional medicine. Among these, nearly 100 are used in the treatment of psychiatric disorders. Employed either as single drugs or in compound prescriptions, such medications are nowadays subgrouped for psychiatric usage. There are applications for 'reducing internal heat', 'tranquillisation and sedation', 'regulating vitality to relieve the liver', 'clearing sputum to invigorate vitality', 'promoting circulation to end stasis', 'regulating the vital function of internal organs', 'nourishing vital energy and blood', and 'inhibiting general prostration and generating body fluids'. Needless to say, such groupings clearly reflect the underlying Chinese traditional medicine concepts of weakness, exhaustion, emptiness, deficiency, and disharmony as the reasons for illness, and regulation, nourishment and vitalisation as the necessary goals for recovery from these maladies.

The Development of Modern Chinese Psychiatry

Despite the early recognition of psychiatric disorders and the development of theories and treatments regarding such illnesses, psychiatry as a branch of medical practice did not fully emerge in China until the last three decades. The first psychiatric sanitarium, the Canton Asylum for the Insane, was built by an American minister and medical doctor, John Kerr, at Guangzhou in 1898 (Kao, 1979). Subsequently, many other institutions were built in Beijing (1906), Shenyang (1919), Suzhou (1923), Dalian (1944), Shanghai (1935) and other cities, but the conditions in such mental institutions were generally poor. Until 1949, for the whole of China, the total number of psychiatric beds was less than 2000, with fewer than 50 designated psychiatrists (Xia and Zhang, 1981).

Several foreign psychiatrists came to China to assist in the teaching of psychiatry around the turn of the twentieth century. Dr A. Woods started the first teaching program in China at Guangdong in 1910, and later at Beijing in 1919. Later, Drs R.S. Lyman, F. Halpern and others came to Shanghai to teach also. In the meantime, many Chinese students went abroad for further training in psychiatry. However, during this early stage there was no integration of the curricular approaches to psychiatry. Instead, every region followed its own system. For example, in the area of Manchuria, due to the influence of Japan and Germany, training in psychiatry was very much shaped by Kraepelin's descriptive school. In the Shanghai area, as a result of the influence of those trained at the Meyer Clinic, the approach was geared towards the psychobiological school; and in Nanjing, Beijing and Chengdu, many psychiatrists were oriented to psychoanalytic theory which has never really taken root in China (Xia and Zhang, 1981).

After the establishment of the new government in 1949, a remarkable change occurred and progress was made, particularly in the early 1950s. Guided by the political ideology which emphasised the need for services for the majority of the common people, psychiatry's development as a discipline was very much emphasised, as was that of other fields of medicine through the effects of massive growth and popularisation of services. Within just one decade, 62 psychiatric institutes were built in 21 provinces. By 1959, in contrast to the situation prior to 1949, the number of psychiatric beds had been increased 19-fold, with 16 times the number of psychiatrists and 20 times the number of psychiatric nurses (Xia and Zhang, 1981). By 1981 there was a total of 270 psychiatric institutes of various kinds, providing more than 40000 beds for treatment, 8800 beds for sanitary care, and 2000 supplementary beds (Xu and Liu, 1981).

As for somatic treatment, antipsychotic agents such as chloropromazine as well as insulin coma therapy and electric coma therapy were popularly utilised in psychiatric care.

During this period in the 1950s, the direction of Chinese psychiatry was very much under the influence of Russian psychiatry. A standard Russian psychiatric textbook in the 1950s was used as the basic reference text, and Pavlov's conditioned reflex and higher nervous activity theories were frequently utilised as the theoretical framework. Additionally, Russian psychiatric classification was used as the basis for the Chinese psychiatric classification established in 1958. Needless to say, Freudian concepts and Meyer's views were very much criticised and denied (Xia and Zhang, 1981).

The official national professional organisation, the Neuropsychiatric Assocation, was formed as a part of the Chinese Medical Association in 1953, and *The Chinese Journal of Neurology and Psychiatry* (*Zhonhua Shenjing-Jingshenke Zazhi*) has been published since 1955. Thus, a complete system of modern Chinese psychiatry was established.

Based on such a foundation, psychiatry made continuous progress during the early 1960s. Hospital administration was improved, and the openward system was adopted. Both individual as well as group therapy was incorporated in the care of inpatients, and work and recreational therapy was also utilised. Many psychotropic drugs were produced domestically for broad usage in the country. In psychiatric orientation, the influence of Russian psychiatry began to fade, and the thoughts of various psychiatric schools such as descriptive psychiatry and psychobiology began to reappear in the textbooks. As a whole, Chinese psychiatry was very much characterised by an emphasis on clinical description, as well as biological research in the fields of genetics, biochemistry, psychophysiology, and psychopharmacology.

The situation changed radically during the period of the Cultural Revolution between 1966 and 1976. Very much influenced by the political ideology of the extreme left, the orientation of Chinese psychiatry was revised, with the psychological factor emphasised as the exclusive cause of mental illness. As a result, in some institutes, somatic therapy, such as insulin coma therapy or electric coma therapy, was completely abandoned and instead 'thought education' was utilised as the primary means for treating and reforming psychiatric patients. Needless to say, all biological research was accordingly discontinued.

Under the influence of such circumstances, several new approaches were enforced in psychiatric institutions in most of the provinces in China. First, entire medical staffs had to leave the urban hospitals and clinics to work, instead, among the people in the countryside. Community-based service was developed, and community education and preventive work were stressed. At various locations throughout the countryside, epidemiological studies were conducted to determine the frequency of mental illness in the community population.

Significant emphasis was directed towards the study and utilisation of Chinese traditional medicine in the actual delivery of medical services. Herbal medicine and acupuncture were applied in the treatment of various kinds of psychiatric disorder including psychoses. However, no scientific measurement was applied to evaluate the effects of such treatments (Xia and Zhang, 1981). Almost all Western psychiatric theories were criticised and the opportunity to communicate with the outside and to exchange knowledge and experience with foreigners was prohibited during that period.

As soon as the Cultural Revolution was terminated in 1976, Chinese psychiatry regained its opportunity for further development. In 1978, the second national Neuropsychiatry Association Meeting was held in Nanjing. At this meeting, several major issues were discussed, namely, the psychiatry classification system, 'group prevention and group treatment', the combining of Chinese and Western psychiatry, and the prevention of relapse in schizophrenia. These topics reflected major concerns of the Chinese psychiatric community at that time, and also served as the primary goals for future efforts.

Several formal psychiatric books were edited and published during the late 1970s. By utilising the expertise of many leading psychiatrists and the key medical schools in the country, the Sichuan Medical School took a major role in publishing a comprehensive three-volume reference book of psychiatry. Volume I, *Basic Psychiatry*, and Volume II, *Clinical Psychiatry* (1984), have been published, and Volume III, *Psychiatry and its Related Issues*, is forthcoming. In addition to this accomplishment, Beijing Medical School also edited *Psychiatry* (1980). Shanghai's First Medical College edited the subsection on psychiatry for the *Chinese Medical Encyclopedia*.

In order to make further advances in psychiatry, several different organisations were formed in different parts of the country. At the Beijing Medical School, a group was formed for teaching and research in medical psychology; Hunan Medical School established a study group for psychological measurement; and the Shanghai Psychiatry Hospital expanded a laboratory for bio-psychiatric research purposes. In the meantime, a subsection of Medical Psychology and a Committee of Ethnopsychiatry were formed within the Chinese Psychological Association, and the Neuropsychiatry Committee was established within the Medical Genetic Subdivision of the Chinese Genetic Association. All of these activities of the late 1970s indicated that Chinese psychiatry was now moving towards the comprehensive and holistic approach rather than adhering to any particular school of thought or special orientation.

After the opening of its doors to the outside world, China rapidly re-established international interaction. Many foreign psychiatrists visited China, and many Chinese psychiatrists took the opportunity to meet counterparts abroad. WHO Collaboration Centres for research and training were established at Beijing and Shanghai with the intention of multiplying such centres in the future. Thus, progress in Chinese psychiatry is once again active. Through contact with international

colleagues and learning from foreign models, Chinese medical personnel are also busy developing a modern discipline of psychiatry which
will fit their unique social environment, cultural background and specific
needs (Xia and Zhang, 1981).

Some Characteristics of Chinese Psychiatry

Although China is characterised by a rather homogeneous population
in terms of ethnic background, with a uniform and centralised hierarchy
system, there still exists some degree of local variation and geographical
difference. This is also true for the health systems, including psychiatry.
Thus, it is rather difficult give a general description without bias. An
attempt will be made, nevertheless, to describe some of the observed
characteristics of Chinese psychiatry.

Community Psychiatric Service for the General Public

In consonance with a political ideology which strives to serve the general
public, the design of a mental health delivery system in China follows
the government's four main principles of health. These are: primary concern for labourers, farmers and soldiers; emphasis on prevention; the
combined use of Chinese traditional medicine and Western medicine;
and the combining of mental health work with mass movements.

The three-level mental health programme developed in Shanghai City
serves as an example of such a grass-roots community mental health
delivery system in China (Xia, 1985). It has been developed with consideration for the pre-existing conditions, that is, an extreme shortage
of mental health facilities, and the advantage of tight neighbourhood relationships and close family ties in Chinese society.

At the street (or commune) level, the neighbourhood health clinic (or
commune health clinic), which provides outpatient and house-call service, is responsible for supervising the so-called '(Psychiatry) Work-
therapy Station' and the 'Psychiatric Home Care Unit'. The Work-therapy
Stations are set up mainly for the supportive and rehabilitation programme
of the chronic decompensated patients in the neighbourhood. The station
is organised under the auspices of the community administrations, that
is, the neighbourhood committee, staffed by paramedical personnel and
retired volunteer workers. Occupational work is the primary mode of
therapy, and this is supplemented with drug and recreational therapy.

The Psychiatric Home Care Programme is another important
neighbourhood project which has been tried out in several places such

as Beijing (Shen, 1985) and Shanghai (Xia, 1985). In this programme, the patient is cared for at home with treatment or rehabilitation. Again, the programme makes good use of the assets of the family and the living environment in the community for the care of the patient, particularly in rural areas where mental health facilities in the form of hospitals and clinics are absent. The units are composed of patients' neighbours, retired workers and family members who assist in the care of mental patients in the neighbourhood. It usually takes two or three people as a team to take care of one patient — to observe the patient's condition, to supervise the taking of medication, to provide guidance and education, and to assist the patient in socio-family rehabilitation.

At the level of the district (or county), the district psychiatric hospital (or country psychiatric hospital) has the facilities to provide both inpatient and outpatient care. At the municipal level, the municipal mental health hospital, in addition to providing ordinary psychiatric care, plays the leading role in the total functioning of the three-level community health delivery system.

With the support of the government on one hand and the co-operation of the community on the other, Chinese colleagues maximally utilise paramedical personnel to expand the scope of the service horizontally. Additionally, the three-level vertical organisation of the mental health care system flows from the municipal to the district to the grass-roots level of the street neighbourhood in the urban area, and from the county to the commune in the rural area. Each level has its own defined function and responsibility, with co-ordinating committees at all levels to ensure adequate co-ordination up and down the three levels of the care system.

Combination of Traditional and Modern Medicine

A unique approach to health systems in contemporary China has been the combination of traditional Chinese medicine and modern Western medicine. This conjunction is observed in the field of psychiatry also. This combining effort is reflected not only at the political-policy and slogan level, but is actually observed in clinical teaching, practice, and research.

The foundation of traditional Chinese medical treatment rests on a symptom complex, and an attempt has been made to correlate concepts and terminology of this symptom complex in traditional medicine with clinical diagnoses made utilising the Western-originated modern classification system (Wu and Zhang, 1979). As a result, attempts have been made to treat psychiatric patients with traditional herbal medication.

For example, physicians have used prescriptions to promote 'circulation to eliminate stasis' in treating cases of periodical psychosis. Psychotic cases due to carbon monoxide poisoning were treated with an aromatic prescription to 'invigorate vitality'. Large doses of radix aconiti praeparata and drugs for 'regulating the vital function of internal organs' are used for some schizophrenics with withdrawal symptoms. Similarly, medicines for 'sedation' and 'regulating vitality to relieve the liver' are widely used in treating neuroses (Xu, 1982). Acupuncture has been applied in the field of psychiatric disorders also in the treatment of schizophrenia, especially for patients experiencing auditory hallucinations. Although most of the psychiatrists involved in such a traditional treatment programme claimed that the results have been encouraging, it has been pointed out by Chinese colleagues that because of the absence of a scientifically controlled study, the ultimate effectiveness of such treatment merits further investigation.

The Predominance of Bio-descriptive Orientation

Despite the fact that, owing to the unique socio-political-historical background, there have occurred several dramatic shifts with regard to theoretical orientation in psychiatry in China over the past three decades, and despite present efforts to move towards the goal of a comprehensive and holistic approach to psychiatry, one can observe, nevertheless, that contemporary Chinese psychiatry is still heavily oriented towards biological-descriptive clinical psychiatry. This orientation is supported by several kinds of evidence, and can be elucidated.

Review and examination of Chinese textbooks on psychiatry reveal that they are characterised by a strong emphasis on clinical description and classification of psychiatric disorders coupled with relatively abundant somatic-biological explanations of aetiology, comparable to the European approach, such as that of Slater, or of the Japanese. Relatively scant attention is paid to the sociocultural and psychological aspects of mental health and illness, not to mention the emphasis on the dynamic orientation of human behaviour, mind and psychopathology evident in some American textbooks.

The reduced emphasis on psychologically oriented treatment and psychotherapy is exemplified in the psychiatry textbook edited by Beijing Medical School, published in 1980. In the 700 pages of this volume there is no special section devoted to the subject of psychotherapy. The concept of psychoanalysis is touched upon in four pages as a part of the introduction to a foreign school of psychiatry. The underplaying of individual psychotherapy, particularly based on an analytic orientation, is not by chance. Rather, such de-emphasis is related to the fact that, particularly during the period of the Cultural Revolution, the traditional individual psychotherapy of Western origin was purposely suppressed by political ideology that criticised this product of 'capitalism' which relied too heavily on the therapist's working only for the benefit of an individual. It was stressed that, under socialism, the purpose of therapy should focus on the cultivation of revolutionary ideology in the patient who could then fight against the illness. This effort was seen to utilise properly the combined assets of the patient, the family, and the medical staff, with the ultimate purpose of serving the mass of the public rather than the single individual. Thus, even the term 'psychotherapy' was considered irrelevant in describing such a 'medical educational approach' (Editing Committee of CJNP, 1966). Following the termination of the Cultural Revolution, these negative attitudes towards traditional individual psychotherapy are becoming less intense. Instead, there is increasing interest in and emphasis on the psychological approach towards the patient's emotional problems (Zhao and Shen, 1983; Zheng and Yang, 1983).

The emphasis on bio-descriptive psychiatry is clearly reflected in the areas of academic research and publication as well. The major psychiatric journal, the *Chinese Journal of Neurology and Psychiatry*, was published for 12 years (1955–1966) and withdrawn for 11 years (1967–1977) during the period of the Cultural Revolution, and resumed publication in 1978. Within these two periods of publication (altogether 18 years up to 1984), a total of 314 psychiatric articles were published in this academic neurology journal of psychiatry. Of these articles, 21.7 per cent dealt with clinical description, psychopathology, and diagnostic matters relating to functional psychoses such as schizophrenic or affective disorders (Xia *et al.*, 1958, 1980; Lu and Zhou, 1984); 14.3 per cent dealt with psychopharmacology; and 11.1 per cent with coma therapy (Table 16.1).

There are some interesting differences between the early period of publication which ended in 1966 and the later period which followed the Cultural Revolution. In the early stage, reviews of Russian psychiatry, subjects of traditional Chinese medicine, the matter of neurasthenia, and various kinds of coma therapy were discussed and studied quite often. These foci of interest faded away or were proscribed during the Cultural Revolution, and after 1977 there is evidently a new interest in the subject of genetics (Xia and Zhang, 1979) and an increased number of reports of epidemiological studies which were carried out mainly during the Cultural Revolution when medical personnel were encouraged to become

Table 16.1: Psychiatric Articles Published in the *Chinese Journal of Neurology and Psychiatry* between 1955–66 and 1978–84

| Category of articles | Period | | | | | |
| | 1955–66 | | 1978–84 | | Total | |
	Number	Per cent	Number	Per cent	Number	Per cent
Foreign (Russian) psychiatry	5		0		5	
Traditional Chinese medicine	12		2		14	
Clinical picture of psychoses	35	17.2	33	30.0	68	21.7
Organic mental disorders	12		4		16	
Neuroses (neurasthenia)	24	11.8	7	6.4	31	7.9
Psychophysiology	7		4		11	
Psychobiochemistry	11		10		21	
Genetics	2		10		12	
Psychopharmacology	31	15.2	14	12.7	45	14.3
ICT, ECT, sleep therapy	35	17.2	0		35	11.1
Psychiatric treatment in general	12		2		14	
Epidemiology	1		9		10	
Community/prevention psychiatry	9		2		11	
Child psychiatry	5		6		11	
Ethnic psychiatry	1		2		3	
Psychological testing	0		4		4	
Others	2		1		3	
Total	204	100.0	110	100.0	314	100.0

involved with the people in rural communities.

Numerous epidemiological surveys have been carried out in various areas of China such as Beijing, Shanghai, Nanjing, Suchang, Shangton, Honang, Sinkian and other places. The total number of the population surveyed exceeds 30 million people. Unfortunately, because methods of investigation were not standardised and levels of sophistication varied greatly, the data collected cannot be cross-compared or statistically handled collectively. Nevertheless, these studies provide a general picture of the prevalence of mental illness in the Chinese population. For example, the prevalence of schizophrenia is revealed to be two to four per thousand, and that of psychoses is five to seven per thousand (Wu and Zhang, 1979). Studies of the sociocultural aspects of the mental health of minority groups, mainly in the form of epidemiological study, are on the rise and numerous reports dealing with such subjects have appeared in the journals recently (Wan *et al.*, 1981, 1982; Ou and Liu, 1984).

Aspects of Sociocultural Interest in Clinical Issues

Radical Eradication of Opium Addiction and Venereal Diseases

Although opium addiction had become a serious social problem among the Chinese by the end of the Qing Dynasty, any attempt to eradicate the problem was in vain when China lost the Opium War. However, such sociopsychopathological problems were solved completely and radically by effectively utilising the social organisation and massive movement within the relatively short period of time of the early 1950s. Initiated by the Government in 1950, a massive movement was organised for the prohibition of opium abuse. All previously addicted persons, estimated to be more than several million in number (Xia and Zhang, 1981), were treated, educated, and 'reformed'. Social networks and organisations were maximally mobilised for campaigns against, education about, and prohibition of drug abuse. As a result, the problems of more than half a century's duration were resolved within less than three years (Shen, 1980).

How the social reorganisation and the system of socialism were effectively utilised for solving problems of sociopsychopathology is well illustrated in China in the case of VD-related psychiatric disorders. Prior to 1949 in Shanghai alone there were more than 20000 prostitutes working in the area and more than 70 per cent of them had syphilis. Among the hospitalised psychiatric patients, 10–15 per cent were suffering from the syphilis-induced dementia paralytica. Under the government's direction, all the prostitutes were treated for VD and participated in the reform programme, with the result that prostitution completely disappeared in the area. By the end of the 1950s, the percentage of dementia paralytica among hospitalised psychiatric patients had been decreased to less than 1 per cent (Xia and Zhang, 1981).

Prevalence of Neurasthenia and Accelerated-Integrated Therapy

According to estimates, more than half of psychiatric outpatients were diagnosed as suffering from neurasthenia in China (Chen, 1955; Geng *et al.*, 1960). Because the diagnostic nosology of neurasthenia is seldom used in the West, and the category is not included in the present American diagnostic classification system of DSM III, it is unclear whether the high percentage of Chinese patients diagnosed with the disorder is related to the pattern of diagnosis or is a reflection of actual high prevalence of the disorder in China. The question deserves further investigation.

Based on clinical study, nearly 90 per cent of such patients are those people who are involved with intellectual pursuits and are relatively less involved with physical work in their daily lives, such as office employees or students. It has also been noted that psychological stress may contribute to the disorder (Li *et al.*, 1959; Geng *et al.*, 1960; Sichuan Medical School, 1960).

The Chinese developed an 'Accelerated-Integrated Therapy' for treating neurasthenic patients, and very positive results have been reported. While China was enthusiastically striving for massive improvement in the 1950s, the dual objectives of psychiatric attention were to enable the majority of psychiatric patients affected by schizophrenia and neurasthenia to recover and to thus permit them to join the work-force for the betterment of the total society.

Neurasthenic patients had previously been treated through individual therapy with poor results. Due to the extreme shortage of mental health workers, such limited treatment did not meet the larger needs of society. The social climate which demanded massive improvement led to the development of accelerated-integrated therapy for the treatment of the majority of psychiatric outpatients who were diagnosed as suffering from neurasthenia (Yan, 1985). The emphasis of this therapy was to integrate all available modes of treatment to deal with the patients as a group and to accelerate the pace of treatment within a short period of time — usually several weeks. In actuality, the treatment programme took several forms:

(a) group therapy with emphasis on educating the patients about their disorders, with the simultaneous cultivation and strengthening of the patients' motivation for improvement;
(b) life-pattern reforming with emphasis on physical activities in addition to the intellectual encouragement;
(c) adjunctive somatic treatment of various kinds including medication, acupuncture and electric therapy.

Such treatments were broadly applied and most of the programmes claimed that results were very gratifying (Chen, Z., 1955; Li *et al.*, 1959; Wang *et al.*, 1964). However, the extent to which such modes of treatment were effective through association with the revolutionary atmosphere of 'massive improvement' during that period of time in the 1950s deserves careful study (Li, 1965; Editing Committee of CJNP, 1966).

Recent Concerns about Minimal Brain Dysfunction among Children

Minimal brain dysfunction (or attention deficit syndrome) among children has received much attention in China since 1979. Although the field of child psychiatry has not yet fully developed in terms of availability of staff and services, schoolchildren in China generally enjoy healthy mental lives (Xu, 1985). However, since 1979, there has been a marked increase in the number of schoolchildren referred to the child clinics in various cities and subsequently diagnosed as suffering from minimal brain dysfunction (Yang, 1985).

There are several reasons for the appearance of such phenomena. Historically, during the 'ten-year turmoil' (Cultural Revolution), there was a disruption in the educational system. Not only higher education, but also the elementary schools were generally affected. Following the end of the turmoil in 1976 and the recovery of the educational system, the teaching curriculum became more organised, with academic education as well as student discipline being more emphasised. Other changes have taken place as well. Now, the door to higher education is more accessible, with competition offering broader opportunities. The traditional Chinese emphasis on the education of children has revived, and parents' expectations of excellence in academic performance have intensified for another reason: they are now concentrated on the 'only child' that couples are permitted to have under the government's new family policy. This interest in the child's academic achievement was coincidental with the publicising of the subject of minimal brain dysfunction in a popular medical magazine and later in newspaper reports which reported that children with such problems could be favourably treated by medications. Therefore, many students who have difficulty concentrating on their studies or who show unsatisfactory academic performance are sent by teachers and parents for psychiatric evaluation. It is clear that the historical background, educational system, and socio-cultural trends of modern China have all contributed to this recent, almost feverish, concern for such dysfunction, and the diminution of such concern can be anticipated as time passes.

The Matter of the Single Child and the Child's Mental Health

Another unique issue relating to the child's mental health in contemporary China is the matter of 'the single child' associated with the national 'one child per couple' family-planning policy. China is the most populous country in the world. Its population was close to one thousand million at the end of 1980, almost one-fourth of the world's total. In order to avoid a population explosion, great efforts in family planning have been exerted and the policy of a single child for each couple has been vigorously supported for many years. According to recent investigation, nearly 95 per cent of young couples living in urban areas have followed the government policy, and 55–60 per cent in rural environments have done so.

The result of such family planning has not only changed the family structure, but has also significantly affected the parent-child relationship as well as the pattern of child-rearing. Traditionally, the Chinese have placed great value on having many children. This was particularly true for farmers who considered an extra child to be an extra hand for the farming. Additionally, there was strong emphasis on having a son to carry on the family name. Thus, the new family-planning policy demands a major social effort to change age-old customs and value systems which include parents' attitudes to and relationships with their children.

What are the merits and demerits of the only child? According to investigations carried out in the Nanjing area in 1980/81, the average body weight and height of only children were higher than those measurements of multiple-sibling children. In relative terms, the only child has better cognitive development and higher intellectual ability than the multiple-sibling child. However, the only child tends to display a more negative behaviour pattern with regard to preference for food, obstinacy, timidity and temper tantrums than does its counterpart. This is attributed to the parents' tendency to spoil their only child (Tao and Chiu, 1985).

A recent community survey of children was conducted in different geographic areas of the Nanjing area in 1984/85. The second investigation included both suburban and countryside areas and utilised a more formal instrument for assessing the mental health of children. This study revealed that negative behaviour is displayed by both the single child and the child with siblings; that is, there is more internalised behaviour in the single child, and more externalised behaviour in the child with a sibling. The study also shows that the difference is related to geographic areas of domicile as well as to parents' educational/occupational background, and is not exclusively a function of the number of children in the family. The difference in the findings of the two investigations in Nanjing may relate to the methods of investigation. Differences may also be interpreted to suggest that the effect of the single-child policy upon child-rearing in China is becoming less intrusive to traditional expectations. Now that such family-planning policies have been mandated and observed for some time, parents no longer react with the heightened sensitivity that they initially evidenced, and they do not, therefore, spoil their single child to the degree they did earlier. Certainly, this very important subject deserves more systematic study since it relates to the personality development and mental health of future generations of Chinese.

Summary

Much influenced by various factors, Chinese psychiatry has emerged and developed over the past three decades to the point where it has developed a nature of its own, in contrast to the approaches to psychiatric medicine of other societies. Because of its unique historical grounding, sociocultural system, political organisation, and the dramatic shift of social conditions in a populous society in past decades. China serves as an example of how the development of psychiatry can be subject to significant impact from such variables.

In spite of frequent shifts of developmental direction and course in the past, it is quite apparent that owing to its fundamental ideological base of socialism, Chinese psychiatry will continue with its primary goal of serving both the political demands of the society and the health-care needs of the general population at large. From an academic point of view, Chinese psychiatry will probably continue to maintain its comprehensive orientation, combining the traditional and modern approaches, and expand towards more psychological and sociocultural orientation based on bio-descriptive investigation. Above all, Chinese psychiatrists will consciously develop their discipline in such a way that it will integrate with their own culture, tradition and social environment, solve their unique mental health problems and promote mental health in a characteristically Chinese style.

References

Chen, C. (1963) 'Some Psychopathological Thoughts in the Book of Tso Chuen', *Acta Psychologica Sinica*, 2, 156–64

Chen, Z. (1955) 'Preliminary Results of the Group Therapy for Neurasthenia Conducted at Nanjing Psychiatric Institute', *Chinese Journal of Neurology and Psychiatry*, 1, 104–6

Editing Committee of *Chinese Journal of Neurology and Psychiatry* (1966) 'Break Through the Tradition, Set up New Direction of Prevention and Treatment in Psychiatry for our Own Country', *Chinese Journal of Neurology and Psychiatry*, 10, 95–7

Geng, Z., Wang, S., Shen, L. and Shu, L. (1960) 'A Clinical Analysis of 100 Cases of Neurasthenia', *Chinese Journal of Neurology and Psychiatry*, 6, 112–15

Kao, J.J. (1979) *Three Millennia of Chinese Psychiatry*, Monograph Series, The Institute for Advanced Research in Asian Science and Medicine, New York

Li, C. (1965) 'Some Issues Concerning the Treatment of Neurasthenia', *Chinese Journal of Neurology and Psychiatry*, 9 (7), 89–90

Li, C., Xu, Y., Geng, Z. and Wang, M. (1959) 'Some Etiological Thoughts and the Preliminary Results of the Accelerated Integrated Therapy of Neurasthenia', *Chinese Journal of Neurology and Psychiatry*, 5 (5), 304–7

Luo, H. and Zhou, C. (1984) 'A Clinical Study of 1,622 Psychiatric Emergency Cases', *Chinese Journal of Neurology and Psychiatry*, 17 (3), 137–9

Ning, Z. and Yang, S. (1982) 'The Establishment of a Sound Prevention-Treatment Network is the Key for Successful Rural Psychiatry Service', *Chinese Journal of Neurology and Psychiatry*, *15* (3), 158–60

Ou, J. and Liu, Z. (1984) 'Cannabis Psychoses in Xinjiang (SingKiang)', in Medical Information Section, Office of Health, Urumuchi City, Xinjiang (eds), *The Collection of Medical Information — Special Issues on Folk Psychology and Folk Psychiatry*, pp. 47–51, Office of Health, Xinjiang

Shen, Y. (1980) 'The Development of Modern Psychiatry in Our Country', in Beijing Medical School (eds), *Psychiatry*, pp. 9–12, People's Medical Publishing Company, Beijing

Shen, Y. (1985) 'Mental Health Home Care Program in the Countryside of Beijing, Haidian District', paper presented at the *Chinese Culture and Mental Health Conference*, Honolulu, 1982, and in W.-S. Tseng and D. Wu (eds), *Chinese Culture and Mental Health: an Overview*, Academic Press, New York

Sichuan Medical School (Neuropsychiatry Research Section) (1960) 'The Analysis of the Etiology of Neurasthenia', *Chinese Journal of Neurology and Psychiatry*, *6* (2), 102–6

Tao, K. and Chiu, J. (1982) 'A One-child-per-family Policy: Psychological perspective', paper presented at the *Chinese Culture and Mental Health Conference*, Honolulu, 1982, and in W.-S. Tseng and D. Wu (eds), *Chinese Culture and Mental Health: an Overview*, Academic Press, New York

Tseng, W.-S. (1973) 'The Development of Psychiatric Concepts in Traditional Chinese Medicine', *Archives of General Psychiatry*, *29*, 569–75

Wan, W., Yu, W., Yang, G., Yang, D., Chen, U., Yang, H., Wu, S., Liu, K., Yang, C. and Bai, L. (1981) 'The Study of Mental Health among the Jino', *Acta Psychologica Sinica*, *4*, 459–63

Wan, W., Yu, W., Yang, G., Yang, D., Chen, U., Yang, H., Wu, S., Liu, K., Yang, C. and Bai, L. (1982) 'Psychoses, Mental Subnormality and Epilepsy in the Jino National', *Chinese Journal of Neurology and Psychiatry*, *15*, 108–11

Wang, J., Li, C., Wang, M., Shen, L., Zhang, W. and Wang, S. (1964) 'A Study of the Mechanism of the Integrated Therapy for Neurasthenia', *Chinese Journal of Neurology and Psychiatry*, *8* (1), 91–6

Wu, Z. and Zhang, J. (1979) 'Our Country's Fifteen-year Development of Psychiatry', *Chinese Journal of Neurology and Psychiatry*, *12* (3), 149–53

Xia, Z. (1985) 'Mental Health Delivery System in Shanghai', paper presented at the *Chinese Culture and Mental Health Conference*, Honolulu, 1982, and in W.-S. Tseng and D. Wu (eds), *Chinese Culture and Mental Health: an Overview*, Academic Press, New York

Xia, Z. and Zhang, M. (1979) 'Family Genetic Study of 294 Index Cases of Affective Psychoses', *Chinese Journal of Neurology and Psychiatry*, *12* (3), 154–7

Xia, Z. and Zhang, M. (1981) 'The Development and the Present Status of Modern Chinese Psychiatry', *Chinese Journal of Neurology and Psychiatry*, *14* (3), 170–3

Xia, Z., Shi, H., Zhang, F., Ning, Y., Hu, Y. and Chen, S. (1958) 'The Clinical Study and the Follow-up Examination of 2000 Schizophrenics', *Chinese Journal of Neurology and Psychiatry*, *4* (2), 89–94

Xia, Z., Zhang, M. and Yan, H. (1980) 'Affective Psychosis: A Follow-up, Retrospective Classification and Heredofamily Study, *Chinese Medical Journal*, *93* (6), 365–8

Xu, S. (1982) 'Traditional Chinese Medicine in Mental Illness', *Chinese Medical Journal*, *95* (5), 325–8

Xu, T. (1985) 'Child Mental Health and Elementary School in China', paper presented at the *Chinese Culture and Mental Health Conference*, Honolulu, 1982, and in W.-S. Tseng and D. Wu (eds), *Chinese Culture and Mental Health: an Overview*, Academic Press, New York

Xu, Y. (1955) 'Our Country's Ancient Psychiatry', *Chinese Journal of Neurology and Psychiatry*, *1* (3), 167–74

Xu, Y. and Liu, X. (1981) 'Our Country's Modern Psychiatry', in *Hunan Medical School*

Psychiatry Teaching/Research Section (eds), *Basic Psychiatry, the Comprehensive Psychiatry, Vol. I,* Hunan Science and Technology Publishing Company, Hunan

Zhang, W. (1979) 'The Experience of Establishing a Three-levels Psychiatry Prevention-Treatment Network in Rural Areas', *Chinese Journal of Neurology and Psychiatry, 12* (1), 14–16

Zhao, Y. and Shen, Y. (1983) 'Psychological Consultation for Women Receiving Sterilization and IUD Contraception Advice', *Chinese Journal of Neurology and Psychiatry, 16* (3), 136–40

Zheng, Y. and Yang, D. (1983) 'Life Events, Psychological Stress and Neuroses', *Chinese Journal of Neurology and Psychiatry, 9* (2), 65–8

Yan, H. (1985) 'Some Psychological Problems as Manifested by Neurotic Patients: Shanghai Examples', paper presented at the *Chinese Culture and Mental Health Conference,* Honolulu, 1982, and in W.-S. Tseng and D. Wu (eds), *Chinese Culture and Mental Health: an Overview,* Academic Press, New York

Yang, X. (1982) 'An Investigation of Minimal Brain Disorders among Primary School Students in Beijing Area', paper presented at the *Chinese Culture and Mental Health Conference,* Honolulu, and in W.-S. Tseng and D. Wu (eds), *Chinese Culture and Mental Health: an Overview,* Academic Press, New York

17 INDIAN AND WESTERN PSYCHIATRY: A COMPARISON

A. Venkoba Rao

Introduction

India, comprising 31 states and 630 million people speaking 15 major languages and hundreds of dialects, is a land of paradox in which opposites exist side by side. Science and superstition, ritual and research, idolatry and iconoclasm, princes and paupers, Boeings and bullock-carts, universities and illiteracy, pacemakers and soothsayers, lofty philosophy and barely filled bellies, and casteism and secularism coexist without apparent conflict. The average Indian practises the opposite doctrines of modernism and traditionalism, reflecting both the strength and the weakness of the culture (Venkoba Rao, 1979). In mimesis, Toynbee (1962) sees a generic feature of all social life and activities. 'In primitive society mimesis is directed backwards towards the older generation and the dead ancestors who stand unseen but not unfelt at the back of the living elders reinforcing their prestige.' Notwithstanding the impact of acculturation on India, the crust of custom has not been broken. The burden of the past sits heavily on the Indian mind, a characteristic that the country shares with several other traditional societies.

Disorders of mind are known from antiquity. The linking of mind with the moon finds mention in *Upanishads*, India's philosophical compositions dating back to 500 BC. The mind was conceptualised as a sense organ by Caraka and Susruta, the Ayurvedic physicians of ancient India. They located the mental faculties in the heart. This was also the view of Aristotle, to whom the brain was but a mere refrigerator, cooling the passions rising from the heart and returning them back to the latter. The Hippocratic insistence on the brain being the seat of the mind finds a parallel in the writings of the ancient Indian physician, Bhela, who assigned the mental faculties to the area lying above the palate within the head. Caraka's medical compendium describes the diseases of the mind elaborately, and there are terms for nearly all the psychological states. One of the Vedas, Atharva Veda, refers to the ghosts, devils and spirits as causal agents of illness and prescribes methods of cures for them. Psychological medicine was separated as a speciality, 'Bhuta Vidya'. The

291

notions that the causes of mental maladies lay in the supernatural and witchcraft and possession were entertained, and remedies were accordingly sought in religious and magical techniques. Such healing practices are resorted to even to this day by visiting notable shrines, through prayers, fasts and offerings, and by taking measures against witchcraft. Amulets were part of therapeutics as much as herbal remedy, the former being an external medicine and the latter an internal one. Whereas, in Europe, millions of the mentally ill were consigned to the flames as 'witches', such executions were never witnessed in India. These allusions to the cultural history of psychiatry are intended to highlight the fact that these beliefs and practices are inextricably woven into the contemporary living of the people of the land and influence psychopathology as well as therapy. For example, a recent report revealed that 51 patients with psychiatric complaints were among the 281 who attended the 'clinic' of a traditional healer. The diagnostic categories included hysteria, schizophrenia, anxiety neurosis and manic depressive psychosis (Sethi *et al.*, 1977).

No more than a kilometre from my centre is a popular shrine, at which hundreds of physically and mentally ill throng on Tuesdays and Fridays with offerings, rituals and sacrifices. In my experience, 30 to 40 per cent of psychiatric-clinic attenders seek some form or other of magico-religious procedures prior to their consultation with us. In some cases, these practices are undertaken concurrently with the modern treatment or following it (Venkoba Rao, unpublished data).

The early scientists and philosophers of India discovered the unity of all things including the inanimate, and observed that any disturbance at any locus has its repercussion on the well-being of the individual. They stressed that, at a fundamental level, matter and mind were alike. However, the Descartian view subsequently ushered in a dichotomy of body and mind, resulting in the neglect of influence of matter over the mind. The recent understanding of the quantum theory and the systems view of life have revived interest and breathed fresh air into the Eastern holistic view of the universe (Capra, 1982). The influence of the sun, moon and the stars besides the immediate environment assumes importance. It is not uncommon to hear that patients' mental states are adversely affected by the lunar phases, both the full and new moon. This was found to be statistically significant in Indian subjects by Verghese (1964). Similar reports are available from the West also, but the absence of the 'Transylvania effect' on suicide behaviour has been noticed by Taylor and Diespecker (1972) and Garth and Lester (1978). There is renewed effort, in the modern sense, to scienticise meditation to help one to achieve the basic unity which is a sign of health. In detail, the cosmic order is reflected in the microcosm. There are hymns in ancient Indian writings dedicated to the planets which were looked upon as sources of health.

Mental illness is estimated to affect some two to seven persons per 1000 population in India. The ratio of psychiatrists to the general population is a little over one psychiatrist to every million people. With so few qualified psychiatrists, with about 45 mental hospitals (some of them more than a hundred years old), with not all of the 110 medical schools in the country offering general hospital psychiatric services, with a qualified doctor to population ratio of 1 : 4000, and with little or no undergraduate training in psychiatry, many psychiatrically ill people resort to indigenous healers, who include shamans. Trivedi and Sethi (1980) observed that 33.2 per cent of their subjects have had treatment from faith healers prior to consulting them. The healers are able to manage neurotic states, hysterical psychoses, convulsions and dissociative states while directing cases of major psychosis to psychiatrists. This appears different from Western psychiatry, which is free from indigenous healers. A sizeable bulk of the patients are also managed by general practitioners, who, by virtue of their authority and social position, exercise an empathic relationship. They also prescribe tranquillisers or antidepressants.

The participation of general practitioners in the in-depth study of mental disorders and their management is not appreciable in the country. The picture in the West appears no different, as reported by Barnes and Prosen (1984) in their project on depression in Canadian general-practice attenders.

Liberalisation of procedures has been effected regarding admission into mental institutions in several Western countries, e.g. the UK. In India, commitment to mental hospital is governed by the Indian Lunacy Act, 1912. The procedure has been simpler for admission into psychiatric wards of general hospitals. General hospital psychiatry started nearly 50 years ago in India, and has been an important contributor for teaching, research and services. Some have tended to become 'mini mental hospitals' within a general hospital campus.

There is nothing like prison psychiatry in India except that separate enclosures for criminal patients are arranged in some mental hospitals. Institutions like Broadmoor and Grendon Underwood are non-existent. Attempted suicide continues to be a legally punishable offence in the Indian subcontinent whereas this has not been so in the UK following the Suicide Act of 1960. In the US, the law exists in some States, and in others it does not. The undergraduate training in psychiatry in Indian medical schools is inadequate. Efforts are in progress to improve this state of affairs. On the other hand, postgraduate training and research in psychiatry have far outstripped training at undergraduate level.

Depressive Illness

Earlier findings were that depressive illness was uncommon in India and that Indian patients rarely complained of depressed mood. The present prevalence rate of the illness in the general population varies from 1.5 to 32.9 per 1000; in the general hospital psychiatric clinics from 6 per cent to 30 per cent. In general medical practice the prevalence varies from 5 per cent to 25 per cent (Venkoba Rao, 1984b). This is less than figures reported from Western countries. The differences are possibly due to the differing measures employed by the investigators. Though in rural India the illness is encountered less often than in urban sectors, the clinical picture is the same in both (Nandi *et al.*, 1977). The tribal population is not immune, and 'in spite of unmistakable cultural differences between a brahmin and a tribal the picture of psychotic brahmin is no different from psychotic tribal' (Nandi *et al.*, 1977). Depressive illness in rural areas escapes perception by the community as well as general practitioners, and this has been commented upon by Wig and Srinivasamurthy (1981). Depressed mood is indeed experienced by Indian patients, and by suitable interrogation it could be brought out. I have pointed out that a sad mood is more often an elicited sign than a spontaneous expression. Its infectious quality manifests in many cases when rapport is possible. I have termed this a reversal of 'praecox' feeling, the opposite of what Rumke described in schizophrenia (Venkoba Rao, 1984a). For those who are knowledgeable about their culture, and also familiar with the patient's culture, the mood becomes obvious by a communication in terms of the nuances of depressed mood. Despondent feeling is no less frequent than in the Western data. It is likely that Indian patients utilise the language of the body to channel the depressed symptoms and hence shift the clinical focus to somatic features. That Western patients too complained of bodily symptoms was reported decades ago by Bonhoeffer (1912). Earlier notions of the predominance of somatic symptoms and the rarity of expressed depressed mood as characteristic of depression in India are not now tenable.

With rarity of expressed depressed mood and preponderant somatic presentation it was naturally suspected that masked depression was the variety that was common in India. However, when it turned out that depressed mood is invariably 'visible', even in patients with somatic complaints, a clearer approximation of Indian depression to the Western depression was noticeable. Support for this changing concept was provided by Chakraborty and Sandel (1984), who cautioned that to assume an inverse relationship between the depressed mood and the somatic complaint was an error. They, on the other hand, observed a parallel relationship. They advanced the hypothesis that in India somatisation is not a substitutive but a normal coping mechanism. They explained this situation on the basis of absence of a concept of dichotomy of mind and body.

Among the clinical features, guilt is less apparent in Indian than in Western patients (Venkoba Rao, 1973). There are others who opine that the content of guilt differs though the frequency is the same (Teja *et al.*, 1971). A point of interest is the possible attribution of the current suffering of the depressive to the misdeeds of his past life (according to the law of Karma). This might naturally be expected to generate guilt. On the contrary, it tends to mitigate it through the mechanism of rationalisation (Venkoba Rao, 1973). An important difference between the Western type of depression and the Indian is in the occurrence of completed suicide as a complication (Venkoba Rao and Nammalvar, 1977). Suicides in depressed patients are much less common in India although the ideation and attempts are as frequent. The failure to proceed to completion is due to the suicide counters acting against the current of suicidogenic thinking. The counters are economic, social, religious and ethical (Venkoba Rao and Nammalvar, 1979). However, there are religious injunctions in every culture against suicide, and the social stigma is no different from country to country. One may have to seek for factors beyond these. However, utterances like: 'But for my children, I would have preferred to die'; 'What will happen to my wife and family if I, the bread winner, die?'; and 'Who will marry my daughter if I commit suicide?' are common. Suicide in ancient cultures was due to the perception of meaning in death as a way for a better after-life. Modern society holds up suicide as a solution for the meaninglessness of life. These perhaps are extreme viewpoints in suicidology, and one has to strain too much to detect them in contemporary India. It is likely that depressive symptomatology emerges from a common mould (biological?) and any difference in their frequency or intensity is determined culturally. That this is so was revealed in a cross-cultural study using Zung's self-rating scale. Master and Zung (1977) reported that whereas there were no differences between those diagnosed as depressive in various cultures, the differences were brought out in the normal adult population.

Earlier reports from Kraepelin (1921) and Lundquist (1945) tended to bestow a benign quality on the affective disorders, thereby injecting a complacent view towards the illness. Subsequently, however, the occurrence of chronic course, poor social adjustment and unfavourable outcome came to be recognised. The subject was reviewed by Venkoba Rao and Nammalvar (1977), who reported on a 13-year follow-up of 122 cases of depression. No recurrence occurred in 28 cases. Forty-two cases became bipolar, and 21 continued to pursue a unipolar course. Manic episodes outnumbered depressive ones. The change of polarity occurred within the first three years after the initial depressive episode, though in others it did so between three and twelve years. The number of episodes of depression before mania varied from one to three. The onset of depression before the age of 40 predisposed to recurrences but the risk of chronicity increased in those who developed the illness after their 40th year. These findings are similar to those reported in the Western literature (Coryell and Winokur, 1982). The finding of 38 per cent bipolar depression closely agrees with the observation of Perris (1982) that the bipolar varies from 10 per cent to 40 per cent among all the manic depressive psychosis. The subject of polar varieties was reviewed by Perris (1982) and Venkoba Rao (1984a). Refractory depressions are being observed in increasing numbers by the present author in his clinical work.

Schizophrenia

There are resemblances and differences in schizophrenia in the West and in India. Elnagar *et al.* (1971) detected no differences in its prevalence and incidence. They found schizophrenia to be distributed in the socially and economically advanced groups, and Rao (1966) too found the disease in the higher-caste groups. These findings do not tally with those of Hollingshead and Redlich (1985). Catatonic forms are known to be more common than other types, a picture dissimilar from the Western pattern. The occurrence of somatic features and the use of the language of the body in the illness in India have been stressed (Hoch, 1963).

The contents of delusional thinking in Indian patients suffering from paranoid states and schizophrenia have been analysed (Kulhara and Wig, 1978). Murder, assault, violence, sex, religion and bodily organs were the main themes among them. In educated and higher socioeconomically placed patients, the delusional contents centred around machines, wireless and technology, as in Western patients. It seems that the thinking in traditional cultures is over such factors as magic and religion, whereas in Western cultures it is around science and technology.

Controversy surrounds the frequency of the Schneiderian first-rank symptoms (FRS) in Indian patients. From the United Kingdom, Mellor (1970) reported their occurrence in 71.7 per cent of cases. Marshall and Silverstein (1978) from the American sample observed FRS in 24 per cent of the material. WHO's International Pilot Study of Schizophrenia revealed FRS in 48 per cent of Indian patients. This discrepancy is ascribed to the predominance of the catatonic type of schizophrenia in the Indian cohorts. In general this finding is uniformly applicable to South-East Asian Psychiatry. The catatonics formed 44 per cent of all the cases in India in the IPSS, compared with 4 per cent in the UK. When the catatonics were excluded from the material, the differences disappear. The excess of catatonic schizophrenia is explained as due to low linguistic competence and ability. One with a high linguistic competence develops delusional symptoms by elaborating his psychic anxiety. That this is so has been suggested by Varma (1982).

Yet another controversial area is the course and outcome of schizophrenia in India. For a Western population the course and outcome of schizophrenia involving more than 1000 cases from Switzerland have now been reported from Zurich, Lausanne and Bonn (Ciompi, 1980). Favourable end-states were found in 53 per cent of cases by Bleuler, 49 per cent by Ciompi, and 57 per cent by Huber *et al.* (Ciompi, 1980). About 30 per cent remain as 'social invalids'. Reporting on the chronicity of schizophrenia from Chandigarh in India, Kulhara and Wig (1978) observed that the chronicity in their cases was no different from that reported by Brown *et al.* (1966) in London. The proportion of patients remaining continuously ill throughout the follow-up period of five years was the same in the London and Chandigarh groups, i.e. one-third, as was the proportion who recovered following the initial episode (another one-third). On the other hand, a favourable prognosis in developing countries including India was reported upon by Cooper and Sartorius (1977) who noticed that severe and chronic forms are more frequent in Europe. This was also borne out by the WHO study (1979). Manfred Bleuler suggests that many acute cases of schizophrenia in the developing countries carry a heavy mortality, and hence this excludes a large proportion who would have pursued a chronic course if they had survived.

A favourable outcome of schizophrenia in India is dependent on the greater tolerance of oddities of behaviour by the family and support from the community. In addition, the joint and extended family offers social support. There are at present no organised after-care and rehabilitative services in the country. It is in this area that India has to catch up with the West. No provision exists for supply of drugs away from the hospital at the patients' home, and the primary health centres are not yet geared to this peripheral psychiatric care. Hence, it is only the family care and a philosophy attendant upon it that complement the psychiatric treatment. It has also been noted that the better the family care the lesser the dose of psychotropic drugs necessary (Venkoba Rao, 1979).

Electroconvulsive Therapy

Though the reports indicate a substantial decline in the use of electroconvulsive therapy in the West; in 3 to 5 per cent of all psychiatric cases in the USA and Sweden (American Psychiatric Association, 1978; Frederiksen and D'Elia, 1979) and in 10 per cent in Denmark (Heshe and Roder, 1976), it continues to be practised in India in a sizeable proportion of cases. In a developing country like India, with few psychiatrists and too many patients, ECT has helped many schizophrenic patients to return to their breadwinning role for their families (Vahia *et al.*, 1974; Shukla, 1981). As a safe, cheap and quick method of treatment in rural India, electroconvulsive therapy has proved useful, and is applied in nearly 15 per cent of all functional psychoses including schizophrenia. It will remain the method of treatment for years to come in the country, especially in the psychiatric institutions for chronic schizophrenic patients and in general hospital psychiatry to stall or treat relapses in patients in the community.

Acute Psychosis

Acute forms of psychosis are common clinical presentations in India. Its incidence has fallen considerably in the West, according to Jilek (1974) (quoted by Sethi *et al.*, 1985). In 'acute psychosis', symptoms start suddenly and soon acquire a psychotic proportion. They usually occur in a younger person, and the clinical profile is one of excitement, socially inappropriate behaviour and fleeting delusion and/or hallucination. Confusional features are uncommon. The symptomatology reaches a crescendo within a fortnight. Preceded by a stressful event in many instances, the episode itself carries a favourable prognosis. No psychiatric illness pre-exists. If relapses occur they are less severe. In some, the remission is accompanied by 'depressive' symptoms — post-psychotic depression, which gradually lifts. 'Withdrawal' may replace 'excitement' in Western patients. In a sizeable number lasting remission is the rule, but in others there may be two or more recurrences resembling the course of a schizophrenic illness. These first-break acute psychosis episodes were described under such titles as psychogenic psychosis (Faergeman, 1933; Mecabe, 1975); reactive psychosis (Pandurangi and Kapur, 1980); and schizo-affective disorder (Kasanin, 1933; Singh and Sachdev, 1981). Recent reports in India have been from Varma *et al.* (1984), Wig *et al.* (1984) and Sethi *et al.* (1985). 'Brief reactive psychosis' (DSM III) fulfils the criteria for acute psychosis. The symptom constellation has been attributed to a culturally sanctioned behaviour serving the function of a wish fulfilment and the appropriation of a psychosis as in conversion symptoms. This is likely in Indian society where a possession state carries a compensation function (Carstairs and Kapur, 1976).

Culture-bound Syndromes

Possession Syndrome

The possession syndrome is common in all parts of India, as is evident from the fact that it has a specific name in almost all Indian languages. It has been described by Varma *et al.* (1970) and Teja *et al.* (1970). Patients show dissociative phenomena and a constricted state of consciousness. Verbal and motor behaviour is governed by the possessing agent, which may be a God, a devil, or an ancestor's spirit. Possession states generally occur sporadically but epidemic forms are known. Varma *et al.* (1970) reported an epidemic of 400 possession cases near Ranchi in eastern India. The age of occurrence was between 26 and 30 and women were the most frequent victims. A lower educational status seemed to predispose to possession. These authors observe that those from urban areas and the more educated are not as vulnerable to possession as tribal and secluded-caste people in villages. Natural calamities such as lack of rain and poor agricultural production precipitate possession in those who believe in animism. To them it is God who brings rain and prosperity, and any rebellion against Him results in drought and possession. Teja *et al.* (1970) reported possession states among hysterics, schizophrenics and manics. In schizophrenic and manic patients, possession was only a part of the main clinical manifestations. In hysterics, possession was often the only symptom and reflected life conflicts. These authors suggest that such hysterical patients be given the diagnosis of 'hysterical psychosis'. Wig and Narang (1969) have also dealt with hysterical psychosis in detail.

Supernatural or religious frenzy is often the climax of possession states, and it is not uncommon to see these states occurring in popular temples where the emotional climate of the rural crowd fosters dissociative phenomena. It is possible to induce possession in psychiatric wards for teaching purposes, which indicates that one can learn to move in and out of a state of possession at will. Many shamans have developed this capacity and believe they are able to become possessed by the spirits whenever they wish.

Venkataramiah *et al*. (1981) reported the one-year-period prevalence of possession to be 3.7 per cent, and 90 per cent of their respondents believed in possession. This belief seems to have played an important part. Clearly this is confined to the societies with such beliefs and is not seen in the Western culture with its modernism.

Sexual Neurosis

Distinct from the sexual symptoms that occur in anxiety neurosis, hysteria, depression and schizophrenia, sexual forms of neurosis which originate from cultural beliefs are well known in India. Among these are the ascetic syndrome (Neki, 1972) and the Indian dhat syndrome (Wig, 1960; Malhotra and Wig, 1975). The ascetic syndrome occurs in adolescents and young adults and arises from a morbid concern over control of sexual impulses. The individual becomes psychosocially withdrawn, sexually abstinent, and loses weight. The Indian dhat syndrome starts with frequent nocturnal emissions which lead to anxiety, hypochondriasis and sexual impotence (Nakra, 1971). In the Indian culture, as in the Chinese, semen is held to bestow robust physical and mental vigour, longevity, and supernatural powers. A frequent involuntary or voluntary loss of seminal fluid is believed to be dangerous to health: hence these culture-bound sexual neuroses.

Koro

Koro (head of turtle) or 'suk-yeong' (shrinking penis) is not exclusively confined to the Chinese and has been reported in non-Chinese subjects. The disorder has been reviewed by Berrios and Morley (1984) who comment that koro-like symptoms in non-Chinese subjects may constitute a behaviour phenotype without any underlying cultural genesis. Descriptively they represent over-valued ideas related to a variety of functional psychiatric syndrome. The symptoms improve once the primary disorders are treated. The culture-specific concept of the syndrome enables a socially meaningful psychotherapeutic approach. However, this is not applicable when it occurs out of the cultural context. Berrios and Morley draw attention to the differences between the typical koro in the Chinese and the picture in non-Chinese patients.

An attentuated form of koro, a syndrome characterised by fear of retraction of the penis into the abdomen, is familiar to psychiatrists in India. Patients suffering from this disorder show impotence and hypochondriacal preoccupation with the size and shape of the penis and the quality and quantity of semen (Carstairs, 1956; Venkoba Rao, 1978). This syndrome is invariably attributed to masturbation. Improved literacy and socioeconomic standard, and sexual education on simple scientific lines help prevent the development of this disorder.

Typical koro, characteristically described among the people of the Malayan archipelago and South China, has also been reported in India. Apart from individual case reports (Shukla and Mishra, 1981; Chakraborty, 1982; Khubalkar and Gupta, 1984) an epidemic of koro was reported recently from areas of Assam (Datta *et al.*, 1982). Its cause has been variously attributed to: reading pornographic material and masturbation; witnessing a koro case; and a peculiar type of sexual neurosis. There was a phase in the history of world psychiatry when masturbation held the pride of place in causing insanity. Even as recently as in the nineteenth century, madness and 'a whole legion of disease' were attributed to masturbation in the writings of English psychiatrists and physicians. However, John Hunter was well ahead of his time when he declared that 'if harm there was in masturbation, it came from the idea rather than the practice' (Hunter and Macalpine, 1964). If in the Eastern parts of the world, masturbation and seminal emission are still believed to cause psychiatric disorders, it is an instance of time lag between the advance in science and the hold of ancient beliefs. The occurrence of the culture-bound syndrome is a distinct contrast between contemporary Western and Indian clinical psychiatry. They are likely to persist until the beliefs get superannuated.

Psychotherapy

In recent times Indian psychiatrists have expressed concern over the suitability of Western psychotherapy for Indian patients. This has inevitably led to publications on the ingredients of a psychotherapeutic system which would be appropriate for the Indian culture. However, no systematic attempts have been made, and the results of the outcome of systems are yet to appear. Surya and Jayaram (1964) were the earliest to draw attention to the basic considerations for the practice of psychotherapy in the Indian setting. They emphasised language, the expectations of the average Indian patient and the conceptual references based on India's culture and philosophy. These authors stressed the need to understand the religion and faith of the individuals. They stressed that the Western concept of ideal mental health involves a search for intrapsychic integration, which is at variance with the Indian concepts because it overlooks faith and religion. The authors also highlighted that whereas in India attempts are made to reintegrate the individual into the family and overcome the individual's attempts at separation from it, in the West, on the other hand, separation and individuation of the person are sought for. That the Oedipus complex is not encountered in the Indian context has been reported by Bose (1921) and Neki (1977). These differences were brought out even in the days when psychoanalysis was popular. It is no more an important aspect even in Western therapy, and fails even as a system of theory (Fisher and Greenberg, 1977).

There are many psychiatrists who have advanced psychotherapeutic principles for use among Indian patients (Bose, 1921; Hoch, 1963; Satyanand, 1972; Vidyasagar, 1973; Neki, 1977). Venkoba Rao (1980) has elaborated on the principles of therapy, taking *Bhagavadgita* as a model. He has drawn attention to the concept of total surrender, eagerness of the pupil to enlighten himself, liberty to interrogate intelligently, desire for knowledge to dispel ignorance, and absence of coercion on the part of the therapist. The fundamental criterion is the guru-chela relationship in psychotherapy. This also underlies group therapy in India (Venkoba Rao, 1983). The relation between the group leader and the members is one of guru-chela type. Members prefer to be led *en masse* rather than to decide between themselves and to rely little on a leader, which characterises the Western system. The father figure of the joint family in India dominates group therapy as well as the individual type. In the Indian philosophical system, emphasis is laid on the understanding of the 'self' which needs a teacher, and the techniques involved are introspection and meditation. The need for the group rarely exists. It is natural that this dyadic relation persists in the group situation too. The members of the group are collectively attached to the leader but between themselves there exists little cohesion. There is a superficial gregariousness but at deeper levels there is social isolation — a state of individual 'islets'.

References

American Psychiatric Association (1978) *Task Force Report-14*, American Psychiatric Association, Washington

Barnes, G.E. and Prosen, R. (1984) 'Depression in Canadian General Practice Attenders', *Canadian Journal of Psychiatry*, 29, 2

Berrios, G.E. and Morley, S.J. (1984) 'Koro-like Symptom in a Non-Chinese Subject (Brief Reports)', *British Journal of Psychiatry*, 145, 331

Bonhoeffer, K. (1912) *Klinische Wochenscrift*, 49, 1. Quoted in Cleghorn, R.A. and Curtis, G.C. (1959) 'Psychosomatic Accompaniments of Manifest Depressive Affect', *Canadian Psychiatric Association Journal Suppl.*, 4, 13–23

Bose, G. (1921) 'The Concept of Repression', D.Sc. dissertation, Calcutta University

Brown, G.W., Bone, M., Dalison, B. and Wing, J.K. (1966) *Schizophrenia and Social Care*, Oxford University Press, London

Capra, F. (1982) *The Turning Point*, p. 263, Bantam Books, London

Carstairs, G.M. (1956) 'Hinjra and Juruan', *British Journal of Medical Psychology*, 29, 128

Carstairs, G.M. and Kapur, R.L. (1976) *The Great Universe of Kota*, Hogarth Press, London

Chakraborty, P.K. (1982) 'Koro — a Peculiar Anxiety Neurosis (a Case Report)', *Indian Journal of Psychiatry*, 24, 181

Chakraborty, A. and Sandel, B. (1984) 'Somatic Complaint Syndrome in India', *Transcultural Psychiatry Research Review*, 21, 212

Ciompi, L. (1980) 'The Natural History of Schizophrenia in the Long Term', *British Journal of Psychiatry*, 136, 413

Cooper, J. and Sartorius, N. (1977) 'Cultural and Temporal Variations in Schizophrenia — a Speculation on the Importance of Industrialisation', *British Journal of Psychiatry*, 130, 50

Coryell, W. and Winokur, G. (1982) 'Course and Outcome' in E.S. Paykel (ed.), *Handbook of Affective Disorders*, pp. 93–108, Churchill Livingstone, Edinburgh

Datta, D., Phookan, H.R. and Das, P.D.M. (1982) 'The Koro Epidemic in Lower Assam', *Indian Journal of Psychiatry*, 24, 370

Elnagar, M.N., Maitra, P. and Rao, M.N. (1971) 'Mental Health in an Indian Rural Community', *British Journal of Psychiatry*, 118, 499

Faergeman, P.M. (1933) *Psychogenic Psychosis — a Description and Follow-up of Psychosis Following Psychological Stress*, Butterworth, London

Fisher, S. and Greenberg, R.P. (1977) *The Scientific Credibility of Freud's Theories and Therapy*, Harvester Press, New York

Frederiksen, S. and D'Elia, G. (1979) 'Electro-convulsive Therapy in Sweden', *British Journal of Psychiatry*, 134, 283

Garth, J. and Lester, D. (1978) 'The Moon and Suicide', *Psychology Reports*, 43, 678

Heshe, J. and Roder, E. (1976) 'Electro-convulsive Therapy in Denmark', *British Journal of Psychiatry*, 128, 241

Hoch, E.M. (1963) 'Psychotherapy in India', *Indo-Asian Culture*, Vol. 12, Indian Council for Cultural Relations, New Delhi

Hollingshead, A.B. and Redlich, F.F. (1985) *Social Class and Mental Illness*, Wiley, New York

Hunter, R. and Macalpine, I. (1964) *Three-hundred Years of Psychiatry, 1535–1860*, pp. 348–491, Oxford University Press, London

Kasanin, J. (1933) 'Acute Schizo-affective Psychosis', *American Journal of Psychiatry*, 13, 97

Khubalkar, R. and Gupta, O.P. (1984) 'Psychodynamics of Koro', *Indian Journal of Psychiatry*, 26, 180

Kulhara, P. and Wig, N.N. (1978) 'The Chronicity of Schizophrenia in North West India — Results of a Follow-up Study', *British Journal of Psychiatry*, 732, 186

Kraepelin, E. (1921) *Manic Depressive Insanity and Paranoia* (transl. M. Barclay), E.S. Livingstone, Edinburgh

Lundquist, G. (1945) 'Prognosis and Course in Manic Depressive Psychoses', *Acta Psychiatrica et Neurologica Scandinavica, Suppl. 35*

Malhotra, H.K. and Wig, N.N. (1975) 'The General Physician and the Psychiatric Patient', *Indian Journal of Psychiatry, 17*, 191

Marshall, L. and Silverstein, M. (1978) 'First Rank Symptoms in the Post-acute Schizophrenic — a Follow-up Study', *American Journal of Psychiatry, 135*, 1481

Master, R. and Zung, W.W.K. (1977) 'Cross-national Survey of Symptoms in Depressed and Normal Adult Indians', *Archives of General Psychiatry, 34*, 972

Mecabe, M.S. (1975) 'Reactive, Psychoses — a Clinical and Genetic Investigation', *Acta Psychiatrica Scandinavica, Suppl. 259*, 133

Mellor, C. (1970) 'First Rank Symptoms in Schizophrenia: (i) the Frequency in Schizoprehenics on Admission to Hospital; (ii) Differences between Individual First Rank Symptoms', *British Journal of Psychiatry, 117*, 15

Nakra, B.R.S. (1971) 'A Psychosocial Study of Male Potency Disorders', MD thesis, Postgraduate Institute of Medical Education and Research, Chandigarh, India

Nandi, D.N., Mukherjee, S.P., Boral, G.C., Banerjee, G., Ghosh, A., Ajmany, S., Sarkar, S. and Biswas, D. 'Prevalence of Psychiatric Morbidity in Two Tribal Communities in Certain Villages of West Bengal — a Cross-cultural Study', *Indian Journal of Psychiatry, 19*, 2

Neki, J.S. (1972) *The Ascetic Syndrome*, All-India Institute of Medical Sciences, New Delhi

Neki, J.S. (1977) 'Psychotherapy in India — Presidential Address', Indian Psychiatric Society, 29th Annual Conference, Calcutta

Pandurangi, A.K. and Kapur, R.L. (1980) 'Reactive Psychosis — a Prospective Study', *Acta Psychiatrica Scandinavica, 61*, 89

Perris, C. (1982) 'The Distinction between Bipolar and Unipolar Affective Disorders', In E.S. Paykel (ed.), *Handbook of Affective Disorders*, p. 45, Churchill Livingstone, Edinburgh

Rao, S. (1966) 'Caste and Mental Disorders in Bihar', *American Journal of Psychiatry, 122*, 1045

Satyanand, D. (1972) 'Dynamic Psychology of the Gita of Hinduism', IBH, New Delhi

Sethi, B.B., Trivedi, J.K. and Sitholey, P. (1977) 'Traditional Healing Practices in Psychiatry', *Indian Journal of Psychiatry, 19*, 9

Sethi, B.B., Bhiman, A. and Trivedi, J.K. (1985) 'One-year Follow-up Study of Acute Psychoses', Paper presented at 37th Annual Conference of Indian Psychiatric Society, Visakapatnam, January 1985

Shukla, G.D. (1981) 'Electroconvulsive Therapy in a Rural Teaching General Hospital in India', *British Journal of Psychiatry, 139*, 569

Shukla, G.D. and Mishra, D.N. (1981) 'Koro-like Syndrome', *Indian Journal of Psychiatry, 23*, 96

Singh, G. and Sachdev, J.S. (1981) 'Acute Schizophrenic Episodes — Are they Schizophrenia?', *Indian Journal of Psychiatry, 23*, 200

Surya, N.C. and Jayaram, S.S. (1964) 'Some Basic Considerations in the Practice of Psychotherapy in the Indian Setting', *Indian Journal of Psychiatry, 4*, 153

Taylor, L.J. and Diespecker, D. (1972) 'Moon Phases and Suicide Attempts in Australia', *Psychology Reports, 31*, 10

Teja, J.S., Khanna, B.S. and Subrahmanyan, T.B. (1970) 'Possession States in Indian Patients', *Indian Journal of Psychiatry, 12*, 71

Teja, J.S., Narang, R.L. and Aggarwal, A.K. (1971) 'Depression across Cultures', *British Journal of Psychiatry, 119*, 253

Toynbee, A.J. (1962) *A Study of History* (abridgement by Dr C. Sommerville), p. 49, Oxford University Press, London

Trivedi, J.K. and Sethi, B.B. (1980) 'Healing Practices in Psychiatric Patients', *Indian*

Journal of Psychiatry, 22, 111

Vahia, N.S., D'ongaji, D.R. and Jeste, D.V. (1974) 'Twenty-five years of Psychiatry in a Teaching General Hospital in India', *Indian Journal of Psychiatry, 16,* 221

Varma, L.P., Srivastava, D.K. and Sahay, R.N. (1970) 'Possession Syndrome', *Indian Journal of Psychiatry, 12,* 58

Varma, V.K. (1982) 'Linguistic Competence and Psychopathology: a Cross-cultural Study', *Indian Journal of Psychiatry, 24,* 107–14

Varma, V.K., Malhotra, S. and Jiloha, R.C. (1984) 'Phenomenology and Outcome of Acute Psychotic States', Paper presented at 36th Annual Conference of Indian Psychiatry Society, Ranchi, 14–16 January 1984

Venkataramiah, V., Mallikarjun, D., Chandrasekhar, C.R., Vasudeva Rao, C.K. and Reddy, G.N.N. (1981) 'Possession Syndrome — an Epidemiological Study in West Karnataka', *Indian Journal of Psychiatry, 23,* 213

Venkoba Rao, A. (1973) 'Depressive Illness and Guilt in Indian Culture', *Indian Journal of Psychiatry, 15,* 231

Venkoba Rao, A. (1978) 'Some Aspects of Psychiatry in India', *Transcultural Psychiatry Research Review, 15,* 7

Venkoba Rao, A. (1979) 'India' in G.L. Usdin (ed.), *World Studies in Psychiatry,* Vol. 3, No. 3

Venkoba Rao, A. (1980) 'Gita and Mental Sciences', *Indian Journal of Psychiatry, 22,* 19

Venkoba Rao, A. (1983) 'Group Psychotherapy in India', in H.I. Kaplan and B.J. Sadock (eds), *Comprehensive Group Psychotherapy,* pp. 325–7, Williams & Wilkins, Baltimore/London

Venkoba Rao, A. (1984a) 'Unipolar and Bipolar Depression — a Review', *Indian Journal of Psychiatry, 26,* 99

Venkoba Rao, A. (1984b) 'Depressive Illness in India', *Indian Journal of Psychiatry, 26,* 801–11

Venkoba Rao, A. and Nammalvar, N. (1977) 'The Course and Outcome in Depressive Illness', *British Journal of Psychiatry, 130,* 392

Venkoba Rao, A. and Nammalvar, N. (1979) 'Death Orientation in Depression', *Indian Journal of Psychiatry, 21,* 199

Verghese, A. (1964) 'Moon and Mental Illness', *Indian Journal of Psychiatry, 6,* 110

Vidyasagar (1973) 'Challenge of Our Times', *Indian Journal of Psychiatry, 15,* 95

Wig, N.N. (1960) 'Problems of Mental Health in India', *Journal of Clinical Society, Medical College — Lucknow, India, 17* (2), 48

Wig, N.N. and Narang, R.L. (1969) 'Hysterical Psychosis', *Indian Journal of Psychiatry, 11,* 93

Wig, N.N. and Srinivasamurthy, R. (1981) 'Rehabilitation of a Depressed Patient in a Developing Country', in J.K. Wing, P. Kielholz and W.M. Zinu (eds), *Rehabilitation of Patients with Schizophrenia and Depression,* p. 82, Hans Huber, Vienna

Wig, N.N., Parhee, R. and Lal, A. (1984) 'A Clinical Study of First Episode Acute Psychosis', Paper presented at 36th Annual Conference of Indian Psychiatric Society, Ranchi, January 1984

World Health Organisation (1979) *Schizophrenia — an International Follow-up Study,* Wiley, New York

18 AFRICAN AND WESTERN PSYCHIATRY : A COMPARISON

T. Asuni

It is often said that comparison is odious. This is when the objective is to show differences in terms of better or worse. The purpose of this chapter is to focus on the etymological idea of comparison — setting together so as to ascertain how far things agree or disagree.

The next issue worth clarifying before going into the substance of the matter is what African psychiatry is, what Western psychiatry is, and what the temporal context is. In this context African psychiatry refers to traditional psychiatry practised by indigenous non-Western-trained specialists. Western psychiatry in the Middle Ages was perhaps no different from African psychiatry last century. In other words, psychiatry is not static. It changes according to fads, and with new knowledge. Furthermore, can one make valid generalisations for the whole of Africa in the same way as one can make generalisations for the West? Attempts at generalisation in both areas are fraught with danger for the same and also different reasons.

Western culture is more similar and homogeneous than African culture. The history of the West is more compact than that of Africa, and the interrelatedness of the West is more intense. Perhaps most important is the level of communication by all media, which is more advanced in the West than in Africa.

Another issue worth discussing is the number of traditional psychiatrists and Western-trained psychiatrists in Africa. From the records of the African Psychiatric Association, it is clear that there are very few Western-trained psychiatrists in Africa. Up till a few years ago, there were some African countries without a single Western-trained psychiatrist. Countries like Kenya and Nigeria fare better in this regard, but even in these two countries the ratio of Western-trained psychiatrists to the total population is very small. Nigeria, for instance, with a population of between 80 and 100 million, has about 55 Western-trained psychiatrists.

Traditional psychiatrists, on the other hand, are many. Here again it is difficult to say how many there are in any African country. There are several reasons for this uncertainty. In the first place, there is no compulsory formal registration of traditional psychiatrists. Secondly,

306

there is no sharp distinction between the various specialisations in the traditional health delivery system by the nature of the traditional medical philosophy, which does not always distinguish illness according to various physiological systems as in the modern Western system since the traditional healer perceives man as a whole. The traditional psychiatrist also may be an obstetrician, a dermatologist and more.

Every community has access to the traditional healing service, but not to modern Western psychiatric services. This is one of the major compelling reasons for advocating the integration of traditional healers into the official health services by the World Health Organization. It is to be noted, however, that the WHO also recommends a deeper study of traditional healing practices.

There are, however, some basic assumptions that might have held true in the past but not now. One is that traditional psychiatrists know the family background of their patients and can weigh psychosocial as well as clinical factors in diagnosis and treatment. This is certainly not true of those who treat patients outside their immediate community. The more renowned a traditional healer becomes, the more patients come to him from outside his community.

Another is that the modern psychiatrist is not familiar with his tradition any more, by virtue of an education which he has acquired away from home. He is therefore not able to understand and empathise with patients from traditional settings. Again this is not altogether true now. Medical education is no longer the monopoly of the upper-class youth. Increasing numbers of young people from traditional communities are now entering medical school and graduating as physicians.

These are only two of the relevant assumptions or 'stereotypes', as Forster (1983) called them, and these are discussed not with the intention of discouraging the incorporation of traditional healers into primary health care programmes, but rather as a caution against the uncritical acceptance of untested or untrue assumptions which will hinder rather than promote sound health policy and planning.

Having said all this, an attempt will be made to find a main thread running through contemporary Western psychiatry and similarly a main thread running through contemporary African traditional psychiatry.

Since psychiatry is usually based on the concept of mental health and mental illness, and also on the cosmic view and the position of the individual within this, the differences in these areas could determine the difference in psychiatry. The history of man suggests that mankind all over the world started with very similar concepts of the cosmos, health, and the position of the individual in those contexts. The concept of the creator of the universe is universal. The differences that have developed over the years are due to climatic, geographical, sociological and other environmental factors.

Examination of the West indicates the impressive technological advancement that has been made over the last few hundred years, especially this century. This technological development has changed not only the cosmic view, but also the position of man in this context. Walking in space and landing on the moon are events which must have tremendous impact on cosmic view. Climate determines to a great extent how people live in terms of interpersonal relationships. Whereas a warm climate allows people to live outdoors most of the year, in cold countries people live indoors when it is cold. Construction of houses also takes account of the climate, and in cold countries everything is built within the walls of the building whereas in warm countries houses are not so compact.

Urbanisation and industrialisation also affect human relationships. People tend to be more individualistic, more self-seeking, in the West than in Africa. In fact independence is highly valued in the West, whereas membership of and belonging to a family and the clan are more important in Africa. Living alone is considered a sign of maturity in the West. In contrast, living alone by choice leads in most parts to Africa, to a person being considered odd.

In Africa respect for age is generally the rule. It is incumbent on children to look after their aged parents, who in turn still have some useful role to play in the family and the community. As a result old people do not feel isolated and worthless.

Child-rearing is another practice which is different between the West and Africa. A child is usually reared in an extended family situation, where, in addition to his natural parents, there are often other parent surrogates. The mother-child relationship is less intense as it is diffused among the 'mothers' and not limited exclusively to the biological mother. The bonding process of the child and others is therefore different between the West and Africa.

Crises — happy, neutral and unhappy — including illnesses are primarily the responsibility of the family and neighbourhood, who are ready and willing to play their role in their resolution.

All these factors and more have implications for psychiatry, not only in terms of prevention of mental illness, but also in terms of recognition and tolerance of mental illness, treatment and rehabilitation. It is against this background of differences that Africa and Western psychiatry will be examined.

Concept of Mental Illness

The concept of mental illness has gone through the stage of demon possession, the four different humours of the body, to the interaction between the individual and his genetic endowment on one hand and his social and physical environment (including his early experiences) on the other. Even at this stage there is still on-going discussion on the dominance of nature or nurture. Emphasis is placed on the cause of mental illness, and a lot of research is being done in this area. This is the situation in the West.

There are different schools of psychiatry, some putting greater emphasis on psychological theories, some biological oriented; yet others believe in the complex interaction between psychology and biology. It appears, however, that the shift which had tended to be from the biological (medical) to the psychological model is now towards eclecticism.

Just as there are different schools of psychiatry in the West, there are also different approaches to psychiatry in Africa. The common thread that runs through most of African psychiatry is the belief in sorcery, witchcraft, the evil eye, the breaking of a taboo, or the neglecting of ritual for ancestral spirits as the cause of mental illness. Biological or physical causes are recognised in varying degrees among the healers in the same as well as in different countries. As an illustration of the different approaches to illness including mental disorders, the case of the Yorubas in south-western Nigeria may be cited. The causes are divided into three categories (Prince, 1964):

(a) natural causes, which include faulty diet, insects and worms, cannabis smoking, and hereditary factors;
(b) preternatural causes, which are malignant magical practices of sorcerers, curses and witchcraft;
(c) supernatural factors, which include the concept of the 'double' and the 'heavenly contact', ancestors and the 'Orisas', which are minor deities.

The practitioners are either essentially herbalists or essentially diviners, but there is considerable overlap in their modus operandi. The difference between them is not as strong as the difference between psychotherapists and psychiatrists in the West.

One major difference between the psychotherapeutic mechanisms used by African and Western psychiatry is that the African uses suggestion, sacrifice, manipulation of the environment, ego-strengthening elements, abreaction, and group therapy, but none of these factors involves the patient's insight into his own deeper motives with resulting expansion of self-awareness and presumably personality maturation as with Western psychotherapy.

Diagnosis of Psychiatric Illness

Considering the difference in the concept of mental illness between African and Western psychiatry, it is not surprising to note that diagnosis is not decided on the same level or factors. Among Western psychiatrists using the same parameters, there are known differences in diagnostic practice. We are aware of the efforts being made by the World Health Organization to standardise diagnostic practice and to continue to review the International Classification of Mental Diseases.

It is difficult to generalise about diagnostic practices in African psychiatry. This is due not only to the lack of a common language base like Greek and Latin for Western medicine, but also and perhaps more important to the lack of common understanding of the dynamics of mental illness. For instance in Uganda (Orley, 1970) the Baganda ascribe diseases to certain parts of the body and also classify them according to three sets of dichotomies. One, those that come by themselves and those that are sent or caused by witchcraft; two, strong and weak, and three, Kiganda and non-Kiganda. Those illnesses which are untreatable by Western medicine or are difficult to treat, as in the case of mental illnesses, are thought to be Kiganda diseases, and are of course strong since traditional forms of therapy are not often very useful either. In contrast the indigenous Yoruba psychiatry (in Nigeria) has names for some psychiatric illnesses.

In the West, diagnosis is made on the basis of mental-state examination and psychological and clinical laboratory tests. African psychiatric diagnosis is made on the basis of divination, sacrifice and questioning, and, in the case of the zar cult (Northern Ethiopia and Sudan), diagnosis is made through demonstration after interrogation (Messing, 1959).

One major difference between Western and African psychiatry is that Western psychiatry tends to include problems of living and coping with situations. Such problems are usually dealt with by the informal social network in Africa. They are not necessarily regarded as illness except in extreme cases.

Coping with and adjusting to loss and bereavement are not referred to traditional psychiatrists. The social-support network, appropriate rituals and ceremonies tend to help the individual concerned to cope with the situation. It is only in extreme cases where the traditional mechanisms fail that the traditional psychiatrist is consulted.

Psychiatric Consultation

In the West, consultation is on a one-to-one basis between the psychiatrist and his patient. In Africa the consultation is between the traditional psychiatrist and usually not the patient alone, but the patient with his relatives. Where necessary there may be consultation with the relatives or patient alone if the situation requires it.

The setting of the consultation is fairly standard in the West, the psychiatrist being the last in a series of intervening stations. In Africa the setting is less formal. Depending on the type of indigenous psychiatry, the paraphernalia and ambience may be quite awe inspiring, and this may well have some psychotherapeutic impact. The process of divination, especially if it is accompanied by the sacrifice of a live animal, can be dramatic for those who are unaccustomed to the proceedings. In some situations a device like ventriloquism is used to give the impression of spirit communication. The Western psychiatrist, especially in a hospital setting, may wear a white coat, whereas the indigenous African psychiatrist may wear an apron or a gown embellished with ritualist objects. The paraphernalia and the embellished attire of the indigenous African psychiatrist give the image of status and power, and a Western psychiatrist may have his office adorned with impressive professional certificates to achieve the same effect.

Treatment

The concept of treatment from the point of view of the indigenous African psychiatrist quite often transcends the phsyical, emotional and psychological to include the social and spiritual parameters. In other words it involves man's relationship with the past, the present and the future, with animate and inanimate objects (inanimate objects are imbued with spirits of their own), and with spirits, especially those of ancestors. This is a generalisation which holds true in spite of minor differences in emphasis. The treatment usually includes physical, psychological, social and spiritual elements.

Physical treatment includes the use of herbs, purgatives, flagellation and the making of incisions to introduce powdered medicine. A procedure as refined and delicate as trephine has been known to be used. Not much work has been done on the pharmacology of the herbs used by indigenous African psychiatrists, but rauwolfia has been identified in West Africa (Prince, 1960). In some cases the notion of sympathetic or contagious magic controls the selection of vegetable or animal medicines. The author has seen patients in deep sleep in some indigenous African psychiatric clinics. In addition all manner of physical restraints are used in cases of violence and refusal to co-operate, but these physical restraints are discontinued when the risk of violence or escape is over.

Physical treatment by Western psychiatrists is not different in principle, but because of the technological advancement of the West it has been possible to identify and extract the active principles of medicinal herbs and plants and also to synthesise them. Furthermore, they are tested on animals before being tried on human beings. The undesirable side-effects are noted, and, if necessary and possible, some additional medication is given to alleviate them. Posology is used in dispensing the drugs. All these refined practices are not observed by indigenous African psychiatrists, and their use of herbs is more by trial and error — not only in relation to dosages but also concerning effectiveness. Furthermore the knowledge of the herbs is very personal and often shrouded in secrecy: it is only passed to apprentices who are usually children or other close relatives of the practitioner.

The plucking of the plant ingredients and the preparation of the medicine is not mechanical. These activities are associated with the recital of incantations and the performance of some rituals, presumably to capture and retain the 'essence' of the herb and to ensure its potency and effectiveness. The use of the herbal medicine by the patient may also be accompanied by some rituals to add another element besides pure pharmacology. This element may be psychological or spiritual.

The presentation of Western medicine in different sizes, colours and shapes may also add more to the whole exercise of drug taking because of its visual attractiveness and taste.

No study has been done on the compliance rate of patients in the use of medicine prescribed and made by the indigenous African psychiatrist, but it will not be surprising if the compliance rate is very high as the medicine is individualised and cannot be bought in the market. In addition to this, the ritual which goes along with the preparation and use of the medicine may also add more to its importance and consequent compliance rate.

Psychological Treatment

This depends on the prestige of the traditional psychiatrist, which tends to enhance reassurance and suggestion. The rituals and sacrifices also have their psychotherapeutic value. Abreaction and group therapy associated with dancing and sometimes possession, as with the zar cult and with the rab cult in Senegal, are potent psychotherapeutic elements. The ego-strengthening elements in the psychological treatment include the recital of incantations, performance of rituals and sacrifices, the wearing of prescribed amulets and other paraphernalia by the patient, and the eating of a specific and sometimes symbolic diet. The technique of manipulation of the environment is also used. Confession is another element of psychological treatment.

An example of a subtle psychological intervention will help to illustrate some of the techniques. A woman in a polygamous setting was running into trouble in her home and this threatened her marriage as the husband wanted to throw her out. The trouble centred on constant fighting and violent arguments with one of her co-wives, who appeared to be the more favoured one. The woman went to an indigenous African psychiatrist to whom she told her plight. The psychiatrist listened patiently and told her to come back in a few days. He did not give any advice or suggestion but assured her that he would do something about it. When the woman came back she was given a small object which the therapist had prepared, and was told that on any occasion when there was a quarrel between her and the other woman she should put this object in her mouth and bite on it. The object, she was told, had the other woman embodied in it. She left. Several weeks later she returned to thank the psychiatrist as not only was the problem over but the other woman had been sent away.

The dynamics of the resolution of the problem was that it was not realistic to tell the woman not to answer back during the quarrels. Rather it was better to give her something to do which would be more painful to the other woman than verbal assault. Biting on the object which symbolised the woman was what she did. Not only was this perceived to be more painful to the other woman: the patient also could not answer her back and bite at the same time. The result was that it was only the other woman's voice that was heard and the people around wondered what was wrong with her shouting to herself. She thus fell out of favour.

Western psychiatry uses the same technique of suggestion and reassurance, and manipulation of the environment. The abreactive technique and group therapy are the same in principle, but different in form.

Behaviour modification technique is also used by indigenous African psychiatrists but not in the standardised form of the West. The example given above illustrates this point.

One major difference between Western and African psychiatry is the area of deep-insight psychotherapy. The division of the psyche into id, ego and super-ego does not exist. The division where it has been studied involves elements of the spirit, especially ancestral spirits, and destiny. It is a different level of division, which is related to the African view of the world. The way this concept is used in therapy is also different. The Western concept tends to focus on 'how', whereas the African concept focuses on 'why'.

In practice the indigenous African psychiatrist does not go into lengthy psychotherapeutic exercise. He does not carry out the type of exploration to bring out the patient's insight into his own deeper motives, but rather he relates the patient's experience to his ancestral spirits and destiny. This type of therapy often points out what to do to placate the spirits and modify the patient's destiny where possible.

Efforts to apply the concept and practice of Western deep-insight psychotherapeutic technique by Western-trained psychiatrists on African patients have frequently not proved successful even though there are some elements of psychoanalytic theory that have been observed in some Africans. These elements have not proved useful in therapy, and appear to be more of theoretical and academic than therapeutic interest and significance. It is doubtful if the psychotherapeutic technique of the West is applicable to Africa — except in the highly Westernised Africans with deeply internalised Western culture.

In any case, neurotic illnesses for which psychotherapy is most applicable are usually handled by the social network and other traditional practices like festivals, ancestral worship and the various cults. It is only when they do not respond to these traditional interventions that the patient seeks specialised help.

Interpretation of dreams is used by both Western and indigenous African psychiatrists, but the interpretations are not usually similar. In the African context they also vary from place to place and this variation depends on the concept of ancestral spirits and cosmic agents.

Social and Group Therapy

The African patient is not treated by the indigenous psychiatrist in isolation from his family and environment. In fact in some cases therapy is a matter of sealing up the breaches in social relationships simultaneously with ridding the patient of his pathological symptoms (Turner, 1964). The therapist is in effect master of ceremonies. Divination in this situation is a form of social analysis, in the course of which hidden struggles among individuals and factions are brought to light so that they may be dealt with by traditional ritual procedures. The therapist's aim is to unravel social complications while also prescribing a course of treatment. The treatment of mental illness in the shrine in Ghana (Field, 1960), in the zar cult in Ethiopia and Sudan, and in the rab cult in Senegal are accentuations of group or social therapy.

Compared with Western psychiatry, African group therapy is more like psychodrama than the verbal group therapy in which patients express their feelings and experiences in words. They let loose their feelings in the dances, ceremonies and rituals. Sometimes the patient's ailment is not removed but he learns to accept it and comes to terms with it by his group membership, as in the case of the zar cult. Membership of a group — the family, the clan, the cult — is a very important element in therapy and appears to be more important than the self-awareness encouraged by Western psychiatry.

Family therapy is taken for granted by the indigenous African psychiatrist as it is almost inconceivable that a patient could be treated without the involvement of the family and outside its context. The objective is to mend rifts and to consolidate the family. The question may be asked 'What if the patient has no family?' This is a rare situation. In most of Africa the concept of family is not limited to blood ties. Continuous propinquity over a long period of time often leads to such close and intimate relationships becoming equivalent to family ties.

This, to some extent, is in contrast to Western psychiatry, where the emphasis is on the individual to the extent that in extreme cases he is encouraged to leave his family so that he can proceed with his personal growth and independence. Whereas in the West the emphasis is on the individual and his growth and independence, it is on the group, group solidarity and interdependence in African psychiatry.

Occupational Therapy

The patients of the indigenous African psychiatrist are not institutionalised, and their life while under treatment is not regimented. They are still free to participate in household chores and sometimes follow their trade, as much as their mental state permits. So the need for formal occupational therapy is not so strong.

Furthermore, emphasis is not so much on occupation as on socialisation. Experience has shown that while occupation *per se* does not necessarily lead to resocialisation, but perhaps to survival, the social obligation can lead to occupational rehabilitation — in that the fulfilment of some social obligation requires money or favours which can be earned by working. This is a point at which economic and social determinants show up very strongly in the practice of psychiatry in the West and in Africa. It has been known that some indigenous African psychiatrists have refused to discharge their patients until their fees are paid, and in some cases the patients have been made to work for the therapist to offset the bill.

In this connection it may be appropriate to mention that indigenous African psychiatrists usually have some other form of occupation, usually farming, to sustain them. It is this other occupation in which their patients participate in the form of occupational therapy — if it can be called so.

Training

The training of the indigenous African psychiatrists is by apprenticeship, and the length of the training varies considerably. It is usually one of the children or nephews or nieces of the psychiatrist who is attached to him for training. The trainee's qualification to set up practice on his own does not depend on examinations but on continuous assessment of his performance.

In some situations the therapists have a guild which determines some code of conduct, but this is not usually the case. Because of the secrecy associated with their *modus operandi* it is difficult to assess the efficacy of the guild in controlling their conduct. On the other hand it can be understood that because of their basic belief in God and the spirits, a common set of values is internalised without it being institutionalised. None the less, the disciplinary role of guilds appears to be less emphasised. For the same reason, the training does not appear to be standardised. Consequently there is theoretically a lot of room for charlatans. Fortunately these charlatans do not last long as they are judged by their efficacy.

In spite of the highly professionalised Western psychiatry with its tough and demanding qualifying tests and the highly selective membership of the professional associations, one does hear of charlatans. Whereas it is not a criminal offence for an indigenous African charlatan to practise medicine and psychiatry, it is a criminal offence for a Western charlatan so to practise.

The status of the indigenous African psychiatrist does not depend on his material wealth and worldly possessions, but on his perceived wisdom and power, which are demonstrated by his achievement in the treatment of his patients, and on his kindness and humanity. The fact that in some cases he still maintains the role of priest in the community confers on him respectability and awe. It can safely be stated that part of the psychotherapeutic success derives from their prestige and respectability within the community. This is why it is difficult for charlatans to intrude. The practice of medicine and psychiatry is still regarded as an honourable one, especially among the traditional communities. The introduction of Western psychiatry has not eroded the place of indigenous psychiatry.

A study (Braito and Asuni, 1977) done in a small town, Abeokuta, in Western Nigeria, which included interviewing some traditional healers, is illustrative even though it was not focused on traditional psychiatrists.

Thirty traditional healers were interviewed at their location using standardised questionnaires with both closed and open-ended questions. The study sought to find out about the process of their recruitment into medicine and how the body of knowledge is acquired, about membership in native healing associations and their codes of practice, and about the referral pattern. The study is exploratory in nature and no claim as to the representativeness of the sample is made.

All but three of the 30 healers were 45 years or older. The three were under 25. Whether this represents a true picture of the age of healers and indicates a lack of recruitment of younger ones into the field or the ageing process demonstrating the length of time needed to acquire the necessary knowledge, or whether it is caused by a lack of knowledge of the existence of younger healers, is not known.

Twenty-three of them had no other occupation apart from healing. Of those who did, six were farmers and one was a trader. (Abeokuta is a town and not a village, where the main occupation would be expected to be farming.) Twenty-four of the healers had not attended any school, three had attended primary school, and only one had attended 'modern' school.

According to 26 respondents, recruitment into traditional healing was from father to son. Only four learnt healing from others. Ten of the healers had taken 16 to 20 years to acquire their knowledge, one took less than 5 years, eight took 6 to 10 years, seven took 11 to 15 years and three had taken 26 to 30 years.

All of them belonged to a traditional healers' association. In order to join, 22 took an oath only, four took an oath and paid dues, one took an oath, took a test and paid dues, one took an oath and took a test, and one paid dues only. Taking an oath appears to be very important.

The components of the oath as expressed by the healers were as follows:

(1) to uphold the ethics of the profession and respect seniors;
(2) not to procure abortion;
(3) to refer difficult cases to competent hands in the union;
(4) not to steal wives of members and not to have sexual relationships with female patients;
(5) to maintain a high standard of health care at all times;
(6) to seek husband's consent before treating a woman;
(7) to pay union dues.

Fifteen healers mentioned items 2 to 6; fourteen items 1 to 4; and one components 1 to 4 and 7. As can be noted, all healers mentioned the rules about not procuring abortions, not stealing wives of members and not having sexual relationships with female patients, and about referring difficult cases to competent hands in the union. Of these 19 healers who reported referring patients, 17 reported referring them to other native healers and two to Western-trained medical doctors.

Even though the study was not focused on traditional psychiatrists, it was found that the most common categories of illness the healers treated were infectious diseases, psychiatric problems, sexual and fertility problems, and convulsions, in that order.

Asuni (1979) pointed out the dilemma of traditional healing and argued that the dilemma faces the traditional healer, the agencies responsible for providing health services, modern doctors and the consumer of the services. He also discussed the issues of co-operation between traditional and Western trained doctors and the integration of the two systems. He concluded his paper with a section on the healing process in traditional and modern medicine, which is worth summarising to conclude this chapter.

The healing process is an interaction between the patient, the therapist and the environment, and this interaction is common to both traditional and modern medicine. The patient goes to the therapist with the expectation and hope of being healed. He has or develops faith and confidence in the therapist. Without these and other related factors, the healing process may be delayed, arrested or neglected. In the interaction these factors may be enhanced or reduced, depending on what happens.

The therapist is seen as having the knowledge and expertise to heal. In addition he has confidence, and he uses impressive paraphernalia which enhances his power of suggestion. It may help if he is charismatic. He has status in society. There are great similarities between the traditional healer and the modern doctor as regards these factors. What makes a difference is the change in the social order and attitudes. The traditional healer has awe-inspiring paraphernalia, in the form of his garb and his dark room; so has the modern doctor, with his glittering equipment and instruments. With the change in attitude about cleanliness, order, etc. the paraphernalia of the traditional healer is losing some of its awe. The status of the traditional healer as a powerful man in society is diminishing by virtue of the changing social order brought about by education, urbanisation, migration and other phenomena. His methods of flogging, beating, purging and chaining of patients are being rejected. I doubt very much if any of my patients have run away from the hospital to go to traditional healers, but I know a few who have run away from the traditional healer to come to the psychiatric hospital, sometimes with the traditional healer at their heels.

On the other hand, the social and physical environment of the traditional healer is more familiar to the patient. He has his relatives with him during treatment, so he does not feel isolated. He wears his own clothes and eats familiar food. Perhaps the reason why more patients do not run away from the unpleasant treatment to which they are constantly exposed is the comforting presence of the relatives and the great expectation of being healed. There is also the fear instilled in them by traditional healers that worse things can happen to them if they run away.

The major differences in the practices of both traditional healer and modern doctor is that the latter talks only in terms of physical factors such as the cause and treatment of illness, whereas the traditional healer evokes factors like the spirit and the supernatural, which are understandable to the patient.

This leads one to the consideration of the components of human existence. It has always been appreciated that there is more to human life than just the physical body. The aspect of soul or mind was also recognised and there was great argument as to which of the two was the main factor. The argument raged for a long time, until it was agreed that one could not be separated from the other psychophysical monism.

This problem came up again when psychoanalysis was born and there were those who laid emphasis on the physical and others on the psyche. It is only recently that they are both being considered as complementing each other.

In neither period was the spirit seriously and persistently considered. If there was a suggestion that this be considered, it got submerged beneath the concept of the mind. True enough, some of the manifestations of the spirit can readily be explained in terms of the mind, but not all. The term 'parapsychology' was invented to take care of some of these phenomena, but it is doubtful if these can be attributed to the mind — even in its extension. Can it truly be said that the phenomenon of the poltergeist, to name only one, is a function of the mind? There are many other such phenomena which cannot be attributed to the function of the mind, even in its extension.

It is true that the concept of the spirit may not fit into the framework of our materialistic and physical concept, but this does not mean that it is a myth. It may not lend itself readily to our present method of scientific inquiry. It may shake to the root some of our cherished notions. However, these are not adequate reasons for turning our backs on the concept of the spirit.

Even if in our concept of the body and mind we examine deeply the aetiology on which it is rational to base treatment, we find that we stop our enquiry at a convenient level at which we can take effective action. For example, we discover some organism or help the body to attack it. The discovery of these organisms is a convenient level. Even at this level we soon find that it is not as simple, for some people exposed to the same organism do not develop the illness, and this leads to the idea of virulence, size of infective agent, immunity, etc. If we pursue our examination beyond the level of the organism, we get to the ultimate or infinity — the greatest dilemma — which perhaps some traditional healing takes into account.

References

Asuni, T. (1979) 'The Dilemma of Traditional Healing with Special Reference to Nigeria', *Social Science and Medicine, 13*, 13, 33

Braito, R. and Asuni, T. (1977) 'Traditional Healers in Abeokuta: Recruitment, Professional Affiliation and Types of Patients Treated'. (Presented at the Western Social Science Association, April, Denver, Colorado, USA.)

Field, M.J. (1960) *Search for Security*, Faber & Faber, London

Forster, G.M. (1983) *An Introduction to Ethnomedicine in Traditional Medicine and Health Care Coverage*, R. H. Bannerman, J. Burton and Ch'en Wen-Chieh (eds), WHO, Geneva

Messing, S.D. (1959) 'Group Therapy and Social Status in Zar Cult of Ethiopia' in *Culture and Mental Health*, M.K. Opter (ed.), Macmillan, New York

Orley, J.H. (1970) *Culture and Mental Illness*, East African Publishing House, Nairobi

Prince, R. (1960) 'The Use of Rauwolfia for the Treatment of Psychosis by Nigerian Native Doctors', *American Journal of Psychiatry, 117*, 147–9

Prince, R. (1964) 'Indigenous Yoruba Psychiatry', in *Magic, Faith and Healing*, A. Kiev (ed.), Free Press, New York

Turner, V.W. (1964) 'A Ndembu Doctor in Practice', in *Magic, Faith and Healing*, A. Kiev (ed.), Free Press, New York

INDEX

abreaction technique 313
Abse, D.W. 33
Abu-Saad, H. 230
accelerated-integrated therapy 284–5
acceptability of psychiatric help 64
achievement motivation 16
acupuncture 277, 281
Adams, F. 107
Adams, R.S. 59
adaptation of social services 200–4
adaptive capacity of migrants 59
Adebimpe, V.R. 150
admissions, hospital 24
    ethnic minorities 97–8
    immigrants 62–3, 182–7, 192
    schizophrenia and 23,25, 27
    see also mental hospitals
adolescence
    and family 243
    anorexia nervosa 264
    fears 263
    identity and self-respect 199, 205,
      206
    overdoses 260–1
    see also children; family
adoption 153–4, 205–7
affirmative action 198–200, 204
Afghanistan 69, 116
Africa/Africans 15
    Bantu psychology 14
    depression 23, 108–9, 115, 117
    emigrants 69, 70, 78–80, 87
    epidemiology 25, 26, 31–5
    ethnography 170
    healers 13, 17, 27, 307, 309, 310,
      317–18
    lack of 'madmen' 9
    language problems 32
    neurosis 29, 34, 81
    possession 254, 313
    psychiatry, comparison with Western
      306–21; consultation 311; mental
      illness concept 309–10; mental
      illness diagnosis 310–11; training
      316–20; treatment 310–16
    racism 143–4, 146–7, 151, 152

    revolt 141
    training 16
    see also individual countries
age
    -adjusted prevalence rate for
      schizophrenia 29
    and admission rates 183–5
    of migrants 71
    oppositions between groups 254
agoraphobia 50, 262–3, 267, 269
Ahmed, S. 210
alcohol abuse 181, 186, 190, 191,
    192–4
Allen, J.J. 97
amok 7, 48, 50
amulets 292
Andrews, J.D.W. 262
anomie 81
anorexia nervosa 50, 263–4, 267, 268
anthropological approach 4, 37–58,
    168, 171, 175
    changing patterns of 50–3
    imperial legacy 38–40
    medical 45–7, 54
    psychopathology, culture-bound
      47–50
    social 40–3; British psychiatry and
      37–8; readings 53–4; schools of
      43–5
Anumonye, A. 79
Anwar, M. 71
anxiety 33
Aponte, H. 237
Apter, M.J. 269
Arab states 7, 78, 117
Arataeus 107
Ardener, E. 44, 54
Ardener, S. 262
Argentina 29, 64
Aristotle 291
armed forces 10–12, 33
Arya, O.P. 81
ascetic syndrome 300
Asia/Asians
    catatonic schizophrenia 297
    emigration 77, 78, 87

immigration 78
racism 147
see also under Britain, immigrants
    and individual countries
assessment and diagnosis 94–6
Astrup, C. 61
Asuni, T. 27, 148, 317
asylums *see* admissions; mental
   hospitals
Atkinson, D.R. 213
Australia 17, 115
   Aborigines 11, 15, 152
   immigrants 62, 68, 186, 190, 249
authority in family 241–2

Babiker, I.E. 80
baby-snatching 267
Bagley, C. 206
Baker, C.M. 229–30
Baker, J.R. 40
Baker, R. 69
Ballard, R. 3, 91–2, 242, 243, 244
Bang, S. 209, 211, 214
Barbosa, D. 7
Barclay Report 201, 202
Barker, J. 202
Barnes, G.E. 293
Barrett, K. 254
Barrett, M. 258, 259
Baruch, G. 109
Bass, B.A. 145
Bateson, G. 45, 54, 253
Baxter, R. 181
Bebbington, P.E. 109, 115
Beck, A.T. 108, 121
Bedford, A. 31
'Begum syndrome' 40, 176
behaviour modification 313–14
Beiser, M. 26
Bell, C. 262
Bell, D. 124
Benedict, R. 44, 45, 54, 116
Benne, K. 228
bereavement 244–6
Berger, J. 68
Berrios, G.E. 300
Bhat, A. 147
Bhate, S. 82
Bibring, E. 130
Biggs, J.T. 97
Binitie, R. 117
bio-descriptive school, Chinese 276,
   277, 281–3

biomedicine *see* psychopathology
Birnbaum, K. 48
Birnbaum, M. 228
Bleuler, M. 297
Bleuler, E. 48
Bluglass, R. 176
Boaz, F. 175
Bolton, P. 146, 151
Bonhoeffer, K. 294
Book, J.A. 114
Borneo 33, 115
Bose, G. 302
Boskind-Lohdahl, M. 264
bouffée délirante 51–3
boundary problems in identification of
   depression 110–11, 119
Bourguignon, E. 19
'brain storm' 268
Braito, R. 317
Branch, M. 228, 229
Brink, P.J. 223
Briquet's syndrome 50, 267
Britain 8–9, 19, 60, 163, 176
   anthropological approach 37, 38,
     40, 53
   armed forces 12, 33
   Asians in 52, 62–5, 113, 125–6,
     159, 224; family therapy
     234–46, 249–50; immigration
     3, 67, 68, 70–1, 124; nursing
     225; psychiatric services 89,
     90, 95–9, 101; social work
     201, 205, 207–9, 213, 215
   Caribbeans in 17, 51–2, 62–3, 87,
     113, 124, 129, 140, 176;
     family therapy 247–8;
     immigration 3, 67, 68; nursing
     225; psychiatric services 90,
     97; repatriated 147–50; social
     work 202, 207, 212–13
   cultural traditions 179–93
   depression 8, 89, 90, 107, 110,
     112–18, 125, 127, 129
   emigration 15, 76, 83–4, 183,
     186–93
   epidemiology 23–5, 33–5
   family therapy 236–50
   immigrants 60; African 17, 79–81;
     Eastern European 62; Latin
     American 64; numbers of 87;
     Tristan da Cunha 51; *see also*
     Asians; Caribbeans *above*
   Jews 112, 116, 127–8

nursing 218, 220–6
psychiatric services 87–102 *passim*
psychosocial problems 87–90
racism 122, 128, 140, 144,
    147–52, 173–4
schizophrenia 297
social work 196–209 *passim*
    213–15
students, overseas 77, 79–83, 230
suicide 293
women 263–4
Brockington, I.F. 62, 63, 90
Broverman, I.D. 258
Brown, C. 87
Brown, G.W. 31, 32, 107, 112, 113,
    114, 121, 297
Brown, M.S. 222, 223, 226
buffering system in family 243–4
Buglass, D.D. 262
Burke, A.W. 100
Burnell, A.C. 7
Burrows, A. 218, 225
Burton, R. 181
Bustamante, J.A. 14
Byng-Hall, J. 249
Byrne, D. 139

Camaroff, J. 255
Cameron, E. 13
Canada
    depression 115, 116, 117
    hospitalisation 182, 183, 184
    immigrants 61, 68, 183–6, 188–91
    nursing 219, 222–3
    publications 12, 14
    students, overseas 230
    training 17
    see also North America
Canning, H. 264
Caplan, R. 84
Capra, F. 120, 292
Caraka 291
Caribbean and Central America 11,
    14, 19
    possession 52–3
    racism 141, 144, 147
    repatriation 147–50
    see also under Britain, immigrants
'Caribbean psychosis' 176
Carothers, J.C. 23, 171, 175
Carpenter, L. 62, 63, 90
Carr, J.E. 49
Carstairs, G.M. 14, 37, 111, 117, 146

on depression 112
on possession 299
psychiatric interviews 26
on somatisation 118, 125, 301
case examples
    family therapy 238, 239–41,
        244–6, 247–8, 250
    racism 151–4
caseness, determination of 31–2
Cashmore, E.E. 109, 110
Catego programme 25, 26, 32, 34
catharsis 255
Cawte, J.E. 15, 16
Central America *see* Caribbean
Chakraborty, A. 159, 295
Chance, N.A. 116
changes in organisation of social work
    200–8
Chapman, R.D. 140
Charcot, J.M. 8, 9
Cheetham, J. 200, 203, 205
Cheetham, W.S. and R.J. 32
Chen, C. 275
Chen, Z. 284, 285
Chesler, P. 256, 269
Cheyne, G. 8, 181
children
    in Africa 308
    fostered or adopted 153–4, 205–7
    minimal brain dysfunction 285–6
    single, in China 286–7
    social services and 205–7
    see also adolescence; family
Chile 64, 68, 77
Chimezie, A. 205
China/Chinese
    disorders 32, 300–1; depression
        116, 117
    family life 234–5, 239–43, 249–50
    psychiatry 274–90; concepts of
        traditional medicine 274–5;
        development of modern 275–9;
        sociocultural interest in clinical
        issues 284–7
Chiu, J. 287
Chrisman, N.J. 45, 54
chronic pain syndrome 50, 267
Ciompi, L. 297
civilisation as pathogenic agent 9
Clarke, M. 230
Clemenets, I. 207
climate 308

clinical assessment, standardisation of
24-6
Cobbs, P.M. 145
Cochrane, R.
on hospital admissions 62, 63, 146,
186, 192
on Irish 66, 191
on schizophrenia 90
sample surveys 65
Cohen, N. 242
collective representation 45
Collomb, H. 16
colonialism 38-40, 50, 51, 122, 142,
169, 171, 175-6
communication *see* feelings; language
community services in China 279-80
'comparative psychiatry' 163-5, 168
Conelly, N. 200, 201, 202, 207
'conflict theory' 44
content and form, distinction between
48, 50
Conti, N. 7
contraception 287
Cooper, J.E. 25, 110, 297
Cooper, S. 210
Coopersmith, S. 129
Cooperstock, R. 260
coping with stress 226
Cornell Medical Index 25
Coryell, W. 296
counselling techniques 212-14
Cox, J. 3
on overseas students and
expatriates 76-86
Cranshaw, R. 264
Crapanzano, V. 46, 54
credibility, social worker's need for
197
Crisp, A.H. 264
Caudill, W. 16
Culpin, M. 83
'cultural distance scale' 80
cultural materialism 43
culture
brokers, doctors as 4
concept of 110, 158-9
depression and 125-33; minority
status 126-8; racism 124,
128-33
nursing and *see* nursing
personality school and 44
role for 34-5
shock: reverse 77, 85; *see also*

ethnic minorities; migration
see also mental health impact;
psychopathology; transcultural
culture-bound psychopathology 47-50
culture-bound syndromes 7, 125, 176
for other people 39, 48-51
in India 299-301
psychopolitics of 266-70
specific 26, 83-4, 176, 154-5,
266; *amok* 7, 48, 50; koro 125,
300-1; *latah* 47, 50, 51;
windigo 40, 48
Western *see* psychopathology
culture-of-poverty school 174
curricula *see* training
Currer, C. 99
Cushion, A.A. 258

Da-Cocodia, L. 151
D'Alembert, J.L. 181
Datta, D. 301
Davidson, B. 108
Davidson, L. 82
De Vos, G.A. 16
D'Elia, G. 298
Dean, G. 62, 63, 90, 146, 186, 191
decadence
genetic 9, 165
moral 8
Defendorf, A. 107
defensive strategies 226
Deloria, V. 169
delusion, defined 2
depression 52, 89, 181, 267
assumed to be rare 23
and guilt 126
in India 294-6
manic 167-8
somatisation and 108, 117, 126
symptoms 222
women 225
depression in ethnic minorities 107-38
Canadian immigrants 188-9
concept of 107-9, 110-11
culture 125-33; minority status
126-8; racism 124, 128-33
individual 120-1
and racism 147
refugees 148
social psychiatry of 123, 124-5
socio-cultural perspectives 109-20
descriptive school, Chinese 276, 277,
281-3

Devereux, G. 12, 45, 54, 239, 269
deviance 16
    features of culture-bound
        syndromes 48-9
    within family 242
Devore, W. 145
diagnosis 94-6
    'diagnostic pitfalls' 64
Diderot, D. 181
Diespecker, D. 292
dieting *see* anorexia
'diminished responsibility' 268
discrimination *see* racism
disease and illness, distinction between
    45
dislocation 254
dissociation 52
Dobash, R.E. and R. 41
Dobson, S. 218, 224
Dohrenwend, B.P. and B.S. 258
Doi, T. 16
Donzelot, J. 257
'double-bind' theory of schizophrenia
    45
Douglas, M. 43, 44, 54
Dove, L. 113
Doyal, L. 175
drugs
    addictive (opium) 285
    Africa 309, 312
    China 275-7, 280-1
    dosage differences 96-7
    healers' use of 27
    herbal 275, 277, 280-1, 292, 309,
        312
    India 292, 297-8
    overdoses 260-1, 266, 267, 268
Dube, K.C. 29
Dummett, M. and A. 128
Durkheim, E. 44, 54, 161, 263

East Indies 11, 12
Eastern Europe 69, 87
eating disorders *see* anorexia; obesity
Eaton, J. 14, 114, 116
Eaton, W.W. 152
education level of Canadian
    immigrants 185-6, 190
    see also training
Edwards, G. 3
Ehrenreich, J. 175
Eisenberg, L. 260
Eitinger, L. 62

Ekman, P. 33
Elder, G.H. 264
elderly and social services 207-8
electroconvulsive therapy 298
elements, Chinese theory of 275
Ellenberger, H. 17, 18, 20, 50
Elnager, M.N. 29, 296
emigration *see* migrants
emotion *see* feelings
Engels, F. 270
Enke, P. 10
epidemiology of mental illness 23-36,
    282-3
    contribution to psychiatry 23-4
    culture, role for 34-5
    depression and 114-19
    migration and 61, 71
    neurosis: detection problems 30-4;
        prevalence of 29, 34
    schizophrenia 26-9
    standardisation of clinical
        assessment 24-6
    see also mental health impact
equality of social work care 198-200
Erickson, E.H. 128
Essien-Udom, E.U. 141, 142
Estroff, S. 20, 46, 54
Ethiopia 310, 315
ethnic minorities 3, 38
    defined 122
    see also depression; migration;
        psychiatric services; racism;
        transcultural psychiatry
ethnocentrism 25-6, 159
ethnopsychiatry 43, 172
ethnoscience 45
Europe 19
    anthropological approach 44, 45,
        49, 52
    awakening 8-9
    colonialism 39, 40, 50, 51, 142,
        169, 171
    'decadence' 9-10
    depression 107, 111, 114, 116
    emigration 1-2, 15, 17, 61, 67-9,
        78, 87, 124, 188-93
    epidemiology 23-4
    folk illnesses 51
    immigration 17, 52, 67, 68,
        163-4; Gastarbeiters 66-8,
        69-71; students 77, 78
    Jews in 114
    psychiatry 176

racism 10, 144–5
repatriation from 148
women 262–3
see also individual countries
Evans-Pritchard, E.E. 41, 54
evil eye 51
exclusion 145–6
exhibitionism 50, 265–6, 267
exiles and refugees 64, 69, 70–1, 77,
    84, 147–8
expatriates 76–7, 83–5

Fabrega, H. 46, 49, 54, 111, 253
Faergeman, P.M. 299
family
    Africa 308, 311, 315
    conflicts of immigrants 89–90
    exiled with expatriate 84
    planning 287
    see also adolescence; children;
        family therapy; kinship; parents
family therapy 234–52, 297
    Africa 315
    China 279–80
    intervention strategies 249–51
    language and communication 248–9
    structure and organisation of family
        234–5, 241–8; adolescence
        243; authority 241–2; extended,
        West Indian 247–8; kinship
        242; marriage 243–6; parenting
        242–3
    symbolic meaning system, different
        238–41
    see also family
Fanon, F. 141, 143, 158, 175
Fanshel, D. 206
Farrar, N. 202
fascination 51
feelings, communication of 32–4,
    211–12, 226, 248–9, 258
Field, M.J. 17, 315
Field, S. 147, 199
Figlio, K. 175
filial piety 234–5, 242–3
Finlay-Jones, R. 31
first-rank symptoms (FRS) 297
Firth, R. 54
Fishberg, M. 10
Fisher, S. 302
Fitch, D. 212
flashing 50, 265–6, 267

followers 73
Forde, D. 43, 54
form and content, distinction between
    48, 50
Forster, G.M. 307
Forsyth, D. 83
Fosdike, H. 224
fostering 153–4, 205–7
Foulds, G.A. 31
Fox, R. 43, 54, 262
France 19, 52, 67, 148, 164, 188–9,
    263
Frederiksen, S. 298
Freire, P. 141
Freud, S. 10–11, 44, 107, 130, 168,
    259, 276
Frey, F. 148
Fromm-Reichmann, F. 116
Froude, J.A. 142, 143
Fry, W.F. 263
Fryer, P. 143
functionalism 43, 54
Funkenstein, D.H. 12
Furnham, A. 81

Gada, M.T. 117
Gaines, A. 38, 46, 54, 253
Galbraith, J. 40
Garetz, F.K. and D. 82
Garfinkel, P.E. 264
Garner, D.M. 264
Garner, V.M. 228
Garth, J. 292
Gastarbeiter 66–8, 69–71
Gaunt, J. 163
Gaw, A. 3
Geertz, C. 41, 54
gender and depression 112–13, 119–20
    see also men; sex; women
General Health Questionnaire 31
general practitioners 4, 293
genetics 9–10, 164–5
Geng, Z. 284, 285
German, G.A. 39, 55, 81
Germany 67, 116, 144, 164
Ghana, 17, 315
Gibbens, T.C.N. 265
Gill, O. 205
Gillis, L.S. 32
Ginsberg, G.P. 261
Godelier, M. 43, 54
Goffman, E. 41, 143, 149
Goldberg, D.P. 31

Goldstein, A.J. 262
Good, B.J. 46, 54
Gove, B.R. 258
grandparents as final authority 237,
    241
Greek-Cypriots in Australia 249
Green, E.M. 108
Greenberg, R.P. 302
Grewel, F. 114
grief 143
    see also bereavement
Grier, W.H. 145
Griffiths, J. 200, 201, 203, 205
Grinder, R.E. 116
group
    -based social work 199
    behaviour in institutions 143
    therapy 302; Africa 313, 314–15
    treatment in China 285
guilt 190, 295
    and depression 107–8, 116, 119,
        126
    and overdoses 261
    and religion 116
Gullahorn, J.T. and J.F. 77
Gupta, O.P. 301
Gypsies 4, 124

Hagnell, O. 30
Hahn, R.A. 39
Haldipur, C.V. 170
Haley, J. 243, 249
Halliday, A. 9
Halpern, F. 276
Hamilton, J.G. 50
Harding, T. 27, 34
Hardman, A. 68
Hare-Mustin, R.T. 243
Harper, S. 212
Harré, R. 42–3, 46
Harris, M. 122
Harris, T. 107, 112, 113, 114, 121
Hart, R. 142
Hashmi, F. 90
Haveli, H.S. 114
Hawton, K. 261
healers, traditional 17, 18
    Africa 13, 17, 27, 307, 309, 310,
        313, 317–19
    India 87, 293, 300
    schizophrenia and 25–6, 27
Heelas, P. 46, 54
Helman, C. 4, 53, 54

Hendin, H. 149
Henley, A. 93
Henriques, F. 247
heredity 9–10, 164–5
Hernderson, D.K. 193
Herodotus 196
Hes, J.P. 114
Heshe, J. 298
Hicks, C. 222
Hicks, D.W. 122
Hippocrates 107, 291
historical development of transcultural
    psychiatry 7–22
Hitch, P.J. 62, 63, 90, 100, 213
Hoch, E.M. 296, 302
Hoffman, L. 237
Hollingshead, A.B. 113, 296
home *see* family
Hong Kong 66, 112, 116
Horney, K. 145
Horwitz, A. 258
hospitals *see* admissions; mental
    hospitals
Huffard, D. 108
Hughes, C.C. 39, 54
Humphrey, D. 149
Hunter, J. 301
Hunter, R. 8, 301
hypochondriasis *see* somatisation
hysteria
    Arctic 50
    conversion 33–4, 50, 225; in 19th
        century 259–60
    Eskimos and 223
    hereditary 10
    possession and 299
    religion and 8
Husband, C. 202

Ibn Khaldun 7
identity, development of 128, 205, 206
    see also individual; self
ideology and politics 158–78, 276
illness and disease, distinction between
    45
immigrants 9, 17
    control 172, 176, 196
    nurses 220–2
    see also migration *and under*
        countries
imperialism *see* colonialism
incidence 24, 28
Index of Definition (ID) 31–2, 34

India
   depression 111, 112, 115, 116,
      118, 294–6
   epidemiology 25, 26, 29, 33
   healers 27, 293, 300
   psychiatry, comparison with
      Western 291–305; culture-
      bound syndromes 299–301;
      depression 294–6;
      electroconvulsive therapy 298;
      psychosis, acute 298–9;
      psychotherapy 301–2;
      schizophrenia 296–8
   see also under Britain, immigrants
indisposition 52
individual
   depression and 120–1
   derogatory attitude and racism
      139–40
   emphasis on 197, 199
   orientation to racism 144
   see also identity; self
Indo-European languages 48
industrialisation 181–20, 308
   anorexia and 263
   migration and 66–8
inferiority of non-Europeans 39
   see also racism
Ingleby, D. 109, 256
institutional racism 132, 139, 151
institutions, group behaviour in 143
internalisation 189–91
interpreters 92, 93–4
intervention strategies in family
   therapy 249–50
inversion and reflexivity 266–70
Iran 69, 115
Irish
   in England 62, 66–8, 87, 124
   in North America 15, 183, 191–2
   see also Britain
isolation 90, 187, 189–90
Israel 51, 61, 68, 114
Italy 15, 17, 19, 67

Jablensky, A. 115
Jackson, B. 205
Jackson, J.A. 59
Jacobson, B. 264
Jaffee, B. 206
Jahoda, G. 44, 53, 54
Janet, P. 9
Janzen, J.M. 46, 54, 270

Japan 16, 266
Jaspers, K. 140, 141
Java
   amok in 7, 48
   mental hospitals in 10, 165–7
Jayaram, S.S. 301
Jews
   depression 113, 114, 116–18, 124,
      126–9
   Nazis and 144
Johnson, P.R. 206
Jones, C. 200
Jones, J.S. 109
Jones, W.H.S. 107
Jordanovna, L.J. 256, 257

Kao, J.J. 273
Kapo, R. 129
Kapur, R.L. 26, 111, 112, 118, 299
Kasanin, J. 299
Katznelson, I. 122
'kayak angst' 266
Kayser-Jones, J. 230
Kelleher, M.J. 191
Keller, S. 257
Kelly, G. 43
Kendell, R.E. 109
Kenny, M.G. 49
Kent, B. 197
Kenya 306
Kerr, J. 275
Kessel, N. 119
Khubalkar, R. 301
Kiev, A. 39, 48–9, 53, 54
Kimura, Van B. 16, 116
King, L.J. 85
King, M.L. 196
kinship 43, 54, 224, 242
   see also family
Kinzie, D. 234
Kirmayer, L.J. 117
Klaf, F.S. 50
Klein, M. 145
Kleinman, A.
   and anthropology 18, 37, 39, 42,
      45, 49, 53, 54, 117
   on 'category fallacy' 111
   on depression 115, 120, 126, 239
   on family therapy 239, 250
   on hospital psychiatrists 3, 4
   on somatisation 126, 239
   phenomenological approach 95
Klerman, A.L. 258

Knight, L. 225
Kogan, N. 227
Korea 68
Koro 125, 300–1
Kovel, J. 169
Kraepelin, E. 276, 295
    influence on training 276
    on 'comparative psychology' 164
    on depression 107, 112, 165–7
    on inferiority of non-Europeans 39,
        165–7, 169
    on universal symptoms 48
    visits to Asian mental hospitals 10,
        166
Kramer, M. 229
Krausz, E. 113
Krupinski, J. 62, 186
Kulhara, P. 296, 297
kuru 47

La Fontaine, J. 256
Lambo, T.A. 17
Lambroso, C. 165
Landy, D. 53, 54
Langner questionnaire 65
language of emotion 32–4
language problems 92, 93–4
    Africa 310
    in family therapy 248–9
    of nurses 224–5
Larose, S. 53
latah 47, 50, 51
Latin America 14, 25, 29
    depression 112, 116
    emigrants 64, 68, 77, 78, 87
Lazarus, A. 262
learned helplessness 130
Lebra, W. 16
Lee, E. 65
Lee, H. 230
Lee, T.R. 230
Leff, J. 3, 49
Leighton, A.H. 25, 31, 34
Leininger, M. 219–20, 223, 229
Leroy, C. 52
Lester, D. 292
Lévi-Strauss, C. 43, 54
Levick, S.E. 250
Levy-Bruhl, L. 109
Lewis, A.J. 37, 107
Lewis, G. 46, 54
Lewis, I.M. 39, 40, 44, 49–50, 53,
    54, 254, 270

Lewis, P. 97
Lewis, S.A. 40
Lewontin, R.C. 48
Li, C. 285
Leinhardt, G. 54
Lin, T. 29, 116
Lindenbaum, S. 47, 54
Linton, R.N. 239
Lipsedge, M. 83
    see also Littlewood, R. and
        Lipsedge, M.
Little, A. 197, 199
Littlewood, J. 261
Littlewood, R. 49
Littlewood, R. and Lipsedge, M. 3, 39
    on culture-based syndromes 40, 47,
        51–2, 96, 223
    on depression 49, 52, 53
    on family 247
    on migration 62, 90, 150
Liu, X. 276
Liu, Z. 283
Lock, A. and M. 46, 54
Logan, W.P.D. 258
loneliness *see* isolation
loss 129–30
Loudon, J.B. 41, 51, 54
Lundquist, G. 295
Luo, H. 282
Lyman, R.S. 276
Lyons, B.G. 107

Macalpine, I. 8, 301
McCord, W. 140
McDermott, J.F. 3
Macfarlane, J. 263
McGoldrick, M. 234, 237, 242, 248
McKay, C. 144
McMichael, R.E. 116
McNeil, W.H. 59
McRae, Prof. K. 83
Madanes, C. 249
magic 39, 309
Magnan 266
Mahy, G.E. 148
Malaysia 33, 51, 115, 301
Malhotra, H.K. 300
Malinowski, B. 11, 43, 54
Malzberg, B. 183, 184, 186
mania 299
manic depression 166–7
manipulation 254
Mannoni, O. 143

Manschrek, T.C. 39, 49
Manson, S.M. 32
marginality 127
Marks, I.M. 262
marriage 243–6
    depression and 112–13, 119–20
    of Canadian immigrants 185
    women's disorders and 258, 262
Mars, L. 11
Marsella, A.J. 33, 46, 52, 54, 108,
    118, 125
Marshall, L. 297
Martin, J.P. 41
Martinu, G. 83
Marx, K. 175
Marxist anthropology 43
masochists, chantage 269
Master, R. 295
masturbation 301
Mauss, M. 40, 44, 54
Mayer, G.G. 229–30
Mayer-Gross, W. 114
Mayor, V. 224
Mead, M. 44, 45, 54, 99, 116, 175
meaning-centred anthropology 42
Mecabe, M.S. 299
mediator role of social workers
    213–14
medical anthropology 45–7, 54
medical graduates 82–3
medicine *see* drugs
melancholia 8, 107, 181
    see also depression
Mellor, C. 297
men
    culture-bound syndromes 254,
        265–8, 269
    domination by 257–9, 302
    see also gender; sex
Mendels, J. 107
Mendelson, M. 107
menopause 267
mental health impact of cultural
    traditions, British 179–95
    admissions, hospital 182–7, 192
    cultural links 189–91
    historical roots and changes 180–2
    Irish and Scots 191–3
mental hospitals 9
    China 275, 276, 280
    India 293
    Java 10, 165–7
    repatriated in 146

    see also admissions
mental hygiene movement 169
mental illness *see* transcultural
    psychiatry
Mental Status Schedule 187
Mercer, K. 146, 149
Merrill, E. 228
Messing, S.D. 310
metaphors, cultural, in family therapy
    249
Metraux, A. 52
Meyer, A. 107, 276
microcosm and macrocosm 275
migration and mental illness 1, 3,
    59–75
    see also ethnic minorities; exiles;
        expatriates; immigrants;
        overseas students
Miller, P.McC. 81
Millman, M. 264
minimal brain dysfunction in children
    285–6
minority status and depression 126–8
    see also ethnic minorities
Minuchin, S. 248
mis-diagnosis 94–5
Mishler, E.G. 49, 54
Mohr, J. 68
Moinat, S.M. 147
moon, effect of 292
Morel, B.-A. 9, 162, 164
Morgenthaler, F. 15
Morley, S.J. 300
Morris, H.S. 122
Muhangi, J. 81
Munoz, L. 77
Murphy, G. 204
Murphy, H.B.M. 3
    on 'comparative psychology' 162,
        163
    on culture-bound syndromes 50,
        223, 253
    on depression 52, 115, 116, 117,
        222
    on guilt 116
    on migration 61, 62
    on overdoses 266
    on schizophrenia 272
Murphy, J. 51
Myer, J. 264
'mystical pressure' 254, 255

Nakra, B.R.S. 300

Nammalvar, N. 295, 296
Nandi, D.N. 29, 294
Narang, R.L. 299
'national character concept' 175-6
Navarro, V. 175
Needham, R. 43, 54
negative selection 65-6, 71
Negi Negi 254
Negrete, J.C. 187
Neki, J.S. 300, 302
Netherlands 81, 114, 148
neurasthenia 284-5
neuroses
    Canadian immigrants 185
    detection problems 30-4
    prevalence of 29, 34
Neutra, R. 40, 49, 54
'New Cross syndrome' 40, 176
New Guinea 33, 43, 180, 254
Newby, H. 262
Newman, P.L. 49
Nigeria 17, 306
    causes of disorder 309
    epidemiology 25, 31-2, 34-5
    healers in 27, 310, 317-18
'noble savage' 8
Norris, U. 112
North Africa 67, 143
North America 3, 19
    anthropological approach 37, 44,
        45
    armed forces 12
    depression 110, 113-18, 120, 129
    electro-convulsive therapy 298
    emigrants 78, 85
    Eskimos 40, 50, 223, 266
    hospitalisation 182-4
    Hutterites 114, 116
    immigrants 1-2, 10, 60, 61, 68,
        182; African 223; Asian 17,
        18, 118; British 15, 183-91;
        German 183-4; Italian 15, 17,
        183-4; Mexican 68; 'poor
        stock' 9; Puerto Rican 12, 222;
        Scandinavian 1-2, 61, 183-4;
        students 77, 78, 82, 230
    Indians, indigenous 32-3, 40, 169,
        222
    Jews 126
    nursing 219, 222-3, 225, 227-30
    racism 141, 144, 145, 147, 172
    schizophrenia 25
    social work 196-201, 204
    suicide 293
    training 17
    women 262
nuclear family, Western, as norm 237
nursing, psychiatric 218-33
    culturological assessment 219-20
    expression of mental illness 222-6
    relationships with patients 220-2
    training 217-19, 227-31
Nylander, J. 263

obesity 263-4, 267, 268
obsessional neurosis and religion 39
occupational therapy 315-16
Odegaard, O. 1, 61
Oklet, J.M. 4
Olins, R. 201
Oman, M. 3, 19
opium addiction 285
Opler, M.K. 12-13, 15
organisation changes in social work
    200-8
Orley, J. 29, 32, 34, 310
Ortigues, M.C. and E. 16
Ortner, S.B. 256
Osborne, O.H. 225, 226, 230
Ou, J. 283
overdoses 260-71, 266, 267, 268
Owens, P. 41

Pahl, J. 41
pain syndromes, chronic 50, 267
Pakistan 69
    see also under Britain, immigrants
Palazzoli, M.S. 250
Pandurangi, A.K. 299
paranoid reaction 225, 226, 296
parents 15-16, 182
    Asian attitudes to 234-5, 237, 241,
        242-3
    functions of 242-3
    in Africa 308
    see also children; family
Parin, P. 10, 15
Parin-Matthey, G. 10, 15
Park, R. 59
Parker, S. 48
Parsons, A. 11, 17
Parsons, P. 262
Parsons, T. 256
past, social workers' preoccupation
    with 214
pathogenic determinants 47-8

pathologisation of other cultures 39,
    91–2
pathoplastic determinants 47–8
patients, women as 256–9
Pattison, E.M. 254
Pavlov 276
Pearce, J.K. 250
Pennell, I. 175
Perris, C. 296
Petri, M. 39, 49
Pfeiffer, W.M. 18, 116
Pfister-Ammende, M. 79, 147
PGI Health Questionnaire 26
Philippe, J.L. 52, 54
Phillips, D.L. 258
piblokto 50
Pilcz, A. 10
Pillay, H.M. 144, 146
Pinel, P. 163
Pinto, R.T. 90
pioneers 73
Pirani, M. 113
Pitt, D. 88
Pobouh Lang 26
Polhemus, T. 265
politics and ideology 159–78, 276
Pollock, H.M. 60
Porter, A.M.W. 112
positive discrimination in social work
    198–200, 204
positive selection 65–6, 71
possession 19, 40, 52–3
    Africa 254, 313
    India 299–300
Power, J. 68
Prange, A.J. Jr 148
prejudice 140–1
    see also racism
Present State Examination 23, 25, 26,
    31–2, 34, 115
presentation of mental illness 90–1
Preto, N.B. 242
prevalence 24
    of neurosis 29, 34
    of schizophrenia 28–9
Primrose, E.J.R. 192–3
Prince, J. 265
Prince, R. 108, 176, 263, 309, 312
Prosen, R. 293
PSE *see* Present State Examination
psychiatric nursing *see* nursing
psychiatric services for ethnic
    minorities 87–106

assessment and diagnosis 94–6
language problems 92, 93–4
presentation 90–1
provision 91–3
psycho-social problems 87–90
psychotherapy 98–102
treatment and management 96–8
psychiatry *see* transcultural psychiatry
psychoanalysis 10–11, 44, 168–9, 319
psychopathology, biomedicine and
    culture 253–73
    agoraphobia 262–3, 267, 269
    anorexia nervosa 263–4, 267, 268
    conversion hysteria 259–60
    domestic sieges 265, 267, 268
    exhibitionism 265–6, 267
    medicalisation of women 256–9
    overdoses 260–1, 266, 267, 268
    psychopolitics of culture-bound
        syndromes 266–70
    shoplifting 265, 267, 268, 269
psychopolitics of culture-bound
    syndromes 266–70
psychoses 283
    acute, in India 298–9
psychosocial problems in Britain 87–90
psychotherapy 98–102, 282, 314
    in India 301–2
pull-factors 65–6, 79
Puritanism 182, 193
push-factors 65–6, 78, 79

racial theories 10, 108–9, 142–3, 163,
    167
racism and mental illness 1, 40, 64,
    88, 139–56
    aspects of 139–43
    case examples 151–4
    current practice 150–1
    defined 128
    depression and 124, 128–33
    institutional 132, 139, 151
    psychological factors 143–7
    repatriation study 147–50
    social work 196, 201–2
Rack, P. 3, 223
    on Bradford Unit 100–1
    on drugs 97
    on elderly 98
    on guilt 108
    on language problems 93–4, 98
    on presentation of illness 90
    on somatisation 108, 126

Racy, J. 117
Radcliffe-Brown, A.R. 43, 54, 175
Raman, A.C. 19, 188
Ramon, S. 261
Ranney, M.H. 60
Rao, S. 296
Rappaport, D. 43, 54
Raskin, A. 119
Rauwolfia 27
Ravenstein, E.G. 62
Rawnsley, K. 51
Redlich, F. 113, 296
Reed, B. 79, 82
Rees, J.R. 12
reflexivity and inversion 266–70
refugees *see* exiles
relationships
    nurses and patients 220–2
    social workers and clients 208–15
religion 182, 188
    and culture-bound syndromes 255
    and guilt 116
    and hysteria 8
    and lifestyle 224
    and obsessional neurosis 39
    and possession 299–300
    and schizophrenia 222–3
    and suicide 295
    healing through 292
repatriation study 147–50
Rex, J. 198
Rhazes 7
Rhela 291
Rhodes, L.A. 46, 54
Richman, N. 113
Rin, H. 2, 29
Rinder, I.D. 126
rituals in family therapy 250
Rivers, W.H.R. 37, 54
Roberts, H. 258, 259
Robins, D. 197, 199
Roder, E. 298
Roheim, G. 11
Romain, J.B. 52, 54
Rooth, F.G. 266
Roscher, C.I. 223
Rose, S. 163–4, 170, 175
Rousseau, J.-J. 8
Rowe, D. 121
Rowe, J. 205
Ruesch, J. 127
Rush, B. 8–9
Rushdie, S. 122

Russell, J. 206

Sachdev, J.S. 299
Sachs, W. 11
sado-masochism of racism 152
Saifullah Khan, V. 128
Sainsbury, E. 209
St Helena 83
Sandel, B. 295
Sanua, V.D. 15, 128, 267
Sar possession 254
Sartorius, N. 115, 297
Sartre, J.P. 129
Satyanand, B. 302
Scandinavia 23–4, 30, 67
    electro-convulsive therapy 298
    emigrants to North America 1–2,
        61, 183–4
Scarman, Lord 199
Scheff, T.J. 250
Scheper-Hughes, N. 192
schizophrenia 15, 283
    and healers 25–6, 27
    Canadian immigrants 185–8, 191–2
    case-finding procedures for 26–9
    catatonic 297
    changing psychopathology of 50
    'double-bind' theory of 45
    ethnocentrism and 25–6
    India 296–8
    International Pilot Study of (IPSS)
        19, 23–4, 28, 32, 46, 297
    overdiagnosis 90
    possession and 299
    religion and 222–3
Schlesinger, E.G. 145
Schneiderian first-rank symptoms 297
Schofield, J. 224, 225
Schooler, C. 16
Schwartz, D. 62
science
    legitimation by 255
    psychiatry and 160, 164, 170
Scotland/Scottish 81
    alcoholism 193–4
    in England 62, 67
    in North America 186, 192–3
    overseas students in 80–1
    see also Britain
screening for neurosis 30–1
Scull, A.T. 162
sculpting in family therapy 250
Segal, B. 258

Seidenberg, R. 260
self
    concept *see* identity
    -consciousness of ethnic groups
        122
    differentiated from other 116
    -esteem 127, 128–31
    -help 197, 204, 207–8, 270
    -poisoning 50; *see also* overdoses
    -respect, adolescents' 199
    -selection hypothesis 60–2
    see also identity; individual
Seligman, C.G. 37, 54
Seligman, M.E.P. 108, 121, 130
Seltzer, W.J. and M.R. 238, 250
Sena, J.F. 8
Senegal 16, 313, 315
senile and arteriosclerotic psychoses
    185–6
separate provision of social work 200,
    204–5, 208
Sethi, B.B. 292, 293, 298, 299
settlers 68–9, 70–1, 76
sex roles 254, 268
    see also gender; men; women
sexual neurosis 300
sexualism, trans- 267
sexuality of women 268
Shackman, J. 248
shaman 39, 51, 293, 300
    see also healers
shame 116
Shapiro, R.M. 128
Shen, Y. 280, 282, 284
Shireman, J.F. 206
Shore, J.H. 32
Shukla, G.D. 301
sick role 255–6
sieges, domestic 265, 267, 268
Sillen, S. 175
Silver, D.B. 46, 54
Silverstein, M. 297
Simons, R.C. 47, 54
Simpson, G.E. 122
Singapore 10, 61, 266
Singh, G. 299
Singh, R. 115
Skynner, R. 235
slavery 142, 144
Small, J.W. 149, 153
Smith, E.J. 212
Smith-Rosenberg, C. 259

social anthropology *see under*
    anthropological
social class and depression 113–14,
    120
social deprivation 146–7
social environment, poor 88
social medicine 160–1
social policy and social work 198–200
social psychiatry of depression 123,
    124–5
social work 196–217
    by ethnic minorities 203–4, 210
    face to face 208–15
    organisation changes 200–8;
        adaptation, forms of 203–4;
        adaptation, need for 200–2;
        child-care services 205–7;
        elderly, ethnic 207–8; separate
        provision 200, 204–5, 208
    social policy considerations
        198–200
sociocultural
    interest in clinical issues, China
        284–7
    perspectives on depression 109–20
sojourners 76–83
Somalia 254
somatisation 46, 90, 181
    and depression 108, 117, 126
    and hysteria 33–4
    and schizophrenia 296
    in India 295, 296
Somerville, C.J. 182
'Soul Kids Campaign' 207
South Africa 14, 26, 32, 141, 144
    racism in 146, 151, 152
Southgate, P. 147
Sow, I. 18
Spiegel, J.P. 250
spirit/s, belief in 309, 320
Spitzer, R.L. 187
Spratlen, L.P. 229
Sri Lanka 30, 111
Srinivasamurthy, R. 294
standardisation in clinical assessment
    24–6
Standardized Assessment of Depressive
    Disorders (SADD) 115
Staplehurst, A. 202
Stark, E. 161
stereotypes *see* racism
Stimson, G. 260
Stoller, A. 186

Stone, M. 129, 150
Stone, R.W.H. 230
Stonequist, E.V. 59
Stopes-Roe, M. 65, 186, 192
stress-of-migration hypothesis 60, 62
structuralism 43
Stuart, R.B. 264
students, overseas 12–13, 69, 77–83, 230
Sudan 310, 315
Sue, D.W. 201, 213
suicide 16, 193, 268
    in India 293, 300
    para- *see* overdoses
Sullivan, H.S. 37
survival strategies, need to learn 205
Surva, N.C. 301
Susruta 291
Susser, M. 164, 166
susto 40
Switzerland 67, 68, 147, 297
symbolic meaning systems, different 238–41
symbolism 44, 54
Symonds, A. 262, 269
Szasz, T.S. 109

Tafjel, H. 121, 122
taijin kyok 266
Taiwan 29, 116
Taller, M. 222, 227
Tao, K. 287
Tarnopolsky, A. 29
tarrantism 51
Taylor, I.J. 292
Teja, J.S. 117, 295, 299
thanatomania 40
Thomas, A. 175
thought, different vehicles of 41
Tikopia 254–5
time, changes over 51
Tirenbaugh, C. 263, 264
Tolsma, F.J. 148
Tonks, C.M. 119
Torrey, E. 77, 109
Toynbee, A.J. 291
training 3–4, 16, 17, 179
    anthropological 37–8
    in Africa 306, 307, 316–20
    in China 276
    lack of, India 293
    medical 3–4, 16, 17
    nurses 218–19, 227–31

social workers 203, 214–15
trances 19
trans-sexualism 267
transcultural psychiatry *see* anthropological approach; culture; depression; epidemiology, family therapy; historical development; ideology; migration; nursing; psychiatric services; psychopathology; racism; social work; *and individual countries and continents*
Treacher, A. 109
treatment and management 96–8
Trezise, L. 81
Tristan da Cunha 51
Trivedi, J.K. 293
'tropical neurasthenia' 83–4
Troyna, R.C. 109, 110
Trumbach, R. 182
Tseng, W.S. 3, 117
Tudor, J.F. 258
Turkey, 67, 68, 124
Turner, B. 256, 257
Turner, V. 45, 53, 54, 254, 270, 315

Uganda
    Asians expelled from 69, 70
    causes of disorder 310
    neurosis 29, 34, 81
United States *see* North America
universal symptoms, pathogenic 48
universalist social work care 198–9
'uprooting problems' 79–80
urbanisation 7, 308
USSR 25, 77, 78
    and psychiatry in China 276, 277

Vahia, N.S. 298
'vapours' 8
Varma, L.O. 299
Varma, V.K. 297, 299
Vega, G. 192
venereal diseases, eradication of 285
Venkataramiah, V. 300
Venkoba Rao, A. 115
Verghese, A. 292
Verma, S.K. 26
'victim' approach to depression 133
Vidyasagar 302
Vietnam, emigration from
    to Britain 64, 87, 214, 239–41, 249

to USA 17, 18
violence, racist 152-3
Virchow, R. 162
voluntary social work 203-4, 207
'voodoo death' 40

Wagley, C. 122
Waitzkin, H. 175
Walvin, J. 142
Wan, W. 283
Wang, J. 285
Waxler, N. 49, 111
Waziri, R. 117
Webb, P. 224, 225, 226
Weber, M. 182
Weil, R. 14, 114, 116
Weinreich, P. 128
Weinstein, E. 48
Weissman, M.M. 258
West Indies *see* Caribbean
Westermeyer, J. 18
Western countries
    assumptions 46
    depression as culture-specific
        variant 49, 52
    culture-bound syndromes *see*
        psychopathology
    nuclear family as norm 237
    psychiatry, comparisons with *see
        under* China; India
    see also individual countries
White, G. 46, 52, 54
Wig, N.N. 26, 294, 296, 297, 299,
    300
Wijesinghe, C.P. 30, 111
Williams, A.H. 12, 33
Williams, E. 144
Willis, R.G. 256
Wilson, A. 64, 65, 225
windigo 40, 48
Wing, J.K. 23, 29, 31, 32, 34, 35,
    115
Winokur, G. 296
Wintrob, R.M. 254
witchcraft 39, 309
Witmer, L.H. 206
Wittokower, E.D. 2
Wolpe, J. 262
women
    agoraphobia 262-3, 267, 269
    anorexia nervosa 263-4, 267, 268
    anthropology 44
    Asian in Britain 225, 243-6

conversion hysteria in 19th century
    259-60
depression 112-13, 114, 225
in male-orientated societies 51
medicalisation of 256-9
overdoses 260-2, 266, 267, 268
sexuality 268
shoplifting 265, 267, 268, 269
West Indian 247-8
Wong, S. and J. 230
Wong, T.J. 139
Woods, A. 276
World Federation for Mental Health
    12
World Health Organisation
    on alcoholism 191
    on classification and diagnosis 179
    on depression 115
    on overseas students 170
    on healers 307
    schizophrenia study 19, 23-4, 28,
        32, 46, 188-9, 297
World Psychiatric Association (WPA)
    13-15, 19
Wu, Z. 280, 283

Xia, Z. 275, 276, 277, 279, 280, 282,
    284
Xu, S. 281
Xu, T. 286
Xu, Y. 274, 275, 276

Yamamoto, J. 94
Yan, H. 285, 286
Yancey, W.L. 124
Yang, D. 282
Yap, P.M. 18, 42, 47, 48, 49, 112,
    116, 125
Yin and Yang 275
Yinger, J.M. 122
Young, A. 255, 256, 261
Young, L. 206
Yule, H. 7

Zeigler, V.E. 97
Zhang, J. 280, 282, 283
Zhang, M. 275, 276, 277, 282, 284
Zhao, Y. 282
Zheng, Y. 282
Zhou, C. 282
Zung, W.W.K. 295
Zwingmann, C.A.A. 79